Gender,
Sexuality,
and the
Cold War

Gender, Sexuality, and the Cold War

A GLOBAL PERSPECTIVE

EDITED BY

Philip E. Muehlenbeck

Vanderbilt University Press
Nashville

Library of Congress Cataloging-in-Publication Data on file
LC control number 2016042790
LC classification number D842 .G445 2017
Dewey class number 327.09/045
LC record available at lccn.loc.gov/2016042790

ISBN 978–0–8265–2142–2 (hardcover)
ISBN 978–0–8265–2143–9 (paperback)
ISBN 978–0–8265–2144–6 (ebook)

Contents

Part III
Masculinities

PREFACE

In the past fifteen years scholarship examining how gender and sexuality have influenced the United States during the Cold War has flourished.[1] Yet, what is striking is the dearth of English-language scholarship that focuses on the ways in which gender and sexuality influenced the domestic and foreign policies of states *other* than the United States during this time period. This volume is an initial step toward rectifying this problem.

Although categorizations of gender and sexuality are interconnected and relational, we have organized this book into three sections—Sexuality, Femininities, and Masculinities—in an effort to aid classroom use. This volume is not comprehensive, of course, nor could such a collection of essays ever hope to be so. We would have preferred to include more chapters on masculinity, for example, but had difficulty finding contributors—which attests to the relative scarcity of studies of masculinities in the Cold War in comparison to those that focus on femininities. Nonetheless, by broadening the study of the Cold War to include gender and sexuality and by moving away from America's shores toward the rest of the world, the volume—with its multidisciplinary approach and emphasis on multiarchival research (primary-source research was conducted in fifteen different countries)—aspires to inspire further research on how gender and sexuality affected the Cold War domestic and foreign policies of states other than the United States.

I thank the following individuals for offering peer-review comments on prospective chapters for this volume: Jeffrey Ahlman, Ben Alziari, Francisca de Haan, Michael Donoghue, Melissa Feinberg, Mary Hawkesworth, Renata Keller, Andy Kirkendall, Pia Koivunen, Brandon Locke, Maxim Matusevich, Stephan Miescher, Rebecca Pulju, Andy Rotter, Kathleen Tobin, Gregory Winger, Jay Winter, and Sergei Zhuk. I also extend special thanks to Jenny Hamilton, a student at George Washington University who assisted me in editing these chapters with an eye toward comprehension by advanced undergraduate students. Finally, Eli Bortz, my acquisitions editor at Vanderbilt University Press, was an integral part of this project from conception to completion. This volume is much better because of his involvement.

Note

1. Influential studies in this subgenre include K. A. Cuordileone, *Manhood and American Political Culture in the Cold War* (New York: Routledge, 2005); Robert D. Dean, *Imperial Brotherhood: Gender and the Making of Cold War Foreign Policy* (Amherst: University of Massachusetts Press, 2002); David Kenneth Johnson, *The Lavender Scare: The Cold War Persecution of Gays and Lesbians in the Federal Government* (Chicago: University of Chicago Press, 2004); and Andrew J. Rotter, *Comrades at Odds: The United States and India, 1947–1964* (Ithaca: Cornell University Press, 2000).

Gender,
Sexuality,
and the
Cold War

INTRODUCTION

Hidden in Plain Sight

The Histories of Gender and Sexuality
during the Cold War

Marko Dumančić

The photograph of Leonid Brezhnev kissing Erich Honecker counts among the most iconic images of the late Cold War era; the two men embrace tightly, with eyes closed and lips touching. Taken by Régis Bossu in 1979, the photo captured the two elderly statesmen exchanging kisses on the occasion of the German Democratic Republic's thirtieth anniversary. The amorous kiss proved sensationalistic enough to receive a two-page spread in *Paris Match*. In 1990, this same photograph attained immortality on a nearly mile-long stretch of the Berlin Wall when Soviet artist Dmitri Vrubel replicated it, cementing it at the center of the German capital's public forum. The mural's title, *God, Help Me Survive This Deadly Love,* unambiguously referenced the Soviet Union's lethal fraternalism. But the passionate kiss became iconic not because of its open allusion to the dysfunction of the Warsaw Pact but rather because of its evocative gender and sexuality politics. Vrubel's piece expressed revulsion toward the USSR and the people's democracies through the politics of sex in a way that made this image more memorable (or worth remembering) than those murals that arguably fit better in the pantheon of Cold War visual imagery, including depictions of brave wall jumpers and other dissenters (such as Andrei Sakharov).

This portrait of two elderly men displaying affection in public reveals how explicitly the politics of gender and sexuality shaped expressions of the Cold War, as well as the memory of conflict between the superpowers. The image is implicitly homophobic, as it codes this act as humorous, bizarre, and grotesque: the "deadly love" in the title not only invokes foreign policy, but also ties the perversion of communist systems to the "perversion" of same-sex affection. Furthermore, the evocation of a "deadly love" at the height of the AIDS epidemic, which was frequently blamed on gay men's sexual habits, adds another sinister dimension to this seemingly playful instance of political satire. The implied homophobia

1

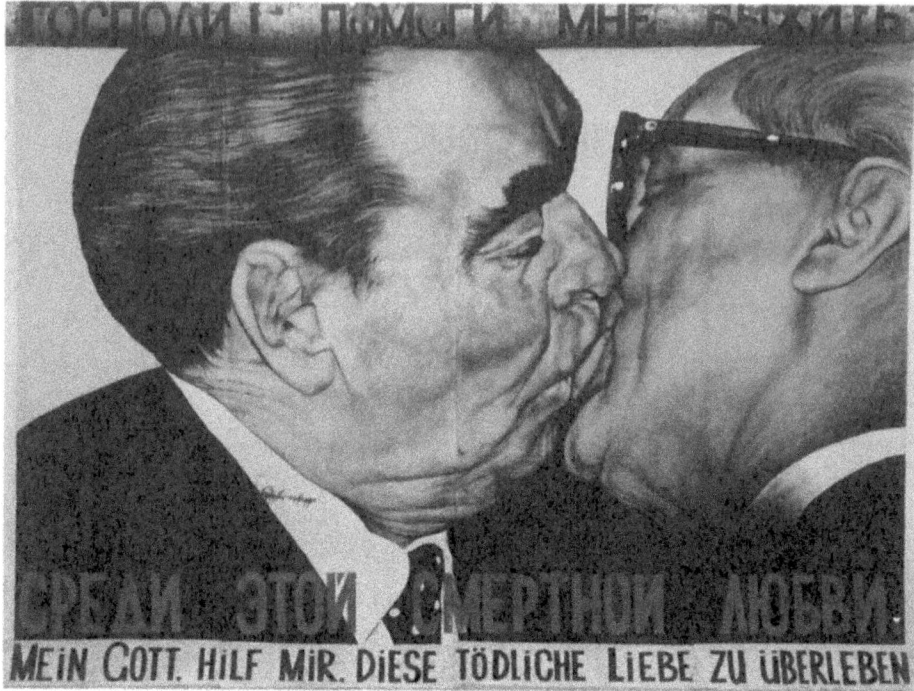

Figure 1. The Berlin Wall's infamous "fraternal kiss" between Leonid Brezhnev and Erich Honecker (Dmitri Vrubel's mural, *God, Help Me Survive This Deadly Love*, based on a 1979 photo by Régis Bossu).

directly mocks the interpersonal customs of a generation of men who led socialist movements, as if invoking the derogatory German slang term for gay men, "warm brothers" (*warmer brüder*). "Tough masculinity," so often demanded of men on both sides of the Iron Curtain, emerged triumphant even as the Cold War gasped its last breath.

My uncomplimentary reading of Vrubel's work aligns with the creator's own reaction to Bossu's photograph when he first saw it in Paris in 1989. He communicated his unease with the picture in the following way: "It was a repulsive, revolting thing that almost made me throw up. But still, as usual, I wanted to preserve in art that which can't be preserved in it, and this painting somehow began to live in my mind by itself."[1] Aversion, rather than sympathy, prompted Vrubel to magnify the scene, make it larger than life, and turn it into a shaming and humiliating spectacle; as such, the mural continues to negatively define popular ideas about the Soviet bloc. The apparent queerness of the situation captured by the French photographer openly ridicules the socialist systems and their standing in the Cold War through a display of emotive excess, or camp. The campiness of the Brezhnev-Honecker kiss has become so recognizable since 1990 that it now adorns mugs, plates, towels, and T-shirts, memorializing the Cold War era with distant, mocking irony. The hundreds of tourists who take photos with the mural in the background enshrine this image as a key part of distorted Cold War memorabilia, making the communist systems seem even more depraved and feeble in retrospect.

This visual document reveals how pivotal gender and sexuality were, first, in manifesting anxieties during the Cold War and, second, in shaping post–Cold War memories. The politics of the Brezhnev-Honecker kiss thus serve as an apt reminder of the focal role that gender and sexuality played how the Cold War was waged, understood, and experienced. Although scholars still debate the definition, chronology, geographic scope, and overall character of the Cold War, it is difficult to consider it without encountering phenomena directly related to gender and sexuality. Ideas about gender both imbued the ways the Cold War was conducted and also defined the representation of Cold War processes; this appears unsurprising if one considers that gender and sexuality reside at the center of human relations, identities, and practices.

Yet, despite the centrality of gender and sexuality in human relations, their scholarly study has played a secondary role in the history of the Cold War. Instead, diplomatic, military, and economic history have, perhaps understandably, dominated the study of the historical era. Possibly the best indication of this trend is that the current master narrative of the Cold War—the three-volume *Cambridge History of the Cold War* (CHCW)—discusses gender only in terms of women, and women only in terms of consumerism. Equally telling is that CHCW does not index or address sexuality as a field of inquiry. Clearly, even a three-volume compilation of essays cannot cover every topic under the sun. At the same time, by investigating the Cold War through the lens of pluralism, the CHCW overlooks a key feature of the very complexity that defined the period: a gender and sexuality perspective.[2]

Gender and sexuality ought to be included in the kind of Cold War analysis Melvyn Leffler called for in a conceptual essay published some fifteen years ago. He observes that the Cold War constituted a system of "complex interactions between a dynamic international system and its constituent units; between governments operating within that system; between peoples and their governments; between factions, parties, and interest groups."[3] If we adopt Leffler's definition, then surely we will find plenty of opportunities for scholars of gender and sexuality to both enrich and redefine the study of the Cold War. I hope this introduction, and the volume overall, will demonstrate that gender and sexuality are more than useful categories of analysis; they are indispensable to understanding the Cold War more fully as a global phenomenon. This volume's essays, along with the published scholarship to date, speak to the ways the study of the Cold War could advance by more purposefully integrating gender and sexuality into the master narrative.

The study of gender and sexuality reveals much about the character and trajectory of the Cold War. For instance, when the CHCW was published with its panoply of wide-ranging topics, some wondered aloud whether the term "Cold War" had come to be applied so loosely as to lose its analytical usefulness. In this sense, we should take seriously Holger Nehring's concern that "the intellectual and methodological pluralism evident in recent writing on the Cold War" has effectively "decentered" the field, moving it away from its military and diplomatic core. In his words, "The meaning of 'Cold War' as a concept has been diluted significantly, so that 'Cold War' lurks everywhere and can be applied to almost everything, from high politics to the history of everyday life, from actions of statesmen to the mundane."[4] While gender and sexuality are often relegated to the personal and commonplace, scholars from a range of disciplines have demonstrated that we cannot effectively analyze decision making at the very top without taking into account the cultural assumptions of the decision makers. Furthermore, the intensity and scope of the Cold War certainly made the personal political and the political personal: few could evade the tentacular grip of the seemingly totalizing logic of the Cold War.

It is impractical to consider wartime without taking into account the dynamics of gender and sexuality. As Joshua Goldstein demonstrates, war and gender are mutually constitutive, regardless of whether war is fought through military or diplomatic means. As he notes, there is a "reciprocal causality" between war and gender/ sexuality; that is, "causality runs both ways between war and gender."[5] Moreover, postcolonial feminist scholarship has observed that wars occur because power hierarchies grounded in constructions of gender, sexuality, nationality, and ethnicity require them. Warring parties deploy difference to justify domination and, in the process, seek to sustain the hierarchies that imbue the system with meaning.[6] The Cold War fits well into this paradigm, since the maintenance of differences of all kinds remained fundamental to both the superpowers and their allies.

As Nehring himself acknowledges, "the Cold War did not come about suddenly and out of nowhere. Rather, policy makers had actively to create it—and they had to believe in it as a way of understanding the world around them."[7] A number of scholars have thus far demonstrated the centrality of gender—and especially masculinity—to foreign policy and policy makers in the United States.[8] Collectively, these scholars illustrate the artificiality of separating the personal and political. Robert Dean's *Imperial Brotherhood*, in particular, demonstrates that male decision makers' gendered identities and experiences had a profound effect on their worldviews and the kinds of policies they adopted. Dean's focus on elite men helps him zero in on how their collective biography, together with the broader cultural context, set the stage on which the Kennedy and Johnson administrations ventured into (and stayed in) Vietnam even though the campaign was a dead end. These men's shared experiences—such as attending Ivy League institutions and serving in WWII—established toughness, stoicism, and fraternal bonds as key markers of their gendered identities. The Lavender Scare further stressed toughness as a key foreign policy marker: a "soft" approach to the "Soviet threat" would imperil a man's career by exposing him to charges of deviant sexuality.

K. A. Cuordileone's work amplifies the idea that policy at the highest level was heavily influenced by popular discursive practices.[9] The linguistic strategies and imagery attending the early Cold War decades defined gendered identities for a whole generation of liberal-leaning politicians, whose masculinity was defined by a culture obsessed with the fear that men were becoming "soft." Liberals went on the offensive as a gendered panic gripped the United States: the Russians were (always) coming, Alfred Kinsey revealed the nonpuritanical sexual practices of American men (1948) and women (1953), and grey flannel suits masked the empty shells that men had become. Understanding this anxiety-ridden cultural landscape makes it easy to grasp how John F. Kennedy became the liberals' response to the accusation that they were a bunch of striped-pants cookie-pushers from

Harvard. In Joseph Alsop's infamous phrase, Kennedy was "Stevenson with balls." JFK not only projected the image of an alluring philosopher-cum-warrior, but also embodied the idea of a "tough liberal." The demand for toughness found itself expressed in an increasingly hawkish foreign policy, and that toughness was on full display during both the Kennedy and Johnson administrations.

Although no analogous examination of a gendered subculture exists for the Kremlin's Politburo or the leaders of the Warsaw Pact, it is not difficult to imagine that the men in charge of socialist governments felt similarly compelled to be true to their (sub)culture's gendered standards.[10] For instance, Nikita Khrushchev's colorful expressions revealed a worldview that had much in common with Kennedy's and Johnson's. In 1962 Khrushchev memorably reflected on Berlin's limbo status: "Berlin is the testicle of the West. When I want the West to scream, I squeeze on Berlin."[11] In a similar manner Johnson commented on the first US airstrikes against North Vietnam in 1964 by observing, "I didn't just screw Ho Chi Minh. I cut his pecker off."[12] Of course, even the genteel patriarch of Camelot was not far off in asserting his penchant for aggression when he declared, "I would rather take my television black and white and have the largest rockets in the world."[13] Soviet leaders, no less than their US counterparts, worried that their nation found itself in permanent danger of becoming physically, mentally, and spiritually soft.[14]

Anxieties about mental and physical toughness consumed not only the leadership of Cold War governments; those in charge of cultural production also found themselves fixated on (re)presenting appropriate versions of masculinity. For instance, in *Discipline and Indulgence*, Jeffrey Montez de Oca uses the concept of a "fortified masculinity" to uncover the ways that militarism had become a "banal aspect of everyday life" during the first decades of the Cold War. He defines fortified masculinity as "the social construction of masculine, white citizens who could fulfill the state's Cold War needs as disciplined, patriotic workers, warriors, and consumers."[15] The fear of Soviet penetration, as well as the pressure to continue projecting US power abroad, turned sports (and physical education more broadly) into training grounds for men's martial mettle. As Montez de Oca convincingly demonstrates, this development was no accident, but a deliberate and carefully orchestrated campaign that brought college football into American living rooms. As college football and the televised broadcast of sports developed in tandem, they sent a mutually reinforcing message about the authentic expression of masculine vigor.

The war-readiness of Soviet men was under no less scrutiny than that of American men. Soviet men, too, lived in a system that invested itself in winning the superpower standoff; red Cold Warriors were essential to the successful execution of this mission. Erica Fraser, for instance, has shown that "cultural anxieties about manhood in the wake of WWII" affected a wide range of predominantly male (homo)social milieus: from officers in training academies to researchers in scientific institutions, from cosmonauts to young conscripts.[16] Other new and important scholarship has demonstrated that the Soviet authorities exhibited concern that men in the post-Stalin era could not be trusted to independently fashion a masculinity that would adequately represent the stamina and wholesomeness of the socialist system. Brandon Gray Miller's dissertation goes a long way toward demonstrating that Soviet men wanted to shape their own practices of consumption, despite unambiguous signals from the state that lifestyle choices—such as clothing, sex, and alcohol—should follow proscribed norms.[17] Versions of the "soft masculinity crisis" circulated in the mainstream cultures of both superpowers, demonstrating that, despite the Iron Curtain, expectations that men live up to the essentialist male social roles recognized no ideological boundaries.

Cold War–era anxieties about a deficient masculinity not only affected men who hewed closely to social expectations for the nations' erstwhile Cold Warriors, but also defined policies against those who in any way differed from prescriptions about martial masculinity. US historians have done a laudable job of demonstrating the ways in which the history of sexuality, and particularly the panic over homosexuality, forms an integral part of the Cold War saga. They provide the context necessary for understanding how and why the very existence of lesbians, gays, bisexuals, and transgender individuals led to an alarmist discourse that equated "sissies" with "Stalin's atom bomb to destroy America."[18]

Without the martial, hypermasculine discourse and logic attending the superpower conflict, the cultural treatment of homosexuality and nonprocreative sexual practices would likely have acquired a different form and tenor in the postwar period. Reproducing and establishing a stable nuclear family was seen as part and parcel of ensuring the nation's security against outside threats. Once this link was established, one's gender/sexual identity, expression, and practices became automatically tethered to the concept of citizenship.[19] The so-called Lavender Scare, waged in the name of national security, devastated the lives of countless LGBT individuals, defining how the US government waged the Cold War at home.[20] Of course, government agencies were not the only ones that discriminated against sexual minorities in their quest to minimize Cold War "security risks." Churches, schools, and mental health organizations all steeled themselves against the "homosexual threat." Recent works on the medical and psychiatric professions demonstrate the ways in which doctors and psychologists pathologized same-sex attraction and enforced heterosexuality as the norm.[21]

To say that sexual minorities were defenseless against the brutal Cold War tactics of their governments would be to obscure the existence of a spectrum of oppression during this period.[22] On the one hand, ordinary citizens felt a palpable pressure to conform to heterosexual and heterosexist norms by remaining closeted.[23] On the other hand, those LGBT individuals who counted themselves among the cultural elites and who remained discreet could both afford themselves more room to maneuver and also shape mainstream culture. Robert Corber's *Homosexuality in Cold War America* reveals that during the 1950s homosexuality was not rendered invisible, despite near-universal insistence that LGBT culture be driven underground. In fact, film noir, as well as the most celebrated early Cold War (closeted) literary figures, injected mainstream culture with homosexual characters and perspectives. Authors including Tennessee Williams, Gore Vidal, and James Baldwin undermined the Cold War consensus by neither aligning gay men with racial and ethnic minorities nor treating gay male identity as a unitary, unproblematic given. Rather, "they stressed the construction of gay male subjectivity across variable axes of difference." Ultimately, these individuals challenged the Cold War consensus "by politicizing private domains of experience even left-wing intellectuals tended to assume were apolitical."[24] Confirming the centrality of queer individuals to mainstream US culture, Michael S. Sherry's *Gay Artists in Modern American Culture* describes how queer artists, such as Edward Albee, Aaron Copland, Samuel Barber, and Montgomery Clift, participated in fashioning the idiosyncratic cultural landscape of US Cold War culture, helping to define American sensibilities in the process. Sherry convincingly maintains that, by at least one metric, gay artists could hardly be considered marginalized. As he observes, "by definition, those who succeeded—who got orchestras to play their music, theaters to mount their plays, movies to do their scripts—were insiders."[25] Far from being outcasts, gay (elite) men proved to be central in advancing a positive US image abroad and thus, ironically, were complicit in extending the empire's reach. Ultimately, the work of such cultural figures spurred the creation of a mentality that was more accepting of difference and diversity. Newer queer histories do more than expand our understanding of LGBT history; they fundamentally reframe our understanding of the sociocultural and political dynamics of the Cold War. Far from being purely oppressive, the insistence that sexual minorities remain invisible, or closeted, indirectly inspired the gay liberation movement that argued for tolerance and visibility.

Although works on sexuality in socialist systems are few compared to the robust body of studies on US sexualities in the Cold War era, they indicate that the Cold War seemed to create pressures "in the East" similar to those in the West. East European socialist elites felt they had to provide a normative model of sexuality while at the same time demonstrating their supposed tolerance for individual expression. But even within socialist systems there existed marked differences, attributable to contrasting national and cultural traditions. For instance, Josie McLellan's masterful *Love in the Time of Communism* tells the compelling story of East Germany's sexual revolution, which in some respects went further than those taking place in West Germany and elsewhere in the developed world. Even more interesting is McLellan's argument that the East German sexual revolution was a "revolution from below" initiated and sustained by "choices people made about their private lives," not by state officials, the Social Unity Party (SED), or medical professionals.[26] Less tolerant of sexual freedom than their East European counterparts, Soviet authorities exhibited a "sexophobic" attitude in the public arena, according to sexologist Igor Kon. However, the negative attitude toward nonprocreative sex outside of marriage seems to have had more to do with the Soviet tradition of emphasizing "cultured-ness" than with Cold War phobia.[27] In fact, the USSR had no equivalent of the Lavender Scare even though homosexuality was as taboo in the Soviet Union as it was in the United States.

The postwar struggle for women's equality constituted no less of a Cold War battle than the one waged to render LGBT communities invisible or the one to "toughen up" men. Women were seen as essential to the health and survival of the nation. The "masculinity crisis" and the ensuing witch hunt for "sexual deviants" cannot be analyzed without bringing into sharp focus the position of women during the Cold War. Aversions to "soft masculinity" and "deviant sexuality" were bound up with disgust at the concept of "momism."[28] The evils lurking beneath the figure of a domineering mother were unambiguously on display in Angela Lansbury's hair-raising performance of "Mother" in John Frankenheimer's *The Manchurian Candidate* (1962).[29] Although this fear did not have a direct equivalent in Soviet culture, the Soviet authorities worried that too many women were obtaining abortions. The Soviet state thus faced a paradox: it had legalized abortion after Stalin's death but simultaneously argued that abortions "deprived women of happiness."[30] Despite claims about their progressive gender politics, both blocs continued to insist that women see themselves primarily as mothers and that they act as caretakers to ensure men grew up to be worthy Cold Warriors.

The pressures women felt were not limited to the domestic realm. Women's social and political movements were initially subsumed under the patriotic priorities of the Cold War, as women's sociopolitical standing became a litmus test for each ideological system's ability to provide for a full half of its citizenry. Helen Laville's work has done the most to show that the Cold War paradigm profoundly impacted the women's rights movement. She observes that, "until the mid-1960s, the business of securing women's rights through declarations, conventions, and treaties had facilitated the imposition of cold war paradigms on the women's rights agenda by fostering an understanding of women's rights as an expression of the relationship between the nation-state and its women citizens."[31] Only with the full blossoming of the Non-Aligned Movement and the emergence of postcolonial independent states did the women's rights movement adopt a grassroots, rather than state-led, approach.

Although debates on women's status that transpired in global forums had an undeniable and palpable effect on the position of women around the world, arguably the more tangible impact was felt domestically. This is because women's sociopolitical clout proved inseparable from the ideological and political stability of Cold War regimes, particularly in socialist countries. As Donna Harsch's superlative monograph *The Revenge of the Domestic* demonstrates, the principle of gender parity destabilized the social equilibrium of the East German regime. She eloquently points to the economic and social consequences of domestication as gradually undermining the ideological and political foundations of the GDR.[32] Between 1949 and 1961 women, collectively and individually, agitated to equate domestic concerns with those of production; women exerted pressure on the East German authorities to make good on their rhetoric of social and political equality. These efforts resulted in the gradual but certain transition from a "productivist dictatorship" to a "welfare dictatorship." By the 1970s, the state was forced by this pressure "from below" to prioritize issues including consumption, reproduction, working conditions, and child care, ultimately conceding to the power of the domestic.[33]

What impresses about the current scholarship on Cold War–era gender and sexuality outlined above are the parallels and echoes that bridge the gap between the mythical East and West. While the Iron Curtain divided Europe and Cold War tensions made cooperation difficult, the world remained integrated. This observation is not surprising, considering that Cold War historians have in the past two decades become expert practitioners of global and international history, successfully demonstrating that international bodies and global transnational processes compelled the opposing factions to discuss shared problems and forced them to the same bargaining table.[34] Furthermore, scholars have identified different kinds of networks—of scientists, medical professionals, demographers, filmmakers, and athletes—that defied rigid Cold War demarcations and created intrabloc cooperation that could work outside the seemingly totalizing framework of the Cold War.[35] One of the most compelling examples of Cold War "networking" and transference can be found in Paula A. Michael's book on the international history of the Lamaze method.[36] Although popularized in France by Dr. Fernand Lamaze during the 1950s, psychoprophylaxis actually originated in the USSR in the late 1940s when the communist authorities were low on pharmacological anesthetics but eager to increase the birthrate. During a tour of Soviet hospitals in the summer of 1951, Lamaze encountered psychoprophylaxis and began promoting it in France. After this method of childbirth declined in popularity in the USSR and France, it became widespread in the United States during the 1960s and 1970s. Although Michaels makes clear that the Lamaze method was never static, always evolving to fit the idiosyncrasies of time and space, it is revealing that at the height of the Cold War there existed a fluid exchange of ideas about reproduction and the nature of gendered power relations in and out of the maternity ward.

On a more general level, the Cold War also created a zeitgeist inhabited by warring ideological blocs. Without denying that the Cold War rivalry erected literal and figurative walls that exacted a heavy toll on those involved, we must recognize the Cold War as a global event that generated a shared sui generis cultural landscape that was international and collective in character. The existence of this cultural ecosystem has, to date, been most successfully illuminated in the context of the 1960s countercultural movements.[37] Jeremi Suri's work indicates that countries as different as France, West Germany, China, and the USSR responded in similar ways to countercultural pressures. Much as dissimilar national governments felt similarly threatened by the social dislocation countercultural protests created, states participating in the Cold War also experienced keen anxiety about their global stature. This eventually translated into the cultural production of "appropriate" and "deviant" models for identities and practices of gender and sexuality. Very different ideological systems produced analogous gendered models and linked citizenship to a set of very specific and restrictive sexual practices. The scholarship on gender and sexuality within a global framework makes it possible to interpret the Cold War as a struggle for hegemony that created a gendered logic that, in turn, fundamentally shaped the course of Cold War events. It is not an exaggeration to say that few were left unaffected by Cold War gender politics; even those who were in charge of producing, disseminating, and enforcing cultural norms were called on to live by the gender and sexuality models into which they breathed life.

Akira Iriye rightfully points out that "the cold war was a minor theme in the broader history of globalization or of such other themes as environmentalism and human rights."[38] The same standard can be applied to gender and sexuality, since the history and evolution of these two concepts is not restricted to the Cold War era. Both idiosyncratic local phenomena and homogenizing global trends can point to the relatively tangential impact of the superpower conflict on identities, expressions, and practices of gender and sexuality. At the same time, to reduce the Cold War to a geostrategic competition would be to miss a crucial, if not fundamental, chapter in the history of gender and sexuality on global and local levels. By the same token, to ignore the profound ways that models of gender and sexuality in the

Cold War affected everything from the evolution of foreign policy to the history of football would be to miss the point that Cold War logic was inseparable from contemporaneous cultural assumptions about gender and sexuality.

Notes

1. Andrey Borzenko, "Brotherly Love, 25 Years On: The Artist behind the Iconic Berlin Wall Mural Tells His Story," *The Calvert Journal*, November 11, 2014, *calvertjournal. com/articles/show/3356/Dmitri-Vrubel-Berlin-Wall-Brezhnev-Honecker-Kiss*.

2. In the preface Leffler and Westad state that "the CHCW aims at being comprehensive, comparative, and pluralist in its approach." Melvyn P. Leffler and Odd Arne Westad, preface to *The Cambridge History of the Cold War*, vol. 1 (Cambridge: Cambridge University Press, 2010), xvi.

3. Melvyn P. Leffler, "Bringing It Together: The Parts and the Whole," in *Reviewing the Cold War: Approaches, Interpretations, Theory*, ed. Odd A. Westad, ed. (London: Frank Cass, 2000), 58.

4. Holger Nehring, "What Was the Cold War?," *English Historical Review* 127, no. 527 (2012): 923.

5. Joshua S. Goldstein, *War and Gender: How Gender Shapes the War System and Vice Versa* (Cambridge: Cambridge University Press, 2001).

6. Francine D'Amico and Laurie Lee Weinstein, *Gender Camouflage: Women and the U. S. Military* (New York: New York University Press, 1999); and Geeta Chowdhry and Sheila Nair, eds., *Power, Postcolonialism, and International Relations: Reading Race, Gender, and Class* (New York: Routledge, 2002).

7. Nehring, "What Was the Cold War?," 927.

8. The most prominent representatives in this grouping include Lucian M. Ashworth and Larry A. Swatuk, "Masculinity and the Fear of Emasculation in International Relations Theory," in *The Man Question in International Relations*, ed. Marysia Zalewski and Jane L. Parpart (Boulder, CO: Westview, 1998), 73–92; Frank Costigliola, "'Unceasing Pressure for Penetration': Gender, Pathology, and Emotion in George Kennan's Formation of the Cold War," *Journal of American History* (1997): 1309–39; Emily S. Rosenberg, *Financial Missionaries to the World: The Politics and Culture of Dollar Diplomacy, 1900–1930* (Cambridge, MA: Harvard University Press, 1999); Melani McAlister, "'The Common Heritage of Mankind': Negotiating Race, Nation, and Masculinity in the King Tut Exhibit," *Representations* 54 (Spring 1996): 80–103; Alexander Deconde, *Presidential Machismo: Executive Authority, Military Intervention, and Foreign Relations* (Boston: Northeastern University Press, 2000); Geoffrey S. Smith, "National Security and Personal Isolation: Sex, Gender, and Disease in the Cold-War United States," *International History Review* 14, no. 2 (1992): 307–37; and Charlotte Hooper, *Manly States: Masculinities, International Relations, and Gender Politics* (New York: Columbia University Press, 2001).

9. K. A. Cuordileone, *Manhood and American Political Culture in the Cold War* (New York: Routledge, 2005).

10. Taubman's masterly biography of Nikita Khrushchev, does, however, go a long way toward providing us with insights about the party secretary's gender identity, even though this is not Taubman's analytical focus. William Taubman, *Khrushchev: The Man and His Era* (New York: W. W. Norton, 2003).

11. Quoted in Frederick Taylor, *The Berlin Wall: A World Divided, 1961–1989* (New York: Harper Collins, 2006), xix.

12. Quoted in Goldstein, *War and Gender*, 358.

13. Quoted in Dean, *Imperial Brotherhood*, 181.

14. This is an area ripe for further investigation that will undoubtedly reveal the centrality of gender in decision-making processes in the Soviet context as well. Since the connection between Vladimir Putin's rule and gender identity has received plenty of scholarly attention, it stands to reason that the conduct of Soviet leaders could benefit from a similar analysis. See, for instance, Valerie Sperling, *Sex, Politics, and Putin: Political Legitimacy in Russia* (Oxford: Oxford University Press, 2014).

15. Jeffrey Montez de Oca, *Discipline and Indulgence: College Football, Media, and the American Way of Life during the Cold War* (New Brunswick, NJ: Rutgers University Press, 2013), 20.

16. Erica Fraser, "Masculinities in the Motherland: Gender and Authority in the Soviet Union during the Cold War, 1945–1968" (PhD diss., University of Illinois at Urbana-Champaign, 2009).

17. Brandon Gray Miller, "Between Creation and Crisis: Soviet Masculinities, Consumption, and Bodies after Stalin" (PhD diss., Michigan State University, 2013).

18. David K. Johnson, *The Lavender Scare: The Cold War Persecution of Gays and Lesbians in the Federal Government* (Chicago: University of Chicago Press, 2006), 37.

19. Carolyn Herbst Lewis, *Prescription for Heterosexuality: Sexual Citizenship in the Cold War Era* (Chapel Hill: University of North Carolina Press, 2010).

20. See Johnson, *Lavender Scare*; and Stacy Braukman, *Communists and Perverts under the Palms: The Johns Committee in Florida, 1956–1965* (Gainesville: University Press of Florida, 2012).

21. See, for instance, Lewis, *Prescription for Heterosexuality*; and Mary Louise Adams, *The Trouble with Normal: Postwar Youth and the Making of Heterosexuality* (Toronto: University of Toronto Press, 1997).

22. I reflect more thoroughly on the concept of an oppression spectrum in a review essay, "Spectrums of Oppression: Gender and Sexuality during the Cold War," *Journal of Cold War Studies* 16, no. 3 (Summer 2014): 190–204.

23. Craig M. Loftin, *Masked Voices: Gay Men and Lesbians in Cold War America* (Albany: State University of New York Press, 2012).

24. Robert J. Corber, *Homosexuality in Cold War America: Resistance and the Crisis of Masculinity* (Durham: Duke University Press, 1997), 191–92.

25. Michael S. Sherry, *Gay Artists in Modern American Culture: An Imagined Conspiracy* (Chapel Hill: University of North Carolina Press, 2007), 93.

26. Josie McLellan, *Love in the Time of Communism: Intimacy and Sexuality in the GDR* (Cambridge: Cambridge University Press, 2011).

27. Dan Healey, "Comrades, Queers, and 'Oddballs': Sodomy, Masculinity, and Gendered Violence in Leningrad Province of the 1950s," *Journal of the History of Sexuality* 21, no. 3 (2012): 496–522.

28. See for instance, Rebecca Jo Plant, *Mom: The Transformation of Motherhood in Modern America* (Chicago: University of Chicago Press, 2010); and Jennifer Terry, "Momism and the Making of Treasonous Homosexuals," in *"Bad" Mothers: The Politics of Blame in Twentieth Century America*, ed. Molly Ladd-Taylor and Lauri Umansky (New York: New York University Press, 1998), 169–90.

29. Kathleen Starck, "The Ultimate Cold War Monster: Exploring 'Mother' in the Film

The Manchurian Candidate," in *The Female of the Species: Cultural Constructions of Evil, Women and the Feminine*, ed. Hannah Priest (Oxfordshire, England: Inter-Disciplinary Press, 2013), 75–90.

30. Amy E. Randall, "'Abortion Will Deprive You of Happiness!': Soviet Reproductive Politics in the Post-Stalin Era," *Journal of Women's History* 23, no. 3 (Fall 2011): 13–38.

31. Helen Laville, "Gender and Women's Rights in the Cold War," in *The Oxford Handbook of the Cold War*, ed. Richard H. Immerman and Petra Goedde (Oxford: Oxford University Press, 2013), p. 534.

32. Donna Harsch, *Revenge of the Domestic: Women, the Family, and Communism in the German Democratic Republic* (Princeton: Princeton University Press, 2007).

33. Soviet historians have also reflected on the increasing importance of the personal and domestic in postwar Soviet life. See, for instance, Deborah Field, *Private Life and Communist Morality in Khrushchev's Russia* (New York: Peter Lang, 2007); Natalya Chernyshova, *Soviet Consumer Culture in the Brezhnev Era* (New York: Routledge, 2013); and Susan E. Reid, "The Khrushchev Kitchen: Domesticating the Scientific-Technological Revolution," *Journal of Contemporary History* 40, no. 2 (2005): 289–316.

34. Helen Laville, *Cold War Women: The International Activities of American Women's Organizations* (Manchester: Manchester University Press, 2009); Akira Iriye, *Global Community: The Role of International Organizations in the Making of the Contemporary World* (Berkeley: University of California Press, 2002); Jocelyn Olcott, "Cold War Conflicts and Cheap Cabaret: Performing Politics at the 1975 United Nations International Women's Year Conference in Mexico City," *Gender and History* 22, no. 3 (2010): 733–54.

35. Erez Manela, "A Pox on Your Narrative: Writing Disease Control into Cold War History," *Diplomatic History* 34, no. 2 (April 2010): 299–323; Bradley Simpson, *Economists with Guns: Authoritarian Development and U.S.-Indonesian Relations, 1960–1968* (Stanford, CA: Stanford University Press, 2008); and Matthew Connelly, *Fatal Misconception: The Struggle to Control World Population* (Cambridge, MA: Harvard University Press, 2008).

36. Paula A. Michaels, *Lamaze: An International History* (Oxford: Oxford University Press, 2014).

37. Martin Klimke, *The Other Alliance: Student Protest in West Germany and the United States in the Global Sixties* (Princeton: Princeton University Press, 2009); Jeremi Suri, *Power and Protest: Global Revolution and the Rise of Détente* (Cambridge, MA: Harvard University Press, 2003); Gerd-Rainer Horn, *The Spirit of '68: Rebellion in Western Europe and North America, 1956–1976* (New York: Oxford University Press, 2007); and Arthur Marwick, *The Sixties: Cultural Revolution in Britain, France, Italy, and United States, c. 1958–c. 1974* (Oxford: Oxford University Press, 1998).

38. Akira Iriye, "Historicizing the Cold War," in Immerman and Goedde, *Oxford Handbook of the Cold War*, 15–31.

PART I

Sexuality

CHAPTER 1

Faceless and Stateless

French Occupation Policy toward Women and Children in Postwar Germany (1945–1949)

Katherine Rossy

By the spring of 1945, Germany was partitioned into four occupation zones. In the German states of Hessen, Bavaria, and north Baden-Württemberg, the Americans structured their German program around the "Four D's" of the Potsdam Agreement—demilitarization, denazification, democratization, and decentralization—while countering the threat of communist expansion in the East.[1] In Thuringia, Saxony, Brandenburg, and Mecklenburg-Vorpommern, the Russians established a new empire in which communism would triumph over Nazism and capitalism while attempting to exploit as many German resources and technologies as possible, all the while "liberating" those under their control through a systematic propaganda apparatus.[2] In Hamburg, Hanover, Schleswig-Holstein, Lower Saxony, and North Rhine-Westphalia, the British sought to reconstruct German society through an intensive re-education program in the hopes of reviving economic cooperation and preserving the balance of power on the continent, all the while buffering Western Europe from Soviet expansion.[3] In Baden, Württemberg, Pfalz, and the Saar, the French exploited German economic resources while exercising zealous cultural and immigration policies designed to engender French "grandeur," a vision in which France would surpass the rest of Europe and once again take its place alongside the world's great powers.[4]

As the occupation took shape, it quickly became evident that postwar reconstruction was not just a matter of repairing shattered infrastructure and denazifying a people influenced by twelve years of fanatical Nazi ideology. Wartime atrocities had ushered in droves of refugees and displaced persons. Among these people were tens of thousands of displaced, orphaned, stolen, and abandoned children who created part of what Tony Judt has called the "human flotsam of war."[5]

While some children were happily reunited with their families after the war, some had no surviving relatives to claim them. Others were too young or traumatized to recall who they were, and many of these children did not have any identity documents or papers in their possession. Some children were the unanticipated consequence of rape or sexual relations between prisoners of war, forced laborers, civilians, and occupation soldiers, while others had been brought to Germany against their will to be put to work or exterminated in concentration camps. These are but several of the possible scenarios that led children to overcrowded cellars and bombed-out buildings, institutions and hospitals, refugee camps, children's homes, transit centers, and repatriation convoys after the war.

As Tara Zahra has argued, "Children were central objects of population politics, nation building projects, and new forms of humanitarian intervention in the twentieth century, as they represented the biological and political future of national communities."[6] For many nations, recovering missing children was the penultimate step toward postwar reconstruction. But theory differed greatly from practice, and locating children in Germany would quickly prove to be one of the most challenging reconstruction policies of the postwar period.

No nation was more concerned with recuperating its missing children than France. To French military authorities and policy makers, recovering and repatriating children who were presumed to be of French origin was a means both of transcending the "dark years" of Vichy collaboration and of solving a decades-long demographic anxiety. The repatriation of French children, furthermore, also symbolized a fundamental element of France's new role on the postwar stage. But finding these children proved to be a most challenging task, as it required the careful cooperation of the military authorities and humanitarian agencies that operated in the French Zone. Under its agreement with the Supreme Headquarters Allied Expeditionary Force in October 1944, the United Nations Relief and Rehabilitation Administration (UNRRA) would act as the principal humanitarian organization during the postmilitary period.[7] Established by U. S. President Franklin D. Roosevelt in Atlantic City in 1943, UNRRA was responsible for coordinating the health, welfare, registration, administration, and repatriation of all United Nations refugees and displaced persons found in enemy or ex-enemy territory between May 1945 and July 1947.[8] The International Refugee Organization (IRO) then resumed UNRRA's activities after its mandate formally ended in July 1947.[9] Unlike the United States and the United Kingdom, France was the only Western occupation authority to exclude UNRRA and the IRO from child search and repatriation efforts. The French chose instead to operate their own child search program through the Tracing Bureau of its Displaced Persons and Prisoners of War branch, whose activities were carried out by the French Red Cross as of December 1945.[10] By choosing to operate outside the international channels championed by the Americans and the British, the French placed the child question within the broader context of the occupation of Germany as a means of furthering concerns about demography, immigration, and the nuclear family across the Rhine. Wedged between two emerging superpowers, the United States and the Soviet Union, French policy toward unaccompanied children marked an attempt to legitimize France as a major power player on the postwar stage as the Iron Curtain began its rapid descent through Eastern Europe.

The "Big Three" and France

When the Nazis unconditionally surrendered on May 8, 1945, the Allies stood at the tail end of a long and bloody succession of wars and occupations against Germany. But the circumstances of defeat had changed, and defeat was now total. The German people were both active and passive perpetrators of some of the most harrowing crimes against humanity that humankind had ever known. Cities were reduced to piles of rubble, and villages were wiped off the map. Entire populations were rendered stateless and driven from their homes, and millions of Jews were systematically exterminated. After Auschwitz, Belzec, Birkenau, and Buchenwald, guilt and denial became deeply engrained in the German collective conscience.[11] In this light, it was not Germany that menaced the Allies after capitulation but a new nemesis in the East, the Soviet Union, an emerging superpower against whom the United States and Britain would square off, leaving France to question the place it was to occupy in a new Cold War order.

It was the French, however, and not the Soviets, who were the outliers during the first phase of the occupation of Germany in 1945. Tensions mounted between the "Big Three" and France during the signing of the German Act of Capitulation in Berlin on May 8, 1945, in Marshal Georgy Zhukov's headquarters in Karlshorst, an episode during which Jean de Lattre de Tassigny, the French signatory, noticed that the French flag was missing:

> I required that France should be represented at this ceremony with her flag in a place of equality with those of her Allies . . . and in fact it was a business! A diplomatic affair to start with, for everyone was not in agreement. A Brigadier-General, learning of my request, had even cried out "And why not China!" It was a practical matter above all, for a French flag could nowhere be found. The Russians decided to make one, with a piece of red stuff taken from a former Hitlerite banner, a white sheet and a piece of blue serge cut out of an engineer's overalls. . . . At last, at 20.00, our national emblem was placed between those of Great Britain and the United States in a cluster surmounted by the Soviet flag.[12]

Charles de Gaulle recalls that even Wilhelm Keitel, Hitler's war minister, was resentful of France's participation in Germany's unconditional surrender, exclaiming, "What? The French too!"[13] Vichy collaboration had made the "Big Three" deeply skeptical of France's participation in the occupation of Germany, especially since Vichy collaborators had fought against the Allies in North Africa in November 1942.[14] Although the Allies did not formally declare war on the Vichy government, they imposed an economic blockade on Vichy France and its colonies.[15] Joseph Stalin had remarked that it was Henri-Philippe Pétain, and not de Gaulle, who symbolized "the real physical France."[16] At Yalta, he told Roosevelt that the "Big Three" was an "exclusive club . . . restricted to a membership of nations with five million soldiers," and had insisted that France had no place as an occupier since "she had not done much fighting in the war."[17] It was Winston Churchill who defended French interests in Germany. Churchill and Roosevelt supported different French émigré governments during the war; Roosevelt backed

Henri Giraud, who controlled French North Africa and claimed to have no political aims, while Churchill supported de Gaulle, who controlled French Equatorial Africa and Oceania from his headquarters in London.[18] As Britain grew more anxious about Soviet expansion by the spring of 1945, Churchill recognized that the key to Britain's survival as a great power lay in a shared occupation effort with France. The need to stabilize a shifting postwar dynamic meant that "Britain had a strong interest in bolstering French power on the Continent as a counterweight to a revived Germany, but more realistically, to the spectre of Soviet communism."[19] Fearful that rapidly expanding Soviet influence would tilt the balance of power in Germany, Churchill telegraphed Roosevelt in November 1944: "How will it be possible to hold down Western Germany beyond the present Russian occupation line? . . . All would therefore rapidly disintegrate as it did last time. . . . I hope however that my fears are groundless. I put my faith in you."[20] Roosevelt was wary of France's ability to sustain the burden of occupation, informing Churchill in February 1944 that he was "absolutely unwilling to police France" and that "France is [Churchill's] baby and will take a lot of nursing in order to bring it to the point of walking alone."[21] But since Roosevelt had initially planned for US troops to occupy Germany for only a two-year period, a plan that was quickly abandoned following the rapid breakdown of American-Soviet relations in 1947, Churchill convinced Roosevelt and Stalin to authorize the creation of a French Zone of Occupation, an hourglass-shaped territory bordering the Rhine created jointly by carved-out portions of the American and British Zones.[22]

For the French, participating in the shared occupation of Germany was as much a means of avenging its long-time *enemi héréditaire* (hereditary enemy) as it was a race to establish hegemony in a new Cold War order. Following Liberation in 1944 and the establishment of the Provisional Government under de Gaulle's leadership, the purge of those considered traitors and collaborators raised many questions about France's rightful place as a victor, ally, and world power. Occupying Germany would provide the French with an opportunity to practice *une grande politique européenne* (grand European policy) through a doctrine known as the "French Thesis."[23] First discussed by Georges Bidault, the French foreign minister, at the London Conference in September 1945, the French Thesis was, in many ways, an intensification of Rhineland policy after the First World War. As Alistair Cole points out, the legacies of the Versailles peace treaty had given way to two lines of reasoning in 1945: the hard-line "Poincaré approach," which sought to punish Germany by imposing a Carthaginian peace with hefty war indemnities, and the more lenient "Briand approach," which sought reconciliation with its former enemy in order to foster European cooperation.[24] The French Thesis was acutely *poincarien* at the beginning of the occupation, in that it was intended to safeguard France from future German aggression by securing French economic interests through the exploitation of German resources, including coal from the Saar. Like Georges Clemenceau before him, de Gaulle needed "to be assured that French forces will be stationed permanently from one end of the Rhine to the other," as he expressed the matter on January 25, 1945; the neutralization of the left bank of the Rhine was non-negotiable for French security.[25] In this regard, coal and security again became the principal aim of the French occupation of Germany.

The French Thesis was intended to do more than secure French economic interests, however. It was also created to finance a costly occupation effort. On June 22, 1945, the four military powers signed an agreement concerning the structure of the German occupation administrations.[26] Much to de Gaulle's displeasure, the French Zone would include only Baden and Württemberg, thus making it the smallest of the occupation zones, while the key cities of Stuttgart and Karlsruhe were absorbed into the American Zone.[27] The French also administered the smallest population, totaling approximately 5.8 million civilians.[28] As the occupation effort began to take shape, it soon became evident that postwar reconstruction, the overarching goal of the dismemberment and occupation of Germany, was not only a matter of denazifying, democratizing, and reeducating the populations under Allied and Soviet control. The very nature of occupation, characterized by civilian displacement, food shortages, health crises, and sexual violence, forced the German people to face the "direct experiences of war and defeat."[29] Since the postwar German population was composed of 36 million German women and just 28 million German men, moreover, it soon became evident that the occupation of Germany was an inherently gendered one.[30]

A Gendered Occupation

The postwar German population was a fusion of women, children, concentration camp victims, displaced persons, refugees, and prisoners of war. By May 1945, 60 percent of Berlin's total population of 2.6 million was composed of women, refugees, and occupation soldiers.[31] Seventy million cubic meters of the city had been reduced to rubble, and aerial bombing had destroyed over 50 percent of homes.[32] A January 10, 1945, Swedish newspaper article describes the shocking sight of war-torn Berlin: "We are struck by the sight of ruins upon returning to Berlin after one year of absence. . . . [S]ometimes it is impossible to find the houses in which we lived several years earlier. The walls are collapsing to the point where they [are] falling into neighboring buildings. . . . We ask ourselves if it will even be possible to rebuild the city in the future."[33] A February 1, 1945, BBC article conveys similar conditions, reporting that "the people of Berlin, already in a miserable state due to Allied aerial attacks, are trembling from cold and are hungry. They have not had coal since last Sunday and are lacking more and more bread and potatoes."[34] Ironically, as Konrad Jarausch points out, the "Aryan master race" now had to "transform itself into a welfare community made up of disabled veterans, widows, orphans, refugees, expellees, and the homeless."[35] Berlin, and Germany more generally, was not just a defeated city but also a "rupture of civilization" that was rife with chaos.[36]

Amid heaps of bombed-out infrastructure and the promise of meager food rations, Germans anxiously awaited the arrival of occupation troops. Fear and uncertainty saturated the postwar climate as each civilian attempted to come to terms with the consequences of defeat and the expectations of military occupation: "Would the Germans be allowed to survive at all, or would their liberated neighbors exact a bloody revenge for the crimes that had been committed against them? How would the occupation powers deal with this defeated people . . . would they grant them a minimal sustenance so that they might live on somehow?"[37] It quickly became evident that German girls and women were to receive very different answers to these questions than their male counterparts.

The inherently gendered experience of occupation forced many girls and women into difficult and deadly predicaments. Rape happened on a mass scale, especially during the "liberation" of Berlin in April 1945 when Soviet shock troops ravaged and pillaged their way through Eastern Europe, raping the young, the pregnant, the elderly, and the sickly as they advanced toward Germany. As Robert Moeller points out, the rape of German women by the Red Army symbolized "the rape of the German nation" and became a means of avenging a people whose regime had murdered millions in the Holocaust and on the Eastern Front.[38] Atina Grossmann, one of the first scholars to break the silence on the Red Army rapes during the 1990s, suggests that Berlin's notorious "Week of Mass Rapes" from April 24 to May 8, 1945, served as a vehicle of humiliation to demoralize the German people.[39] Frederick Taylor claims that Soviet propaganda encouraged the Red Army to rape German women who had "sat safe at home while the men of the Wehrmacht ravaged Belarus, the Ukraine, the Caucasus, the plains before Moscow."[40] Antony Beevor makes a different claim by arguing that the Red Army viewed German women as "sexual spoils of war" instead of "substitutes for the Wehrmacht on which to vent their rage," raping girls as young as nine and women as old as ninety.[41]

Rape quickly paved the way toward fraternization, which became a preferred method of escaping the gendered realities of defeat. Wartime rape and fraternization are not mutually exclusive, however. As Atina Grossman argues, fraternization is "the putatively 'other,' but frequently difficult-to-disentangle side of the rape story."[42] As Grossmann points out, the permeable boundary between forced sex and consensual sex within the context of occupation makes it difficult to distinguish between those who are raped and those who fraternize, often semi-willingly.[43] Although the gendered nature of occupation forced girls and women into impossible predicaments, this did not arouse much sympathy from the rest of the civilian population. The use of degrading terms like *Schokoladenhure* (chocolate whore) to describe women who fraternized with occupation soldiers in exchange for commodities like chocolate bars and cigarettes reflects German men's interpretation of fraternization as a humiliating symbol of defeat.[44] Fraternization thus sparked violent backlash by German civilians and returning Wehrmacht soldiers who punished women who engaged with the occupier. Fraternization lists were circulated throughout the occupation zones, subjecting many women to violent attacks such as the humiliating practice of haircutting and head shaving.[45] This gendered practice was also commonplace in Liberation France, where French civilians and returning prisoners of war engaged in public haircutting rituals to shame Frenchwomen who had collaborated with Wehrmacht soldiers during the German occupation of France.[46]

Fraternization motives become especially clear within the context of mass food shortages that submerged the postwar German population into desperate hunger. A former enemy people, the German population now depended on the victors for survival. The hunger crisis of the winter of 1946–1947 marked a record low for zonal food rationing, reaching an alleged 950 calories in the American Zone, 850 calories in the British Zone, and 450 calories in the French Zone, a far cry from the average 1,550 calories needed to sustain basic metabolic function.[47] Hunger had particular ramifications on women, who made up a larger portion of the population. The gendered nature of occupation meant that women often had the task of "negotiating the impossible food situation," Alice Weinreb argues.[48] The harsh realities of the immediate postwar period also placed women in what Petra Goedde calls a "paradoxical position," in that they provided for their families while depending on occupation soldiers for basic necessities and foodstuffs.[49] Grossmann argues that since women were often more negatively affected by food shortages than men, the food crisis also became a convenient way to punish women for their involvement in Nazi organizations; they were often given *Himmelsfahrkarte*, low-level ration cards that were nicknamed "ticket to heaven" cards.[50]

The gendered nature of food rationing also shifted German women's roles, forcing women to rummage the streets, forage for food, and build ersatz shelters to house children, the sick, and the elderly. As German anthropologist Hilde Thurnwald noted in her study of 498 Berlin families, "women [had] moved into the central position as providers" by 1947.[51] German women "queued for a handout of butter and dry sausage, while men emerged only to line up for an issue of schnapps," a reality Beevor finds ironic following twelve years of sexist Nazi family policy.[52] A predominately female population therefore meant that German women now assumed the roles of provider and protector in addition to those of caretaker and nurturer.

These women, who Moeller calls the *Trümmerfrauen* (women of the rubble), "cleared away the ruins of bombed German cities to pave the way for a new beginning."[53] In many ways, the backbreaking work of the *Trümmerfrauen* marked the beginning of German women's social and political mobilization during the postwar period. Being bombed out of their homes drove German women out of the domestic sphere and into the public eye, which became the site of many early democratization efforts. Democratization was a process hindered by the physical realities of the postwar period, however. As Peter Duignan points out, "The very infrastructure required for political life seemed shattered beyond repair—meeting halls and office buildings were in ruins, newspaper presses halted, funds scarce, Allied licenses required for all party work."[54] Yet, political life gradually resumed. Despite a chaotic start, the Soviet Military Administration was the first to provide German women with a relative degree of agency, provided that they pledged their loyalty to the Communist Party. In June 1945, Soviet authorities authorized Germans to mobilize into antifascist political parties.[55] The Soviet authorities likewise permitted the *Trümmerfrauen* to assemble into antifascist groups, and in 1946 members of the Sozialistische Einheitspartei Deutschlands (Socialist Unity Party of Germany) began to rally support from the Women's Branch of the Soviet administration to push for the creation of the Demokratischer Frauenbund Deutschlands (Democratic Women's League), which boasted a membership of 484,075 by January 1950.[56]

The British, who were initially skeptical about political activity in the British Zone, authorized the formation of political parties in September 1945, which led to a revival of social democratic and communist parties in their zone.[57] British women, however, were the first to support German women's social and political empowerment, which is not surprising considering that the United Kingdom had a long, successful history of feminist activism. In August 1946, the Townswomen's Guild and the National Federation of Women's Institutes petitioned the Labour Party to improve the status of German women in the British Zone; in November 1947, six British women's organizations, including the National Federation of Business and Professional Women's Clubs, the National Council of Women of Great Britain, and the YWCA, wrote to Ernest Bevin, the British foreign secretary, to ask that German women be included in the reconstruction effort.[58] Soon thereafter, the British Military Government established a Women's Affairs Branch in 1947, whose personnel began to collaborate with the Relief Team of the British Red Cross to address women's issues.[59]

The Americans were next to acknowledge the importance of a democratized female population. Female journalists and politicians had urged the Office of Military Government, United States (OMGUS) to sanction women's associations in the US Zone as early as 1946.[60] In November 1947, the OMGUS Civil Administration Division asked the members of the Carrie Chapman Catt Memorial Fund, an organization founded in April 1947 to promote awareness about the workings of democracy, to establish a German women's organization in the US Zone and to sponsor visits by German women to the United States.[61] Following public pressure from female journalists in the *New York Times*, US General Lucius D. Clay established the Women's Branch on January 23, 1948.[62] The branch then sanctioned German women's participation in social and political affairs by authorizing, in 1946, the revival of women's magazines, many of which had been banned following Hitler's seizure of power in 1933. These magazines celebrated German women's return to public life and even promoted women's participation in traditionally male-dominated jobs.

Although these advancements by no means symbolized an attempt to fully empower women, they nevertheless marked a key step toward the democratization of the German civilian population. But the democratization of women in the French Zone unfurled in a radically different manner, if at all. Four regime changes in six years meant that France had its own politics to contend with.[63] Since Frenchwomen had only been enfranchised in 1944, it should come as no surprise that German women were disempowered in the French Zone. Unlike their British, American, and Soviet counterparts, who had each established a women's branch and sanctioned women's social and political activity by 1948, the French did not establish a women's branch in their occupation administration, nor did they sanction women's activities or authorize the creation of women's organizations. A reluctance to acknowledge the inherently gendered nature of occupation resulted in the complete absence of policy toward women in the French Zone, an absence that was, in many ways, overshadowed by an abundance of French policy toward children. Much to the detriment of women under occupation, the French were determined to secure the moral and material future of the French nation through the safeguarding of French children. And the solution lay, as it had many times before, in demography.

Depopulation, Occupation, Repatriation

The three basic objectives of de Gaulle's Provisional Government were to modernize the French public service, to nationalize industry, and to reform family and immigration policy.[64] The third objective would have a direct effect on occupation policy toward children across the Rhine. In his state of the nation speech during the spring of 1945, de Gaulle told the French people that "since the French population would not multiply, and since the French nation could not be a bright light going out," France needed to produce "twelve million bonnie babies in ten years" by decreasing infant mortality rates and introducing new immigration schemes.[65] This meant that France desperately needed children, and quickly. But the French obsession with depopulation was by no means new. Postwar family policy merely continued a long tradition of natalism that had dominated French domestic policy as early as the mid-nineteenth century. Reforms in postwar family and immigration policy were strongly rooted in "populationism," an ideology that attempted to reconstruct the French demographic along the lines of "nation, race, ethnicity, and gender."[66] This was not an innovation of the French Provisional Government either, but rather the continuation of a natalist obsession that had led countries like Italy, Russia, and Germany to experiment with ways to strengthen their populations.

In Fascist Italy, depopulation concerns led to a failed pronatal and pronuptial campaign that Benito Mussolini had hoped would act as a "demographic jolt" to raise the low Italian birthrate. He unsuccessfully imposed a bachelor tax on unmarried men and introduced severer penalties for women who illegally terminated their pregnancies.[67] Stalin also experimented with pronatal policies and failed. The criminalization of abortion in 1936 as well as generous compensation for women who had six or more children marked attempts to increase the Russian birthrate.[68] Nazi family policy was also based on demographics, however its focus on eugenics characterize it as a most extreme form of populationism. Nazi policy sought to redesign the "Aryan race" along highly selective, racialized lines at the expense of all who did not fit into Hitler's murderous worldview. The resulting antinatal and anti-Semitic policies of the Third Reich, such as the Law for the Prevention of Genetically Diseased Offspring (1933) and the Nuremberg Laws (1935), prevented millions of Jews, Roma people, political enemies, and individuals who were deemed "racially," physically, and psychologically "unfit" from having children.

French domestic policy had long been entangled with the natalist obsession. The low national birthrate had been used to fuel Germanophobia and *révanchisme* following France's defeat in the Franco-Prussian War of 1870–1871, sentiments that were intensified after the First World War had left half of all Frenchmen between the ages of eighteen and thirty-five dead.[69] The tumultuous political climate of interwar France reinforced "female domesticity" and traditional gender roles, portraying the French mother as a "cultural representation of [a] longing to heal and forget" the horrors of war in an attempt to revive the war-torn nation.[70] These sentiments echoed in the government's criminalization of contraceptives in 1920, which imposed harsh penalties for women who had abortions and created family allowances and financial compensation for childbirth.[71] Demographic anxieties continued to saturate the domestic policies of the Third Republic until the eve of the Second World War. On July 29, 1939, the Daladier government introduced the Code de la Famille, whose natalist policies would later form the basis of family policy under the Pétain and de Gaulle governments. The code made demography a mandatory subject in school curricula, increased penalties for abortion, and offered financial compensation to mothers who gave birth to children within the first two years of marriage.[72] Pronatal movements such as the Alliance Nationale would continue to obsess over depopulation by supporting the taxation of unmarried individuals and the criminalization of public awareness about birth control.[73]

Demographic anxieties further intensified in Vichy France, where abortion was made a capital offense in 1941.[74] The patriarchal elements of Vichy familialism created separate gender spheres in which women were expected to be nurturing mothers and dutiful housewives while men were to be patriarchs and providers.[75] Fernand Boverat, the leader of the Alliance Nationale, insisted to Pétain that they must "defeat depopulation" and that "a family that produces only two children in each generation is condemned to disappear. . . . The minimum family is the family of three children, and there is no more indispensable truth to be imposed on the minds of Frenchmen than this."[76] In November 1941, Alexis Carrel, the founder of the Foundation for the Study of Human Problems, was allocated an annual budget of 40 million francs to conduct research on ways to physically and morally strengthen the French demographic by encouraging the "strongest" and "fittest" to procreate.[77] The legacies of Vichy eugenics and demographic reconstruction resonated in post-Liberation policy as well. In 1945, the Ministry of Health was renamed the Ministry of Population and Public Health, proving that French demographic anxieties were as rampant as ever.[78] This obsession with depopulation resulted in new demographic policies that directly affected unaccompanied, displaced, orphaned, and abandoned children in the French Zone of occupied Germany.

By the spring of 1945, the French had begun to consider the mass hodgepodge of children across the Rhine as a means of remedying the decades-long concern about depopulation. On July 26, 1946, French officials circulated a secret memorandum regarding the demographic potential of the children of French prisoners of war, deportees, and workers who were left stranded in Germany after the war: "The majority of them are abandoned children who we cannot leave in Germany because the fate of France's demography is at stake. It would be one thing to have Germany benefit from a population increase that it certainly does not deserve, which would contradict our thesis on the necessity of reducing the German population. These children of unknown parentage are a wealth that a country of weak population density must not ignore."[79]

It was next to impossible to accurately determine the extent of the unaccompanied child problem, however. By March 1947, UNRRA had processed a staggering 11,861 children's cases in the three Western occupation zones: 2,364 children were repatriated, 1,398 children were resettled, and 881 were settled under other circumstances, including "reunion(s) with relatives, reaching 18 years, marrying, death, etc."[80] Of this number, only 7,218 unaccompanied children of United Nations parentage in the French, British, and American Zones of Occupation were successfully located and identified, including 4,278 Jewish children and 2,940 non-Jewish children.[81] Although there were an estimated 135,000 displaced children living with parents and close family members in Displaced Persons camps in the three western zones, the total number of unaccompanied children in Germany after the war could not accurately be determined.[82] As one June 1947 UNRRA report pointed out, "For over a year after the war ended, populations were milling back and forth across Europe, communications were destroyed and there was no possibility of determining who or how many were missing."[83]

The case of children in Germany who were presumed to be French was equally difficult. Following the fall of France in May 1940, a sizable number of children of French parentage wound up on German soil, some through deportation and others through relations between prisoners of war, forced laborers, and German civilians. According to an August 1946 article in Le Monde, the French commissioner of German affairs estimated that there were between four thousand and five thousand children ready to be repatriated to France from the French Zone in Germany.[84] In Berlin, a French Red Cross worker informed the chief of the French Displaced Persons Bureau that between 1943 and 1945 approximately one thousand French children were born to French female laborers, the majority of whom were illegitimate.[85] In June 1947, French authorities submitted to the German authorities a list of five thousand children, most of whom were not "unaccompanied or eligible under the definition of United Nations' children" since evidence suggested that only a small number of unaccompanied children had actually been evacuated to the French Zone.[86] Nevertheless, the French insisted that "a large number of children of French origin [were] still in Germany," even though there was "no possible way of estimating the number of French children born in Germany [since] to date only a very few such children have been found."[87]

Repatriation was one of the Allies' main concerns during the first six months of the occupation. With an estimated nine million people already displaced by war by 1944, UNRRA had hoped to repatriate up to 35,000 refugees a day within the first six to seven months of the postwar period with the help of the military authorities and the International Red Cross.[88] Between May 1945 and July 1, 1947, on the eve of IRO takeover, nearly seven million displaced persons were repatriated.[89] By May 31, 1946, 5,888,400 refugees and displaced persons had already been repatriated from German assembly centers while a further 792,850 remained behind.[90] The majority of the repatriates were French (1,562,800) and Polish (2,039,200), and most of those remaining were either Polish (427,320) or of undetermined nationality (118,830).[91]

By February 28, 1947, there were a remaining 223,107 displaced persons receiving UNRRA assistance in the British Zone, 370,090 in the US Zone, and 36,066 in the French Zone.[92] Of this number, there were 11,939 Jewish displaced persons in the British Zone, 125,580 in the US Zone, and 2,333 in the French Zone.[93] By this same date, the total number of unaccompanied children receiving UNRRA care and maintenance was 1,352 in the British Zone, 4,917 in the US Zone, and 123 in the French Zone.[94] Refugees and displaced persons were temporarily clothed, fed, and accommodated in 359 assembly centers scattered across the three Western zones, including 144 in the US Zone, 179 in the British Zone, and 36 in the French Zone.[95] All assembly centers in the American and French Zones were administered by UNRRA; in the British Zone, however, which housed the largest number of refugees and displaced persons, 109 were run by UNRRA, 52 were administered by the military, and 18 were run by voluntary agencies.[96] Although the proportion of unaccompanied children receiving UNRRA aid in the French Zone seems small in comparison to its neighboring zones, this is because the French military authorities retained complete control over the care, maintenance, and repatriation of all unaccompanied and displaced children found in their zone.

The search for French children in Germany was already well underway by the summer of 1945. On November 25, 1947, a proposal was put forth for the search and repatriation of "French children or presumably such" by Emile Laffon, administrator general of the French Zone:

> A representative of the Ministry of Public Health and Population has stated the conditions for repatriation and the precautions to be taken before carrying them out. The children in question are broken down into 3 categories:
>
> 1. Children who have been indefinitely abandoned by their families or born to unknown French parents,
> 2. A child who has at least one unknown or missing parent,
> 3. Children for repatriation whose parent(s) have asked for an extended delay.
>
> Children in the last two categories must remain in nurseries until
>
> — The investigation is finished and a decision is reached about their fate,
> — The families can collect them.[97]

Children of suspected French parentage, viewed as potential candidates for French immigration, were placed in *pouponnières* (nurseries) and *maisons d'enfants* (children's homes) across the French Zone. By March 8, 1948, there were four nurseries and children's homes in operation in Appenthal, Bad-Durkheim, Nordrach, and Unterhausen.[98] The Ministry of Public Health and Population instructed each nursery to "house children who are up to and including fourteen years old, of French origin or presumably such as found in Germany, for repatriation to France."[99]

Conditions in the children's homes were generally difficult, much like the rest of postwar Germany. There were instances in which children of assumed French parentage were given preferential treatment, as was the case in August 1947 when a "colony" of two hundred French children reportedly received special fruit and vegetable rations while the majority of German children did not receive "a single gram of fat."[100] The majority of the children in nurseries and homes suffered from malnutrition, however. The only nursery in operation in Berlin, for example, reported a desperate shortage of nursing staff, clothing, flour, and milk in February 1947.[101] A French Red Cross worker in Berlin similarly reported that low food rations meant that children aged between one and six received only half a liter of milk per day; many of these children, she added, did not have suitable shoes and clothing.[102] A frustrating shortage of ambulances and medical supplies often prevented Red Cross workers from repatriating children altogether; one August 1945 memo states that more ambulances were needed to "retrieve the French who are still hospitalized in German hospitals in the Russian Zone."[103]

Although there were many well-intentioned child welfare officers and voluntary workers who saw repatriation as a means of relieving a grave humanitarian crisis, the criterion on which the French Military Government based its children's policy is problematic in that it revolved around determining the origins of unaccompanied children who were abandoned or orphaned with no known relatives, had no documents or paper in their possession, or might have been too young or traumatized to speak or recall details about their past. The key phrase in the Laffon Memorandum, "French children or presumably such," underscores the nebulous nature of French repatriation policy toward unaccompanied children. The term "repatriation," the act of returning a citizen back to his or her homeland, suggests one's rightful claim to French citizenship. According to Deborah Cowen and Emily Gilbert, citizenship implies an "official membership in the nation-state, achieved by either birth or 'naturalization'" and comprises elements of "identity, belonging, status, rights, and responsibilities."[104] But as one UNRRA welfare guide points out, "the identity of some children may be unknown; some children may conceal their identity," and "younger children may not be able to supply the information required."[105]

The dark legacies of National Socialism further complicate matters. A July 1946 UNRRA report on the issue of "stolen" and "hidden" children points out that many children who were presumed to be Germans after the war were, in fact, kidnapped by the Nazis during the war from countries such as Poland, Czechoslovakia, and Yugoslavia in order to "deplete the population of the countries which Germany was trying to conquer" in order to "replenish her own population" with supposed "ethnically German war orphans."[106] The issue of "stolen" and "hidden" children, therefore, became a major point of contention for the Allied occupiers. Attempting to determine the ethnicities, nationalities, and backgrounds of children with no known relatives was a guessing game with no end in sight. In the case of children who were presumably French, however, this could be easily remedied with the right papers. A memorandum to the commissioner general in Germany from the Ministry of Health and Population on July 10, 1946, proposed a solution for the nationality and civil status of children repatriated from the French Zone:

> I believe that it would be preferable that these children, and eventually the people who take them in, ignore their foreign origins and that in the future all traces of their alienage disappear. Regarding their civil status, they can in fact be legally given a certificate of origin that would act as a birth certificate in all cases that would require it. This certificate, delivered by the Prefect, who would become the sponsor of the child, *could* also designate the child under a new name that would not indicate the place of the child's birth.[107]

With the mechanisms in place to begin repatriation, arrangements were hastily made for the return of children to France. On August 4, 1946, thirty-seven children from a nursery in Tübingen, Germany, boarded a repatriation train and were brought to France "under very good circumstances, despite the hot weather."[108] Having waited since March at a children's center in Commercy, where the children were well fed and cared for and frequently examined by a doctor who found them to be in "good condition," the convoy brought the children to the Children's Assistance Service in the Meuse department in northeastern France. Upon arrival, the children were lodged in the hospital barracks and spent only a short time there before being placed with families for adoption.[109]

The August 4 repatriation journey from Tübingen to Commercy is merely one example out of dozens, if not hundreds, of similar convoys that left Germany for other parts of Europe and the world. Apart from official logs and records, it is difficult to determine what happened to these children once they left the care of the military authorities to be taken in by new families. One certainty remains, however. When the Tübingen children reached the Franco-German border, they were unaccompanied foreigners; when they crossed it, they became French boys and girls.

Faceless and Stateless: Concluding Thoughts

The death and destruction of the Second World War ushered in a new age of humanitarianism, but the fate of children in French-occupied Germany was not determined by humanitarian action alone. Although French policy toward these children was driven partially by a motive to clothe, feed, and shelter vulnerable children, such policies were ultimately designed to secure national aims and political agendas, much to the detriment of girls and women under French occupation. To the French, the primary goal was to strengthen a weakened demographic and to transform France into a world power, one that would take its rightful place alongside the major power players of the postwar era.

French aims in Germany, designed to crush the German threat once and for all while legitimizing France's status as a victor and Cold War ally, were anchored in matters of national security. Recovering all that was lost to France was, simply put, the entire point of the occupation of Germany. Just as stolen artwork was restituted and prisoners of war were repatriated, faceless and stateless children were exploited for the broader purposes of postwar reconstruction.

Notes

I would like to thank Phil Muehlenbeck for his hard work and dedication in putting together this volume. I am also grateful to Rebecca Pulju for her comments and criticism on earlier drafts. Thank you also to Andy Rotter and my fellow panelists at the 2015 SHAFR Annual Meeting in Arlington, Virginia, for their many insightful comments and helpful feedback. This contribution is partially based on my master's thesis, which would not have been possible without the guidance and mentorship of my MA supervisor, Rosemarie Schade. Finally, I am grateful to the Social Sciences and Humanities Research Council for its continued support.

1. John Gimbel, *The American Occupation of Germany: Politics and the Military, 1945–1949* (Stanford: Stanford University Press, 1968), xiii.

2. Norman Naimark, *The Russians in Germany: A History of the Soviet Zone of Occupation, 1945–1949* (Cambridge: Harvard University Press, 1995), 1–2.

3. Ian D. Turner, *Reconstruction in Post-War Germany: British Occupation Policy and the Western Zones, 1945–1955* (Oxford: Berg, 1989), 4, 218.

4. Frank Roy Willis, *The French in Germany, 1945–1949* (Stanford: Stanford University Press, 1962), passim.

5. Tony Judt, *Postwar: A History of Europe since 1945* (New York: Penguin, 2006), 21.

6. Tara Zhara, *The Lost Children: Reconstructing Europe's Families after World War II* (Cambridge, MA: Harvard University Press, 2011), 20–21.

7. "Agreement between UNRRA and SHAEF," October 14, 1944, Archives pour l'Organisation Internationale pour les réfugiés, Archives nationales, Pierrefitte-sur-Seine, France, AJ/43/14.

8. Any Displaced Person or Refugee who claimed that his or her country of origin was a member of the United Nations was considered eligible for UNRRA care and maintenance. Members of ex-enemy nations, such as Austria, Bulgaria, Germany, Hungary, Japan, Romania and Siam, were excluded from the mandate. This meant that German Jews were, by definition, excluded from the mandate as well.

9. "Intergovernmental Committee on Refugees Seventh Plenary Session," May 25, 1947, Archives pour l'Organisation Internationale pour les réfugiés, Archives nationales, Pierrefitte-sur-Seine, AJ/43/25.

10. "Project de convention entre la Direction des Personnes Déplacées et du Croix Rouge Française," December 13, 1945, Ministère des Affaires étrangères et européennes, Centre des Archives diplomatiques, La Courneuve, France, PDR 3/58.

11. See Theodor Adorno, "Schuld und Abwehr," in *Guilt and Defense: On the Legacies of National Socialism in Postwar Germany*, ed. Jeffrey K. Olick and Andrew J. Perrin (Cambridge, MA: Harvard University Press, 2010), 51–188.

12. Marshal de Lattre de Tassigny, *The History of the First French Army* (London: George Allen and Unwin, 1952), 517–18. The concept of the "Big 3 and France" was coined in John Young's article, "The Foreign Office, the French and the Post-War Division of Germany, 1945–46," *Review of International Studies* 12, no. 3 (July 1986): 223–34.

13. Charles de Gaulle, *Mémoires de Guerre, Tome III, Le Salut, 1944–1946* (Paris: Librairie Plon, 1959), 187–88.

14. Robert Paxton, *Vichy France: Old Guard and New Order* (New York: Columbia University Press, 2001), 282.

15. Willis, *French in Germany*, 3.

16. Susan Butler, *My Dear Mr. Stalin: The Complete Correspondence between Franklin D. Roosevelt and Joseph V. Stalin* (New Haven: Yale University Press, 2008), 188.

17. Willis, *French in Germany*, 9.

18. Ibid., 5.

19. Turner, *Reconstruction in Post-War Germany*, 13.

20. Martin Gilbert, *Churchill and America* (New York: Free Press, 2005), 318.

21. Butler, *My Dear Mr. Stalin*, 188; Bianka J. Adams, *From Crusade to Hazard: The Denazification of Bremen Germany* (Lanham: Scarecrow, 2009), 3.

22. Willis, *French in Germany*, 8–9.

23. "Sujet de l'Allemagne occidentale," August 19, 1947, Service des missions de

liaison, Ministère des Affaires étrangères et européennes, Centre des Archives diplomatiques, La Courneuve, France, SL 11/1.

24. Alistair Cole, *Franco-German Relations* (Essex: Longman, 2001), 3.

25. Willis, *French in Germany*, 30.

26. Ibid., 20.

27. Ibid., 107.

28. Ibid., 104.

29. Atina Grossmann, "Trauma, Memory, and Motherhood: Germans and Jewish Displaced Persons in Post-Nazi Germany, 1945–1949," in *Life after Death: Approaches to a Cultural and Social History of Europe during the 1940s and 1950s*, ed. Richard Bessel and Dirk Schumann (Cambridge: Cambridge University Press, 2003), 94.

30. Henry P. Pilgert, *Women in West Germany: With Special Reference to the Policies and Programs of the Women's Affairs Branch* (Office of the US High Commissioner for Germany, 1952), 3–4, Archiv der deutschen Frauenbewegung, Kassel, Germany.

31. Atina Grossmann, *Jews, Germans, and Allies: Close Encounters in Occupied Germany* (Princeton: Princeton University Press, 2007), 2.

32. Elise Julien, *Les Rapports Franco-Allemands à Berlin 1945–1961* (Paris: Éditions L'Harmattan, 2000), 32–33.

33. "Berlin en ruines," *Stockholms-Tidningen*, January 10, 1945, Service historique de la Défense, Vincennes, France, 7P161.

34. Norman Macdonald, "Life in Berlin with Refugees from the East," February 1, 1945, 7P161.

35. Konrad Jarausch, *After Hitler: Recivilizing Germans, 1945–1999* (Oxford: Oxford University Press, 2006), 61.

36. Jarausch, *After Hitler*, 3–18.

37. Ibid., 4.

38. Robert Moeller, *Protecting Motherhood: Women and the Family in the Politics of Postwar West Germany* (Berkeley: University of California Press, 1993), 7.

39. Atina Grossmann, "Trauma, Memory, and Motherhood: Germans and Jewish Displaced Persons in Post-Nazi Germany, 1945–1949," in *Life after Death: Approaches to a Cultural and Social History of Europe during the 1940s and 1950s*, ed. Richard Bessel and Dirk Schumann (Cambridge: Cambridge University Press, 2003), 100.

40. Frederick Taylor, *Exorcising Hitler: The Occupation and Denazification of Germany* (London: Bloomsbury, 2011), 49.

41. Antony Beevor, *The Fall of Berlin 1945* (New York: Penguin Books, 2003), 326.

42. Atina Grossmann, "The 'Big Rape': Sex and Sexual Violence, War, and Occupation in Post–World War II Memory and Imagination," in *Sexual Violence in Conflict Zones: From the Ancient World to the Era of Human Rights*, ed. Elizabeth Heinemann (Philadelphia: University of Pennsylvania Press, 2011), 147.

43. Grossmann, *Jews, Germans, and Allies*, 70.

44. Perry Biddiscombe, "Dangerous Liaisons: The Anti-Fraternization Movement in the U. S. Occupation Zones of Germany and Austria, 1945–1948," *Journal of Social History* 34, no. 3 (Spring 2001): 627.

45. Ibid., 619.

46. Ibid., 621.

47. John Dietrich, *The Morgenthau Plan: Soviet Influence on American Postwar Policy* (New York: Algora Publishing, 2013), 116. See also: Alice Weinreb, "'For the Hungry

Have No Past nor Do They Belong to a Political Party': Debates over German Hunger after World War II," *Central European History* 45 (2012): 50–78; and Atina Grossmann, "Grams, Calories, and Food: Languages of Victimization, Entitlement, and Human Rights in Occupied Germany, 1945–1949," *Central European History* 44 (2011): 118–48.

48. Weinreb, "For the Hungry Have No Past" 54, 52.

49. Petra Goedde, *GIs and Germans: Culture, Gender, and Foreign Relations, 1945–1949* (New Haven: Yale University Press, 2003), 108.

50. Grossmann, "Grams, Calories, and Food," 123.

51. Moeller, *Protecting Motherhood*, 11.

52. Beevor, *Fall of Berlin*, 310–11.

53. Moeller, *Protecting Motherhood*, 11.

54. Peter Duignan, *The Rebirth of the West: The Americanization of the Democratic World, 1945–1958* (Lanham: Rowman & Littlefield, 1992), 240.

55. Adams, *From Crusade to Hazard*, 44.

56. Ibid., 42–43.

57. Ibid., 44.

58. Patricia Meehan, *A Strange People: Germans under the British* (London: Peter Owen, 2001), 261–62.

59. Denise Tscharntke, *Re-Educating German Women: The Work of the Women's Affairs Section of British Military Government, 1946–1951* (London: P. Lang, 2003), 123; Meehan, *Strange People*, 261–62.

60. Detlef Junker ed., *The United States and Germany in the Era of the Cold War, 1945–1990* (Cambridge: Cambridge University Press, 2004), 391.

61. Helen Laville, *Cold War Women: The International Activities of American Women's Organizations* (Manchester: Manchester University Press, 2002), 76.

62. Pilgert, *Women in West Germany*, 6–7.

63. These regime changes are the Third Republic (1870–1940), the Vichy Regime (1940–1944), Liberation and the French Provisional Government (1944–1946), and the Fourth Republic (1946–1958).

64. Karen H. Adler, *Jews and Gender in Liberation France* (Cambridge: Cambridge University Press, 2003), 71.

65. Raymond Ruffin, *La vie des Français au jour le jour: de la Libération à la victoire, 1944–1945* (Coudray-Macouard: Editions Cheminements, 2004), 188.

66. Adler, *Jews and Gender in Liberation France*, 72.

67. Simonetta Falasca-Zamponi, *Fascist Spectacle: The Aesthetics of Power in Mussolini's Italy* (Berkeley: University of California Press, 2000), 158; Carl Ipsen, *Dictating Demography: The Problem of Population in Fascist Italy* (Cambridge: Cambridge University Press, 2002), 73.

68. Paul Ginsborg, "The Politics of the Family in Twentieth-Century Europe," *Contemporary European History* 9, no. 3 (2000): 414, 427; David L. Hoffman, "Mothers in the Motherland: Stalinist Pronatalism in its Pan-European Context," *Journal of Social History* 34, no. 1 (Autumn 2000): 41.

69. Elisa Camiscioli, *Reproducing the French Race: Immigration, Intimacy, and Embodiment in the Early Twentieth Century* (Durham, NC: Duke University Press, 2009), 28.

70. Mary Louise Roberts, *Civilization without Sexes: Reconstructing Gender in Postwar France, 1917–1927* (Chicago: University of Chicago Press, 2009), 149, 211.

71. Hoffman, "Mothers in the Motherland," 39; Camiscioli, *Reproducing the French Race*, 44.

72. Kristen Stromberg Childers, *Fathers, Families, and the State in France, 1914–1945* (Ithaca, NY: Cornell University Press, 2003), 40.

73. Camiscioli, *Reproducing the French Race*, 25; Paul Dutton, *Origins of the French Welfare State: The Struggle for Social Reform in France, 1914–1947* (Cambridge: Cambridge University Press, 2004), 8; Anne Cova, *Féminismes et néo-malthusianismes sous la IIIe République: "La liberté de la maternité"* (Paris: Editions l'Harmattan, 2011), 34.

74. Adler, *Jews and Gender in Liberation France*, 89.

75. Childers, *Fathers, Families, and the State in France*, 84.

76. Ibid., 168.

77. Ibid., 125.

78. Adler, *Jews and Gender in Liberation France*, 72.

79. "Rapatriement des Enfants en Partie Français Nes en Allemagne," July 26, 1946, PDR5/242.

80. "Statistical Report on Unaccompanied Children in U.S., British and French Zones of Germany as of March 1st, 1947," March 24, 1947, AJ/43/596–97; "Closure Report of United Nations' Unaccompanied Children in Germany," June 1947, AJ/43/596–97.

81. "Statistical Report on Unaccompanied Children."

82. Eileen Blackey, "Summary Statement on Unaccompanied Children in Germany," March 24, 1947, AJ/43/596–97.

83. "Closure Report of United Nations' Unaccompanied Children."

84. Henri Fesquet, "Les Enfants Nés en Allemagne Pendant la Guerre," *Le Monde*, August 6, 1946, PDR 5/238.

85. "Les Enfants de Berlin," undated, PDR 5/8.

86. "Closure Report of United Nations' Unaccompanied Children."

87. Ibid.

88. "UNRRA and Its Tasks," *Times* (London), September 9, 1944.

89. Section 8, June 1948, AJ/43/170.

90. Appendix 1, July 8, 1946, AJ/43/19.

91. Ibid.

92. Table 1, UNRRA Statistics, February 28, 1947, AJ/43/169.

93. Table 4, UNRRA Statistics, February 28, 1947, AJ/43/169.

94. Table 8, UNRRA Statistics, February 28, 1947, AJ/43/169.

95. Appendix 4, July 8, 1946, AJ/43/19.

96. Ibid.

97. "Rapatriement d'enfants français ou présumés tells," November 25, 1947, PDR 5/213.

98. "Convention," March 8, 1948, PDR 3/58.

99. Ibid.

100. "Sujet de l'Allemagne occidentale," August 19, 1947, SL/11/1.

101. "Letter from J. Meillon to Madame Coppinger," February 22, 1947, PDR 3/81.

102. "Letter from Madame Smol to Monsieur le Commandant de Rosen," December 14, 1945, PDR 3/81.

103. "Letter from Monsieur le Commandant Rochau to Monsieur Juhel," August 22, 1945, PDR 3/81.

104. Deborah Cowen and Emily Gilbert, *War, Citizenship, Territory* (London: Routledge, 2008), 10–11.

105. *UNRRA Welfare Guide*, February 15, 1945, AJ/43/16.

106. "Report on Unaccompanied United Nations' Children in Germany," UNRRA, July 31, 1946, The National Archives, Kew, United Kingdom, FO 1052/356.

107. "Memorandum from Le Ministère de la Population à Monsieur le Commissaire Général aux Affaires Allemandes et Autrichtiennes," July 10, 1946, PDR 5/242.

108. "COMPTE-RENDU de la Mission du 4 aout," August 9, 1946, PDR 5/242.

109. Ibid.

References

Archives

Archiv der deutschen Frauenbewegung, Kassel, Germany

Archives Nationales, Pierrefitte-sur-Seine, France

Ministère des affaires étrangères et européennes, La Courneuve, France

National Archives (of the United Kingdom), Kew, United Kingdom

Service historique de la Défense, Vincennes, France

Selected Published Works

Adler, Karen H. *Jews and Gender in Liberation France*. Cambridge: Cambridge University Press, 2003.

Beevor, Antony. *The Fall of Berlin 1945*. New York: Penguin Books, 2003.

Biddiscombe, Perry. "Dangerous Liaisons: The Anti-Fraternization Movement in the U. S. Occupation Zones of Germany and Austria, 1945–1948." *Journal of Social History* 34, no. 3 (Spring 2001): 611–47.

Camiscioli, Elisa. *Reproducing the French Race: Immigration, Intimacy, and Embodiment in the Early Twentieth Century*. Durham, NC: Duke University Press, 2009.

Childers, Kristen Stromberg. *Fathers, Families, and the State in France, 1914–1945*. Ithaca, NY: Cornell University Press, 2003.

Cova, Anne. *Féminismes et néo-malthusianismes sous la IIIe République: "La liberté de la maternité."* Paris: Editions l'Harmattan, 2011.

Dietrich, John. *The Morgenthau Plan: Soviet Influence on American Postwar Policy*. New York: Algora Publishing, 2013.

Dutton, Paul. *Origins of the French Welfare State: The Struggle for Social Reform in France, 1914–1947*. Cambridge: Cambridge University Press, 2004.

Falasca-Zamponi, Simonetta. *Fascist Spectacle: The Aesthetics of Power in Mussolini's Italy*. Berkeley: University of California Press, 2000.

Gimbel, John. *The American Occupation of Germany: Politics and the Military, 1945–1949*. Stanford: Stanford University Press, 1968.

Goedde, Petra. *GIs and Germans: Culture, Gender, and Foreign Relations, 1945–1949*. New Haven: Yale University Press, 2003.

Grossmann, Atina. "The 'Big Rape': Sex and Sexual Violence, War, and Occupation in Post–World War II Memory and Imagination." In *Sexual Violence in Conflict Zones from the Ancient World to the Era of Human Rights*, edited by Elizabeth Heinemann, 137–51. Philadelphia: University of Pennsylvania Press, 2011.

———. "Grams, Calories, and Food: Languages of Victimization, Entitlement, and Human

Rights in Occupied Germany, 1945–1949." *Central European History* 44, no. 1 (March 2011): 118–48.

Ipsen, Carl. *Dictating Demography: The Problem of Population in Fascist Italy.* Cambridge: Cambridge University Press, 2002.

Judt, Tony. *Postwar: A History of Europe since 1945.* New York: Penguin, 2006.

Julien, Elise. *Les Rapports Franco-Allemands à Berlin 1945-1961.* Paris: Éditions L'Harmattan, 2000.

Moeller, Robert. *Protecting Motherhood: Women and the Family in the Politics of Postwar West Germany.* Berkeley: University of California Press, 1993.

Paxton, Robert. *Vichy France: Old Guard and New Order.* New York: Columbia University Press, 2001.

Roberts, Mary Louise. *Civilization without Sexes: Reconstructing Gender in Postwar France, 1917-1927.* Chicago: University of Chicago Press, 2009.

Ruffin, Raymond. *La vie des Français au jour le jour: de la Libération à la victoire, 1944–1945.* Coudray-Macouard: Editions Cheminements, 2004.

Weinreb, Alice. "'For the Hungry Have No Past nor Do They Belong to a Political Party': Debates over German Hunger after World War II." *Central European History* 45 (2012): 50–78.

Willis, Frank Roy. *The French in Germany, 1945–1949.* Stanford: Stanford University Press, 1962.

Zhara, Tara. *Lost Children: Reconstructing Europe's Families after World War II.* Cambridge, MA: Harvard University Press, 2011.

CHAPTER 2

Patriarchy and Segregation

Policing Sexuality in US-Icelandic Military Relations

Valur Ingimundarson

After World War II, the US government believed that the military importance of Iceland depended on continued territorial access to the country and on integrating it into a global base system. Icelandic political elites were fully aware of Iceland's strategic location in the middle of the North Atlantic after experiencing a "friendly" occupation by the British during the war. But while they had consented to a US wartime request to replace the bulk of the British contingent, they did not think that the American military presence in Iceland should be a permanent fixture following the defeat of Nazi Germany. For one thing, the stationing of foreign troops conflicted with Iceland's policy of neutrality in foreign affairs as stipulated in the Act of Union with Denmark in 1918. For another, the enormous social and cultural impact of foreign troops during the war was seen as a potential threat to the fabric of Icelandic society. The number of US soldiers in Iceland had reached a peak of 50,000 in 1943 in a country whose population did not exceed 130,000, and for a time they outnumbered the whole Icelandic male population. Needless to say, this gender imbalance created not only social but also sexual tensions.

To be sure, attempts by Icelandic officials to stigmatize Icelandic women as national traitors for consorting with troops and to control their sexual behavior through surveillance methods and, in some cases, punitive measures reflected traditional patriarchal ideas. Icelandic men's resentment of the competition for Icelandic women clearly influenced government and media attitudes toward fraternization with soldiers, even if real concerns about the sexual mistreatment of minors also played a role. Similarly, warnings about female depopulation as a result of marriages with soldiers were grossly exaggerated. Only four hundred Icelandic women married British and American soldiers during World War II.[1] But the social disruption stemming from the wartime presence of foreign troops should not be underestimated. There was much public support in Iceland for policies aimed at minimizing civil-military relations. Even if Iceland profited greatly in economic terms from World War II, there was no interest in the postwar period in extending and normalizing what was seen as a state of wartime exception.

Hence, US demands on Iceland in the name of Cold War solidarity created immediate pressure on its domestic political system, sharpening ideological divisions. Pro-Western Icelandic politicians ultimately managed to ensure Iceland's integration into the Western Alliance in the late 1940s and early 1950s, reflecting a preponderant support for Iceland's Western orientation. But as a nonarmed nation—with strong nationalist and neutralist leanings as well as considerable pro-Soviet support—the acceptance of Western military policies was severely conditioned. The memory of the political, social, and cultural ruptures of the military presence in World War II was not the only factor explaining this response. The foundation of the Icelandic Republic in 1944 led to a nationalistic revival that made it impossible for Icelandic political elites to agree to a US request, in 1945, for long-term rights to military bases on the island. Even a much less ambitious agreement on temporary landing rights for US military aircraft in 1946 led to the downfall of a right-left unity government, which had been formed in 1944. When Iceland joined the North Atlantic Treaty Organization (NATO) as a founding member in 1949, it witnessed the most serious riots in its history. The US-Icelandic Defense Agreement, which was concluded in 1951 on the basis of the North Atlantic Treaty—added another sharply contested element to Iceland's foreign policy. Indeed, during the Cold War, two left-wing governments in the 1950s and 1970s sought—unsuccessfully, it turned out—to abrogate the agreement and to expel US forces from Iceland.[2] Not until the 1980s were such challenges abandoned, even if the military relationship with the United States continued to be a sensitive domestic political issue until the end of the Cold War.

In this chapter I explore the US-Icelandic military relationship from the perspectives of sexual politics and relations between the troops and community. First, I show how Icelandic politicians "appropriated" gender as a negotiating tool with the United States and as a domestic political mechanism to prevent fraternization between US soldiers and Icelandic women. Second, I explore the rationale for the policing of sexuality. In its quest to "protect" the Icelandic female population and to reduce the social impact of the US presence, the Icelandic government imposed a stringent system to control off-base movement of troops—a system that was kept intact throughout the Cold War. It was also tied to a secret racist ban on the stationing of black soldiers in Iceland from the early 1950s until the mid-1960s.

I argue that the antifraternization policy had the double function of enabling center-right pro-Western elites to maintain a defense relationship with the United States in the face of domestic opposition and to institutionalize Iceland's pro-American foreign policy. Conversely, it also served the aims of Icelandic nationalist and left-wing forces that contested Iceland's close military alignment with the United States on political, social, and cultural grounds. The consensus on segregating the troops did not eliminate a critical domestic political discourse on the links between gender and the military. Sexual imagery was frequently used to fight the US presence in Iceland. But the policy of exclusion served both sides because of its underlying patriarchal motivation: the need to maintain a homogeneous national body through the social control of women.

Finally, I put the topic within the larger social context of the US system of military bases during the Cold War. Drawing on feminist critiques, I contend that the Icelandic case differed in important respects from the situation in other Asian and European countries. Despite the vast power disparities between the United States and Iceland, the Americans were never in a position to dictate the terms of civil-military relations. On the contrary, because of the controversy of the military presence, the United States had to accept strict segregation policies enforced by the Icelandic government. Given Iceland's strategic importance—and the presence of a large Socialist Party—the bargaining position of Icelandic political elites vis-à-vis the United States proved strong until the end of the East-West conflict.

Sexual Containment: Icelandic Policies on Civil-Military Relations

When the Icelandic government concluded the Defense Agreement with the United States in May 1951—in the wake of the Korean War—the number of US troops who came to Iceland was far lower than that stationed in Iceland during World War II. The Icelandic government had insisted on a ceiling of less than five thousand. It wanted to preempt a public backlash and to blunt political opposition, especially from the anti-American Socialists who enjoyed the support of 15 to 20 percent of the electorate. In contrast to the political turmoil caused by Iceland's membership in NATO, the reaction to the arrival of the US troops proved anticlimactic. The Socialists were the only political force that protested the decision, reminding the government of Iceland's precondition for NATO membership: that no foreign troops be stationed in Iceland in peacetime. They had been isolated, however, in Icelandic politics after they left the government in 1946. The anticommunist environment created by the Cold War had also reduced their influence. While the three other Icelandic political parties had different views on the extent and nature of Iceland's Western military integration, they all supported the Defense Agreement as part of a general introduction of US troops to Western Europe after the outbreak of the Korean War.

Yet, from the beginning, the question of the impact of the military presence on Icelandic society remained a sensitive one—not only on political grounds but also on cultural and social ones. When the first contingent of US soldiers came to Iceland, they were ordered to stay at Keflavik Airport—the site of the military base—and, to minimize the social impact, were not permitted to travel to the capital, Reykjavik, for the first month. For that reason, the abolition of most restrictions on off-base movement after the first month, which can probably be explained by a desire to accommodate American wishes for recreational opportunities, proved surprising. The government did not anticipate that the US soldiers—who were mostly young, single, and far better paid than the average Icelander—would flock, in their leisure time, to Reykjavik and other smaller towns in the vicinity of the Keflavik base in search of entertainment and nightlife. Their presence prompted immediate local resentment—made worse by a display of open hostility on the part of the Socialists.

In addition to Socialist opposition, nationalist politicians, especially those active in the National Defense Society—which had fought against US attempts to get a military base in Iceland in the postwar period—sought to deny soldiers admission to Reykjavik's restaurants and clubs. To them, a recurrence of the wartime practice of Icelandic women fraternizing with American soldiers had to be prevented at all costs.[3] Some of these politicians actually saw the US military presence as a necessary evil and had voted for the Defense Agreement. But they thought the government had made a big mistake by failing to exclude single men from what became known as the "Iceland Defense Force." They warned against the "danger" of letting soldiers—most of whom were in their early twenties—go out with Icelandic women. This would only strengthen the opposition to the military base and increase political support for the Socialist Party.[4] Several Icelandic women's organizations also echoed concerns about the detrimental impact of the military presence on sexual morality, demanding that the soldiers be confined to the Keflavik base to prevent them with fraternizing with Icelandic women.

At first, however, the government ignored calls for a strict regulation of contacts between the US military and Icelandic civilians, underestimating their political and popular appeal. As a result, the opposition to the US military presence increased steadily in 1952. It was not only the off-base movements of American troops that troubled many Icelanders. US requests for additional military facilities in Iceland, including a new air base for the Strategic Air Command—operating US nuclear strike forces—fueled fears that the country would be turned into a military bastion for US Cold War interests. The practices of the American military contractors, Metacalf, Hamilton, Smith, and Beck Companies, were also controversial, not only because the construction boom in the Keflavik area attracted laborers from other parts of the country but also because of frequent labor disputes.[5]

Just before the 1953 elections, a new party, the National Defense Party, was founded to resist the US presence. It was kind of a successor organization to the National Defense Society, which had become dormant after Iceland's entry into NATO. Dominated by non-Socialist nationalistic intellectuals, this party did well in the elections, capturing 6 percent of the vote. The success of the party had a huge impact on the domestic political scene in Iceland, and it also forced the government to react to the growing opposition to the base. Admittedly, the senior coalition partner, the pro-American Independence Party, was reluctant to close off the base to minimize fraternization between Icelanders and the troops. But the junior coalition partner, the rural/centrist Progressive Party, which was far more skeptical of the US presence, insisted on it, conjuring up stark memories of what was dubbed the "situation" during World War II—sexual relations between Icelandic women and foreign troops.

The political realignment in Iceland undermined the position of the United States in Iceland. In December, Kristinn Guðmundsson, the new foreign minister, delivered the first blow by demanding the revision of the Defense Agreement. The goal of the Progressives was to seal off the military area in Keflavik by erecting a sort of a "Mending Wall"—a fence around the base and imposing far stricter rules on off-base movements. Moreover, they insisted on replacing all foreign workers at the base with Icelandic ones and on withdrawing the business license of the American contractor.

The bilateral negotiations, which began in the spring of 1954, were long and arduous and put a strain on US-Icelandic relations. The Eisenhower administration was prepared to meet some of the Icelandic demands, but it was reluctant to accede to others. For one thing, the Americans argued that the erection of a fence to close off the base was bound to lower the morale of the troops and to cause a great deal of resentment. They also doubted that an Icelandic contractor would be in a position to assume the function of the American one. It was not until the Progressives threatened—indirectly—to revoke the Defense Agreement that the Americans finally gave in. Fearing the worst, they accepted, in 1954, the replacement of the US contractor with an Icelandic one. As a result, an Icelandic company, Prime Contractors, soon took over all military construction work from the Americans.

What is more, the US military began erecting fences around the base, ironically enough, to "protect" the host nation from the presence of its "protectors." In no other country did the US military face such harsh restrictions. The United States also respected the demand of the Icelandic government to ban the stationing of black soldiers in Iceland, in contradiction to President Harry S. Truman's 1948 order to desegregate the military. The perceived need to "protect" Icelandic women motivated this racist policy, which Iceland enforced with more vigor than other countries. After World War II, Greenland (under Danish jurisdiction), Canada, Newfoundland, Bermuda, and British possessions in the Caribbean were also on a US list of places where black soldiers were not welcome. But all—except Iceland—were removed from it in the 1950s, even if there were cases of black troop assignments to such countries as Turkey being canceled because of "domestic political considerations."[6]

The Impact of Gender Politics on US-Icelandic Military Relations

As many feminist scholars such as Anne Tickner and Cynthia Enloe have stressed, mainstream realist accounts of international affairs have systematically ignored gender as an analytical tool.[7] What needs to be avoided however—as Katherine H. S. Moon has pointed out in her study on the US military presence in Korea—is oversimplifying the nature of bilateral state relationships by focusing on nominal power disparities. The case has often been made that the weakness of a small state leaves its women unprotected and vulnerable to violence, abuse, and exploitation by a strong state and its agents.[8] Similarly, interstate relations have been interpreted in such gendered terms: with the "masculine" power dominating the "feminine" one, and with sexual imagery and language used to drive home the point.[9]

Yet the US-Icelandic military relationship was never characterized by a dichotomy of domination and exploitation, on the one hand, and submission and victimization, on the other.[10] As Saundra Pollock Sturdevant and Brenda Stoltzfus have argued, the potential sexual control of a strong state over a weak one often hinges on economic factors. When the Americans arrived in Iceland in 1951, they were dealing with a nation that had not experienced wartime brutalities and that had maintained one of the highest living standards in the world. True, the purchasing power of US soldiers was considerably greater than that of Icelanders in the 1950s. But the material disparities were by no means comparable to most other places with US bases after World War II. Moreover, in the 1960s, a reversal slowly took place as Icelandic living standards increased, making Iceland an expensive location for US troops. In Okinawa, where a similar change occurred later, Philippine women were imported to provide sexual labor for US soldiers in an effort to "protect" Okinawan women from foreigners. But this was not an option in Iceland, where a militarized sex industry never existed. In other words, the institutionalization of prostitution around US overseas bases was not universal.

Another variable that has to be considered is the marital status of US troops abroad. In Asia, most US soldiers were single and young, which reinforced the sexual industry around the bases. It was, however, much more common to send married men to Europe, reducing the "need" to provide sexual services to soldiers. West Germany is a case in point, where this policy was enforced since the 1980s, even though it had never experienced a nationalist backlash against the presence of US troops. The main reason for the Icelandic government's insistence that married men replace single men was to prevent sexual relations between Icelandic women and American soldiers. From the 1970s on, most soldiers at the Keflavik base were accompanied by their families.

In the 1950s and 1960s, the center-right "internationalists," who were in control of Iceland's foreign policy, thought that it was imperative to make concessions to Icelandic nationalism in view of the widespread opposition to the militarization of the island. That Iceland had no army made it much more difficult to grant a foreign power military rights. For this reason, many pro-Western Icelandic politicians were willing to adopt segregationist policies vis-à-vis the US military. Mindful of the controversy surrounding sexual relationships between Icelandic women and American soldiers during World War II, they wanted to be in a position to defend Icelandic manhood by controlling the sexuality of Icelandic women. Hence, they supported the racist policy of excluding black soldiers from Iceland on the grounds that their presence posed a direct threat to Icelandic women and—by extension—to the Icelandic nation.

The Icelandic left—non-Socialists and Socialists alike—fought Iceland's close alignment with the United States and sought to minimize the impact of the military presence by stressing the need to maintain Iceland's political, socioeconomic, and cultural traditions. It was, for example, common for critical novelists in the 1950s and 1960s to use sexual imagery to make political points against the military relationship with the United States. Icelandic politicians were compared to prostitutes for providing the Americans with a military base.[11] Not only politicians were feminized and charged with corrupting Icelandic national values; Icelandic women were also accused of failing in their roles as "national protectors" and of betraying their country. Such misogynist views were not universal; the women who consorted with soldiers were often portrayed as victims of American predators. But in any case, women had no agency in the Icelandic nationalistic discourse on the base issue.

During World War II, the Icelandic government had imposed tight controls on young Icelandic girls who fraternized with soldiers, even to the point of incarcerating them (between thirty and forty girls were treated in this way).[12] The Icelandic government never contemplated such drastic moves during the Cold War. Nonetheless, some nationalist opponents of the base saw a clear link between the need to stave off a perceived "threat" to the purity of the Icelandic nation and to Icelandic manhood, on the one hand, and the need to prevent interethnic marriages between Icelandic women and US servicemen, on the other. There had only been a handful of such marriages since 1951 (most stemmed from World War II). Nonetheless, this attitude was only a stepping-stone away from harsher eugenic demands made by xenophobic nationalists during World War II. Some had even gone so far—unsuccessfully—as to demand the sterilization of women considered "susceptible" to having children with foreign soldiers.[13]

After the Keflavik military base was sealed off in 1954, US soldiers seldom ventured off the base to make the tightly regulated trip to Reykjavik in their leisure time. Most of the soldiers—almost 95 percent of the Iceland Defense Force—were not allowed to leave the base from ten o'clock at night until six in the morning, except for Wednesdays (the only day of the week when it was prohibited to serve alcohol in Icelandic restaurants), when the curfew lasted from midnight until six in the morning. The Icelandic government was prepared to make one exception, though: those soldiers who were joined by their families at Keflavik did not have to abide by the ban, but only if they were accompanied on their trip off the base by at least one family member. That this was a device to make sure that they would not fraternize with Icelandic women was obvious. The ban on off-base movement applied only to the enlisted men at the Keflavik base, not the officers, betraying an additional class motive behind this policy. At the outset, all soldiers had to wear uniforms to distinguish themselves from the Icelanders. In 1960, the Icelandic government modified the policy, but only slightly: only the lowest-ranking soldiers—a group of 740, or 25 percent of the total number of troops—had to wear uniforms outside the base.

To be sure, the US soldiers sometimes circumvented the off-base ban on wearing civilian clothes. After leaving the base, some hid their uniforms nearby before continuing by taxi to social clubs in the capital. But Icelandic police officers who patrolled the route from Keflavik to Reykjavik often confiscated the uniforms and handed them over to the US military police in Keflavik. When the soldiers discovered on their return trip that their uniforms had been removed, they opted, in some cases, to reenter the base illegally through holes in the fence surrounding the base. Because of the cooperation between the Icelandic police and US military police, the offenders were typically captured the day after. But they were usually treated leniently by the American military authorities; they were not incarcerated and received a nonjudicial punishment ("article 15"), usually in the form of extra duty.[14] The US response suggests that the American military superiors sympathized with the troops and saw the Icelandic rules regarding off-base movements as far too strict.

There was some fraternization between Icelandic women and American soldiers— especially during the 1950s and early 1960s, when the US soldiers had money to spend. Icelandic women also consorted with soldiers in clubs at the military base. Some relationships resulted in marriages, but, as noted, that was not common.[15] US military commanders usually discounted negative reports about the fraternization between Icelandic women and US soldiers. They even argued that the soldiers were the innocent victims of female aggression, blaming the families of young girls for not taking adequate care of them and the Icelandic authorities for not "controlling" them.[16]

It was nothing new that the American military castigated women for the "sexual entrapment" of troops; this was common in the United States, for example, where women were pictured as seducers or, in extreme cases, as "ravening wolves at the gates of our camps and posts."[17] In Iceland, there were instances of soldiers raping women and underage girls attending social clubs frequented by troops. The reaction of the Icelandic government and press usually depended on the social background of these women. One woman, who filed a charge against four US servicemen for raping her, received no public sympathy because she had been arrested later for trying to enter the Keflavik base illegally.[18] Four soldiers were found guilty of the crime and sentenced by an Icelandic court, but their jail sentences ranged from only three to fifteen months.[19]

The conservative prime minister Bjarni Benediktsson, who, as foreign minister, was instrumental in concluding the 1951 US-Icelandic Defense Agreement, told the Americans in 1964 that it must seem absurd for US soldiers to be subjected to the severe off-base movement rules. But he added that he believed the rules served both Icelandic and US interests by preventing conflicts between the troops and the community.[20] He also had to deal with difficult cases involving the failure of US servicemen to pay alimony to Icelandic women. The president of Iceland, Ásgeir Ásgeirsson, also showed sympathy for the troops using typical Cold War language: they were, he said, in Iceland under difficult circumstance in the "service of freedom so far away from their homeland."[21] But such sympathetic words did nothing to change the official Icelandic attitude. Given the controversy over the stationing of US troops, the pro-Western parties did not want to draw additional attention to their presence. There is, however, nothing to suggest that conservative politicians, such as Bjarni Benediktsson, were motivated by a simultaneous desire to stymie the spread of youth culture in the 1950s or counterculture in the 1960s. To be sure, during this period, the Icelandic Socialists and nationalists voiced their criticism of US mass culture, and, in the early 1960s, they targeted the Keflavik base's television station, whose programs could be viewed by Icelanders, for monopolizing this medium. But with the introduction of Icelandic TV in the mid-1960s, followed by concrete measures to confine the base's TV programming to military areas in Keflavik, such nationalist cultural criticisms became less salient.

The off-base rules were deeply resented by the troops, not least after the best restaurants in Reykjavik began to deny uniformed soldiers access in the early 1970s. This had, of course, clear class-based political implications: the lowest-paid soldiers, who had to wear uniforms, were unable to dine at these restaurants, while their superiors, who were under no such obligation, were allowed to do so.

The Pentagon pressed the Icelandic government to abandon its policy. To the

Americans, it was inexplicable to exclude soldiers from restaurants that were frequented by "hippies dressed in rags" without any restrictions.[22] Such an analogy, where no difference was made between men in military uniforms and citizens in civilian clothing, even if fanciful, lacked credibility. Hence, they suggested that the rules requiring the lowest rank to wear uniforms should be abolished. In addition to pointing out the discriminatory aspect of this policy, American officials argued that it could spoil Iceland's image abroad. Many US servicemen who were forced to abide by these rules while on duty in Iceland felt resentment toward the country.[23] In March 1971, the Nixon administration formally handed the Icelandic government an aide-mémoire, detailing its complaints and formally asking for changes, arguing that "nowhere in the world were US troops subjected to such stringent restrictions like in Iceland, neither in democratic nor authoritarian states."[24]

The Icelandic government was reminded that the presence of US soldiers was far less conspicuous than in the 1950s, when there was only "one good restaurant" to be found in Reykjavik. Finally, the Nixon administration pointed out that US servicemen were far less keen to go to Reykjavik in their leisure time after facilities for social and recreational activities had been constructed at the Keflavik base.[25] Despite US pressure, the Icelandic government refused to change the rules. And when a left-wing government—formed later in 1971—sought the withdrawal of US forces from Iceland, the Americans backed off. The Icelandic government, it turned out, was divided on the base issue. Nothing was done about ending the military presence before the government was brought down by internal squabbles in 1974.[26] The episode again showed that the Americans were not willing to challenge the prohibitive Icelandic policies on off-base movements. This underscores the exceptional nature of the Icelandic case: while most of these restrictions were eventually removed in countries with US military installations, they remained largely intact in Iceland.

Preserving "Racial Purity": The Ban on the Stationing of Black Troops

As was the case with the limitations on contact between US troops and Icelanders, the need to preserve the social and racial homogeneity of the Icelandic nation lay at the heart of Iceland's policy to prevent black soldiers from serving at Keflavik in the 1950s and 1960s. There was a historical precedent for this move. When US troops arrived in Iceland in 1941, the Icelandic prime minister, Hermann Jónasson, insisted that only "elite forces" should be among the troops—a code for white soldiers only.[27] Because of President Truman's desegregation order, it became far more difficult for the US military establishment after World War II to accede to demands by foreign governments to exclude black troops. But when the United States and Iceland negotiated the 1951 Defense Agreement, Icelandic government officials used the same arguments they had in 1941. Foreign Minister Bjarni Benediktsson wanted to make sure that "none of our black friends" would be among the US troops stationed in Iceland, at least not in the first contingent.[28] The Truman administration accepted this demand, and throughout the 1950s top US military officials were convinced that it would be impossible to force the Icelandic government to change its policy.

In 1957, the Eisenhower administration formally requested the lifting of the ban on stationing black troops in Iceland because it feared that it could face domestic problems at home if the policy became publicly known. At the time, the left-wing government in power in Iceland wanted to expel all US troops from Iceland; it abandoned its policy, however, following the Hungarian Revolution and after receiving economic assistance from the United States. When approaching the Icelandic government on the race issue, US officials argued that it would look far better on paper if a few black soldiers were sent to Iceland. A token presence would be enough; it was not so much a question of ending racial barriers as appearing to do so. Even this modest demand was too much for the Icelandic government, which rejected it on the grounds that it would cause domestic troubles.[29] As a result, the Americans abandoned their efforts to have the ban reversed.

Two years later, American newspapers, including the *New York Times*, broke the news about the ban on the stationing of black troops in Iceland. The Icelandic government responded disingenuously that no such policy was being enforced because it was not part of the US-Icelandic Defense Agreement. But despite the negative publicity, two years passed before the issue was addressed seriously. The Kennedy administration even contemplated making it public that the Icelandic government was fully responsible for the exclusionary practice.[30] Only at that point did the Icelandic government agree on a new informal policy, which it conveyed to the US government as follows: "The Icelandic government will not oppose the inclusion of three or four colored soldiers in the Defense Force, but hopes that they will be carefully selected in light of the special circumstances prevailing in Iceland. . . . On the other hand, it should be stated there are no racial restrictions or any other restrictions."[31]

This statement only reaffirmed the previous policy without acknowledging it publicly; it also stated, incorrectly, that no racial discrimination was practiced in Iceland. Therefore, the Kennedy administration was unwilling to accept the Icelandic proposal. A stalemate ensued, and no black soldiers were sent to Iceland for the next two years. The United States did not make a further attempt to get the Icelanders to abandon the racial ban until 1963. Again, the overture was met with skepticism and resistance by the Icelandic government. This time, Icelandic officials were blunt about the real reason for their reluctance to permit black soldiers to stay in Iceland: it would create a domestic backlash because of the "threat" of intimate relations with Icelandic women. What was more, the reaction of Icelandic men would be harsh. In other words, the same arguments were made in 1963 as had been made in World War II and the early Cold War: it was imperative to protect Icelandic blood and manhood. The Icelandic government was, however, willing to make the same concession as two years earlier: "to allow three or four carefully selected married blacks" to be stationed at Keflavik if their arrival would be arranged without much fanfare. The US ambassador to Iceland believed that this solution would basically eliminate the main opposition—namely, the "boy/girl problem"— demonstrating the patriarchal reasons behind the policy.[32]

With increased domestic political attention in the United States focused on the civil rights movement and protests against the segregation policies enforced in the

South, it was impossible to continue to ignore discriminatory practices within the armed forces. Indeed, a presidential commission appointed by John F. Kennedy on racial equality in the US military showed interest in what became known as the "Iceland problem."[33] US officials feared that if this commission highlighted the situation in Iceland, it would not only result in bad publicity but also seriously damage US relations with Iceland.[34] After an African American US congressman, Charles Diggs, put pressure on the Defense Department, the Pentagon made plans to send "three or four" black soldiers to Iceland.[35] This corresponded fully with the Icelandic wish to minimize the number of blacks and to select only "family men." Even President John F. Kennedy took a personal interest in the case, wanting to know what kind of "gentleman's agreement" existed between the US and Icelandic governments on racial matters.[36] Moreover, he ordered the Department of Defense to begin immediate talks with the Icelandic government on sending "a few blacks" to Iceland.[37] But again, as in 1957, the question was only about tokenism, not about ending racial discrimination. At the outset, only a few black soldiers were chosen to serve in Iceland, in accordance with the Icelandic government's wishes. No racial tensions ensued between black US servicemen and Icelanders. There were instances of marriages between black soldiers and Icelandic women. But they were few, and Icelandic women faced family pressure not to enter into interracial relationships.[38] The number of black soldiers in Iceland increased steadily, and in the 1970s and 1980s no restrictions were placed on their number. The Icelanders had shown themselves "ready" to accept black troops but, of course, within the confines of the strict rules regarding off-base movements—rules that were, as noted, not abolished until after the Cold War.

Conclusion

Despite their sharp differences over Iceland's foreign policy, the supporters and opponents of the US military presence agreed on one thing: fraternization between US troops and Icelandic civilians should be kept to a minimum. Those who supported the US-Icelandic Defense Agreement wanted to make sure that the military presence did further polarize Icelandic society or dent their anticommunist and pro-Western agendas. The opponents wanted to prevent any socializing with soldiers because they believed that the majority of Icelanders opposed the stationing of American troops and because it could facilitate the creation of a sexual industry.[39] Thus, as I have shown here, gender was at the core of the segregationist policies, whether they were couched in "domestic stability" or antimilitaristic language. The underlying rationale for sealing off the Keflavik base was a patriarchal need to protect Icelandic women from having sexual relations with foreigners. And even if women had almost no parliamentary representation in Iceland during this period, women's organizations generally supported this policy. Thus, in contrast to what took place around US bases in Okinawa, the Philippines, or South Africa, to name a few well-publicized examples, there was never the problem of institutionalizing prostitution as part of the American military presence in Iceland. The Icelandic government was in a very strong position when it came to civil-military relations, shaping the terms and rules throughout the Cold War.

The Icelandic policy of preventing sexual relationships between Icelandic women and black soldiers did not change from World War II until the mid-1960s. The fear of "brown babies" was definitely part of this agenda—but even though there were instances of interracial relationships, this never became an issue in Iceland after the ban was lifted. The ban only applied to soldiers. Black tourists had no problem visiting Iceland and were not subject to hostility—and when famous black artists, such as Louis Armstrong, came to Iceland, they were greeted with enthusiasm. This does not, of course, draw attention away from the fact that to minimize the damage to Iceland's image abroad, Icelandic officials lied repeatedly about the policy. The US government tried to have the Icelandic government modify its stance, but it was, in fact, satisfied with cosmetic changes. When the Defense Agreement was modified in 1974 following the downfall of the second left-wing government, race did not become an issue in the bilateral relationship. And even if the number of blacks was proportionally smaller than that of whites after the racial ban was lifted, those proportions changed in the late 1970s and early 1980s. By that time, the racial balance in Iceland did not differ from that of other US military bases in the world. Of 3,133 soldiers stationed in Iceland in 1989, 15.3 percent were black and 5 percent were classified as "other," most likely Filipino and Hispanic.[40]

In their dealings with the Icelanders, the Americans claimed that that the discriminatory practices of the Icelandic government violated human rights, though the US government was willing to make substantial compromises. But to the opponents of the military base, efforts to minimize contacts between soldiers and civilians made its presence more bearable. Because the ban was so "successful," the fraternization issue never became a domestic political problem after the base was sealed off. Many US-Icelandic marriages ended in divorce, and Icelandic authorities often had difficulty tracking down American fathers of illegitimate children. Soldiers commonly denied having sexual relations with women who bore their children or refused to pay child allowance.[41] Thus, US overtures to abolish or modify the curfew rules made no impression on the Icelandic government and met with no success whatsoever. Fearing a political backlash, the pro-American Icelandic government, which was in power from 1959 to 1971, did not want to fight for an unpopular issue in the domestic domain. The government was only prepared to make one minor concession: soldiers were permitted to go to Reykjavik without family members when the curfew did not apply.[42] Later, off-base hours were extended a bit, but only on weekends. In 1979, an Icelandic foreign minister tried to suspend the restrictive off-base rules for a trial period of four months.[43] But his decision, which he justified on human rights grounds, was met with such hostility by his left-wing coalition partners that he was immediately forced to rescind it.[44] The curfew was not abolished until 1989.

After the end of the Cold War, restrictions on off-base movements in Iceland were completely lifted, giving US troops freedom to go to Reykjavik and other places in their leisure time. The move encountered no resistance by Icelanders, reflecting the reduced force of nationalism and the removal of Cold War tensions. But during the Cold War, successive Icelandic governments isolated the base to lessen the impact of the military presence, to "protect the nation" from too much polarization over its pro-Western foreign policy, and to "protect" Icelandic women against fraternization with foreign soldiers, especially blacks. While the cause of this policy was domestic and patriarchal, it also served foreign policy ends: to maintain a relationship with the United States in the face of domestic opposition and to cement Iceland's pro-Western foreign policy course. The irony is that, after the end of the Cold War, the Icelanders were the ones pressing for a continued US military presence. When the United States decided—unilaterally—to close down the Keflavik military base in 2006, it acted against the wishes of a center-right Icelandic government. The US-Icelandic Defense Agreement, however, remains in place—even if in a much reduced deterritorialized and rotational form and without a permanent American military presence.

Notes

1. The US military authorities forbade such marriages from 1942 to 1944 as a way of preventing them from adversely affecting the relationship between the United States and Iceland. See Íris Cochran Lárusdóttir, "'Það er draumur að vera með dáta.' Ástandið frá komu Bandaríkjahers 1941 til ársloka 1943" [It is a "dream to be with a soldier": The "situation" from the arrival of the US military 1942 until the end of 1943] (BA thesis, University of Iceland, 2011), 29–36.
2. On Iceland foreign policy relations with the United States, see Valur Ingimundarson, *The Rebellious Ally: Iceland, the United States, and the Politics of Empire* (Dordrecht: Republic of Letters, 2011); Ingimundarson, *Í eldlínu kalda stríðsins. Samskipti Íslands og Bandaríkjanna 1945–1960* [In the crossfire during the Cold War: The US-Icelandic Relationship, 1945–1960] (Reykjavik: Vaka-Helgafell, 1996); Ingimundarson, *Uppgjör við umheiminn. Samskipti Íslands, Bandaríkjanna og NATO 1960–1974* [A reckoning with the outside world: Iceland, the United States, and NATO 1960–1974] (Reykjavik: Vaka Helgafell, 2001); Thor Whitehead, "Leiðin frá hlutleysi [The path away from neutrality]," *Saga* 29 (1991): 63–121; Whitehead, *The Ally Who Came In from the Cold. A Survey of Icelandic Foreign Policy, 1946–1956* (Reykjavik: University of Iceland Press, 1998); Elfar Loftsson, *Island í NATO—partierna og försvarsfrågan* [Iceland in NATO: The political parties and the defense question] (PhD diss., University of Gothenburg, 1980).
3. See Ingimundarson, *Í eldlínu kalda stríðsins*, 225–26.
4. Ibid., 226.
5. Ibid., 248, 256–68.
6. See Morris J. MacGregor Jr., *Integration of the Armed Forces, 1940–1965* (Washington: The Free Press, 1986; Project Gutenberg Ebook edition, 2007), ch. 15: "The Role of the Secretary of Defense 1949–1951." See *www.gutenberg.org/files/20587/20587-h/20587-h.htm#page379*.
7. See Ann Tickner, *Gendering World Politics: Issues and Approaches in the Post-Cold War Era* (New York: Columbia University Press, 2001); Cynthia Enloe, *Bananas, Beaches and Bases: Making Feminist Sense of International Politics* (Berkeley: University of California Press, 1989); Enloe, *Maneuvers: The International Politics of Militarizing Women's Lives* (Berkeley: University of California Press, 2000); Enloe, *The Morning After: Sexual Politics at the End of the Cold War* (Berkeley: University of California Press, 1990).
8. Katherine H. S. Moon, *Sex among Allies: Military Prostitution in U.S.-Korea Relations* (New York: Columbia University Press, 1997), 49–52.

9. See, for example, Frank Costigliola, "The Nuclear Family: Tropes of Gender and Pathology in the Western Alliance," *Diplomatic History* 21, no. 2 (1997): 163–83.

10. On the sexual and gender aspects of US military bases overseas, see Catherine Lutz, ed., *The Bases of Empire: The Global Struggle against U. S. Military Posts* (London: Pluto, 2009); Maria Höhn and Seungsook Moon, eds., *Over There: Living with the U. S. Military Empire from World War Two to the Present* (Durham, NC: Duke University Press, 2010); Sara Kovner, *Occupying Power: Sex Workers and Servicemen in Postwar Japan* (Stanford: Stanford University Press, 2012); Christine De Matos and Rowena Ward, eds., *Gender, Power, and Military Occupations: Asia Pacific and the Middle East since 1945* (New York: Routledge, 2012); Andrew Yeo, *Activists, Alliances, and Anti-U. S. Base Protests* (Cambridge: Cambridge University Press, 2011); Na Young Lee, "The Construction of Military Prostitution in South Korea during the U. S. Military Rule, 1945–1948," *Feminist Studies* 33, no. 3 (2007): 453–81; Saundra Pollock Sturdevant and Brenda Stoltzfus, eds., *Let the Good Times Roll: Prostitution and the U. S. Military in Asia* (New York: New Press, 1993); Brenda Gayle Plummer, *Window on Freedom: Race, Gender, and Policy after World War II* (Chapel Hill: University of North Carolina Press, 2003); Moon, *Sex among Allies*; Aurora Camacho de Schmidt, "Voices of Hope and Anger: Women Resisting Militarization," in *The Sun Never Sets . . . Confronting the Network of U. S. Military Bases*, ed. Joseph Gerson and Bruce Birchard (Boston: South End, 1991), 107–19; Ann Tickner, *Gender in International Relations: Feminist Perspectives on Achieving Global Security* (New York: Columbia University Press, 1992); Rebecca Grant and Kathleen Newland, eds., *Gender and International Relations* (Bloomington: Indiana University Press, 1991); Jeanne Vickers, *Women and War* (New York: Basic Books, 1987); Beth Baily and David Farber, *The Alchemy of Race and Sex in World War II Hawaii* (New York: Free Press, 1992); Mire Koikari, "Exporting Democracy? American Women, 'Feminist Reforms,' Politics of Imperialism in the U. S. Occupation of Japan, 1945–1952," *Frontiers: A Journal of Women Studies* 23, no. 1 (2002): 23–45; Mire Koikari, "Rethinking Gender and Power in the U. S. Occupation of Japan, 1945–1952," *Gender & History* 11, no. 2 (1999): 313–35; and Marguerite R. Waller and Jenifer Rycenga, eds., *Frontline Feminisms: Women, War, and Resistance* (New York: Garland, 2000).

11. Ingimar Erlendur Sigurðsson, *Borgarlíf* (Reykjavik: Helgafell, 1966), 280.

12. See Thor Whitehead, "Ástandið og yfirvöldin. Stríðið um konurnar 1940–1941" [The "situation" and the authorities: The war over [Icelandic] women, 1940–1941], *Saga* 51, no. 2 (2013): 92–142; Bára Baldursdóttir, "'Þær myndu fegnar skifta um þjóðerni.' Ríkisafskipti af samböndum unglingsstúlkna og setuliðsmana" [They would have gladly changed their nationality: State interference in relationships between young girls and troops], in *Kvennaslóðir* [Women's paths], ed. Anna Agnarsdóttir, Erla Hulda Halldórsdóttir et al. (Reykjavik: Kvennasögusafn Íslands, 2001), 301–17; Baldursdóttir, "'This Rot Spreads Like an Epidemic': Policing Adolescent Female Sexuality in Iceland during World War II" (MA thesis, University of Maryland, College Park, 2000); Bjarni Guðmarsson and Hrafn Jökulsson, *Ástandið. Mannlífið á hernámsárunum* [The situation: Social life during the occupation period] (Reykjavik: Tákn, 1989); Katherine Connor Martin, "The Role of Nationalism, Internationalism, and Gender in the Icelandic Anti-Base Movement, 1945–1956" (MA thesis, University of Iceland, 2003); Herdís Helgadóttir, *Úr fjötrum—íslenskar konur og erlendur her* [Liberated: Icelandic women and a foreign army] (Reykjavik: Mál og menning, 2001); Helgadóttir, "Konur í hersetnu landi: Ísland á árunum 1940–1947" [Women in a militarized country: Iceland, 1940–1947] (MA thesis, University of Iceland, 2000); Inga Dóra Björnsdóttir, "Public View and Private

Voices," in *The Anthropology of Iceland*, ed. E. Paul Durrenberger and Gísli Pálsson (Iowa City: University of Iowa Press, 1989), 98–118; Gunnar M. Magnúss, *Virkið í norðri. Hernámsárin, I* [The fortress in the north], 3rd ed. (Reykjavik: Virkið, 1984); and Þóra Kristín Ásgeirsdóttir, *Herbrúðir* [Military brides] (Reykjavik: Fróði, 1994).

13. See Unnur Birna Karlsdóttir, *Mannkynbætur. Hugmyndir um bætta kynstofna hérlendis og erlendis á 19. og 20. öld* [Eugenics: Ideas about improving races in Iceland and abroad in the 19th and 20th centuries] (Reykjavik: Sagnfræðistofnun, 1998), 111; see also Baldursdóttir, "Þær myndu fegnar skifta um þjóðerni," 306.

14. See Garðar Kristinsson, "Upphaf og starfsemi lögreglunnar á Keflavíkurflugvelli 1946–1960" [The origins and operations of the police in Keflavik Airport 1946–1960] (BA thesis, University of Iceland, 2011), 35–36.

15. See Ásgeirsdóttir, *Herbrúðir*.

16. US Embassy (Reykjavik) to Department of State, December 15, 1966, NA, RG 59, General Foreign Policy Papers, 1964–1966, Politics & Defense, Box 2280.

17. Saundra Pollock Sturdevant and Brenda Stolzfuz, "Disparate Threads of the Whole: An Interpretive Essay," in Pollock and Stolzfus, *Let the Good Times Roll*, 309.

18. US Embassy (Reykjavik) to Department of State, December 15, 1966.

19. See *Morgunblaðið*, August 22, 1967.

20. *Morgunblaðið*, September 30, 1964.

21. Memorandum between Robert Dennison and Ásgeir Ásgeirsson, May 17, 1961, NA, RG 59, 740B.58/5–1761, Box 1655.

22. Report, "Takmarkanir á frelsi varnarliðsmanna," March 8, 1971, Þjóðskjalasafn Íslands [Þ.Í] (the National Archives of Iceland) Reykjavik, Sögusafn utanríkisráðuneytis, 77, 3, Varnarmál, 1974–1975

23. Ibid.

24. Aide-memoire, March 1, 1971, Þ.Í, Sögusafn utanríkisráðuneytis, 77, 3, Varnarmál, 1974–1975.

25. Ibid.

26. See Ingimundarson, *Rebellious Ally*, 99–134.

27. See *Alþingistíðindi*, 1941 (Reykjavik, 1942), 24; see also Thor Whitehead, "Kynþáttastefna Íslands" [Iceland's racist policy], *Lesbók Morgunblaðsins*, January 13, 1972. See also Karlsdóttir, *Mannkynbætur*, 105–6.

28. Edward B. Lawson to Secretary of State, May 2, 1951, Naval History and Heritage Command (NHHC), Washington, D.C., Operational Archives, Politico-Military Policy Division, Box 209; see also Background Briefing Memorandum: Stationing of Non-Caucausian Servicemen in Iceland, January 31, 1961, NHHC, Operational Archives, Politico-Military Policy Division, Box 209.

29. Background Briefing Memorandum: Stationing of Non-Caucasian Servicemen in Iceland, January 31, 1961.

30. Foy D. Kohler to Tyler Thompson, February 23, 1961, NHHC, Operational Archives, Politico-Military Division, Box 209.

31. William C. Burdett to William P. Bundy, August 11, 1961, NHHC, Operational Archives, Politico-Military Policy Division, Box 209.

32. Navy Chief of Staff to Chief of Naval Operations, May 7, 1963, NHHC, Operational Archives, Politico-Military Policy Division, Box 209.

33. Memorandum of a Conversation with the US Ambassador in Iceland on Colored Troops in Iceland, May 17, 1963, NHHC, Operational Archives, Politico-Military Policy Division, Box 209.

34. William E. Lang to Keld Christiansen, April 12, 1963, NA, RG 59, Deputy Under Secretary for Political Affairs, Correspondence concerning the Establishment and Defense of US Military Bases and Naval Bases Overseas, 1957–1963, Box 1.

35. Dean Rusk to James Penfield, June 14, 1963, NA, RG 59, Central Foreign Policy Files, 1960–1963, Box 3725.

36. Memorandum, "Staff Problems in Iceland," June 20, 1963, NHHC, Operational Archives, Politico-Military Policy Division, Box 209.

37. Memorandum (Norman S. Paul), [June 20, 1963?], NHHC, Operational Archives, Politico-Military Policy Division, Box 209.

38. See Ásgeirsdóttir, *Herbrúðir*, 170–77.

39. See Enloe, *Maneuvers*; Moon, *Sex among Allies*; Ruth Ann Keyso, *Women of Okinawa: Nine Voices from the Garrison Island* (Ithaca, NY: Cornell University Press, 2000); and Sturdevant and Stoltzfus, *Let the Good Times Roll*.

40. Information supplied by Friþór Eydal, former press officer for Icelandic Defense Force, May 14, 2003.

41. "Störf sendiráðsins árið 1962," report, January 29, 1963, Þ.Í., Sögusafn utanríkisráðuneytisins, 40, 5, sendiráð Íslands í Washington.

42. Aide-Memoire, April 14, 1971, Þ.Í., Sögusafn utanríkisráðuneytisins, 77, 3, Varnarmál 1974–1975.

43. See *Morgunblaðið*, July 4, 1979.

44. *Morgunblaðið*, July 4 and 7, 1979.

References

Archives

National Archives II, College Park, Maryland
Naval History and Heritage Command (NHHC), Washington, D.C.
Þjóðskjalsafn Íslands [Þ.Í] (The National Archives of Iceland), Reykjavik

Selected Published Works

Ásgeirsdóttir, Þóra Kristín. *Herbrúðir*. Reykjavik: Fróði, 1994.

Baily, Beth, and David Farber. *The Alchemy of Race and Sex in World War II Hawaii*. New York: Free Press, 1992.

Baldursdóttir, Bára. "'Þær myndu fegnar skifta um þjóðerni.' Ríkisafskipti af samböndum unglingsstúlkna og setuliðsmana." In *Kvennaslóðir*, edited by Anna Agnarsdóttir, Erla Hulda Halldórsdóttir et al., 301–17. Reykjavik: Kvennasögusafn Íslands, 2001.

Baldursdóttir, Bára. "'This Rot Spreads Like an Epidemic': Policing Adolescent Female Sexuality in Iceland during World War II." MA thesis, University of Maryland, College Park, 2000.

Björnsdóttir, Inga Dóra. "Public View and Private Voices." In *The Anthropology of Iceland*, edited by E. Paul Durrenberger and Gísli Pálsson, 98–118. Iowa City: University of Iowa Press, 1989.

Costigliola, Frank. "The Nuclear Family: Tropes of Gender and Pathology in the Western Alliance." *Diplomatic History* 21, no. 2 (1997): 163–83.

De Matos, Christine, and Rowena Ward, eds. *Gender, Power, and Military Occupations: Asia Pacific and the Middle East since 1945*. New York: Routledge, 2012.

Enloe, Cynthia. *Bananas, Beaches and Bases: Making Feminist Sense of International Politics*. Berkeley: University of California Press, 1989.

———. *Maneuvers: The International Politics of Militarizing Women's Lives*. Berkeley: University of California Press, 2000.

———. *The Morning After: Sexual Politics at the End of the Cold War*. Berkeley: University of California Press.

Gayle Plummer, Brenda. *Window on Freedom: Race, Gender, and Policy after World War II*. Chapel Hill: University of North Carolina Press, 2003.

Grant, Rebecca, and Kathleen Newland, eds. *Gender and International Relations*. Bloomington: Indiana University Press, 1991.

Guðmarsson, Bjarni, and Hrafn Jökulsson. *Ástandið. Mannlíf á hernámsárunum*. Reykjavik: Tákn, 1989.

Helgadóttir, Herdís. *Úr fjötrum—íslenskar konur og erlendur her*. Reykjavik: Mál og menning, 2001.

Höhn, Maria, and Seungsook Moon, eds. *Over There: Living with the U. S. Military Empire from World War Two to the Present*. Durham, NC: Duke University Press, 2010.

Ingimundarson, Valur. *The Rebellious Ally: Iceland, the United States, and the Politics of Empire*. Dordrecht and St. Louis: Republic of Letters, 2011.

———. *Í eldlínu kalda stríðsins. Samskipti Íslands og Bandaríkjanna 1945–1960*. Reykjavik: Vaka-Helgafell, 1996.

———. *Uppgjör við umheiminn. Samskipti Íslands, Bandaríkjanna og NATO 1960–1974*. Reykjavik: Vaka-Helgafell, 2001.

Karlsdóttir, Unnur Birna. *Mannkynbætur. Hugmyndir um bætta kynstofna hérlendis og erlendis á 19. og 20. öld*. Reykjavik: Sagnfræðistofnun, 1998.

Keyso, Ruth Ann. *Women of Okinawa: Nine Voices from the Garrison Island*. Ithaca, NY: Cornell University Press, 2000.

Koikari, Mire. "Exporting Democracy? American Women, 'Feminist Reforms,' Politics of Imperialism in the U. S. Occupation of Japan, 1945–1952." *Frontiers: A Journal of Women Studies* 23, no. 1 (2002): 23–45.

———. "Rethinking Gender and Power in the U. S. Occupation of Japan, 1945–1952." *Gender and History* 11, no. 2 (1999): 313–35.

Kovner, Sara. *Occupying Power: Sex Workers and Servicemen in Postwar Japan*. Stanford: Stanford University Press, 2012.

Kristinsson, Garðar. "Upphaf og starfsemi lögreglunnar á Keflavíkurflugvelli 1946–1960." BA thesis, University of Iceland, 2011.

Lárusdóttir, Íris Cochran. "'Það er draumur að vera með dáta.' Ástandið frá komu Bandaríkjahers 1941 til ársloka 1943." BA thesis, University of Iceland, 2011.

Lee, Na Young. "The Construction of Military Prostitution in South Korea during the U. S. Military Rule, 1945–1948." *Feminist Studies* 33, no. 3 (2007): 453–81.

Lutz, Catherine, ed. *The Bases of Empire: The Global Struggle against U. S. Military Posts*. London: Pluto, 2009.

MacGregor, Morris J., Jr. *Integration of the Armed Forces, 1940–1965*. Washington: Free Press, 1986. Ebook edition, 2007, www.gutenberg.org/files/20587/20587-h/20587-h.htm.

Magnúss, Gunnar M. *Virkið í norðri. Hernámsárin*, I [The fortress in the north]. 3rd ed. Reykjavik: Virkið, 1984.

Martin, Katherine Connor. "The Role of Nationalism, Internationalism, and Gender in the Icelandic Anti-Base Movement, 1945–1956." MA thesis, University of Iceland, 2003.

Moon, Kathiner H. S. *Sex among Allies: Military Prostitution in U.S.-Korea Relations.* New York: Columbia University Press, 1997.

Pollock Sturdevant, Saundra, and Brenda Stoltzfus, eds. *Let the Good Times Roll: Prostitution and the U. S. Military in Asia.* New York: New Press, 1993.

Sigurðsson, Ingimar Erlendur. *Borgarlíf.* Reykjavik: Helgafell, 1966.

Sturdevant, Saundra Pollock, and Brenda Stolzfuz, "Disparate Threads of the Whole: An Interpretive Essay." In *Let the Good Times Roll: Prostitution and the U. S. Military in Asia*, edited by Saundra Pollock Studevant and Brenda Stolzfus, 300–34. New York: New Press, 1993.

Tickner, Ann. *Gendering World Politics: Issues and Approaches in the Post–Cold War Era.* New York: Columbia University Press, 2001.

———. *Gender in International Relations: Feminist Perspectives on Achieving Global Security.* New York: Columbia University Press, 1992.

Waller, Marguerite R., and Jenifer Rycenga, eds. *Frontline Feminisms: Women, War, and Resistance.* New York: Garland, 2000.

Whitehead, Thor. *The Ally Who Came in from the Cold: A Survey of Icelandic Foreign Policy, 1946–1956.* Reykjavik: University of Iceland Press, 1998.

———. "Ástandið og yfirvöldin. Stríðið um konurnar 1940–1941" [The "situation" and the authorities: The war over [Icelandic] women, 1940–1941]. *Saga* 51, no. 2 (2013): 92–142.

———. "Kynþáttastefna Íslands" [Iceland's racist policy]. *Lesbók Morgunblaðsins*, January 13, 1972.

———. "Leiðin frá hlutleysi." [The path away from neutrality] *Saga* 29 (1991): 63–121.

Yeo, Andrew. *Activists, Alliances, and Anti-U. S. Base Protests.* Cambridge: Cambridge University Press, 2011.

CHAPTER 3

Queering Subversives in Cold War Canada

Patrizia Gentile

In a 1959 memorandum, Don Wall, secretary of Canada's Security Panel, described homosexuals as defiant toward society:

> Sexual abnormalities appear to be the favourite target of hostile intelligence agencies, and of these homosexuality is most often used. . . . The nature of homosexuality appears to adapt itself to this kind of exploitation. By exercising fairly simple precautions, homosexuals are usually able to keep their habits hidden from those who are not specifically seeking them out. Further, homosexuals often appear to believe that the accepted ethical code which governs normal human relationships does not apply to them. . . . From the small amount of information we have been able to obtain about homosexual behaviour generally, certain characteristics appear to stand out—instability, willing self-deceit, defiance towards society, a tendency to surround oneself with persons of similar propensities, regardless of other considerations—none of which inspire the confidence one would hope to have in persons required to fill positions of trust and responsibility.[1]

During the Cold War era in Canada, the discursive link between "instability" and "trust and responsibility" was a core ideological construction of homosexuals as suffering from character weaknesses. In Canadian national security discourse, the deceitful, unstable, and abnormal homosexual was yet another prime target of "hostile intelligence agencies," framed as the unreliable citizen capable of subverting the foundations of society and the gender and sexual codes that sustained it. As the secretary of the Security Panel, an interdepartmental advisory committee responsible for coordinating national security that answered to the Cabinet Committee on Security and Intelligence and the prime minister, Wall played a central role in deploying the homosexual as security risk.

"Character weakness" was a key collecting category in the queering and gendering enacted by the Cold War national security regime in Canada. It was contained within another collecting category, the term "subversive," and used extensively by Canadian security police forces and security policy makers against communists, immigrants, feminists, leftists, and Quebec separatists. "Subversive" was an ideological and administrative tool, linked to other terms like "national security risk" and even "terrorist" (especially in reference to Quebec separatists).[2] At particular historical moments, this term was used to help sort social and political practices deemed against the interests of the state. This chapter will examine how the queer(ing) of subversives in the Canadian Cold War context was used to sort gender and sexual practices as "outside" of the normal and national social and political fabric of society.

Defined as suffering from "character weaknesses" and living outside the boundaries of normative sexual and social discourses, gays and lesbians in Canada were the focus of state-initiated and state-organized security campaigns from the mid-1950s to the 1990s. This security regime reorganized gay and lesbian space and communities in such cities as Victoria, Toronto, Montreal, Ottawa, and Halifax. The investigative practices of the federal, provincial, municipal, and military police forced gay and lesbian communities to establish new social and communal sanctuaries in regard to space, networks, and social relations.

Although "character weakness" included a number of "afflictions" that could supposedly result in a person being blackmailed, the term became increasingly "homosexualized" in the late 1950s and 1960s. Within the national security discourse, homosexuality was presumed to be a distinct form of sexual practice, and anyone who engaged in same-gender sex, or was perceived to be doing so, was considered to be homosexual and pervert.

Secretary Wall was influenced by US antihomosexual national security discourse. David Johnson's investigation of the antigay purges in the State Department from 1947 to the late 1960s, for instance, would have been known to Canadian security officials. In the US context, the loyalty/security program, originally established in 1947 by the Truman administration to oust communist sympathizers employed in the federal government, played a critical role in the vetting and dismissal of subversives such as homosexuals, including Sumner Wells, undersecretary of state to Franklin Roosevelt.[3] Moreover, by the mid-1950s the Eisenhower administration was pressing allies such as Britain, Canada, and Australia to comply with security policies that excluded homosexuals from government positions.[4] As Johnson points out, failure to follow US policies on this issue jeopardized close ties with American intelligence officials at a time when national security was an international obsession. Not surprisingly, then, Wall quotes a former CIA director, Admiral Roscoe Hillenkoetter, in his document to the Security Panel outlining the "homosexual problem":

The consistent symptoms of weakness and instability which accompany homosexuality almost always represent danger points of susceptibility from the standpoint of security. . . . The moral pervert is a security risk of so serious a nature that he must be weeded out of government employment. . . . In addition homosexuality frequently is accompanied by other exploitable weaknesses such as psychopathic tendencies which affect the soundness of their judgement, physical cowardice, susceptibility to pressure, and general instability. . . . Lastly, perverts in key positions lead to the concept of a government within a government. . . . One pervert brings other perverts.[5]

Hillenkoetter's fear was based on two fronts: first, homosexuality was a weakness that could be "exploitable," presumably by enemy spy agencies, and, second, if "one pervert brings other perverts," the potential security threat posed by homosexuals was daunting.

In the late 1950s, homosexuals were conceptualized as gender inverts who engaged in unnatural sexual acts. Unlike the adulterer or the alcoholic, two other collecting categories labeled as suffering from weak character, the homosexual subverted the reproductive order of the patriarchal nuclear family.[6] Homosexuals were understood to be duplicitous: they kept parts of their lives secret, subverted gender codes, and worked to hide their sexuality. Many lived double lives as husbands or wives with children.

The construction of heterosexuality as normal, natural, clean, and healthy has a long history but is solidified in the Cold War era as a way to protect against the evils of communism and one of its tenets, homosexuality.[7] In 1960, Countess Rosa Goldschmidt Waldeck published "Homosexual International," an article that outlines the logic behind this association: "Without being necessarily Marxist they [homosexuals] serve the ends of the Communist International in the name of their rebellion against the prejudice, standards, ideals of the 'bourgeois' world. Another reason for the homosexual-Communist alliance is the instability and passion for intrigue for intrigue's sake, which is inherent in the homosexual personality."[8] Connecting the homosexual's "personality" with communism played a critical part in making homosexuality a subversive category. For Waldeck, homosexuals were not just antithetical to normal heterosexuals but also presented a clear political danger and a national security risk. Homosexuals were bent on "rebelling" against capitalist values in the interest of intrigue (we will encounter this theme again in the context of the 1970s gay and lesbian liberation movement). Waldeck's connections echoed the Canadian government documents used to construct homosexuals as national security threats based on their "character weakness."

National security policy in Cold War Canada was based largely on Cabinet Directive 29, established in 1955, and Cabinet Directive 35, a version of the former security directive introduced in 1963. Cabinet directives governed security policies and procedures for all departments, crown corporations, and industries involved in government business. These documents anchored two critical aspects of the Canadian national security regime: first, they highlighted the merits of preserving the security of the nation against the civil liberties of Canadians, and, second, they made loyalty, reliability, and strength of character factors in determining security risks. The administrative logic underpinning these two security discourses helped to sustain bureaucratic, police, and administrative procedures that organized homosexuals as subversives and security threats. For example, Cabinet Directive 35 included the following categories to define "unreliability": "a person who is unreliable, not because he is disloyal, but because of features of his character which may lead to indiscretion or dishonesty, or make him vulnerable to blackmail or coercion. Such features may be greed, debt, illicit sexual behaviour, drunkenness, drug addiction, mental imbalance, or such other aspect of character as might seriously affect his reliability."[9] Despite this long list of possible reasons one could be considered unreliable, one cannot understate the security regime's emphasis on homosexuals. In a document titled "Security Cases involving Character Weaknesses, with Special Reference to the Problem of Homosexuality," government officials "make the case" for a systemic purge of homosexuals working in the Canadian federal government because of the definitions outlined in Cabinet Directives 29 and 35 and the need to synchronize these security policies with those already dictated by Allied forces including the United States, United Kingdom, and Australia.[10]

Several historians have written on the social and political history of the Cold War era.[11] This research on Cold War surveillance practices and national security discourses shows that Canadians were not spared the trauma that Americans endured under the McCarthy campaigns. Despite this extensive research, many Canadians today, as a result of the highly secretive nature of the Canadian security and surveillance systems, operate under the illusion that the Canadian government did not conduct "witch hunts." Unlike Americans living through the McCarthy trials, Canadians were not exposed to the same level of publicity and visibility associated with the investigations and trials organized by the House Committee on Un-American Activities. Conversely, the Canadian government in the Cold War era worked under the veil of secrecy, protecting it from public debates concerning civil liberties. Moreover, Canadians caught in the national security and surveillance net did not have access to an appeal process.

The secretive nature of the Canadian security system did not go unnoticed. In a 1956 article examining this issue in the *Civil Service News*, the author describes the "Canadian approach" as suppressing individual rights in favor of those of the state:

> Canada . . . has a stringent program to protect Government secrets against subversives, cocktail party talkers, and people who associate with Communists. . . . Policies and standards are set by a committee of high officials representing several Canadian agencies [the previously mentioned Security Panel]. The Special Branch of the Royal Canadian Mounted Police . . . has a representative on the policy-making panel. The identity of individual members of this panel is not disclosed to the public. Only a few in Government know who the members are. The panel meets in secret. The Government refuses to tell who makes the major decisions about security or what those decisions are. . . . In Canada, the security system is a tough one. There is less concern than in the United States about the rights of individuals involved. To Canadian officials, safety of the state comes first.[12]

The "safety of the state comes first" or "in the interest of national security" were key operating mandates in the Canadian context. Hiding the existence of the Security Panel and its membership from the Canadian public was considered paramount to this mandate. The absence of an appeal process and lack of knowledge regarding the extensive surveillance and security net that hovered over Canadians helped the social and political organization of the Canadian national security state endure and led to destructive effects for many Canadians.

In the early 1960s, Prime Minister John Diefenbaker defended the government's position in the debate between the "safety of the state" and the preservation of individual civil liberties. In the following, Diefenbaker makes specific reference to the recruitment of homosexuals in the former USSR, braiding the discourse of loyalty, reliability, the danger of blackmail, and the recruitment of homosexuals with the debate on the "fundamental rights of the individual":

> How are you going to maintain security while at the same time preserving and maintaining the fundamental rights of the individual? It is a difficult problem. It is so easy to criticize, but it is so much more difficult, having that responsibility, being desirous of maintaining those freedoms, to be able to carry out one's wishes. Loyalty is expected of all Canadians. It is imperative as a quality of public service. There are many cases in which the loyalty of the individual is not a question. But that individual may still not be reliable as a security risk . . . because of defects of character which subject him to the danger of blackmail. . . . It is a fertile field for recruiting by the USSR, where public servants are known to be the companions of homosexuals. Those are the people that are generally chosen by the USSR, in recruiting spies who are otherwise loyal people within their countries.[13]

By conflating security risk with homosexuality, Diefenbaker made the case for queering subversives in the context of the Cold War and in the fight against communism in the West. Placing homosexuality at the center of the debate between civil liberties and the safety of the state legitimized the secrecy behind Canada's security practices and particularly those tactics mobilized against queers. Curtailing civil liberties in the face of the de facto unreliability of homosexuals based on their "defects of character" was deemed justified and became the basis for security policy in Cold War Canada.

These secretive security policies were effective. Jim Egan, one of Canada's first visible gay activists, says that he had very little knowledge of the scope of Canadian antihomosexual security practices despite writing extensively about the McCarthy campaigns and the purging of queers in the US context throughout the 1950s: "I guess what I did was spend far more time reading American literature because it was easier to get your hands on."[14] Nonetheless, the surveillance and investigative tactics employed against homosexuals by many groups—including the Royal Canadian Mounted Police (RCMP), Ottawa's police force, and the military police—began to be felt by the community. By word of mouth, public servants working in federal government became aware of the security campaigns, even if that knowledge was based on rumors or third-party experiences.

Firsthand accounts from the people directly affected by the purges underline the social character of the queering of subversives, but they also reveal the multiple narratives that disrupt the "official" text forwarded by declassified security documents. In Ottawa, many homosexuals had knowledge of the security purge, even if most Canadians were oblivious to the policies. One man, referring to an incident that took place around 1964 in the basement tavern of an Ottawa institution, the Lord Elgin Hotel, remembered: "We even knew occasionally that there was somebody in some police force or some investigator who would be sitting in a bar. And you would see someone with a . . . newspaper held right, and if you . . . looked real closely you could find him holding behind the newspaper a camera, and these people were photographing everyone in the bar." The response to this surveillance tactic demonstrates that the security purges were common knowledge and shows how some members of the community resisted: "We always knew that when you saw someone with a newspaper held up in front of their face . . . that somebody would take out something like a wallet and do this sort of thing [like snapping a photo]. . . . You would see somebody . . . and you would catch everyone's eye and you would go like this [snapping a photo]. And everyone knew [to] watch out for this guy." Police forces photographed people in establishments frequented by homosexuals, conducted surveillance, and engaged in entrapment exercises to collect information as part of the security purge regime. The RCMP's central aim was to confirm the identities of homosexuals working in the federal government and military forces, but this mandate often resulted in the surveillance and interrogation of people not employed in these areas of work.

RCMP investigators often used photo albums filled with pictures of people entering known homosexual establishments. These photos were shown to people taken to RCMP headquarters in Ottawa, a common practice for homosexuals under suspicion, as a means to help the federal police move individuals from the "suspected" and "alleged" categories to the "confirmed" column. These categories were a critical organizing tool and played an important part in dismissals, the denial of internal transfers, and the failure to grant security clearances or promotions for thousands of individuals trapped by the security net. For example, it was reported in 1960 that in the Royal Canadian Navy (RCN), 123 members had been confirmed as homosexuals and another 76 were suspected of being homosexual.[15] The same 1960 report stated that 59 suspected homosexuals had been identified in the Department of External Affairs (DEA) and that, of these, 9 had resigned, 1 had been released, 1 retired, and 2 were deceased. These numbers for the DEA were based on 363 people classified as "confirmed," "alleged," or "suspected" homosexuals, 117 of whom had died, resigned, retired, been transferred, or been released.[16] Meticulously documented in the RCMP Annual Report throughout the 1960s, the categorization of suspected, alleged, and confirmed homosexuals entrenched the security regime with an administrative logic that had real consequences in the lives of gay and lesbian people.

Locating so-called subversive elements, especially homosexuals, became a veritable obsession for security forces and officials. While surveillance, interrogations, and entrapment tactics worked, the members of the Security Panel quickly recognized their inefficiencies in terms of time, effort, and, most importantly, resources. In an attempt to streamline the detection process, the Security Panel sought the services of Frank R. Wake, a psychology professor at Carleton University who also worked as a medical researcher between 1954 and 1958 for the Royal Commission on the Criminal Law Relating to Criminal Sexual Psychopaths.[17] Throughout the

Cold War era, governments relied on psychologists to guide their actions[18] Scientific knowledge was used to frame homosexuality as disease, abnormality, deviance, and perversion, and this played a key role in making and queering subversives in the Canadian context. Technologies to facilitate the ferreting out of these subversive elements were appealing and enthusiastically embraced by the Security Panel.[19]

A January 1961 Security Panel document offered the potential for a device that could detect homosexuals so as to purge them from the civil service and also to prevent their being hired:

> Consideration be given to setting up a program of research . . . with a view to devising tests to identify persons with homosexual tendencies. It is hoped that such tests might aid in the identification of homosexuals already employed in the government service, and eventually might assist in the selection of persons who are not homosexuals for service in positions considered vulnerable to blackmail for intelligence purposes. (The Commissioner of the RCM Police feels that these tests should be extended to prevent, where possible, the initial engagement of homosexuals in the government service on the grounds that they are usually practising criminals under Section 147 and 149 of the Criminal Code of Canada.)[20]

For Wake, the Security Panel's enthusiasm was lucrative, and it also enabled him to delve into research methods that applied the pseudoscience widely associated with theories about the "homosexual personality." By 1961, the Security Panel secured $5,000 to fund Wake's "Special Project."[21] In addition, Wake was funded by the Department of National Health and Welfare to travel to the United States to research detection technologies.[22]

The report written by Wake detailed a series of tests to identify a person's masculinity or femininity tests (M/F tests), word association tests, and the use of pupillary measurement (based on the Hess-Polt apparatus introduced by Eckhar H. Hess and his assistant J. M. Polt from the University of Chicago) to detect homosexuality. Wake also recommended the plethysmograph, which measures blood volume in the finger by electronic or pneumatic means; the Palmer sweat test, which measures perspiration; and the span of attention test, which measures the time spent attending to various images. Dubbed the "fruit machine" by RCMP officers, the battery of tests was considered an important step in ridding the federal government and military of homosexuals.

M/F tests used gender assumptions to code homosexuality as deviant by linking gay men to effeminacy and lesbians to masculinity. Subjects taking the tests were asked to answer "true" or "false" to statements grounded in gender stereotypes emphasizing heterosexual performances of masculinity and femininity. Some of the statements in the M/F test included the following:

> I want to be an important person in the community.
> I'm not the type to be a political leader.
> When someone talks against certain groups or nationalities, I always speak up against such talk even though it makes me unpopular.
> I like mechanics magazines.

I think I would like the work of a librarian.

I'm pretty sure I know how we can settle the international problems we face today.

I like to go to parties and other affairs where there is lots of loud fun.

If I were a reporter I would like very much to report news of the theatre.

I would like to be a nurse.

I very much like to hunt.

I would like to be a soldier.

It is hard for me to start a conversation with strangers.

I think I would like the work of a building contractor.

I think I would like the work of a dress designer.[23]

Although Wake felt the M/F tests had limitations (perhaps he knew that the answers could be manipulated by subjects), he insisted that "intensive research" was needed to verify their usefulness for the detection of homosexuals.[24] With this recommendation, Wake demonstrated that he was not prepared to abandon the gender stereotypes embedded in shaping homosexuality as opposed to heteropatriarchy.

Wake was not deterred by his own observations about the M/F tests and continued to recommend a combination of the word association test with the Palmer sweat test as more effective in detecting homosexuals. In the document, Wake placed asterisks next to words he deemed to have homosexual meaning, such as queen, circus, gay, bell, whole, blind, bull, camp, coo, cruise, drag, dike (dyke), fish, flute, fruit, mother, punk, queer, rim, sew, swing, trade, velvet, wolf, blackmail, prowl, bar, house, club, restaurant, tea room, and top men.[25] Subjects would be connected to a device measuring palm sweat or attached to a plethysmograph to test their reactions to the words, which were interspersed with so-called neutral words. The presumption was that a greater level of anxiety in response to homosexual-related words indicated sexual proclivity.

Finally, Wake found the pupillary response test to be quite "productive" with regard to detecting homosexuals. It measured different interest patterns by means of a machine that simultaneously projected a visual stimulus and photographed the pupil of the eye. In the test, research subjects peered through an opening in a box. This procedure was supposed to produce an involuntary "response that [could not] be controlled by the subject."[26] To illustrate the pseudoscience on which this contraption was based, the images used to illicit reactions from the subjects were based on physique magazines and other pictures of nude bodies. Presumably, "real" homosexuals would not be able to control their reactions to these photographs or images and would involuntarily reveal themselves as indicated by dilated pupils. As in the word association test, so-called neutral images would be added to the mix.

Operationalizing this battery of tests proved prohibitive, and, in the end, the Special Project never materialized as a functioning detection device. The project would have required many staff people, including full- and part-time scientists, between $5,000 and $10,000 of annual funding, and a team of RCMP officers to coordinate the collecting of subjects. In their 1965–1966 *Directorate of Security and Intelligence (DSI) Annual Report*, the RCMP brass reported that "to date the tests have been inconclusive, the main obstacle to the Program being a lack of suitable subjects for testing purposes." The result did not improve the following year: "Although the research group has made some progress, the objective has not, as yet been achieved."[27] The project was officially abandoned in 1967, and Wake went back to his academic work, eventually becoming the chair of the Department of Psychology at Carleton University.

Screening for homosexuals continued to occupy the resources of the Canadian government, despite the failure of the "fruit machine." Arguing for the security screening of all civil servants, not just those who had access to classified information, the 1969 *Report of the Royal Commission on Security* (also known as the Mackenzie Commission after Maxwell Mackenzie), waded in on the "question of homosexuals" in paragraph 100:

> The question of homosexuality is a contentious area as social mores change. It is a fact demonstrated by a large number of case histories, that homosexuals are special targets for attention from foreign intelligence services. What is more, there seem to us clear evidence that certain types of homosexuals are more readily compromised than non-deviate persons. However, we feel that each case must be judged in the light of all its circumstances, including such factors as the stability of the relationships, the decency of the incidents, the public or private character of the acts, the incidence of arrests or convictions, and the effects of any rehabilitative efforts.[28]

While this quote might seem liberal compared to other stances, identifying homosexuals as "special targets" for foreign intelligence services continues to place them as security risks. The attempt to differentiate among homosexuals by deeming some as "decent" or "nondeviant" and others as criminals, such as those who engage in public sex, echoed the partial decriminalization of homosexual sex introduced by the 1969 omnibus bill. While this positioning diminished some of the pressure for homosexuals, it did not stop them from being understood as "subversive" and being marginalized. Even in this reiteration, homosexuals suffered from an abnormality, but some were more abnormal than others.

The Mackenzie Commission played a critical role in putting knowledge of Canadian security policies and practices into public view, often repeating parts of Cabinet Directives 29 and 35. Despite the attempts to "soften the blow" against homosexuals by creating a false differentiation between "good" and "bad" queers, the Mackenzie Commission was clear about its mandate to purge homosexuals with access to classified information. By invoking "the interests of the state" as the basis for their administrative logic but feigning concern for the individual, the authors of the report stated that, "in the interests of the individuals themselves as well as in the interests of the state, homosexuals should not normally be granted clearance to higher levels, should not be recruited if there is a possibility that they may require such clearance in the course of their careers and should certainly not be posted to sensitive positions overseas."[29] Limiting or revoking security clearances worked to discipline and exclude gay and lesbian people in recruitment, diplomatic postings, and employment.

The antihomosexual security purges continued into the 1970s, at the height of the gay and lesbian liberation movement in Canada. Canadian security officials and the RCMP were not deterred by the fact that the gay and lesbian liberation movement had a major impact on society's view of homosexuality. Increasingly visible, the gay, lesbian, and bisexual communities were breaking down the idea that homosexuals were a threat because they harbored a secret. The August 1971 protest on Parliament Hill by Toronto Gay Action, known as "We Demand," was the first national protest organized by homosexuals in Canada. The protestors' demands focused on the employment of homosexuals and called for antidiscrimination policies. Specifically, the We Demand document, which was read to the protestors, included reference to paragraph 100 of the Royal Commission on Security in which the authors "tackle" the "question of homosexuality." The activists' aim was to showcase the flawed logic in paragraph 100 given the "changes taking place in our social mores."[30] Here, the We Demand activists turned the tables on a security regime that constructed homosexuals as security risks based on their secrets by standing in public on the steps of Parliament Hill in the nation's capital—an unprecedented act of resistance.

The demands, publicity, and protests that erupted forced Canadian government and police security forces to shift how they queer(ed) subversion. A declassified document dated June 21, 1976, regarding the National Gay Rights Coalition of Canada (NGRC) reveals a reconceptualization of the "gay political activist":

> The gay political activists are predominantly young, ranging in the age of 20–25 years old, and unlike the older homosexuals they are eager to display their homosexuality through such acts as demonstrating. Interestingly, these individuals have been joined in loose alliance with certain lesbian communes in the city as both groups see they have a common cause. It must be noted that the gay political activists are non-violent and their tactics have always followed those of pressure groups who are without political power and view themselves as a minority.[31]

Despite recognizing the nonviolent character of the gay and lesbian liberation movement and their lack of political power, Canadian security forces continued to link homosexuality with threats to national security. This time, the participation of homosexuals in what were called "unaligned Marxist groups," such as the League for Socialist Action, enabled the Canadian security regime to recalibrate the association between subversives and sexuality and to revise its tactics (monitoring meetings, meeting places, planting informants, and the like).

At the core of this shift was the threat gays and lesbians involved in leftist organizations posed as "radicals" ready to subvert the capitalist system, not just as "queers":

> The gays have received little public support as the public still views homosexuals in a negative light. However, certain of the ultraleft groups, mainly Trotskyists, have been involved in gay groups in attempts to radicalize them. (It has been found that those ultra left members involved in gay groups were also homosexuals). This is part explains why some of the gay political activists have been increasingly taking on a Marxist analysis of their position, equating homosexuals as an oppressed minority in a capitalist system.[32]

In addition to the danger homosexuality posed to the heteropatriarchal gender order and nuclear family, the belief that "only a radical social change can bring about gay liberation" was seen as subverting the socioeconomic system of liberal democratic societies. The lengthy report contained newspaper clippings and a description of every gay and lesbian liberation organization active by 1976.

The surveillance of gay and lesbian organizations was extensive. In the course of researching *The Canadian War on Queers* we acquired declassified documents on almost every gay and lesbian organization established on university campuses across the country as well as national organizations such as the aforementioned NGRC, the Gay Liberation Front (organized in various cities such as in Vancouver in 1970), and the various chapters of the Gay Alliance Towards Equality.[33] The surveillance of lesbians, lesbian feminists, and feminists also became a particularly critical component in the security regime. Archival documents show the extensive surveillance of the 1970 Abortion Caravan and the Royal Commission on the Status of Women and describe feminists and lesbians as a threat to national security because they allegedly subvert the gender order, noting the "unfeminine clothing" and "slovenly attire" that some of the women under surveillance supposedly wore.[34]

The fight for legal recognition of sexual orientation in the repatriated Canadian constitution, known as the Charter of Rights and Freedoms, in 1982 did not lead the RCMP and military officials to modify security practices against queer communities. Shifts in social visibility and tolerance for queers as well as national campaigns for inclusion in the charter did not sit well with RCMP and military officials. They initiated calls for exemptions from adhering to constitutional equality rights for gays and lesbians serving in the RCMP and military because they posed an "operational impediment."[35] The appeals for exemptions ultimately failed, however, and the investigation and surveillance of queers serving in the RCMP and the military continued unabated throughout the 1980s. Although these tactics were not necessarily sanctioned by cabinet ministers or high-ranking security officials, they were certainly not challenged by these segments of the government. The discourse and practices born of the Cold War panic that established homosexuality as a security risk, as evidence of disloyalty, and as a mark of character weakness informed the vetting of homosexuals in the federal police force and military in the 1980s.

The antihomosexual national security purge in Cold War Canada was an organized and systemic process involving the highest levels of government, including the prime minister, the Cabinet Committee on Security and Intelligence, and the Security Panel. Working with the RCMP commissioner and the Security Service branch of the federal police force, Canadian security officials coordinated various surveillance, entrapment, interrogation, and investigation schemes targeting gay and lesbian communities across the country to ferret out what they believed were unreliable and disloyal subversives who could be blackmailed. This queering of the subversive was anchored in an administrative logic that drew on heteropatriarchal codes of sexuality and gender as well as a pseudoscientific conceptualization of personality defects in homosexuals. In the language of the Canadian security regime, homosexuals suffered from a "character weakness" that made them dangerous to the "interests of the state."

Notes

This chapter is based on research and interviews on the national security campaigns against queers conducted for *The Canadian War on Queers: National Security as Sexual Regulation* (Vancouver: University of British Columbia Press, 2010), coauthored with Gary Kinsman.

1. Gary Kinsman and Patrizia Gentile, *The Canadian War on Queers: National Security as Sexual Regulation* (Vancouver: University of British Columbia Press, 2010), p. 7.
2. The Front de libération du Québec fought for Quebec sovereignty from 1963 to 1970, beginning with the kidnapping and murder of Pierre Laporte, minister of labor with the Liberal Party of Quebec. These actions culminated in what is now known as the October Crisis and the instituting of the War Measures Act by Prime Minister Pierre E. Trudeau.
3. David Johnson, *The Lavender Scare: The Cold War Persecution of Gays and Lesbians in the Federal Government* (Chicago: University of Chicago Press, 2009), 76.
4. Ibid., 133.
5. Quoted in Kinsman and Gentile, *Canadian War on Queers*, 8. Hillenkoetter is quoted in the memo authored by Don Wall. See also Daniel J. Robinson and David Kimmel, "The Queer Career of Homosexual Security Vetting," *Canadian Historical Review* 75, no. 3 (1994): 319–45.
6. Don Wall lists the various categories of character weakness in his memo to the Security Panel titled "Security Cases involving Character Weaknesses, with Special Reference to the Problem of Homosexuality," May 1959. On page 2 of this document, Wall lists "desire for money," "drinking," and "sex: adultery and homosexuality" as "the most common character weaknesses."
7. On the containment of gender values and codes in the Cold War era see the classic by Elaine Tyler May, *Homeward Bound: American Families in the Cold War Era* (New York: Basic Books, 1988). For a Canadian version see Mary Louise Adams, *The Trouble with Normal: Postwar Youth and the Making of Heterosexuality* (Toronto: University of Toronto Press, 1997).
8. R. G. Waldeck, "Homosexual International," *Human Events*, September 29, 1960, 453–56. According to Erin G. Carlston, Waldeck first published this article in 1952. For more on Waldeck and the conflation of communism with homosexuality see chapter 5, "The Ganelon Type," in her *Double Agents: Espionage, Literature, and Liminal Citizens* (New York: Columbia University Press, 2013).
9. R. G. Robertson, Secretary to the Cabinet, "Memorandum for Deputy Ministers and Head of Agency: Revised Cabinet Directive on Security," December 27, 1963, Canadian Security Intelligence Service (CSIS), Access to Information Request (AIR) 91–088. Appendix: Cabinet Directive No. 35: Security in the Public Service of Canada, December 18, 1963. The memorandum gives a summary of the contents of Cabinet Directive No. 29.
10. D. F. Wall, "Security Cases Involving Character Weaknesses, with Special Reference to the Problem of Homosexuality," May 12, 1959, CSIS, AIR 91–088.
11. For a full historical overview of the Canadian national security state, see Reg Whitaker and Gary Marcuse, *The Making of a National Insecurity State, 1945–1957* (Toronto: University of Toronto Press, 1994). On surveillance in the academy, see Steve Hewitt, *Spying 101: The RCMP's Secret Activities at Canadian Universities, 1917–1997* (Toronto: University of Toronto Press, 2002). For the latest work on the security police forces in Canada, see Reg Whitaker, Gregory Kealey, and Andrew Parnaby, *Secret Service: Political Policing in Canada from the Fenians to Fortress America* (Toronto: University of Toronto Press, 2012).

12. An excerpt from an article originally published in *US News & World Report*, a magazine read by US federal civil servants. Their Canadian counterparts would have read " 'How Canada Fights Spies': Security of State Is Put before That of Individual," *Civil Service News*, April 1956, 5.

13. *House of Commons Debates*, Canada, October 25, 1963, 4049. The Bill of Rights, Canada's first piece of legislation formally protecting Canadians' rights, was established under the John Diefenbacker (Progressive Conservative Party of Canada) government in 1960.

14. Gary Kinsman and I conducted approximately fifty-two interviews for our book, *The Canadian War on Queers*. On Jim Egan, see his *Challenging the Conspiracy of Silence: My Life as a Canadian Gay Activist* (Toronto: Canadian Gay and Lesbian Archives, 1998); and *Jim Egan: Canada's Pioneer Gay Activist* (Toronto: Canadian Lesbian and Gay History Network, 1987). See also the film *Jim Loves Jack*, produced and directed by David Adkin (New York: Cinema Guild, 1996). For samples of Egan's work, see "Most Fantastic Witch-Hunt since Inquisition War Followed by Dismissal of Homosexuals by the Hundreds from US Government Offices," *Justice Weekly*, March 13, 1954, 13; and his "Persecution of Homosexuals Gets Blamed for Their Increased Activity in Public," *Justice Weekly*, April 13, 1954, 13.

15. Appendix A, "Homosexuality within the Federal Government Service—Statistics," to J. M. Bella, Director of Security and Intelligence, to the RCMP Commissioner, "Homosexuality within the Federal Government Service," April 29, 1960, 2, 4. CSIS, AIR 92–008.

16. Directorate of Security and Intelligence (DSI), Annual Report, 1961–1962, 22, CSIS, AIR 91–088.

17. Wake was known to government and military officials through his work in the Royal Commission on the Criminal Sexual Psychopaths. For more on the commission, see the chapter titled "The Criminal Sexual Psychopath in Canada" in Elise Chenier, *Strangers in Our Midst* (Toronto: University of Toronto Press, 2008).

18. On the psychological profession in the Cold War era, see Ellen Herman, "The Career of Cold War Psychology," *Radical History Review* 63 (Fall 1995): 52–85. On the psychologist/psychiatrist gaze and homosexual bodies, see Jennifer Terry, *An American Obsession: Science, Medicine, and Homosexuality in Modern Society* (Chicago: University of Chicago Press, 1999); and Terry, "Momism and the Making of Treasonous Homosexuals," in *"Bad" Mothers: The Politics of Blame in Twentieth Century America*, ed. Molly Ladd-Taylor and Lauri Umansky (New York: New York University Press, 1998), 169–90.

19. On security procedures and the use of fingerprinting in the making of the national security state, see Larry Hannant, *The Infernal Machine: Investigating the Loyalty of Canada's Citizens* (Toronto: University of Toronto Press, 1995).

20. J. M. Bella, director of Security and Intelligence, Memo to the Commissioner, "Homosexuality within the Federal Government Service," April 29, 1960, 6, CSIS, AIR 92–008. Note the RCMP commissioner's use of the criminalization of homosexual sexual practices.

21. Ibid. See also F. R. Wake, "Report on Special Project," December 19, 1962, CSIS, AIR 91–088.

22. Several of the documents we obtained through the Access to Information Act uncovered the direct link between US security policies on homosexuals and Canadian security practices, but the document that makes explicit reference to Wake, US security

policy, and psychiatry is the report of C. W. Harvison, the RCMP commissioner, to the Directorate of Security and Intelligence outlining a meeting he had with the then minister of justice: "Meeting to Consider Reports of Dr. Don Wall and Dr. F. R. Wake on the Problem of Character Weaknesses in the Government Service," March 4, 1963. In this document, Harvison mentioned meetings between US security officials, Wall, and Wake in minute detail. These meetings led Canadian security officials to modify their security procedures in light of what they learned from their US counterparts. In addition, we also learned how eager Wake was to apply the psychiatric strategies used in the United States to help vet homosexuals in the State Department. He seemed to believe that the United States was more advanced in this area.

23. Wake, "Report on Special Project."
24. Ibid.
25. Ibid., Appendix A, "Word Association List," 1–3.
26. Wake, "Report on Special Project."
27. Directorate of Security and Intelligence Annual Report, 1965–66, 33, CSIS, AIR 91–088.
28. Report of the Royal Commission on Security, Canada (Mackenzie Commission), 36, s. 100.
29. Ibid., 36, s. 98.
30. "Community Homophile Association Toronto, Ont.," Library and Archives Canada, Record Group 146, vol. 3115.
31. Ibid.
32. Ibid.
33. For more on spying in the academy, see Hewitt, *Spying 101*.
34. "Gays of Ottawa," LAC, Record Group 146, vol. 3121, 34. For more on the surveillance of the feminist movement in Canada, see Christabelle Sethna and Steven Hewitt, "Clandestine Operations: The Vancouver Women's Caucus, the Abortion Caravan, and the RCMP," *Canadian Historical Review* 90, no. 3 (2009): 463–95. The Abortion Caravan was the first cross-country feminist action instigated by the Vancouver Women's Caucus. The protest resulted in thousands of women congregating on the steps of the Parliament Building in Ottawa in 1970. The protesters demanded that changes be made to the 1969 amendments of the Criminal Code that legalized only therapeutic abortions. The Royal Commission on the Status of Women, also known as the Bird Commission, was established in 1967 and published its final report in 1970. It included reports on Canadian women's political, social, economic, and health welfare.
35. See Kinsman and Gentile, *Canadian War on Queers*, 351.

References

Archives

Canadian Lesbian and Gay Archives, Toronto, Canada
Library and Archives Canada, Ottawa, Canada

Periodicals

Civil Service News
Justice Weekly

Selected Published Works

Hannant, Larry. *The Infernal Machine: Investigating the Loyalty of Canada's Citizens.* Toronto: University of Toronto Press, 1995.

Hewitt, Steve. *Spying 101: The RCMP's Secret Activities at Canadian Universities, 1917–1997.* Toronto: University of Toronto Press, 2002.

Johnson, David. *The Lavender Scare: The Cold War Persecution of Gays and Lesbians in the Federal Government.* Chicago: University of Chicago Press, 2009.

Kinsman, Gary, and Patrizia Gentile. *The Canadian War on Queers: National Security as Sexual Regulation.* Vancouver: University of British Columbia Press, 2010.

Robinson, Daniel J., and David Kimmel, "The Queer Career of Homosexual Security Vetting." *Canadian Historical Review* 75, no. 3 (1994): 319–45.

Waldeck, R. G. "Homosexual International." *Human Events*, September 29, 1960, 453–56.

Whitaker, Reg, and Gary Marcuse, *The Making of a National Insecurity State, 1945–1957.* Toronto: University of Toronto Press, 1994.

Whitaker, Reg, Gregory Kealey, and Andrew Parnaby. *Secret Service: Political Policing in Canada from the Fenians to Fortress America.* Toronto: University of Toronto Press, 2012.

CHAPTER 4

"Nonreligious Activities"

Sex, Anticommunism, and Progressive Christianity in Late Cold War Brazil

Benjamin A. Cowan

In September 1975, spies from Brazil's Air Force Intelligence Service (Centro de Informações da Aeronáutica, or CISA), one of several agencies in the byzantine repressive apparatus of the country's dictatorship, leveled very serious accusations against a young French missionary then residing in the state of Minas Gerais. Benjamin Thierry Lefebvre, according to a secret report emanating from Rio de Janeiro, not only had participated in the French student disturbances of 1968 but had immediately thereafter shown up in Brazil, "wearing a plaster cast to correct a fracture or dislocation resulting from a parachute jump, incurred while training for or participating in guerrilla warfare, perhaps in Africa."[1] Curiously, this rather alarming alleged activity did not draw further attention from security agents in Brazil. Instead, they exhaustively investigated several other aspects of Lefebvre's life, aspects that to police eyes appeared inextricable, and of paramount importance: his sexuality, his contact with young students, and his alleged promotion of Marxism. The secret file on Lefebvre listed his "nonreligious activities," indicating that (1) he had taught not only at a state university but also at a local high school, where (2) he had "formed youth groups, principally drawn from drug addicts, pretending to recuperate them" when actually he himself was "addicted to drugs"; (3) these youth groups were in fact "political-ideological" indoctrination sessions, designed to create Marxist leaders; and (4) Lefebvre had nefariously cultivated the "admiration of his students by his facility of expression, intelligence, and knowledge of the political-social situation, always letting his opposition to the Government be known." Finally, the CISA agents took pains to clarify one crucial point: "He isn't a homosexual, as was presumed, and in fact has been considered a lothario, . . . always accompanied by young girls with whom he is said to carry on sexual escapades outside the city."[2]

Several critical aspects of life under military rule in late Cold War Brazil come into focus here. The report on Lefebvre evokes the ways that sexuality framed political policing in that context—in this case, via a climate of suspicion surrounding and conflating so-called subversion, sexual and gender behavior, young people, pedagogy, and the emergence of progressive Christianity. Youth, religion, social justice–oriented politics, teaching, and sex formed a nexus of anxiety for Brazil's powerful—and fearfully abusive—Cold Warriors in the 1970s. The spies who surveilled Lefebvre were, in a sense, foot soldiers in a campaign of terror, intimidation, torture, murder, and disappearance waged by Brazil's anticommunist military dictatorship against its enemies, both avowed and perceived. The dictatorship itself began with a coup in 1964 and cycled through the administrations of four generals who assumed the presidency and ruled with varying degrees of authoritarian repression. The years between 1968 and 1973, often called the *anos de chumbo*, or "years of lead," saw a climax of legal and extralegal repression and state violence, both overt and covert, committed by paramilitary and official agents of the regime. By 1974, the government had ruthlessly eliminated the handful of enemies of the state who actually did take up arms against it. Yet even as redemocratization slowly commenced—it would be a ten-year process, culminating with massive demonstrations in 1984 and elections in 1985— intelligence and security forces continued to operate in a context of high Cold War alert. Through the end of dictatorship, the regime's spies and atrocity perpetrators perceived enemies all around them, and pursued those enemies with sometimes-paranoid alacrity.

As I have argued elsewhere, this pursuit had long been gendered and sexualized; indeed, sex became one of several vital axes along which Cold War blurred into culture war, part of a process that I, in company with other researchers, have begun to trace hemispherically. In Brazil, as elsewhere in the Americas and even further afield, Cold Warriors saw themselves fighting a "total war," a battle conceived on almost infinite fronts, but often with very specific foci. These foci signally included behaviors and cultural production linked with sexuality, gender, and changes—real and perceived—in "traditional" social, institutional, and family structure.[3] The infamous countersubversive conflation of "communists and queers" extended beyond North American McCarthyites into hemispheric notions of a global, Marxist conspiracy to subvert the family, traditional manhood and womanhood, and moral and aesthetic standards, most seminally by promoting deviant sexual behavior and the gender-sexual denaturing of wayward youth. Where Ronald Reagan, campaigning in 1966, famously equated student protest with "Communism" and "sexual misconduct," right-wing activists sang a similar tune from Argentina to Mexico, insisting—to quote anticommunists in the latter country—that student "disturbances" were "sexual in origin" and the result of "smoking marijuana . . . watching pornography . . . [reading] degenerate comics," and attending "seminars led by Marxist priests."[4]

In this chapter I illustrate one way in which sexuality colored the policing of emergent threats in 1970s Brazil. As noted above, countersubversion generally was gendered and sexualized; here I present a case study in one realm of policing. I analyze a particular confluence of anxieties that coalesced into one focus of the "war" against subversion: a node of eroticized concerns revolving around sex, pedagogy, religion, and putative subversion. The story of liberation theology and its political legacy in Cold War Brazil and Latin America is widely known; by the period in question, Brazil's Catholic hierarchs and activists found themselves the acknowledged champions of human rights in the face of what some euphemistically called the "excesses" of the military regime.[5] As I have elsewhere noted, Catholic progressives were often just as staunchly conservative in matters of sex as their authoritarian counterparts—but were ironically the targets of state suspicion and surveillance when it came to sex. Here I show that Christian evangelicals, too, played a role in this struggle over the intertwined meanings of social justice, sexual liberation, and communist infiltration.[6] In fact, the emergence of liberation theology simultaneously created divergences among Brazil's Protestants and fostered a cross-denominational movement taking up the mantle of ecumenism. The ecumenical alliance lent itself to progressive causes ranging from human and civil rights to social justice.[7] This development led to several reactions, some of which gained notoriety even at the time: the persecution of outspoken Protestant progressives, including the murder by security forces of Paulo Stuart Wright, son of American missionaries and the brother of Presbyterian pastor Jaime Wright, and the enduring schism between progressive Protestants (associated with liberation theology, social justice initiatives, antiregime protest, and ecumenism) and conservatives. The latter derided their liberation-minded coreligionists not only as communists but as dissolute—as, that is, a total package of sexual, doctrinal, and political depravity.[8]

As the state began persecuting religious liberationists of several stripes, then, it developed an alliance with right-wing Christians who, like security forces themselves, associated liberation theology, human rights advocacy, and social justice simultaneously and inextricably with communist "subversion" *and* with sexual dissipation. Right-wing evangelicals adopted an agenda that linked reactionary sexual moralism, anticommunism, and opposition to Protestant and ecumenical liberalism as their pet cause, and in doing so grew closer to the regime. As one right-wing pastor put it, conservative evangelicals considered themselves firmly in "our territory" when they opposed the combined threats of liberalized sexuality ("eroticism and pornography"), communism, and religious innovation.[9] This reactionary agenda, as I demonstrate here, mirrored attitudes within the state, especially in the shadowy circuits of the regime's secret police and intelligence services. Indeed, to this nexus of concerns about religion, sex, activism, and subversion, security forces added one further, critical element, likewise shared with conservative pastors (some of whom cooperated, overtly and covertly, with security officials): pedagogy and the suspected infiltration of schools by religiously, sexually, and politically deviant "subversives." In short, as the dictatorship matured and entered its twilight, and as the hemispheric Cold War began a new phase (focused on Central America as the "doorstep" of the West), a set of conflations focused the attentions of Brazil's political police on a seminal knot of anxieties linking sexuality, religion, progressive politics, youth, and pedagogy. This was, of course, not the only way conservatives, evangelical and nonevangelical, within and outside of the state, envisioned and understood their adversaries. Indeed, each component issue constituted the locus of long-standing animosity on the part of the regime. Yet, by the middle 1970s, those animosities had combined in a particular configuration, drawing the suspicions of security forces down on progressive, religious pedagogues presumed to be sexually, doctrinally, and politically subverting their young charges.

Students, Sex, and Subversion

Almost from its inception, the regime had reserved perhaps its most pronounced animosity for young people, especially students and the institutions to which they pertained. As a venerable tradition of Brazilianist historiography has catalogued, protest and persecution marked the history of the country's largely middle- and upper-class students in the 1960s. Secondary schools and universities furnished many of those who supported major social, political, and economic reforms (*reformas de base*) during the heady administration of President João Goulart (1961–1964). When Goulart, accused by a civilian-military conspiracy of complicity with communist plotting, was deposed by a coup, high school and college students took center stage in protests that rocked the country in the middle 1960s and especially in 1968. Partly as a result, young people, many of them linked with what came to be known as the "student movement," formed a key face of opposition to the regime—and suffered the brunt of repression.[10]

This repression included the dismantling of student organizations and led student organizers to go into hiding and—in some cases—to engage in armed resistance to the government. Between 1968 and 1974, the state eradicated its enemies, armed and unarmed, via a fearsome campaign of intimidation, secret detention, torture, disappearance, and urban and rural counterguerrilla operations. In the midst of these violent disruptions, the gender, sexuality, and cultural penchants of youth and students quickly became a focus. One exemplary incident gained notoriety even at the time: when police and military officials raided student housing at the University of São Paulo (USP) in December 1968, they appropriated "subversive" paraphernalia and paraded it for the press. The incriminating items included, according to a military intelligence report, "great quantities of weapons, explosives, propaganda material, communist ideological proselytizing," "subversive publications," and "strong indications of sexual liberty among students . . . such as birth-control and abortifacient materials."[11] As historian Victoria Langland indicates, "The display of the pills provided a double message to the attentive journalists and their readers: not only did young women get involved in these confrontational and dangerous activities (for only women take birth control pills), but they came prepared to do more than just discuss politics. In the vision of the police-sponsored press conference, Molotov cocktails and female student sexuality posed equally alarming risks to the established order."[12]

By the 1970s, the decade that concerns us here, this kind of anticommunist vigilance vis-à-vis student sexuality had expanded well beyond female students and their birth-control devices. Police surveillance of male and female students' gender and sexuality become de rigueur, a regular part of the even more regular policing of schools, teachers, pupils, and educational materials. That is, the sexual policing of pedagogy was a rule of security forces' ideology, surveillance, and repression in military Brazil. Indeed, a 1976 report compiled by Air Force intelligence agents in São Paulo referred back to the USP incident as a reminder of the duration and consistency of the battle against moral subversion in the nation's institutions of learning: "Looking back a few years, the Student Movement was very active, terrorism was taking shape; an 'invasion' with subversive roots took place at the USP Residential Center . . . the 'invaders' settled in and fortified themselves and the [dormitory] came to have communist cells, terrorism, drug-trafficking, and sexual degradation."[13]

Indeed, by some measures, countersubversive concern over pedagogy grew more and more pronounced over the course of the 1970s—particularly when it came to the confluence of anxieties surrounding young students, morality and moral education, and, as we shall see below, religious instruction. Partly to address the perceived crisis of subversive youth behavior, conservatives had successfully instituted Moral and Civic Education as a required discipline at all levels of education in 1969. The new discipline was designed to combine sexual, moral, and political reform, inculcating anticommunism alongside abstinence.[14] Yet as the decade wore on, anticommunists within and outside of security forces fretted about the quality of the teaching staff in general—and most of all about the vetting of those who taught courses in Moral and Civic Education. As the regime's authoritarianism and violence increased between 1968 and 1974 (with a very slow *distensão*, or "opening," thereafter), the state and its repressive foot soldiers became overtly and covertly concerned with the quality (the countersubversive and moral quality, that is) of teaching. Under the aegis of Institutional Act No. 5 (the regime's most notorious single act of authoritarian legal wrangling), the state sought the "technical control and new relations of domination inside of schools."[15] As one report from local National Intelligence Service (SNI) agents in Curitiba explained, "In diverse Learning Establishments, public and private, the existence has come to be known of elements indicted under the Institutional Acts or possessing negative ideological backgrounds, who are now teaching."[16]

Teachers, then, became a regular focus of surveillance—and moral education a particular focus of that scrutiny. The state's spies and enforcers worried, according to a 1971 report, that "there have even been attempts to distort the General Program of [Moral and Civic Education] elaborated by the National Education Council, by means of various artifices . . . where controversial themes are brought up, by people who are not always qualified." In this case, SNI agents fretted that school officials had invited "people, who though knowledgeable about problems, do not possess pedagogical attributions to permit the transmission of useful instruction." They poured out the most concern, however, about "speaking on Sexual Education" and the role of "elements with subversive ideas" in promoting pedagogical techniques the SNI deemed highly suspicious (such techniques, according to agents, included "scavenger hunts.")[17]

This hand-wringing on the part of intelligence agents was consistent with their broader preoccupation with pedagogy, sexuality, morality, and one further element: what security forces called the *linha progressista* (progressive line) of Christian authorities and laypeople. This category included Catholics, but heightened suspicion extended to developing evangelical groups and alliances, such that the byzantine matrix of state spies and enforcers lent extra attention to religious figures of several stripes. Surveillance of teachers, administrators, and schools in general reached a level of high alert where concerns about students and sexuality collided with those about religious subversion. Indeed, officials discerned a grand plot drawing together suspect developments in Christian sectarianism, teaching, and moral-sexual corruption. Thus, a series of reports compiled as part of a new initiative to coordinate intelligence-gathering at the federal level alleged a crisis in education, arguing, by way of introduction, that "among the factors to be considered in the distortion of the moral and civic formation of Brazilian youth are those of spiritual, moral, and social nature." Replete with accusations about such "distortion," the reports displayed the broad suspicions of spies at the SNI, the Ministry of Justice, the Ministry of Education and Culture, and the fearsome Intelligence Operations Detachment (DOI), who charged that schools, "especially at the high school level," were promoting the "bastardization of morality and of the family" via everything from drug abuse to "interviews with prostitutes and pederasts." Such tactics, according to representatives from across these security agencies, constituted part of "the constant psychological work of communists, today reinforced by the thinking and action of the progressive line of [Christians, which] foregrounds aspects of Marxism which attract youth."[18]

The report leveled charges against specific schools (religious and nonreligious) alongside the wider claim that "another aspect to be considered, and which by dint of its subtlety merits a good deal of attention, is the religious aspect." That "attention," as we shall see, zeroed in on new developments in the evangelical world. Here, in the same breath, intelligence officials fretted over drug abuse, sexual education, student protest, "activities of various subversive organizations," "deviance committed against the moral and civic formation of youth" at specific schools, and the influence of Testemunhas de Jeová (Jehovah's Witnesses) in schools in São Paulo and elsewhere. SNI agents ruminated that the Witnesses' approach to pedagogy and schools "might develop into yet another area of subversive exploitation."[19]

The New Right, Religion, and the Regime

Jehovah's Witnesses and their fundamentalist counterparts, however, did not usually bear the brunt of security forces' attention; that dubious distinction generally fell to those identified with liberationist or social justice–oriented theology.[20] As the 1970s wore on, Protestantism (and particularly Pentecostalism) gained adherents and visibility in Brazil. Several developments clarified the relationship between the regime's enforcement agencies, Pentecostals, older Protestant denominations, and the shifting terrain of national politics. When politicized divisions began to emerge between right- and left-wing Protestants, security forces monitored these divisions and consciously sided with rightist evangelicals who took up the banners of moralism (especially vis-à-vis sexuality), anticommunism, and authoritarianism. Eventually, this would mean a convergence of interests (or, perhaps better stated, of enmities and animosities) among state spies and the more intransigent members of Brazil's evangelical "community." Opposition to ecumenism, to democratization, to progressive politics, and to social justice initiatives drew the burgeoning evangelical Right closer to the regime—and closer to its dungeon keepers, for whom, it appears, the enemy of an enemy was a friend. Significantly, this enemy appeared as an amorphous, conflated amalgam of ecumenical cooperation, progressive Christianity, suspected moral and sexual deviance, and putatively subversive pedagogy. The evangelical Right and the regime and its allies shared animosity toward this amalgam. In other words, sexuality was not the only, or even the paramount, concern that framed right-wing countersubversives' vision of their enemies, yet it *was* an essential part of that vision, one that extended into each specific realm of authoritarian policing. Here, it distinctly colored the developing politics of Christianity, where sexual and moral conservatism fused with anticommunism, in much the same way these had come together within the repressive apparatus more generally.

Excellent scholarship has unearthed histories of interaction between evangelical Christianity, the Cold War, and military authoritarianism; indeed, the connections between American evangelical missionaries, local congregations, and the terrorist states of 1980s Central America are the stuff not only of historiography but of popular knowledge.[21] Brazil, however, is something of a special case in the history of evangelical Protestantism in Latin America. In the 1970s, Brazilian Protestantism stood on the verge of an explosion of visibility and popularity, with new adherents flocking to Pentecostalism and to a glittering new televangelism industry. By 1972, the first evangelical preacher had appeared in a *telenovela*, an oft-heralded sign of the times; in the decade or so following, evangelicals of several stripes left behind a studied, even doctrinal apoliticism and entered formal politics.[22]

In this context, even more than in decades past, evangelicals could be found inhabiting points throughout the political matrix. Nationally, Brazil saw the rise of prodemocracy organizing and of social movements for several key identitarian causes (such as feminism, black power, and gay rights). By the late 1970s, participants in these social movements, alongside social justice, antipoverty, and human rights advocates (including representatives of the Catholic Church) garnered both attention and increasing success in their demands for democratization. As the military regime grew more and more unpopular—its demise would be cemented by massive street demonstrations in São Paulo and Rio de Janeiro in 1984—the stage was set for a schism among evangelicals. In the simplest terms, this can be understood as a face-off between conservatives who supported the regime and progressives who gravitated toward the currents of liberation theology. In fact, the story was much more complicated; each side identified with a set of issues at the heart of a polemic that gave rise to an evangelical New Right. By the time of Brazil's 1987–1988 constitutional convention—in which evangelicals would play a notable role—that New Right had coalesced around opposition to a conflated set of perceived evils: democratization, ecumenism, leftist social justice initiatives, communism, and sexual-moral dissolution.[23]

The debates that shook Brazilian society, then, certainly divided evangelicals: on one side were progressives who supported ecumenism, democratization, and social justice, and on the other side was something resembling a New Right, vehemently rejecting their progressive counterparts and convening support for the regime with a conservative politics of sexuality, morality, and the Cold War. Baptist pastor José dos Reis Pereira, for example, pertained decidedly to the latter camp and, as such, echoed the anticommunist moralism that pervaded right-wing and hard-line circles inside and outside of the government.[24] Pereira denounced "moral" dissolution, gambling, "the excessive tolerance of eroticism and pornography," and "ecumenism," exhorting his fellow evangelical conservatives to "combat theological liberalism" and "reveal the errors of the so-called 'theology of liberation' and its close relative, international communism."[25] Tensions between liberationists and the likes of Pereira grew pronounced enough that progressives were persecuted not only by security forces but by members of their own denominations and congregations.[26]

Conservative evangelicals, meanwhile, often made common cause with the regime and its enforcers, who had long been engaged in a battle against what one general referred to as "a true sexolatry." To both conservative anticommunists in the military government—especially the notoriously hard-line "intelligence community"—and evangelical rightists, sexuality in public culture represented deviance and a simultaneous affront to Western capitalism, democracy, and Christianity. As one 1972 report would have it, a "movement of eroticism" including "incentives to pornography" sought the "dissolution of the Christian customs of the Brazilian people" such that "the Revolution would be won."[27] Based on such ideas, the regime took steps to combat sexual deviance—real and perceived—in the name of national security. Pornography and obscenity, already subject to censorship, were further criminalized as communist threats; suspected subversives were surveilled sexually as well as politically; and the dictatorship's ideologues and enforcers saw infractions against sexual conservatism as of a piece with political subversion. Sexual deviance, or even unconventionality, was presumed to indicate Marxist plotting, and vice versa; these became two inextricable parts of the framework of authoritarian policing.[28]

Security forces, in other words, shared conservatives' fixation on progressive Christianity (Catholic or evangelical), ecumenism, moral and sexual deviance, and young people and pedagogy as sources and manifestations of communist subversion. On the Right, as in the headquarters and secret detention and information centers of the state's intelligence services, "ecumenical," "Marxist," "progressive," and "sex" caused hostile ears to prick up. These became associated taboos, read as enemy tactics designed to undermine church and society, largely via the nation's students.

Security forces made no secret of their loyalties. Aware of the yawning divisions between right-wing and left-wing evangelicals, the state's repressive workers sympathized with the Right—against *progressistas*, their putative Marxism, and alleged cultural disruptions. Security officials and right-wing Protestants found themselves in utter agreement when supporting a traditionalism within the nation's churches. This traditionalism fused doctrinal and gender-sexual conservatism—progressives were daubed concomitantly communist and threatening to the extant gender, sexual, and familial order. The São Paulo SNI, for example, spoke with undisguised approval of the conservative Confederation of Fundamentalist Evangelical Churches of Brazil (CIEF), an antiprogressive coalition. Admirers at the SNI described CIEF as "a national movement of religious clarification, Christian confraternity, bearing witness in the service of biblical and historic Christianity and combating all the forms of theological and moral change in the heart of the Church of Christ in our days." The state agents were particularly pleased with a missionary pastor representing CIEF who railed against Marxist interference in gender, sexual, and social relations, "pitting children against parents, women against men . . . creating social, moral, and political anarchy."[29] Spies posted at a southern university in 1982 noted that "evangelicals are organizing around two divergent poles, one representing the traditional conservative wing of the Church" and the other opting for "the doctrine of liberation theology." Reporting to the regional SNI headquarters, these spies openly sympathized with the former, affirming that the "leftist drift [*esquerdização*] of the Evangelical Clergy" was cause for political and moral alarm. The ecumenical, progressive organizations CONIC and CLAI, in this view, served as proof positive that "the Protestant Churches in Brazil have come to suffer the influence of leftist ideologies, although a few [churches] of conservative tradition still resist the investitures of the Marxist Clergy." Left-leaning churches, then, were assumed *not* to have resisted such "investitures." As evidence, the report recurred, predictably, to suspicion of gender, sexual, and doctrinal trouble, all rolled into one. The SNI agents registered their displeasure with a Methodist pastor who "placed himself against all types of discrimination and domination" including "machismo, of the oppression of women," and the treatment of "prostitution." To these police eyes, Marxism, via *progressista* Protestants, had made common cause with feminism and prostitution.[30]

Notably, the pastor's speech drew the attention of police because of its title: "Foundations, Guidelines, Politics, and Objectives of the Methodist Educational System." This is consistent with the ways in which particular concern focused on pedagogy, evangelical educational institutions, and the exposure of young people to progressive evangelicalism and its associated political and cultural evils. Several of the police files described above, in fact, revolved around these issues. The Curitiba SNI's report alleging "communist infiltration in the religious sector," for example, bore the heading "Communist Infiltration—Sector of Religion and Education—Paraná." The file began with denunciations of two pastors, alleged to be "manifestly subversive and communist" and extremely dangerous because of their role in a local school. According to the denunciation, which SNI officials affirmed, "In the educational establishments, [the pastors] take advantage of inexperienced youth . . . to inject all sorts of leftist ideas. . . . And how the seed of evil germinates rapidly and profusely!" The danger was the more pronounced because students were allegedly encouraged to hide "all sorts of ideas" from their parents.[31]

Pastors, Pederasts, and Pedagogues

The byzantine corpus of declassified police records makes clear that, by invoking "all sorts of ideas," anticommunists envisioned evangelical teachers imparting a combination of political, religious, moral, and sexual dissolution. Police heavily surveilled progressive Christian pastors, schools, and teachers and with dogged inevitability convinced themselves that they had found what they set out to find: sexual subversion of young people emanating from leftist religious figures linked with an ecumenical, global, Marxist plot. Doubtless there were progressive evangelicals working with or in educational establishments across Brazil, and certainly some of these *progressistas* would have been interested in sharing their liberationist, antiregime, or even Marxist ideas with students. Security officials, however, like their right-wing evangelical allies, had a vision that took on a life of its own—in which progressive religious interpretation, sex, ecumenism, Marxism, and pedagogy formed interwoven strands of a shadowy and unseemly underworld. This is all the more interesting from a historical standpoint because, as a developing scholarship has suggested, the hardened core of the regime's left-wing opponents often waxed at least as moralistic as religious and authoritarian conservatives in this period.[32]

At all scholastic levels, but particularly among secondary school and university students, police were wont to investigate progressive Christian activists and leaders as combined sexual and political threats—alluring demagogues, like the missionary with whom this essay began, or drug-addicted, sexually deviant debauchees, bent on using their religious authority to promote promiscuity alongside propaganda, sex mingled with subversion. In the aftermath of the dormitory raid at the University of São Paulo, mentioned above, police investigated a ring of suspected terrorists at the school, led, according to reports, by an adept, subversive Anglican pastor. Linked with ecumenical progressivism and the Catholic Left, military investigators argued, the pastor was not a student himself. Instead, he hung around the university, preying on students influenced by those currents and establishing an "amplification cell" at the university, with a "high degree of subversion" and the goals of "enticing people into subversive and clandestine activities . . . executing plans of agitation and inciting armed struggle against the social and political regime ruling the country . . . [and] distributing pamphlets and bulletins."[33]

The goal, then, was armed struggle—but perhaps more significant were the pastor's alleged methods, which consisted of winning over unsuspecting youths via demagoguery and, sometimes, literal seduction. A pied piper of subversion, he used his "cultured, intelligent" affect to attract students into his "evil activity," but the methods of attraction also included overt sexuality.[34] The report made several mentions of "amorous" or "sentimental" links used to "entice" new converts into the subversive plot. Indeed, the agents alleged the pastor had drawn a young woman away from her family, into his own home, before handing her off into an affair with another malefactor: "For amorous and sentimental reasons, Lucinda abandoned the home of her parents, going to live afterward in the apartment of [the pastor], where she also would meet Pablo who sometimes slept there. This attitude of Lucinda can be attributed to the fact that her family . . . did not approve of her flirtation." Condemned in absentia to six years in prison, the pastor fled into exile, where he and his family suffered continued surveillance. His liberationist intellectual and political activities (particularly his ecumenism and connection to the World Council of Churches) attracted the ongoing suspicion and condemnation of Brazilian spies.[35]

In other cases, police investigated the institutional deployment of the dissolute, Marxist-ecumenicist plot. That is, they often envisioned such subversion relying less on individual malefactors and more on evangelical schools thought to serve as centers of sexualized subversion. In one particularly salient example, security forces focused their attentions on a Presbyterian school precisely because its progressive administration—linked to celebrated pastor Jaime Wright—had broken with conservatives in the national Presbyterian hierarchy. Officials from the Navy Intelligence Service (CENIMAR) scrutinized the school, its professors, administration, and relationships with external organizations and people. The resulting classified report showed the CENIMAR satisfied that the *colégio* had exposed students to a familiar combination of moral, sexual, ecumenical, and Marxist deviance. The report featured several prime suspects, among them a pastor "linked with the Ecumenist Wing of Protestantism, inspired by the World Council of Churches, of indubitable Marxist influence." In Brazil and beyond, some affiliates of the World Council of Churches (WCC) *did* engage, to varying extents, with Marxism; anticommunists, in turn, denounced the WCC en bloc as a subversive conspiracy. In this climate, the CENIMAR report's authors wrung their hands over "ties to the Left," "attempts at immersing the students in subversive ideology," and professors' "attitudes of seduction." In keeping with their general vision of a web of sex, students, subversion, and evangelicalism, they cast about, searching for sexually maleficent pastors, teachers, and students—and were, at first, surprised *not* to find them. "Despite the fact that some of the members [of the school's administration] preach ideology contrary to the Revolution of 31 March 1964," related the dubious CENIMAR account, "no indication was obtained of the existence of promiscuous habits or customs among the students at the *colégio*."[36]

Disappointed in their expectation that leftist, evangelical, ecumenist educators would, as a matter of course, combine sexual and political malfeasance, intelligence agents nevertheless dwelled on the general profligacy, parasitism, and decadence of these putatively communist and corrupt Christians. The agents even hinted at the potential homosexuality of two of the pastors, who had always "lived together" in what might otherwise be referred to as confirmed bachelorhood.[37] Such hints were no coincidence—indeed, direct allegations of homosexuality among these "subversive" clergy and their supposedly suborned students arose in a separate security report (from the Army Intelligence Service) on this very school. The army intelligence officials alleged, almost as a matter of course, that sexual, doctrinal, and political subversion had united at the school. This report described the teachers not only as "communist activists" who used their positions to "share their subversive ideas," but as "ultra-modernists in the administration of the *colégio*, allowing ample promiscuity" among students. This "promiscuity," they alleged, "ranges from homosexuality to the use of drugs."[38] Promiscuity, homosexuality, subversive ideas, and pharmacology formed an alarming, if anticipated, cocktail. Army spies confirmed what their counterparts at the navy had been expecting to find: that this school was another example of evangelical clergy ("the Ecumenist Wing") gone astray, leading students down a path of sexual, religious, and political subversion.

The Presbyterian school could be seen as "another example" because it was certainly not the only site where intelligence and security officials envisioned evangelical leftists deploying subversion in the form of religious and sexual deviance. A 1977 information-gathering endeavor shared by Rio's fearsome General Department of Special Investigations (DGIE), one of several branches of political police, with the CISA, the CENIMAR, and the intelligence divisions of the army and the Ministries of Justice and Education and Culture produced a police file entitled "Communist Infiltration in the Student Milieu." In this account and related follow-up reports by the SNI and other agencies, security monitors remarked on supposed subversion at several evangelical schools, concluding that "the present intelligence goes to show the effort that the communist-subversive plot has been making . . . in the educational sector." The report expressed particular concern about private schools, including evangelical institutions, where the "privileged classes" might be initiated in "anti-regime theses." Indeed, several "institutions of different religious denominations . . . manifest different types of perversion of democratic ideals."[39]

Authorities surveilled specific individuals and institutions where, according to officials and their informants, such "communist-subversive" efforts were manifest. One Methodist school in Rio de Janeiro attested to DGIE officers and other security workers the presence of alarming infiltration in that denomination—infiltration detected in the combination of progressivism, "pornography," and drugs.[40] Operationalizing their knowledge of divisions within the evangelical community and their affinity for those who viewed *progressismo* with hostility, the political police made contact with an anticommunist informant, a pastor relatively new to the school's administration. This informant, who "accepted his position in order to try to control the communist infiltration in the Methodist Church, to which the Institute is subordinated," described subversive professors promoting "a climate of tendencies contrary to the regime." The state's agents saw "the greatest danger" in the exposure of primary school students, whose "low degree of maturity" made them "easily manipulated by the teachers." As a result, police alleged, an atmosphere of "riotous indiscipline" reigned in the school, serving the infiltrated teachers' subversive ends. The SNI and Ministry of Justice reported "a large proportion of drug-addicted students, who obtain drugs at the very doors of the *colégio*." The intelligence files waxed particularly alarmist at a "more insistent and less subtle" tactic of encouraging students to read the alternative newspaper *O Pasquim*, which was critical of the regime and considered "pornographic" by many in the security and intelligence ranks.[41]

Surveillance at another Rio de Janeiro *colégio* demonstrates security officials' penchant for making doubtful allegations based on a murky combination of assumptions and reconnaissance. Ministry of Justice and army spies classified this school among the "institutions of different religious affiliations" (though in fact the school itself was not formally parochial), where the "perversion of democratic ideals" was again "less subtle." Distressed informants reported that "the book *The Subversives* was being leafed through by one of the teachers" at the same time that another teacher "looked at a photograph of the terrorist Leila Khaled and commented: 'This woman is formidable.' The literature used by teachers of Portuguese, constantly, encompasses negative themes like sex, violence, the under-world, etcetera, highly prejudicial to the age group of the students, who range from 14 to 18 years old.["]42 Several items stand out here: First, the book in question was likely J. Bernard Hutton's *Subverters of Liberty*, making the report's alarm yet more misplaced, as the book was a wildly *anticommunist* tract sometimes used to train security forces themselves. Second, state agents from several agencies once again conflated sexuality and a moral "underworld" with progressive politics, ecumenism, and subversion (in this case linked with global terrorism). It is quite possible that some teachers and students at the school opposed the regime, that some expressed admiration for Leila Khaled, certainly that some supported ecu-menism and liberation theology, and even that some engaged in the use of illegal drugs. Security forces, however, presumed not only that all of these things were indeed happening but that they were all *linked* to each other and, furthermore, that they were products of a grand, global design by the ever-invoked "MCI," or "International Communist Movement," a paranoid fantasy of countersubversives. The MCI, often described as near-omnipotent, was always improbable—not least so when state agents and anticommunists envisioned it at work in this Rio Janeiro *colégio*, weaving together ecumenism, sexual deviance, religious heterodoxy, and pedagogy as avenues of massive infiltration.

Powerful forces within the regime, including security forces themselves, looked with undisguised approval on alliances triangulating their own ranks, agents of extrajudicial right-wing repression (often intimately linked with formal state agencies), and anti-*progressista* reactionaries within the evangelical com-munity, particularly when it came to youth, morality, and pedagogy. Indeed, General João Figueiredo, the last of the military presidents, shared a morality-based, gendered, and sexual anticommunism with Brazil's burgeoning evangelical Right. Figueiredo, who had publicly argued that young people became subversives because of a failure to adopt proper family and sexual values, developed work-ing relationships with several conservative Protestant groups whose moralism he openly admired. Agreement with the regime's moral agenda drew conservative evangelicals into the halls of power, sometimes literally. In 1982, celebrating a planned crackdown on pornography, Figueiredo welcomed a group of evangeli-cal pastors to his office for a moment of prayer and solidarity. In a videotaped ceremony, the pastors presented Figueiredo with a Bible and praised his "taking a stand" against pornography and immorality. Emphasizing "just how much it repulsed me, my government, my friends—the [material of a sexual nature] that I was reading, that I was seeing, that I was hearing," Figueiredo responded that he was taking action against "indecency" because he "just could not stand by." He then thanked and praised the pastors as pillars of Brazil's moral community who were helping to "defend our families," as well as the "interests of Christian society" and the *Pátria* (homeland) itself from the machinations of immoral communists.43

Security forces, meanwhile, carried this alliance with Protestant conservatives into the realm of policing pedagogy, sexuality, and suspected "subversion." For example, representatives from several agencies reported on the tumultuous events of the late 1960s and early 1970s at the Mackenzie Institute, a Presbyterian university in São Paulo. Recognizing Mackenzie as "one of the largest and oldest establishments of private education in Brazil," the SNI continued to monitor potential subversion at Mackenzie in 1971, three years after *rightist* Mackenzie University students had clashed bloodily with left-wing, antiregime students from the neighboring University of São Paulo. The SNI feared that the influence of progressive Christians had made Mackenzie a bastion of "extremist ideas, not only among students, but among professors," and in fact had "transformed [the University] into one of the most active centers of communist irradiation in the country." After some investigation, the SNI report expressed relief at several developments, all of which indicated that Mackenzie had come under the control of those who combined sexual moralism with anticommunism: First, Esther Figueiredo Ferraz, a noted sexual conservative, moralist, and pet of the regime, had taken charge of the university. Second, Command for Hunting Communists, a far-right terrorist group known for staging anticommunist attacks on "immoral" cultural productions and publications, had set up a "base of operations" at Mackenzie. Third, a schism in the Presbyterian Church of Brazil (IPB) had brought the reactionary Reverend Boanerges Ribeiro to power, inaugurating a wave of internal moralism and persecution of progressives and ecumenists. Ribeiro oversaw a church whose critiques of progressivism crowded the institution's principal journal, *O Brasil Presbiteriano*, with articles that demonstrated—to the evident satisfaction of SNI agents—the conflation of sex, subversion, endangering students, and progressive Christianity. References to liberation theology were summed up in the headline "Liberty . . . or Libidinousness?" At Mackenzie, the SNI related, the conservative, moralistic takeover of the hierarchy had "transformed" the school "into one of the greatest centers of resistance against subversion, and defense of the regime installed in March 1964."[44]

This was critical, to political police eyes, because of IPB's general, and Mackenzie's particular, combination of religion, politics, morality, and pedagogy. The school was a key piece of the national higher education framework, "one of the most important educational establishments in the country," specializing in the critical "issues of instruction . . . the intellectual, moral, and even physical formation of our youth." The conservative wing of the IPB, the SNI affirmed, would cultivate the kind of morally and patriotically irreproachable young people on whom the national security state must depend. That is, conservative evangelical pedagogy, unlike its progressive challengers, would "care for youth, whose character it wishes to see ennobled and solidified by righteousness and honesty and whose spirit it wishes to see reinforced by pure patriotism, by love of work, and by dedication to countrymen and fellow man, in general."[45] Following the schism among Presbyterians and what became a court battle for control of the school and of the IPB, the SNI characterized Mackenzie's current president as a corrupt, "insatiable 'wolf of the steppes'" who ignored or lied about the "subversive aspect" at the university ("Wolf of the steppes" may have been a literary reference, an allusion to the Soviets, or both). SNI officials were thus thankful for and sympathetic to the steerage of Reverend Ribeiro, a notorious anticommunist hard-liner who oversaw the IPB during its most dramatic schism and who supported the dictatorship throughout the harshest years of repression. As early as September 1968,

Ribeiro had emerged as the leader of the "ultraconservative" faction of the IPB, and his "inquisitorial" and "dictatorial spirit," applied to eradicating progressives and ecumenists from the church hierarchy, were said to be causing a "grave internal crisis" in the IPB.[46] Ribeiro and his ilk, according to the SNI, deserved credit for preventing Brazil's Presbyterians—and most importantly Mackenzie—from "compacting with extremist activities, particularly Leftists. Thanks to [Presbyterian conservatives'] Christian and democratic orientation, the Marxist doctrine never managed to take hold in the heart of [Mackenzie], where the revolutionary movement of 1964 [the military coup] has always been defended."[47]

Conclusion

The crisis in Brazil's evangelical churches, like that in the Catholic Church, was very real and in some cases had deep effects, on people as well as on institutions. Indeed, security officials' suspicions—conflations and exaggerations notwithstanding—did sometimes rest on grains of truth. There *were* liberalizing currents flowing through certain Christian communities in Brazil and beyond. In terms of social justice, anticommunism, and relative support for the regime, evangelicals found themselves divided—and certainly some, especially from the traditional denominations, did opt for reformist or liberationist politics and theological interpretations. For the most part, moderation marked these moves, though some activists and progressives would eventually criticize or more actively oppose the regime. Still, most progressive Christians (Catholic as well as Protestant) remained anticommunist and certainly did not equate their penchants for ecumenism and liberalization with Marxism, much less with sexual and gender deviance. Conservative evangelicals, meanwhile, reacted with outrage and anger, moving, in the words of historian Lyndon Santos, "to purge leaders who had come to be seen as sowers of modernist, ecumenist, and communist ideas."[48]

Security officials shared this reaction, aligning themselves with what began to take shape as an evangelical New Right. When evangelical reactionaries left the pulpit for the political sphere in the 1970s, they declared war on an amalgam of menaces: communism, ecumenism, and moral-sexual dissolution.[49] The state's security outfits engaged in precisely this conflation, a focus that manifested itself in their surveillance of youth, pedagogy, and evangelical educational institutions and instructors. This was, of course, not the sole way agents of the SNI and the various intelligence divisions and political police units understood and monitored supposed subversion; the work of countersubversion and of "war" against the imagined "International Communist Movement" (MCI) entailed tasks that included cataloging terrorist and guerrilla activity, censoring cultural production, and, of course, managing the massive apparatus of state repression.

Nevertheless, this particular confluence is revelatory: those who saw the inside of the regime's dungeons, or who fled into exile to avoid persecution, included those accused of involvement in a progressive evangelical grand design that, security forces supposed, combined ecumenism (especially via the WCC), communism, opposition to the regime, pedagogy and access to youth, and moral and sexual deviance. When, in 1977, CENIMAR officials described the "leftist ideas

and seductive attitudes" of a teacher "linked to the Ecumenist Wing of Protestantism, inspired by the World Council of Churches, of clear Marxist influence," they
drew on a narrative that extended to many evangelical conservatives and to other
security agencies. The emergence of Brazil's evangelical New Right cannot, in this
sense, be separated from the military regime's persecution of progressive evangelical pedagogues and pastors as sexually and doctrinally deviant malefactors, bent
on "seducing" young students into dissolute Marxist subversion.

Notes

1. All names from classified intelligence reports have been changed to protect identities.
   It is worth noting that agents from the Centro de Informações da Aeronáutica (CISA)
   misspelled the real name of the man I have called "Lefebvre" so badly as to make
   him nearly unrecognizable—calling into question the source and accuracy of their
   information about his supposed parachuting activities in Africa.
2. Centro de Informações da Aeronáutica, Quarta Região Militar, "Informe 050,"
   September 5, 1975, Arquivo Nacional do Brasil, Coordenação Regional no
   Distrito Federal (hereafter AN/COREG), Fundo CISA, BR-AN-BSB-VAZ-084-0006,
   1–2.
3. Benjamin A. Cowan, *Securing Sex: Morality and Repression in the Marking of Cold War
   Brazil* (Chapel Hill: University of North Carolina Press, 2016).
4. Ariel Rodríguez Kuri, "El lado oscuro de la luna: El momento Conservador en 1968,"
   in *Conservadurismo y Derechas en la História de México*, vol. 2, ed. Erika Pani (Mexico
   City: Fondo de Cultura Económico, 2009), 529; Jaime Pensado, *Rebel Mexico: Student
   Unrest and Authoritarian Political Culture during the Long Sixties* (Stanford: Stanford
   University Press, 2013), 224; Valeria Manzano, *The Age of Youth in Argentina: Culture,
   Politics, and Sexuality from Perón to Videla* (Chapel Hill: University of North Carolina
   Press, 2014).
5. Among Latin America's most remarkable contributions to Christian theology,
   liberation theology marked a major reorientation for its adherents, Protestant as
   well as Catholic. The renovators argued that Christians should seek to follow Christ's
   teaching not only by saving souls but also by improving the material conditions of
   those suffering poverty and other forms of injustice. See, for example, Iain S. Maclean,
   "Brazil: Nation and Church during the Cold War," in *Religion and the Cold War: A
   Global Perspective*, ed. Philip E. Muehlenbeck (Nashville, TN: Vanderbilt University
   Press, 2012), 229–47.
6. The terminology here is problematic. I have followed unofficial convention, using
   the term "evangelical" as a translation of the Portuguese *evangélico*, used in Brazil to
   refer to almost all Protestants, with little regard for the distinctions made in English
   between "evangelicals" and "Protestants." Hence, mainline Protestants in Brazil are
   almost always referred to as *evangélicos* and rarely as *protestantes*.
7. Michael Löwy, *The War of Gods: Religion and Politics in Latin America* (London:
   Verso, 1996); João Dias de Araújo, *Inquisição Sem Fogueiras* [*Inquisition without Fire*]
   (Rio de Janeiro: Instituto Superior de Estudos da Religião, 1982); Valdir Gonzalez
   Paixão Junior, "Poder, memória e repressão: a Igreja Presbiteriana do Brasil no
   período da ditadura militar (1966-1978)," *Bauru* 2, no. 2 (2014): 20-40; Leonildo
   Silveira Campos, "Os políticos de Cristo: uma análise do comportamento político
   de protestantes históricos e pentecostais no Brasil," in *Os votos de Deus: evangélicos,*

política e eleições no Brasil, [The Votes of God: evangelicals, politics, and elections in Brazil] ed. Joanildo Burity and Maria da Dores Campos Machado (Recife: Fundação Joaquim Nabuco, 2006), 29–90; Paulo Julião da Silva, "O alinhamento protestante ao Golpe Militar e a repressão aos 'crentes subversivos,'" *História e-História* 1, no. 1 (2009): 1–16, *www.historiaehistoria.com.br/materia.cfm?tb=alunos&id=270*; Rubem A. Alves, *Protestantismo e Repressão* (São Paulo: Editora Atica, 1979).

8. Benjamin Cowan, "'Nosso Terreno': Crise Moral, Política Evangélica e a Formação da 'Nova Direita' Brasileira," *Varia História* 30, no. 52 (2014): 101–25.

9. Ibid., 111.

10. Archdiocese of São Paulo, *Brasil: Nunca Mais* (Petrópolis: Vozes, 1985); Marcelo Ridenti, *O fantasma da revolução brasileira* (São Paulo: Unesp/Fapesp, 1993), 119; Victoria Langland, *Speaking of Flowers: Student Movements and the Making and Remembering of 1968 in Military Brazil* (Durham, NC: Duke University Press, 2013); Maria Paula Nascimento Araujo, *Memórias estudantís: da Fundação da UNE aos nossos dias* (Rio de Janeiro: Relume Dumará, 2007).

11. Serviço Nacional de Informações (hereafter SNI), "Quadro geral da evolução da Guerra Revolucionária no País," February 4, 1969, AN/COREG, Fundo CGI-PM, BR-DFANBSB-AAJ-IPM-091.

12. Victoria Ann Langland, "Birth Control Pills and Molotov Cocktails: Reading Sex and Revolution in 1968 Brazil," in *In from the Cold: Latin America's New Encounter with the Cold War*, ed. Gilbert M. Joseph and Daniela Spenser (Durham, NC: Duke University Press, 2008), 309.

13. Ministério da Aeronáutica, "Situação Política e Psicossocial na area de São Paulo no Período de 1 a 31 Dez 76," January 7, 1977, AN/COREG, Fundo CISA, BR-AN-BSB-VAZ-001-0063, 6.

14. Cowan, *Securing Sex*.

15. Selva Guimarães Fonseca, "O Ensino da história e o golpe militar de 1964," in *1964–2004, 40 anos do golpe: ditadura militar e resistência no Brasil* (Rio de Janeiro: 7Letras, 2004), 368–69.

16. SNI, Agência Curitiba, "Educação Moral e Cívica," November 12, 1971, AN/COREG, Fundo PF, Caixa 06-B, 741–42.

17. Ibid.

18. Ministério do Exército, 1° Exército, D. O. I. [Destacamento de Operações de Informações], "Declarações do Interrogado," n.d., AN/COREG, Fundo SNIG, AC-ACE-47259-71.

19. Ministério da Justiça, Divisão de Segurança e Informações (hereafter DSI/MJ), "Informação No. 371/71/DSI/MJ," October 27, 1971, 1, 4; Ministério da Educação e Cultura, Divisão de Segurança e Informações, "Informação No. 89/71/DSI/MEC"; SNI, Agência Rio de Janeiro, "Informação No. 949/71/ARJ/SNI," November 30, 1971, 1–3; Ministério do Exército, "Declarações do Interrogado."

20. Alves, *Protestantismo e Repressão*; Lyndon de Araújo Santos, "O púlpito, a praça e o palanque: os evangélicos e o regime militar brasileiro," in *A Ditadura em debate: Estado e Sociedade nos anos do autoritarismo*, ed. Adriano de Freixo and Oswaldo Munteal Filho (Rio de Janeiro: Contraponto, 2005), 151–82; Burity e Machado, *Os votos de Deus*.

21. Virginia Garrard-Burnett, *Terror in the Land of the Holy Spirit: Guatemala under General Efraín Ríos Montt, 1982–1983* (Oxford: Oxford University Press, 2010); David Stoll, *Is Latin America Turning Protestant? The Politics of Evangelical Growth*

(Berkeley: University of California Press, 1990); Angela Lahr, *Millennial Dreams and Apocalyptic Nightmares: The Cold War Origins of Political Evangelicalism* (New York: Oxford University Press, 2007); Löwy, *War of the Gods*; Virginia Garrard-Burnett and David Stoll, eds., *Rethinking Protestantism in Latin America* (Philadelphia: Temple University Press, 1993); Paul Freston, ed., *Evangelical Christianity and Democracy in Latin America* (New York: Oxford University Press, 2008).

22. Santos, "O púlpito, a praça e o palanque."

23. Cowan, "Nosso Terreno."

24. Cowan, *Securing Sex.*

25. Ibid.; José Dos Reis Pereira, "Orações pela Convenção," *Jornal Batista*, January 3, 1988, 3; José Dos Reis Pereira, "Ponto Final," *Jornal Batista*, April 24, 1988, 3.

26. Löwy, *War of Gods*; Silva, "O alinhamento protestante"; Saulo Baptista, *Pentecostais e neopentecostais na política brasileira: um estudo sobre a cultura política, estado e atores coletivos religiosos no Brasil* (São Paulo: Annablume, 2009).

27. SNI, "Corrupção de costumes por intermédio dos veículos de comunicação no Brasil," December 28, 1972, AN/COREG, Fundo DSI/MJ, BR-RJANRIO-TT-0-MCAP-AVU-0203-D001, 11–13; Cowan, *Securing Sex.*

28. Cowan, *Securing Sex.*

29. SNI, Agência São Paulo, "Atividades da Confederação de Igrejas Evangélicas Fundamentalistas do Brasil (CIEF)," December 11, 1981, AN/COREG, Fundo SNIG, E0096453-1981.

30. Assessoria de Segurança e Informacões da Fundação Universidade Estadual de Londrina (ASI/FUEL), "Conselho Latino-Americano de Igrejas," March 12, 1982, AN/COREG, Fundo ASI/FUEL, N0029282-1982.

31. SNI, Agência Curitiba, "Infiltracão Comunista—Setor Religioso e de Ensino—Paraná," March 14, 1977, AN/COREG, Fundo SNIG, AC-ACE-103658-77, 5–7; SNI, "Carta," November 23, 1976, AN/COREG, Fundo SNIG, AC-ACE-103658-77, 1–2.

32. The relationships between left-wing political activism, guerrilla fighting, counterculture, and sexual mores were of course variable and complex in this period, especially at the level of individual behavior. Nevertheless, key scholarly and primary accounts attest to a decided moralism on the Left, from progressive Christians (moderate as well as radical) to avowed Marxists and guerillas. James N. Green, "(Homo)sexuality, Human Rights, and Revolution," in *Human Rights and Revolutions*, ed. Jeffrey N. Wasserstrom, Lynn Hunt, Marilyn B. Young, and Gregory Grandin (Lanham, MD: Rowman and Littlefield, 2007); James N. Green, "'Who is the Macho Who Wants to Kill Me?': Male Homosexuality, Revolutionary Masculinity, and the Brazilian Armed Struggle of the 1960s and 70s," *Hispanic American Historical Review* 92, no. 3 (2012): 449; Christopher Dunn, "Desbunde and Its Discontents: Counterculture and Authoritarian Modernization in Brazil, 1968–1974," *Americas* 70, no. 3 (2014): 454–56; Fernando Gabeira, *O crepúsculo do macho* (Rio de Janeiro: Codecri, 1980); Zuenir Ventura, *1968: O Ano que não terminou* (Rio de Janeiro: Editôra Nova Fronteira, 1988), 36; Cowan, *Securing Sex.*

33. Departamento de Ordem Política e Social, São Paulo, Delegacia Especializada de Ordem Política, "Qualificação dos Indiciados," August 8, 1969, AN/COREG, Fundo CGIPM, BR-DFANBSB-AAJ-IPM-0498-D, 8.

34. Ibid., 8–9.

35. Departamento de Ordem Política e Social, São Paulo, Delegacia Especializada de Ordem Política, "Qualificação dos Indiciados,"; Centro de Informações

da Aeronáutica, Rio de Janeiro, "[Name]—Infiltração no corpo docente de estabelecimento de ensino," March 12, 1980, AN/COREG, Fundo CISA, BR-AN-BSB-VAZ-055-0162. I have changed the names to protect the identities of those surveilled; "Lucinda" and "Pablo" are pseudonyms.

36. Ministério da Marinha, 2° Distrito Naval, "Informação No. 1374/77," September 30, 1977, AN/COREG, Fundo SNIG, ASV-ACE-3215-82; SNI, Agência Salvador, "Informação No. 0329/116/ASV/77," December 13, 1977, AN/COREG, Fundo SNIG, ASV-ACE-3215-82. The World Council of Churches, founded in 1948, arose out of ecumenical movements and has historically promoted progressive theology, social justice initiatives, and left-wing political and social programs. It has also been the site of decades of controversy, drawing the ire of anticommunists, Christian conservatives, and some moderate critics who allege that the WCC shows favoritism toward left-wing governments. In Brazil, the WCC's most famous adherents included Paulo Freire and Richard Shaull, both known for their pronounced progressivism and their use of Marxist scholarship to construct a Christian social justice agenda. See Andrew J. Kirkendall, *Paulo Freire and the Cold War Politics of Literacy* (Chapel Hill: University of North Carolina Press, 2010); and Christian Smith, *The Emergence of Liberation Theology: Radical Religion and Social Movement Theory* (Chicago: University of Chicago Press, 1991), 31.

37. Ministério da Marinha, "Informação No. 1374/77."

38. Ministério do Exército, IV Exército, 6a Região Militar, 2a Secção, "Pedido de Busca No. 125/E2–06/D," August 22, 1977, AN/COREG, Fundo SNIG, P0036377-1982.

39. Ministério do Exército, Gabinete do Ministro, "Infiltração Comunista no Meio Estudantil," January 14, 1977, AN/COREG, Fundo SNIG, AC-ACE-100373-77; SNI, Agência Central, "Informação No. 056/16/AC/77," February 10, 1977, AN/COREG, Fundo SNIG, AC-ACE-100373-77.

40. Divisão de Segurança e Informações, Ministério da Justiça (hereafter DSI/MJ), "Informação No. 173/77," February 28, 1977, AN/COREG, Fundo SNIG, AC-ACE-100373-77; DSI/MJ, "Informação No. 664/76," August 9, 1976, AN/COREG, Fundo SNIG, AC-ACE-100373-77.

41. SNI, Agência Central, "Informação No. 056/16/AC/77"; DSI/MJ, "Informação No. 664/76."

42. SNI, Agência Central, "Informação No. 056/16/AC/77."

43. "Governo João Figueiredo," Arquivo Nacional, Acervo Secretaria de Imprensa e Divulgação, DX/VID.0085 (VHS #219), March–April 1982.

44. SNI, Agência Central, "Instituto Mackenzie—São Paulo," October 12, 1971, AN/COREG, Fundo SNIG, AC-ACE-58764-72; SNI, Agência São Paulo, "Informação No. 2840271/1971/ASP/SNI," October 4, 1972, AN/COREG, Fundo SNIG, AC-ACE-58764-72.

45. SNI, Agência São Paulo, "Informação No. 2840271/1971/ASP/SNI," 5.

46. Ibid.; SNI, Agência Central, "Instituto Mackenzie—São Paulo"; Karina Kosicki Bellotti, *A Mídia Presbiteriana no Brasil: Luz Para o Caminho e Editora Cultura Cristã (1976–2001)* (São Paulo: Fapesp, 2005), 31; "Presbiterianos também atingidos," *Correio da Manhã*, September 1, 1968, 1° caderno, 3.

47. SNI, "Informação No. 041/SNI/GAB/72," October 27, 1972, AN/COREG, Fundo SNIG, AC-ACE-58764-72, 1.

48. Santos, "O púlpito, a praça e o palanque," 177–78.

49. Cowan, "Nosso Terreno."

References

Archives

Arquivo Nacional do Brasil, Coordenação Regional no Distrito Federal, Brasília
Arquivo Nacional do Brasil, Rio de Janeiro
Biblioteca Nacional do Brasil, Rio de Janeiro

Periodicals

Correio da Manhã
Jornal Batista
O Brasil Presbiteriano

Selected Published Works

Alves, Rubem A., *Protestantismo e Repressão* [Protestantism and repression]. São Paulo: Editora Ática, 1979.

Burity, Joanildo, and Maria das Dores Campos Machado, eds. *Os votos de Deus: evangélicos, política e eleições no Brasil.* [The Votes of God: evangelicals, politics, and elections in Brazil] Recife: Fundação Joaquim Nabuco, 2006.

Cowan, Benjamin A. *Securing Sex: Morality and Repression in the Making of Cold War Brazil.* Chapel Hill: University of North Carolina Press, 2016.

———. "'Nosso Terreno': Crise Moral, Política Evangélica e a Formação da 'Nova Direita' Brasileira" ["Our territory": Moral crisis, evangelical politics, and the formation of a Brazilian "New Right"]. *Varia História* 30, no. 52 (2014): 101–25.

de Araújo, João Dias. *Inquisição Sem Fogueiras.* [*Inquisition without Fire*] Rio de Janeiro: Instituto Superior de Estudos da Religião, 1982.

Langland, Victoria. *Speaking of Flowers: Student Movements and the Making and Remembering of 1968 in Military Brazil.* Durham, NC: Duke University Press, 2013.

Löwy, Michael. *The War of Gods: Religion and Politics in Latin America.* London: Verso, 1996.

Santos, Lyndon de Araújo. "O púlpito, a praça e o palanque: os evangélicos e o regime militar brasileiro" [The pulpit, the public square, and the stage: Evangelicals and the Brazilian military regime]. In *A Ditadura em debate: Estado e Sociedade nos anos do autoritarismo* [*The Dictatorship Under Discussion: State and Society in the Years of Authoritarianism*], edited by Adriano de Freixo and Oswaldo Munteal Filho, 151–82. Rio de Janeiro: Contraponto, 2005.

CHAPTER 5

Manning the Enemy

US Perspectives on International Birthrates during the Cold War

Kathleen A. Tobin

Cold War fears and competitive behaviors in the second half of the twentieth century took many forms, not the least of which were related to regional populations. Historical competitions—through war and peacetime alike—had pitted tribe against tribe and nation against nation for millennia, commanding attention to the size of one's enemy forces. Numbers influenced the success of campaigns, and casualties took the lives of young men who would otherwise begin families, threatening future populations, encouraging pronatalist policies, and raising expectations for women to bear more children.[1] Twentieth-century weaponry devastated populations even further, claiming the lives of both military personnel and civilians. Air warfare was responsible for much of the destruction, and the presence of atomic and hydrogen bombs at midcentury created the possibility of complete obliteration of populated areas. In his *Fatal Misconception: The Struggle to Control World Population*, historian Matthew Connelly argues that "the international politics of population control did not fit into Cold War categories."[2] The complexities of intention and perspective in population analyses and programs did not align neatly in communist or noncommunist realms, or what would be termed the First World and Second World. Ultimately, population concerns and efforts at control would be directed toward the developing countries, or Third World.[3] In addition, and very importantly, population fears were often irrational and not substantiated by reliable data. Historian Jay Winter and demographer Michael Teitelbaum point this out in their 1985 work, *The Fear of Population Decline*, and their 2013 work, *The Global Spread of Fertility Decline: Population, Fear, and Uncertainty*.[4] Even without accurate demographic data—and accuracy was continually disputed—or with data that countered US concerns, Cold War tensions drove policy analysts to examine birthrates in various parts of the world very carefully.

Some research related to concerns over military capacity; however, these arguments weakened as experts reminded policy makers that modern war relied more on technology than on numbers of soldiers. Of increasing concern were population rates as they related to economic capacity. The Cold War was a conflict grounded in differing economic ideologies after all. The post–World War II era ultimately proved to be one of economic advantage for the United States, but there was no guarantee in the 1950s and 1960s that capitalism would be victorious. The superpowers of the Soviet Union and China held enormous populations, and state policies in both regions worked to convert demographic doctrines into productivity and efficiency. In the Cold War of the 1970s and 1980s, US attention was drawn to population rates in Latin America, South Asia, and the Middle East. In less developed countries of those regions, the United States feared that poverty, masses of youth, and radical politics could threaten access to the resources needed to maintain geopolitical dominance. Not only did the United States want to prevent nations from turning communist for political reasons, it also wished to maintain its capitalist economic advantage by stabilizing the flow of oil and precious metals.

Demography

The field of demography—a subdiscipline of sociology—had expanded during the first half of the twentieth century to include and consider more countries and more social and political implications of demographic changes. Shifts in relations between men and women, marriage practices, birthrates and family size, and the devastating effects of military brutality affected the geopolitical balance, and numbers mattered in new ways to policy makers. As municipal, state, and national governments took increasing responsibility for the health and welfare of their populations, an increase or decrease in birthrates and the corresponding size of the younger sector placed added demands on schools and housing development planning. Often, demographers and policy makers operated on traditional notions that increasing population was good, beneficial, and in the best interests of a nation. Government officials relied on the work of demographers to support their concerns regarding population growth in regions of the world considered dangerous and unstable. In the eyes of the United States, the global balance of power appeared to hinge on population numbers and birthrates, and government officials warned that the workforce in the Soviet Union and China, for example, threatened competition with the capitalist world of the West. Later, perceived threats that rapid population growth in the developing world could lead to international instability, internal insurgency, and war intensified. US devotion to studying demographic patterns and their international implications continued in subsequent decades, but with an alternative premise. Rapid population growth was viewed as a detriment to an underdeveloped region's economy and potentially destabilizing. At the same time, advanced countries with strong population growth might exert more international influence.[5]

In his 1958 essay, "Population and Power in the Free World," demographer Kingsley Davis detailed reasons that population was a major determinant of national power. He wrote:

First, the magnitude of the total population is the principal factor in the size of the labor force, and it is impossible to substitute completely other factors of production for labor. In fact, as an economy develops the price of labor increases because its level of living rises, so that, from a cost standpoint, the share of labor in production remains high. In the United States in 1951, for example, the payments of salaries and wages in manufacturing establishments amounted to 55 per cent of the value added by manufacture. Second, given the adequacy of resources, the larger the population integrated in one economic system, the greater the potential advantages of scale to be gained from mass production and mass distribution. Third, since military personnel is drawn most heavily from restricted age groups, a large population is necessary to furnish a sizable army and to sustain losses in fighting strength. Fourth, the consolidation of a victory in war often requires a sizable occupation force, which cannot be supplied if the population is small.[6]

In 1950, the average communist country was larger than the average noncommunist country, as China and Russia comprised much of the communist population. If all other factors were equal, said Kingsley, the communist world was at an advantage in having a large population concentrated within one political unit rather than divided into several units. However, it was more complicated than that. Within the communist realm, resources per unit of land were not greater, the efficiency with which resources were used was not greater, and the population lay above the optimum for the best utilization of resources given technological capacity. If communist populations grew or at least remained stable and systems there became more technologically advanced and productive while more efficiently using resources, the United States perhaps had as much to fear as it would from an atomic attack.[7]

The potential effect of nuclear destruction on population was taken into consideration, and densely populated industrial centers would likely suffer the greatest impact. While Kingsley and other demographers examined population rates in a conventional military sense—in terms of fighting capacity and prospects for postwar occupation—they could not ignore the fact that the nature of war had changed. An examination of population research during the 1950s demonstrates an increased emphasis on economic concerns. If Soviet and Chinese economies could compete with those of the United States and its allies, they might be considered victors. This would prove not only an economic setback but a political one, as ideological battles centered on the sanctity of the free market. If communist systems could produce in better ways and ultimately raise the standard of living of all, they might earn a better reputation than the world's capitalist systems. US demographers and policy makers continued to watch international birthrates and population trends for military reasons, but the significance of their economic concerns cannot be denied.[8]

Demographer Quincy Wright argued that competition through population should be considered a policy of the past. Industrial development and urbanization naturally led to lower birthrates, and by the mid-twentieth century education and technology were seen as competitive advantages, regardless of numbers. The Cold War threatened stability of the entire world, and Wright maintained that if leaders "abandon ideological imperialism, and, at the same time, co-operate to increase the standard of living everywhere, and build a stable political order in the world within which ideological competition can proceed by peaceful persuasion, world tensions might gradually be reduced." He added that "the public and politicians should be educated on population problems both here and abroad. This will make it possible for population changes and problems to be viewed in proper perspective. With such education the public will be in a position to make decisions based on reason, and avoid the hysteria always possible in a nation that has been thrust into world leadership." According to Wright, the principal population problems for the United States stemmed from overpopulation in poorer countries. The United States had long been a host for migrants and refugees leaving poverty and strife for a better life. While this would continue, some argued that the United States should play a larger role in stabilizing populations in the less developed world. This would require international cooperation in technological aid, education, and capital export.[9] Eventually, technological aid and education came in the form of birth control.

Soviet Union

Depletion of a population due to war often leads to pronatalist policies as a strategy to rebuild. Such was the case in France following the First World War and in Germany during the reign of Hitler. Because the Soviet Union had lost twenty to thirty million people in the First and Second World Wars, its adversaries watched very closely.[10] However, Soviet opinions on women's responsibility to bear children for the good of the state were not clear-cut or unified. US economists and social researchers pointed to Soviet policies since the 1930s that encouraged women to enter the workforce and legalized abortion as examples of new messages regarding childbearing.[11] Compared to American women, Soviet women's participation in the workforce was much greater (some research included instances of forced labor), and they appeared to have greater access to birth control. This perplexed some researchers who saw little parallel between government pressure on women to have children and legislative realities that placed checks on growth.[12] Noting that the Soviet Union's crude birthrate fell between 1938 and 1950, Johns Hopkins University demographer Warren W. Eason looked to urbanization trends and other causes. In 1952, he wrote, "This is a curious development in view of continued state encouragement of large families. Perhaps psychological and sociological factors are at work similar to those which caused birthrates to fall in other industrializing countries."[13]

The Soviet government also watched the birthrate. Abortion had been legalized in the Soviet Union in 1920 as a result of economic strife and concern over the danger to women who sought illegal abortions. Abortion was prohibited in 1936 because Stalin feared the military implications of a declining birthrate. Following his death, the Soviet government made abortion legal once more because women demanded it, not because the military threat had become less significant. Housing conditions were crowded, and a significant number of women were working. Surveys conducted by the Soviet government in 1958 and 1959 indicated legalized abortion was having a significant impact on family size. While the practice of abortion continued even when it was illegal, abortions had now increased to more than five million per year. The surveys included questions regarding work in an effort to determine whether abortion rates for women of childbearing age paralleled their employment. Data indicated there were 105.5 abortions per thousand working women per year, and 41.5 abortions per thousand nonworking women. Further calculations concluded there were more abortions than live births. This posed a dilemma for policy makers favoring a strong Soviet Union, as many sought higher birthrates while also valuing women in the labor force.[14]

The Soviet government encouraged changing roles for women as an attempt to implement ideas of the family articulated by Karl Marx, Friedrich Engels, and Vladimir Lenin. At the core of their models were marital equality, the emancipation of women from household duties, and women's active participation in politics and economic expansion. In order to facilitate these goals, the government guaranteed equality for women, permitted easy access to marriage and divorce, and legalized abortion. In addition, it provided infrastructure to support the communal upbringing of children and communal performance of cooking and other household chores. The family would no longer serve as an economic unit; rather, women, as laborers, would be integral to the economy of the nation. Russia needed women as well as men working in factories and on farms to ensure the country returned to normal as quickly as possible. At the same time, a new and healthy generation was possible only by encouraging every healthy man and woman to have a family.[15] Working women were aware they lived in a system professing equal rights and asked that they have the right not to give birth to children they did not want. As there was little access to contraceptives, abortion became the preferred method of controlling births. Opponents of abortion (on medical grounds, women's protectionist grounds, or population grounds) succeeded in implementing programs to minimize the number of abortions through improved housing, maternity care, and child care. While birthrates never soared, each child was provided nourishment, health, and education. They were considered the future of a strong Soviet Union.[16]

In 1960, the US Central Intelligence Agency (CIA) presented data on population and workforce comparing the United States with the Soviet Union; the data indicated potential development and increased competition over the next decade. The findings supported earlier research illustrating the economic significance of such development. Population changes in the United States were expected to expand the labor force and high school and college enrollments by 1970. These rates had slowed during the 1950s because of fewer births during the Great Depression, but the post–World War II baby boom was perceived as benefiting the United States by establishing a greater competitive edge in workforce by the early 1970s. On the other hand, Soviet birthrates remained comparatively stable during the 1930s and, after a decline during the war, rose only in the late 1940s. The wartime decline resulted in smaller numbers of high school students and entrants into the workforce in 1960. However, the CIA warned that postwar birthrate increases would accelerate growth in the Soviet labor force very quickly in the 1970s. Constant fertility rates compounded with declining birthrates would aid in fulfilling the workforce and school enrollment goals laid out in the Soviet Seven Year Plan (1959–1965).[17]

The CIA looked carefully at Soviet policies affecting birthrates, population growth, and ultimate strength in workforce. Fertility rates remained stable in the 1950s, but some changes, such as continued urbanization, legalized abortion, and wider dissemination of birth-control information, could result in a significant decline. Nevertheless, the CIA argued the effects would likely be offset by continued government subsidies to mothers of large families and unmarried mothers, improved housing, and lower ratio of men to women of marrying age. In 1959, there were 107 women for every 100 men thirty years old and older in the United States, while there were 158 women for every 100 men of the same age in the Soviet Union. This discrepancy was due to the significant number of Soviet lives lost during the world wars and internal crises. The ratio affected Soviet women's chances for marriage, which might in turn affect population growth. However, because the government provided subsistence to unmarried mothers, the number of children born was not affected. CIA research concluded that the population of high school–age youth in the Soviet Union would outpace that of the United States. More importantly, the population of working-age adults in the Soviet Union would grow significantly more than that in the United States, with a projected 116 million in the Soviet Union compared to 90 million in the United States. Adding to the economic and workforce advantages was the higher rate of employment among Soviet women.[18]

Soviet birthrates declined in the 1960s, from 212 births for every 10,000 people in 1963 to 174 for every 10,000 people in 1967. The pattern became more apparent to US demographers by this time, and more worrisome to Soviet demographers. The overall increase in population from 1920 to 1970 was due to lower infant mortality and increased longevity, placing greater economic pressures on programs caring for the young and the old. From the Soviet perspective, demographic shifts posed an additional problem in relation to abundant natural resources. Petroleum and other reserves were largely unexplored and untapped, in part because of a chronic shortage of workers. There was little chance of workers, including women, being released from work or granted a shorter workday; consequently, birthrates among workers would likely continue to decline. In *Our Soviet Sister*, author George St. George describes birthrate stimulation policies, such as the bachelor tax and cash payments for children, as an insult to women.[19] Soviet couples—with easy access to contraceptives and abortions—were making childbearing decisions on their own, often for family economic reasons. Soviet journalist V. Perevedentsev described this trend in his 1969 *Literaturnaya Gazeta* article, "How Many Children?":

> Of course the question of family planning rests on many considerations, but the economics one should not be dismissed. The cost of bringing up children has increased, and the fruits are collected primarily by the society. Therefore it would be only just that the society take upon itself a larger share of such cost. The raising of children requires much labor, and hard labor at that. The weight of this labor falls mostly upon women. . . . The fact is that families with many children inevitably find themselves at an economic disadvantage in comparison with small families.[20]

Although Soviet competition through population was unlikely, US fears were real.

China

For many of the same reasons identified in the Soviet case, China's population drew significant attention from the United States following its successful transition to communism in 1949. China's population was the largest in the world, and should the government succeed in employing its prospective workforce effectively and exploiting its natural resources efficiently, communism might confront the capitalist system in noticeable ways. Mao Zedong, chairman of the Communist Party and China's head of state, understood that. In 1949, he stated:

> It is a very good thing that China has a big population. Even if China's population multiplies many times, she is fully capable of finding a solution; the solution is production. . . . [R]evolution plus production can solve the problem of feeding the population. . . . Under the leadership of the Communist Party, as long as there are people, every kind of miracle can be performed. We believe that revolution can change everything, and that before long there will arise a new China with a big population and a great wealth of products, where life will be abundant and culture will flourish. All pessimistic views are utterly groundless.[21]

China reported a population of 582.6 million in 1953, with increasing urban density and more questions regarding food supply. At this time, however, the government did not implement control measures addressing birthrate; rather, the official policy was to better organize and effectively employ the rural workforce. Leaders did not see economic and social challenges as familial or behavioral, but as institutional.[22] In traditional China, prior to the revolution, women were expected to bear children soon after being married, for the sooner pregnancy resulted from marriage the more fortunate it was deemed. Among classes above the peasantry, women's fertility rates seemed higher, likely because they were healthier and better nourished. In revolutionary China, it was expected that women of all classes be equally nourished, resulting in healthier pregnancies and greater survival among all infants. Gender and family roles in "transitional" China shifted. Wives were considerably less responsible for their mothers-in-law; family units comprised only husband, wife, and nonadult children; and young women were increasingly employed as teachers in public schools. However, expectations regarding family size initially remained the same.[23]

In the 1950s, the US Department of Commerce and the Bureau of the Census researched and published a number of reports on international population, including "The Population of Communist China, 1953." A publication that stood out among the rest, however, was "The Population and Manpower of China: An Annotated Bibliography," produced by the US Department of Commerce and Foreign Manpower Research Office of the Bureau of the Census under contract with the Office for Social Science Programs of the Air Force Personnel and Training Research Center of the Air Research and Development Command. The authors prefaced the work by saying that the subject of Chinese population and workforce seemed to be of increasing interest and importance to American scholars, public officials, and the general public, and they warned that the communist publications included therein—very often articles appearing in *People's China*—sought to present the Chinese social and economic picture in the best possible light and were likely inaccurate.[24]

By the 1950s, Cold War concerns over Chinese population tied growth to economic transition and prospective competition. In a report titled "The Demography of the Asian 'Big Three,'" sponsored by the Technical Military Planning Operation of the General Electric Company, author Charles G. McClintock described the Chinese economy as industrializing at a rapid rate via a program patterned after "that which has proved successful in the USSR." He added, however, that China faced significant impediments that Russia did not. "In the first place, China has the largest population in the world, and people in great numbers, making substantial demands for food and consumer goods, produced conditions under which it is difficult to channel materials for production into non-consumer goods such as are necessary." In addition, "Large populations living at a minimum level of subsistence inhibit the movement of persons from rural to urban areas. . . . By restricting young people to rural areas there is an intensification of the pattern of high birth rates which characterizes these areas, making the task of maintaining a bare minimum level of subsistence even more difficult." As with many less developed countries, China had a young population with more than 40 percent of its people under the age of eighteen. This placed high demands on social services from those who could not yet enter the labor force. McClintock estimated that thirty million, or approximately 11 percent of the total labor force, was employed in manufacturing and mining. Land reform measures underway could free an additional hundred million to enter the industrial force without decreasing food production. In 1953, China's urban population was 13.3 percent of its total population; around the same time, 64 percent of the US population lived in urban areas. McClintock provided this comparison, noting that birthrates tended to fall with urbanization, stabilizing economies and raising the standard of living.[25]

Expectations—both inside and outside China—regarding urbanization and industrialization were positive, though McClintock maintained China was not "destined to attain her visionary goal of being one of the industrial giants of the world." Population was the problem, primarily high rural birthrates. While nationalistic pride under communism strongly encouraged the overall growth of the Chinese population, leaders saw continued high birthrates as detrimental to industrial and economic growth. The Chinese government initiated a program to promote birth control and delay marriages, but in the 1950s it was difficult to imagine any significant impact for decades. In the meantime, McClintock saw the possibility that China might turn to the Soviet Union for economic assistance, just as other less developed countries turned to wealthier ones in other parts of the world. Such an association could prove disastrous for the United States. McClintock concluded that "much of the world's political, economic, and military future may rest upon the nature of this relationship."[26]

In the late 1950s and early 1960s the Chinese government began to address population policies in addition to implementing land, food production, and employment policies. Concerted efforts at birth control emerged in 1957 and 1958.[27] John S. Aird, head of the China branch of the US Census Bureau, continued to follow

China's population carefully, but by the 1970s he expressed desperation in his attempts to secure accurate numbers. He hypothesized that health improvements were resulting in lower infant mortality and greater longevity, and that efforts at birth control were not affecting fertility rates in any significant way. He estimated China's 1953 population at 576.05 million and predicted significant growth each year until the population reached 909.2 million in 1974. Aird prefaced his findings by saying China population researchers had long been accustomed to the problem of working without adequate data. "Official data issued during the First Five-Year Plan period were subject to varying and often indeterminate degrees of incompleteness and inaccuracy. Officials of the State Statistical Bureau (SSB) acknowledged at that time that their figures were defective." He added, "Since the First Five-Year Plan period, most of the data collection systems of the [People's Republic of China] seem to have ceased to function, and many types of data have become virtually nonexistent." Aird predicted a growing interest in accurate population statistics on the part of both Chinese and non-Chinese researchers, and criticized the government for failing to implement a registry system.[28] He acknowledged that the size of a population was not necessarily an indicator of favorable or unfavorable socioeconomic conditions—a large population may reflect the failure of the economy to supply incentives for fertility control, while a small one may reflect an economy's failure to address mortality. And although data was not entirely reliable, both he (through his work with the Foreign Demographic Analysis Division of the US Bureau of the Census) and the United Nations anticipated, with certainty, a substantial population increase in the immediate future that would demand address by the Chinese government.[29] Observers noted that China continued to face decisions regarding employment and food production in the face of this rapid growth and that women were important to China not only as bearers of children but as active members of the industrial, agricultural, and domestic labor forces.[30]

Latin America, Africa, the Middle East, and South Asia

The Cold War of the 1960s and beyond drew increased attention to Latin America, Africa, and Asia. The First World (the United States and its allies) vied with the Second World (the communist world and its allies) for influence and control in the Third World (underdeveloped regions lying primarily in the Global South). The United States had a unique interest in Latin America; since the Monroe Doctrine of 1823, it considered the region as part of its geopolitical sphere. When any hint of communist leanings appeared—as was claimed to be the case in Guatemala in 1954—the United States was quick to quash it, either overtly or covertly. The same was true in other parts of the world. Often, new nationalist, anti-imperialist movements embraced Marxist or Maoist ideology and were targeted as threats to US national security. Even when the ideological bases were unclear, the United States worked to protect political structures that would in turn protect its interests. Population played into this in a number of ways. Where populations teemed, increasing numbers left their homelands for better opportunities, often migrating to the United States. This was particularly true for Mexico. The Immigration and Nationality Act of 1965, also known as the Hart-Celler Act, eliminated national origins quotas favoring Europeans and opened the doors to Asians, Africans, and Latin Americans at unprecedented levels. US policy makers often saw this demographic shift as a threat to security.[31] In addition, many economists theorized that rapid population growth in the Third World contributed to poverty rather than development, causing instability and the possibility of Marxist and Maoist populists taking on leadership roles, threatening the existing global balance. Furthermore, when these unstable or radical populations resided near natural resources, US security experts feared they would hinder access to those materials.

Comparatively little was said about Latin America's birthrates or their implications for US security until the 1960s. President John F. Kennedy's Alliance for Progress, a program to develop economic cooperation, drew attention to Latin America in 1961, but population was not addressed in any significant way. In a few short years, however, concerns over Latin America's population grew exponentially. Under Lyndon Johnson's administration, with Secretary of Defense Robert McNamara's influence, population growth in Latin America was viewed as a problem that had reached crisis proportions.[32] The work of demographer and Princeton University Population Council founding director Frank W. Notenstein exemplified an approach to Latin America that contrasted with conventional demography. Some argued that Latin America did not have a "population problem" because the region—except for rapidly growing urban areas such as Mexico City—was sparsely populated compared to Europe. Notenstein contended that population density held a different significance for traditional, self-sufficient agrarian economies (in Latin America and elsewhere) than for highly diversified and capitalized economies (such as Europe and the United States) that relied on modern energy and use of resources. In traditional economies, density contributed to poverty, while in Europe's case, high population density did not serve as a major obstacle to achieving high per-capita income. In addition, sparsely settled agrarian societies did not need larger populations to bring them national, political, or military power, as was commonly understood. Rather, power was derived from advanced technology, and even more so in the nuclear age. Military might in the twentieth century was no longer obtained through raw numbers.[33]

While population size and density might not pose significant problems, rates of population growth did, Notenstein argued: such growth impeded the process of modernization. The situation in Latin America was unique because high birthrates compounded with death rates lower than in Africa and Asia, for example, led to more rapid population growth. Reducing birthrates would decrease the percentage of population under the age of fifteen, a group that placed high demands on the food supply, health care, and education. In addition, there would be a greater ability to save and invest, creating capital necessary for modernization and the adoption of new technology, and an increase in per-capita income. Historically, this modernization coincided with urbanization and industrial development as the shift naturally led to lower birthrates. Agricultural societies valued large numbers of children and allowed fewer opportunities for women, while modern societies presented opportunities for women beyond childbearing. The fear lay, however, in Marxist assertions that birth control in Latin America was unnecessary.[34]

Gender roles, the Latin American family, and the Catholic Church were considered key among the institutional forces responsible for high fertility. In addition, post-1945 peace and prosperity did not result in a rapidly growing middle class. The landed class, historically holding the majority of wealth and power, saw its large estates dwindle through inheritance to large numbers of children, forcing many of its sons into positions in law, government, the church, or the military. These occupations were traditionally considered middle class, sought after by those of a lower sector in a growing economy, but the lower sector seemed bound by poverty—due, some argued, to political uncertainty in the region. George Washington University sociologist Carr B. Lavell, in research funded by the Draper Foundation, described political institutions that had not yet evolved to stimulate consistent long-range social and economic planning: "The predominance of the executive makes the legislative process a figment of the political imagination. The rise (and fall) of dictators is less the machinations of neo-Machiavellians than it is the immature desire not to frustrate the hopes placed in them by their peoples. Due to a combination of causes governmental stability and tranquility is the exception to the rule in several of these countries." According to Lavell, the typical Latin American social-class structures made up of a small elite at the top and a large, impoverished, and uneducated population at the bottom were "not conducive to a republican form of democracy. Instead, governments [were] more likely to be dictatorial (either of the individual or the military junta type) than democratic, and the power to regulate economic activity . . . more a matter of control than of regulation, and for immediate and capricious rather than long-term and universal ends." High birthrates exacerbated these situations.[35] Such reports motivated population policy in Latin America.

By the early 1970s, US Agency for International Development (USAID) worked to slow population growth in Latin America; however, administrators quickly pointed out that their actions should not be categorized as "population control." According to Robert Black, director of USAID's Office of Population Programs in 1971, "We're talking in the way of providing options through family planning so parents can choose the timing and the number of children that conform with their own free preference." He added, "As a foreign policy matter we of course are interested in demography, which is what economic population planners take into account. . . . But the focus is on the individual, not just from a technical viewpoint but from a human one as well."[36] USAID's priorities included the following: (1) developing a greater awareness of the undesirable impact of high population growth on economic and social progress, (2) assisting family-planning programs with the intention of integrating them into national health care programs, and (3) assisting multilateral organizations and governments in planning and developing national population policies and effective family-planning services. Black saw cultural and religious barriers to smaller family size as falling away and expressed hope that by the year 2000 the gap between population growth and economic and social opportunities would begin to close.[37]

Latin America as a whole was sparsely populated compared to other regions, with numbers increasing only moderately in the first half of the twentieth century. From 1950 to 1975, however, the severity of population growth drew increasing attention from the United States, who wished to maintain stability and order in the region. Modernization and successful public health programs contributed to lower infant mortality and longer lifespan, adding to the number of people residing in Latin America, particularly in Venezuela, Mexico, Colombia, and Brazil, countries that held nearly two-thirds of Latin America's entire population. Birthrates did not rise significantly, at least in part because of strong cultural traditions and adherence to Catholic teachings that discourage limiting family size. US demographers benefited from more accurate data coming from their Latin American counterparts by 1970, facilitating policy making.[38] Demographer T. Lynn Smith warned of too-rapid urbanization and the impact of population shifts on food supply.[39] He also pointed to increased migration to the United States when Latin America could not meet the economic needs of families. Several hundred thousand Cubans left their homeland during the 1960s and 1970s, the majority destined for the United States; Mexican workers traveled to farms and ranches in the United States, many of them without permission; and, also without permission, citizens of the Dominican Republic migrated to New York. Smith argued that each of these situations was exacerbated by Latin American women's tendency to have many children.

From the 1970s into the 1980s, US population policy toward Latin America was tempered by programs supporting human rights and meeting basic human needs. These approaches provided for the poor to spur stable economic development that might ultimately stabilize the population. Some economists argued that Latin America had large spaces and great potential with room for population growth that would enhance economic development if regions themselves remained secure.[40] However, as the Cold War intensified, policy makers argued for a reconsideration of population control. They met with resistance from those who viewed US population programs as evidence of imperialism, from the Catholic Church, which was prevalent in Latin America, and from the US conservative base, which aligned itself increasingly with religious fundamentalism. Cornell University sociologist J. Mayone Stycos wrote extensively on population and family planning in Latin America, integrating political debates within his work. He described the region as "deeply dedicated in spirit to freedom and liberty but often bound in fact to political tyranny and economic dependence." He linked this political tyranny to Marxism, whose influence was growing among Latin American intellectuals, and pointed to population theories rooted in the Soviet Union. In recent decades the United Nations' Soviet bloc argued repeatedly that the West misrepresented population concerns in self-serving ways, and Stycos warned of the anti-Malthusian nature of communism and its pronatalist efforts to rebuild workforce. Stycos linked the Soviet stance to Latin American Marxists who saw economic strength in population growth and who described international birth-control programs as imperialist.[41]

Economic theories related to population were applied differently to the United States and to the Global South.[42] The capitalist model of development embraced neo-Malthusian principles, arguing that, left unchecked, population growth would lead to starvation, chaos, and war. The intense growth of population in Latin America, Africa, the Middle East, and South Asia was viewed by the

United States as a precursor to instability and thus in need of control. To policy makers in the United States, influencing a culture so that women had fewer children would erase poverty and underdevelopment.[43] Not all Third World leaders held this position. Many advocated for nationalist agendas tying population growth to economic development, arguing that growth would stimulate agricultural development (with more people to feed and more hands to work the land), deliver more natural resources, and increase productivity by linking it to standard of living. Marxist ideology drew no correlation between the economy and population. Rather, they pointed to birth-control programs funded by the United States and other economically advanced countries as imperialist and argued that neo-Malthusian cries ignored the true fundamental causes of poverty—namely, the greed and exploitation of the wealthy, whether at home or abroad.[44] Development patterns in the United States differed clearly from those in other countries in birthrates and family size. Because advancements in agriculture and industrialization in the United States (and Europe) coincided with a decline in birthrates, one might assume the same would happen elsewhere. However, women's labor was still used in agriculture, often to meet temporary needs, and that labor did not significantly affect the number of children they bore. Urbanization was understood to naturally result in decreased family size because children were less valuable in cities than they had been as farm laborers. But that was not the case everywhere. In many industrial centers, child labor laws were essentially nonexistent; thus, so as long as children could add to the family income with their meager wages, there was no financial incentive to limit their numbers.[45] This lack of incentive on the part of the women in the developing world to bear fewer children inspired international organizations to distribute contraceptives and contraceptive information more widely. Intrauterine devices were often considered the method of choice among organization leaders, regardless of the fact that they were deemed unsafe in the United States. In addition, sterilization programs were implemented widely in Puerto Rico and India.[46]

Perhaps the most significant US statement about international population rates can be found in the confidential 1974 National Security Study Memorandum 200, "Implications of Worldwide Population Growth for US Security and Overseas Interests," also known as the Kissinger Report. Declassified in 1989, the report called for various development measures, heavily emphasizing birth control. Education and improved employment opportunities for women in the less developed world could slow population growth, the report argued, but not quickly enough. Education should include contraceptive information influencing women, especially rural women, to desire fewer children. If family size could be quickly limited to replacement level—two or fewer children—the population explosion in the less developed world might be curbed.[47] The Kissinger Report argued that effective measures to reduce fertility urgently needed to be initiated in the 1970s and 1980s if future numbers were to be "kept within reasonable bounds." While under other circumstances modernization might lower the birthrate, population growth had been too rapid in comparison to development, likely slowing development even further and widening the gap between rich and poor. Numerous potential political effects—ultimately threatening US national security—included increased child abandonment, juvenile delinquency, food riots, separatist movements, communal massacres, and revolutionary actions. "Such conditions also detract from the environment needed to attract the foreign capital vital to increasing levels of economic growth in these areas. If these conditions result in expropriation of foreign interests, such action, from an economic viewpoint, is not in the best interests of either the investing country or the host government." It went on to reinforce the notion that political conflicts often have demographic roots.[48]

The report blamed demographic factors and population pressures for the war between El Salvador and Honduras, as well as for conflicts in Nigeria and between Pakistan, India, and Bangladesh. In order to stabilize situations there and elsewhere, the National Security Council recommended increasing birth control assistance and, in areas where US political influence and diplomatic relations were less favorable, encouraged donations from other countries and from international organizations. It placed primary emphasis on the largest and fastest growing developing countries "where the imbalance between growing numbers and development potential" most seriously risked "instability, unrest, and international tensions." The targeted countries included India, Bangladesh, Pakistan, Nigeria, Mexico, Indonesia, Brazil, the Philippines, Thailand, Egypt, Turkey, Ethiopia, and Colombia. In addition to recommending field studies and contraceptive education, the council urged programs to make oral contraceptives, intrauterine devices, tubal ligations, vasectomies, and injectable contraceptives available.[49]

Unimpeded access to natural resources was very important to US national security, and population was seen as playing a vital role in providing or hampering that access. The resources at stake included aluminum, copper, iron ore, lead, nickel, tin, uranium, zinc, and petroleum (both oil and natural gas). The negative effects of excessive population growth on economic development and social progress affected countries' internal stability, and the United States had become increasingly dependent on mineral and petroleum imports from developing regions. "The real problems of mineral supplies lie, not in basic physical sufficiency, but in the politico-economic issues of access, terms for exploration and exploitation, and division of the benefits among producers, consumers, and host country governments." The National Security Council warned of extreme cases where population pressures led to famine, food riots, and the breakdown of social order. "Whether through government action, labor conflicts, sabotage, or civil disturbance, the smooth flow of needed materials will be jeopardized. Although population pressure is obviously not the only factor involved, these types of frustrations are much less likely under conditions of slow or zero population growth."[50]

During the 1980s, US population concerns in Latin America intensified as civil wars raged and political unrest transformed into turmoil. The Cold War raged in Latin America under the Reagan administration, and population research reflected developments there. Howard J. Wiarda, professor of political science at the University of Massachusetts, associate at the Harvard University Center for International Affairs, and director of the Center for Hemispheric Studies at the American Enterprise Institute for Public Policy Research, warned that population growth in Latin America was not subsiding, as had been predicted by those believing demographic transition would take hold there by the late twentieth century. He predicted an increase of 42 percent in the last two decades of the twentieth century, with serious political, economic, social, strategic, and other implications not just for the region but also for the United States. The workforce would double or triple in some countries, while employment opportunities remained stagnant. According to Wiarda, "Social unrest will surely grow. The level of tension, violence, and conflict will increase. Social and political systems are very likely to unravel under these pressures, and revolution and increased international conflict will result. All these prospective changes carry profound implications for the United States and for U. S. foreign policy."[51]

The high birthrate would contribute to a growing population of young people, which, Wiarda pointed out, would lead to additional problems. Not only did they face unemployment, he argued, but they also had a tendency to lean toward the radical Left. He said, "What is certain is that in Latin America virtually an entire generation of university-trained young people is Marxist. The figures we have indicate that whereas in the United States only 2–3% of the college-age population could be classified as activist in a political sense, in Latin America the figures may be 40–45%." He broke the numbers down further, explaining, "State universities tend to be more radical and politicized in Latin America than private ones: the law and arts and letters faculties tend to be more activist than those in engineering or other technical fields." He added, "Socialism occupies the middle of the political spectrum, with social democracy on the right; there are no groups of what Americans would call conservatives on most Latin American college campuses. Part of the ideology of these young persons is virulent anti-Americanism."[52] He also outlined threats to US security, including crowding and internal tension, pressures on land, refugee problems, economic frustrations, the unraveling of political systems, and the potential for war, continually pointing to unchecked population as a primary source and the radical Left as a key element.

The United States held similar views of population pressure and radical youth in other regions. The student uprising and taking of US hostages in Iran in 1979 served as proof to some. The US Department of State had sought to maintain strong relations with Iran in the 1970s. It had found an ally in Iranian head of state Mohammad Reza Shah Pahlavi, who protected US interests against insurgents and the Soviet Union. Iran shared a long border with the Soviet Union and was witness to Soviet influence in nearby Afghanistan and Iraq. Interestingly, the State Department pointed to Iran's large population as a strength, claiming it served an advantage in warding off enemies. From a US perspective, Iran's large population worked hand in hand with rapid social and economic development, allowing it to exercise leadership in the Persian Gulf region. The United States welcomed Iran's greater security responsibilities and agreed to sell Iran defense materials, including aircraft and naval vessels.[53] A confluence of factors, including Cold War tensions, population issues, political instability, and anti-American politics among Iranian youth, led to the deposing of the Shah.

By the 1970s, USAID had become a principal provider of contraceptives and contraceptive information in less developed countries and became a catalyst for non-US and international population agencies to do the same. Much of that assistance was directed toward the Middle East, Africa, and South Asia. USAID annual budgets for population assistance increased from $106 million in 1975 to $190 million in 1981. In 1979, approximately $90 million (52 percent of the budget) was directed to private intermediary organizations. Of this, 85 percent was channeled through fourteen agencies that provided technical assistance to countries where bilateral assistance was "not always appropriate." Nongovernmental organizations (NGOs) based in the United States delivered population assistance to sixty-four less developed countries, including nine in the Middle East.[54] Achievements in population assistance and programs in Iran and Turkey were detailed in "The Middle East and North Africa," published in *Studies in Family Planning*, the journal of the Population Council, in 1975.[55] The United States was most successful in assisting with population control in Egypt. In much of the Middle East, cultural traditions prevented most women from using contraceptives, but Egyptian women were more open to their use.[56]

Rapid population growth in less developed countries of the Middle East influenced social, economic, and political factors in ways that threatened stability and therefore US security interests. "These interests include such tangible commodities as oil, chromium and vanadium imported by the United States," with less tangible, but very important, interests surrounding the "global balance of power."[57]

> In the long run, levels of US population assistance, like other forms of US development aid, will be determined by an overall assessment of the importance of population growth to US interests. The Middle East provides an important example. Because higher levels of Security Supporting Assistance have been appropriated for Middle Eastern countries, population assistance for Egypt is a major effort, well justified by US security interests. Population assistance for Egypt can be expected to increase in recognition of the "Arc of Crisis" countries in that region.[58]

The US intention to control population via birth control assistance was apparent. Concerns differed from those early in the Cold War when the Soviet Union and China garnered the most attention from US demographers, policy analysts, and government officials. But their foundations were the same. Both were rooted in economics and the desire to preserve and expand the US global position in the name of national security.

Notes

1. For recent perspectives on pronatalism, see Carole H. Browner and Carolyn F. Sargent, eds., *Reproduction, Globalization, and the State: New Theoretical and Ethnographic Perspectives* (Durham, NC: Duke University Press, 2011); Laura L. Lovett, *Conceiving the Future: Pronatalism, Reproduction, and the Family in the United States, 1890–1938* (Chapel Hill: University of North Carolina Press, 2007); Leslie Tuttle, *Conceiving the Old Regime: Pronatalism and the Politics of Reproduction in Early Modern France* (New York: Oxford University Press, 2010); and David L. Hoffmann, *Mothers in the*

Motherland: Stalinist Pronatalism and Its Pan-European Context (Columbus: Ohio State University Press, 2000).

2. Matthew Connelly, *Fatal Misconception: The Struggle to Control World Population* (Cambridge, MA: Belknap Press of Harvard University Press, 2008), 152.

3. Ibid., 115–54.

4. Michael S. Teitelbaum and Jay M. Winter, *The Fear of Population Decline* (London: Academic Press, 1985); Jay Winter and Michael Teitelbaum, *The Global Spread of Fertility Decline* (New Haven: Yale University Press, 2013).

5. Ronal R. Krebs and Jack S. Levy, "Demographic Change and the Sources of International Conflict," in *Demography and International Security*, ed. Myron Weiner and Sharon Stanton Russell (New York: Berghahn, 2001), 62. For a recent overview on population and economics, see David E. Bloom, David Canning, and Jaypee Sevilla, *The Demographic Dividend: A New Perspective on the Economic Consequences of Population Change* (Santa Monica, CA: Rand, 2003).

6. Kingsley Davis, "Population and Power in the Free World," in *Population and World Politics*, ed. Philip M. Hauser (Glencoe, IL: Free Press, 1958), 199.

7. Ibid., 203–13.

8. Frank Lorimer, "Population Policies and Politics in the Communist World," in Hauser, *Population and World Politics*, 214.

9. Quincy Wright, "Population and United States Foreign Policy," in Hauser, *Population and World Politics*, 260–70.

10. Frank W. Notestein et al., *The Future Population of Europe and the Soviet Union: Population Projections, 1940–1970* (Geneva: League of Nations and Office of Population Research, Princeton University, 1944), 15–19, 38–39.

11. For more on Soviet women's roles in the family and the workforce before 1945, see J. Grunfeld, "Women's Work in Russia's Planned Economy," *Social Research* 9, no. 1 (February 1942): 22–45; and S. M. Kingsbury and M. Fairchild, *Factory, Family and Woman in the Soviet Union* (New York: Putnam, 1935).

12. See chapter 3, "Stalinist Family Values," in David L. Hoffmann, *Stalinist Values: Cultural Norms of Soviet Modernity, 1917–1941* (Ithaca, NY: Cornell University Press, 2003), 97–104.

13. Warren W. Eason, "Population and Labor Force," in *Soviet Economic Growth: Conditions and Perspectives*, ed. Abram Bergson (Evanston, IL: Row, Peterson, 1953), 104–5.

14. David M. Heer, "The Childbearing Functions of the Soviet Family," in *The Role and Status of Women in the Soviet Union*, ed. Donald R. Brown (New York: Columbia University Teachers College Press, 1968), 125–27. Also see *Annual Economic Indicators for the U.S.S.R.*, prepared for the Joint Economic Committee, 88th Congress (Washington, DC: US Government Printing Office, 1964), 44–45; and James W. Brackett, "Demographic Trends and Population Policy in the Soviet Union," in *Dimensions of Soviet Economic Power*, studies prepared for the Joint Economic Committee, 87th Congress (Washington, DC: US Government Printing Office, 1962).

15. Urie Bronfenbrenner, "The Changing Soviet Family," in Brown, *Role and Status of Women in the Soviet Union*, 99–101. Also see Leon Trotsky, *Women and the Family* (New York: Pathfinder Press, 1970); and Vladimir Ilich Lenin, *Soviet Power and the Status of Women: International Women's Day* (Moscow: Foreign Languages Publishing House, 1954), originally published in *Pravda*, no. 249 (November 6, 1919). For Soviet ideals regarding women and families before the Cold War, see Alice Withrow Field,

Protection of Women and Children in Soviet Russia (New York: E. P. Dutton, 1932), 57–59.

16. Field, *Protection of Women and Children in Soviet Russia*, 75–81. Also see Lenin, *Soviet Power and the Status of Women*.

17. US Central Intelligence Agency, *Comparison of U. S. and Soviet Population and Manpower* (Washington, DC: Central Intelligence Agency Office of Research and Reports, 1960), i. Also see US Department of Labor, *Manpower: Challenge of the 1960s* (Washington, DC: U. S. Department of Labor, 1960); and US Central Intelligence Agency, *Soviet Manpower: 1960–70* (Washington, DC: Central Intelligence Agency Office of Research and Reports, 1960).

18. US Central Intelligence Agency, *Comparison of U. S. and Soviet Population and Manpower*, 3, 5–8. Also see Harold Wool, *Working Memorandum on Statistics of Population, Labor Force, and Employment in the Soviet Union* (New York: Study of Economic Growth, National Bureau of Economic Research, 1959); and J. William Leasure and Robert A. Lewis, *Population Changes in Russia and the USSR: A Set of Comparable Territorial Units*, Social Science Monograph Series 1, no. 2 (San Diego: San Diego State College Press, 1966).

19. George St. George, *Our Soviet Sister* (Washington, DC: Robert B. Luce, 1973), chapter titled "To Beget or Not to Beget," 155–76.

20. As cited in St. George, *Our Soviet Sister*, 172. Also see Norton T. Doge, *Women in the Soviet Economy: Their Role in Economic, Scientific, and Technical Development* (Baltimore: Johns Hopkins University Press, 1966); and Helen Desfosses, ed., *Soviet Population Policy: Conflicts and Constraints* (New York: Pergamon, 1981).

21. Mao Tse-Tung, *Selected Works of Mao Tse-Tung*, vol. 4 (Peking: Foreign Languages Press, 1961), 453–54; in H. Yuan Tien, "The Demographic Significance of Organized Population Transfers in Communist China," *Demography* 1, no. 1 (1964): 220–22.

22. Tien, "Demographic Significance of Organized Population Transfers," 220–21.

23. Marion J. Levy Jr., *The Family Revolution in Modern China* (Cambridge, MA: Harvard University Press and the Institute of Pacific Relations, 1949), 111–15, 299–304. Also see C. K. Yang, *Chinese Communist Society: The Family and the Village* (Cambridge, MA: Massachusetts Institute of Technology Press, 1959), 17–20.

24. US Bureau of the Census, *The Population of Communist China: 1953*, International Population Reports P-90, no. 6 (Washington, DC: US Government Printing Office, 1955); US Bureau of the Census, *The Population and Manpower of China: An Annotated Bibliography*, International Population Reports P-90, no. 8 (Washington, DC: US Government Printing Office, 1958). For a sample of Communist perspectives in *People's China*, see Central Committee of the Chinese Communist Party, "Decisions on Agricultural Cooperation," *People's China* 23 (1955): 24; Chang Ching, "Shanghai in the First Year of the First Five-Year Plan," *People's China* 3 (1954): 20–27; Chou En-lai, "Report on the Proposals for the Second Five-Year Plan," *People's China* 21 (1956): 27; Mao Tse-Tung, "The Question of Agricultural Cooperation," *People's China* 12 (1955): 3–20; and Chou Wei-pin, "Our First Scientific Census," *People's China* 7 (1955): 17–23.

25. Charles G. McClintock, *The Demography of the "Big Three"*, (Santa Barbara, CA: Technical Military Planning Operation, General Electric Company, 1958), 6–10.

26. Ibid., 20–21.

27. For more on early birth control policies in China, see H. Yuan Tien, "Birth Control in Mainland China: Ideology and Politics," *Milbank Memorial Fund Quarterly* 41, no. 3 (1963): 269–90; H. Yuan Tien, "Population Control: Recent Developments in

Mainland China," *Asian Survey* 2, no. 5 (1962): 12–16; and John S. Aird, "Population Policy in Mainland China," *Population Studies* 16, no. 1 (1962): 38–51.

28. John S. Aird, *Population Estimates for the Provinces of the People's Republic of China: 1953 to 1974*, International Population Reports P-95, no. 73 (Washington, DC: Bureau of Economic Analysis and Social and Economic Statistics Administration, US Department of Commerce, 1974), 1, 4, 22. Also see Morris B. Ullman, *Cities of Mainland China: 1953 and 1958*, International Population Reports P-95, no. 59 (Washington, DC: Bureau of the Census, US Department of Commerce, 1961).

29. John S. Aird, "Population Growth," in *Economic Trends in Communist China*, ed. Alexander Eckstein, Walter Galenson, and Ta-Chung Liu (Chicago: Aldine, 1968), 312–16.

30. Alexander Eckstein, Walter Galenson, and Ta-Chung Liu, "Introduction," in Eckstein, Galenson, and Liu, *Economic Trends in Communist China*, 1–16. Also see *Chinese Women in the Great Leap Forward* (Peking: Foreign Languages Press, 1960).

31. See Michael C. LeMay, *Guarding the Gates: Immigration and National Security* (Westport, CT: Praeger Security International, 2006).

32. Jurgen Wesphalen, "Effects on Development of the Population Explosion in Latin America," *Intereconomics* 1, no. 2 (1966): 10–15. Also see Paul R. Ehrlich, *The Population Bomb: Population Control or Race to Oblivion* (San Francisco: Sierra Club, 1969).

33. Frank W. Notestein, "Some Economic Aspects of Population Change in the Developing Countries," in *Population Dilemma in Latin America*, ed. J. Mayone Stycos and Jorge Arias (Washington, DC: Potomac Books, 1966), pp. 89–91. For more statistics, see Giorgio Mortara, *Characteristics of the Demographic Structure of the American Countries* (Washington, DC: Pan American Union, 1964).

34. Notestein, "Some Economic Aspects of Population Change," 93–97; Ansley J. Coale and Edgar M. Hoover, *Population Growth and Economic Development in Low-Income Countries* (Princeton, NJ: Princeton University Press, 1958); and T. Lynn Smith, *Latin American Population Studies*, University of Florida Monographs, Social Sciences no. 8 (Gainesville: University of Florida Press, 1960).

35. Carr B. Lavell, *Population Growth and the Development of South America*, Population Research Project, Department of Sociology and Anthropology, George Washington University (Washington, D.C.: George Washington University Press, 1959), 42–44.

36. Robert Black, "Options for Latin Parents—Through Family Planning," in *Population and Urbanization Problems of Latin America, A Conference Held under the Auspices of the Committee on Latin American Studies, University of Houston*, ed. Philip B. Taylor Jr. and Sam Schulman (Houston: Latin American Studies Committee, Office of International Affairs, University of Houston, 1971), 43.

37. Ibid., 43–45.

38. T. Lynn Smith, *The Race between Population and Food Supply in Latin America* (Albuquerque: University of New Mexico Press, 1976), 51–56. Also see Inter-American Statistical Institute, "Situación Demográfica," in *América en Cifras: 1974* (Washington, DC: Organization of American States, 1974); and US Bureau of the Census, *World Population: 1973, Recent Demographic Estimates for the Countries and Regions of the World* (Washington, DC: US Government Printing Office, 1974).

39. For statistics on urbanization, see Richard W. Wilkie, *Latin American Population and Urbanization Analysis, Maps and Statistics, 1950–1982* (Los Angeles: University of California Los Angeles Latin American Center Publications, 1984).

40. See Phyllis T. Piotrow, *World Population Crisis: The United States Response* (New York: Praeger, 1973); Julian L. Simon, *The Ultimate Resource* (Princeton, NJ: Princeton University Press, 1981); Simon, *The Economics of Population Growth* (Princeton, NJ: Princeton University Press, 1977); *Report of the United States Delegation to the United Nations International Conference on Population, Mexico City, Mexico, August 6–14, 1984* (Washington, DC, 1984); and Ben Wattenberg and Karl Zinsmeister, eds., *Are World Population Trends a Problem?* (Washington, DC: American Enterprise Institute, 1985).

41. J. Mayone Stycos, "Politics and Population Control in Latin America," in *The Dynamics of Population Policy in Latin America*, ed. Terry L. McCoy (Cambridge, MA: Ballinger, 1974), 7–12; and Stycos, *Human Fertility in Latin America: Sociological Perspectives* (Ithaca, NY: Cornell University Press, 1968), 32–56. For more on imperialist considerations and international birth control, see Connolly, *Fatal Misconception*; Bonnie Mass, *Political Economy of Population Control in Latin America* (Montreal: Editions Latin America, 1972); and Mass, *Population Target: The Political Economy of Population Control in Latin America* (Toronto: Latin America Working Group, 1976).

42. For more on approaches to population in this context, see Michael S. Teitelbaum and Jay Winter, *A Question of Numbers: High Migration, Low Fertility, and the Politics of National Identity* (New York: Hill and Wang, 1998). Chapter 7, "A Generation of Demographic Debate in the United States" (127–53), details related US concerns, including shifting immigration patterns after 1965.

43. Connolly, *Fatal Misconception*, 195–236. Connolly conducted extensive research on the work of USAID and other international funding organizations in supplying and supporting sterilization in the developing world.

44. Patricia J. O'Brien, *Population Policy, Economic Development, and Multinational Corporations in Latin America: Issues and Impacts*, Working Paper on Women in International Development, originally presented at the 1982 North Central Sociological Association Meeting, Detroit, Michigan, May 5–8 (East Lansing: Michigan State University Press, 1982), 2–4. For nationalist population ideology in this period, see Colin Clark, *Population Growth and Land Use* (New York: St. Martin's, 1967); and Ester Boserup, *Women's Roles in Economic Development* (New York: St. Martin's, 1970). For Marxist population policy in this period, see Ronald Meek, *Marx and Engels on the Population Bomb* (New York: Ramparts, 1971).

45. O'Brien, *Population Policy, Economic Development, and Multinational Corporations*, 12–13.

46. Connolly, *Fatal Misconception*, 203–7. Connolly addresses the application of these methods throughout his chapter "Controlling Nations," 195–236.

47. US National Security Council, *NSSM 200: Implications of Worldwide Population Growth for U. S. Security and Overseas Interests* (Washington, DC: National Security Council, 1974), 9, appendix.

48. Ibid., 8.

49. Ibid., appendix and "Part Two: Policy Recommendations."

50. Ibid., appendix.

51. Howard J. Wiarda, *Population, Internal Unrest, and U. S. Security in Latin America*, Occasional Papers Series no. 18 (Amherst, MA: Program in Latin American Studies, 1986), 2–5. This report was first prepared for the Population Growth in Latin America and US National Security Conference held at Mississippi State University's Center for International Security and Strategic Studies.

52. Ibid., 11–12. Also see S. M. Lipset, ed., *Rebellion in the University* (Chicago: University of Chicago Press, 1976).

53. US Department of State, *U. S. Policy in the Middle East: November 1974–February 1976* (Washington, DC: United States Government Printing Office, 1976), 100, 105.

54. US Congress, Office of Technology Assistance, *World Population and Fertility Planning Technologies: The Next 20 Years* (Washington, DC: US Government Printing Office, 1982), 182.

55. Joel G. Montague and Gerald I. Zatuchni, "The Middle East and North Africa," *Studies in Family Planning* 6, no. 8 (1975): 302–4.

56. See Elizabeth M. Edmands, *Concepts and Issues in Family Planning: Guidelines for Nurses, Midwives, and Other Health Personnel: Focus on Africa and the Middle East* (Chapel Hill: University of North Carolina School of Medicine, Institute for International Training in Health, 1984).

57. Office of Technology Assistance, *World Population and Fertility Planning Technologies*, 51.

58. Ibid., 196.

References

Selected Published Works

Connelly, Matthew. *Fatal Misconception: The Struggle to Control World Population.* Cambridge, MA: Belknap Press of Harvard University Press, 2008.

Eason, Warren W. "Population and Labor Force." In *Soviet Economic Growth: Conditions and Perspectives*, edited by Abram Bergson. Evanston, IL: Row, Peterson, 1953.

Eckstein, Alexander, Walter Galenson, and Ta-Chung Liu, eds. *Economic Trends in Communist China.* Chicago: Aldine, 1968.

Edmands, Elizabeth M. *Concepts and Issues in Family Planning: Guidelines for Nurses, Midwives, and Other Health Personnel; Focus on Africa and the Middle East.* Chapel Hill: University of North Carolina School of Medicine, Institute for International Training in Health, 1984.

Hauser, Philip M., ed. *Population and World Politics.* Glencoe, IL: Free Press, 1958.

Lavell, Carr B. *Population Growth and the Development of South America.* Population Research Project, Department of Sociology and Anthropology, George Washington University. Washington, D.C.: George Washington University Press, 1959.

Mass, Bonnie. *Population Target: The Political Economy of Population Control in Latin America.* Toronto: Latin America Working Group, 1976.

McClintock, Charles G. *The Demography of the "Big Three."* Santa Barbara, CA: Technical Military Planning Operation, General Electric Company, 1958.

Smith, T. Lynn. *The Race between Population and Food Supply in Latin America.* Albuquerque: University of New Mexico Press, 1976.

St. George, George. *Our Soviet Sister.* Washington, DC: Robert B. Luce, 1973.

Stycos, J. Mayone. "Politics and Population Control in Latin America." In *The Dynamics of Population Policy in Latin America*, edited by Terry L. McCoy. Cambridge, MA: Ballinger Publishing, 1974.

Stycos, J. Mayone, and Jorge Arias, eds. *Population Dilemma in Latin America.* Washington, DC: Potomac Books, 1966.

Taylor, Philip B., Jr., and Sam Schulman, eds. *Population and Urbanization Problems of Latin America, a Conference Held under the Auspices of the Committee on Latin American Studies, University of Houston.* Houston: Latin American Studies Committee, Office of International Affairs, University of Houston, 1971.

Teitelbaum, Michael S., and Jay Winter. *A Question of Numbers: High Migration, Low Fertility, and the Politics of National Identity*. New York: Hill and Wang, 1998.

——. *The Fear of Population Decline*. London: Academic Press, 1985.

Tien, H. Yuan. "The Demographic Significance of Organized Population Transfers in Communist China." *Demography* 1, no. 1 (1964): 220–26.

United States Bureau of the Census. *The Population and Manpower of China: An Annotated Bibliography*. International Population Reports P-90, no. 8. Washington, DC: U. S. Government Printing Office, 1958.

United States Central Intelligence Agency. *Comparison of U. S. and Soviet Population and Manpower*. Washington, DC: Central Intelligence Agency Office of Research and Reports, 1960.

United States Congress, Office of Technology Assistance. *World Population and Fertility Planning Technologies: The Next 20 Years*. Washington, DC: US Government Printing Office, 1982.

United States National Security Council. *NSSM 200: Implications of Worldwide Population Growth for U. S. Security and Overseas Interests*. Washington, DC: National Security Council, 1974.

Wiarda, Howard J. *Population, Internal Unrest, and U. S. Security in Latin America*. Occasional Papers Series 18. Amherst, MA: Program in Latin American Studies, 1986.

Winter, Jay, and Michael Teitelbaum. *The Global Spread of Fertility Decline*. New Haven, CT: Yale University Press, 2013.

PART II

Femininities

CHAPTER 6

Indian Peasant Women's Activism in a Hot Cold War

Elisabeth Armstrong

The twentieth-century pan-Asian women's movement did not begin as a peasant women's movement, but by the 1940s it became one. Women who gained their livelihood through agricultural labor brought energy, relevance, and an exhilarating unpredictability to the pan-Asian women's movement as a whole. They powerfully shaped the postwar women's movement in the Global South, and pressured both communist and anticommunist international women's movements in the Global North. As a mass movement, peasant women formed the core of the leftist women's movement in the Global South. Yet our histories of the Cold War give little space for peasant women's activism in the mid-twentieth century. The bifurcation between the Euro-American West and the Soviet East in standard narratives of the Cold War obscures the formative class struggles that shaped anti-imperialist women's activism in the Global South. Even in Europe, the Cold War as a geopolitical framework rarely questions the subjects, goals, or demands of the class conflict between capitalism and socialism.

Mass movements of women in the Global South reveal two critical facets that Cold War scholars of the 1940s and 1950s too often ignore. First, local, national, and regional class conflict rather than international arm-twisting fueled the polarity between communism and anticommunism in Asia. In the context of India, class-based political differences between peasant women and elite women—not Soviet or US promises of support—split the formerly unified nationalist women's movement. Second, the Cold War in Europe was a hot war across the continents of Asia and Africa. Peasant women's organizing as a mass force emerged during the intensified military repression against insurgent populations by colonial forces.[1] Anti-imperialism integrally shaped these leftist women's movements in the Global South as a critical site for pan-Asian and Afro-Asian women's solidarity. They wielded this solidarity among colonial and

Originally published in *Communist Histories*, vol. 1, edited by Vijay Prashad (New Delhi: LeftWord Books, 2016). Used with permission.

postcolonial nations in the international women's forums reenergized by the end of the war in Europe and Japan.

Scholars have documented varied pan-Asian movements against imperialism that began in the 1920s, by parties such as the Kuomindang in China founded by Sun Yat-sen, alongside communist parties in China and the USSR.[2] In India, the nationalist movement recognized the importance of mobilizing as many Indian people as possible into its struggle for an independent nation-state. Most Indian people were peasants, which included artisans, small farmers, landless agricultural workers, tenant farmers, and fishing people. By the 1920s, they were central to the widespread nationalist anticolonial mobilizations across the country.[3] As with peasant men, Indian peasant women's activism developed out of nationalist, communist, socialist, and anti-casteist peasant movements in the 1930s and 1940s.[4] Peasant groups, called *kisan sabhas* in India, sought to build rural men's leadership and to represent the demands of dispossessed agricultural people. In India until 1945, peasant women were peripheral to rural organizing campaigns, holding no leadership positions in the All India Kisan Sabha, the India-wide multiparty farmers' organization that began in 1936. By 1945, separate meetings for peasant women were structured into their national conferences.[5] Peasant women's activism also developed from the nationalist women's movement, particularly in the late 1930s and 1940s.

The All India Women's Conference (AIWC) began in 1927 as a nonsectarian, social reform organization to promote Indian women's education and health.[6] The AIWC was not directly linked to the nationalist movement, nor did it espouse the cause of women's activism. Its members were from elite, princely families and the educated middle classes, though these women espoused a wide range of political viewpoints and affiliations. At its inception, at least, the AIWC seemed an unlikely instigator of peasant, poor, and working-class women. Yet, as its name attests, the AIWC aspired to represent and lead all women of India under its umbrella, regardless of their religion, language, or political affiliation. By the early 1940s, not only did the AIWC overtly support women's activism in the Indian independence movement, but it also sought to reach the masses of rural, peasant Indian women.

Sarojini Naidu was a leading figure in India's nationalist feminism of the mid-twentieth century. She joined the Indian freedom movement in 1905, spoke to Lord Chelmsford and Mr. Montagu in favor of women's right to vote in 1918, and was the Congress Party president in 1925. She led the AIWC as president in 1930. For nationalist members like Naidu, to describe AIWC as a "nonpolitical" group meant that it was an omnipolitical one. All women, they argued, were welcome. In 1944, Naidu defended the right of communists and members from the Muslim League to participate in the Indian National Congress. "'In times of great crisis,' she said, 'humanity is greater than all political parties.'"[7] Addressing Congress Party members, she added, "Why did you not organize—ban or no ban—to give relief to the distressed? Why did you leave the work of relief to the communists?"[8] Naidu pointedly named the discomfiting power of communists within the independence movement derived from their active relief work in the countryside and cities during the Bengal famine that began in 1943. Nationalist feminists, like leftist feminists, sought to strengthen the women's movement by organizing among rural peasant women. Their methods of mobilizing rural, dispossessed women to support the Indian independence movement, however, were not attuned to peasant women's demands or their methods of organizing. Without addressing peasant women's daily needs for survival alongside the systemic injustice that made their survival so precarious, nationalist feminist efforts fell short.

Leftist regional women's groups, like the Mahila Atma Raksha Samiti (MARS) in Bengal and the Punjab Women's Self-Defense League, also organized among working-class and poor women in cities and peasant women in rural areas. Leftist organizers allied (and often shared membership) with the AIWC in these struggles over wages, fair working conditions, and food distribution. During the Bengal famine in 1943 and 1944, the AIWC with other women's groups set up and ran rehabilitation centers for destitute women in the cities of Kolkata, Krishnanagar, and Barisal.[9] This mass-based work increased the AIWC's membership numbers dramatically. By April 1944, the AIWC's membership had risen two and a half times over one year, from ten thousand to twenty-five thousand women.[10] The AIWC convention resolutions from 1942 to 1946 reveal the political pressures of holding together social reform feminism with nationalist feminism and leftist feminism. AIWC conference resolutions show the AIWC's increasing breadth of issues: in favor of food distribution "for the entire population" in 1943 during the Bengal famine, against the "barbaric practice of whipping of political and other prisoners" also in 1943, against the Nizam of Hyderabad's sexual and physical violence against Andhra women in 1945, and in favor of postal workers' rights in 1946.[11] Its increasing radicalism clashed with the entrenched interests of its powerful members and began to tear at the seams of the AIWC's proclaimed All India unity.

In 1946, the AIWC finally split over its restrictive membership policies that charged dues too costly for most women to pay. The desire to lead peasant women did not mean the desire to organize as equals alongside them or to heed their demands. Nationalist feminists allied with social reformist members to maintain the AIWC's higher membership dues, thus excluding the large numbers of working-class and peasant women radicalized by their rural activism. In December 1946, the AIWC membership allowed local clubs to decide whether to reduce their fees from three rupees to four annas (a quarter of one rupee) to allow more rural and working-class women to join. Without the explicit support for the fee reduction at the national level, communist members lost the possibility of transforming the AIWC into a national women's organization that represented all Indian women. After this defeat, most of its left-wing members withdrew from the organization to concentrate their efforts organizing a national, mass-based women's movement from the scattered regional leftist women's groups.[12]

Importantly, communist and socialist women did not leave the AIWC because of its anticommunism as such. Many nationalist leaders of the AIWC sought a unified group of women from all political parties and wanted to lead peasant women. Instead, leftist members left the one welcoming national women's organization to create a women's movement substantively shaped and led by peasant women. After 1946, leftist women's groups gave voice to increasingly radical demands at local and regional levels, since they had no alternative national women's organization. They sought to overturn gendered caste hierarchies, rural power relations between the landed and the land-poor, and women's sexual norms as a unified class politics, not niche demands for indigenous, Dalit (oppressed caste), and working-class women and men.[13] The antiviolence demands of the peasant women in India confronted local patriarchal and casteist norms as well as the intertwined character of European colonialism with regional feudal class relations.[14] Leftist women's groups also joined the fight by peasant groups for greater rights to land and crops, for example, in the Tebhaga movement of Bengal in 1946 and 1947. They worked alongside activists in the Communist Party of India (CPI), in communist and socialist unions, and in student groups. They developed a mass-based leftist women's movement in India because of the large numbers of women organized into women's groups, but also because of the politics they espoused.

After 1945, Euro-American-aligned organizations like the International Alliance of Women actively wished to recruit Asian women's groups into their folds on anticommunist terms, and they sought to reach (and guide) these masses. In no small part, peasant women's militancy on class issues, alongside their anti-imperialism, spurred Euro-American, anticommunist interest in peeling away some nationalist and Third Worldist women to incorporate them into pro-Western international work. On the pan-Asian level, peasant women's politics also shaped the Cold War discourse of the international women's movement. The Women's International Democratic Federation (WIDF) gained respect among leftist and nationalist women's groups in Asia for forcefully denouncing colonialism in its opening antifascist program.[15] Asian and North African participants in the opening meeting of WIDF in December 1945 successfully fought to widen "antifascism" to include "anti-imperialism."

The Three Strands of Indian Feminism

Before independence in 1947, the Indian women's movement had three distinct, yet often overlapping feminist ideologies: social reformist, nationalist, and leftist. Social reform feminism sought to allow women access to education and other material benefits and fostered political subjectivities for women's activism in the private sphere. Social reform feminism by the 1930s was intercommunal. It linked women and men from different religions and regions to push for wider resources for women and girls. Social reform activists sought changes to restrictive norms for girls and women largely from within the private spheres of the family and the religious or ethnic community. In contrast, nationalist feminism saw women's education and health as goals that could support women's equal rights and their full participation in public life. Mrinalini Sinha argues that nationalist feminism supported an openly political and public subject bounded not by familial community but by the patriarchal benevolence of the nation.[16] Through a focus on legal reform, nationalist feminists in the AIWC and elsewhere sought laws to support women's rights to equal citizenship. Women's full citizenship also contested the legitimacy of the British colonial order in India, since neither Indian women nor Indian men enjoyed this status. Leftist feminism shared with nationalist feminism a commitment to anticolonialism and to women's legal and state-based inclusion into the public sphere. However, leftist feminism was also anti-imperialist and anticapitalist. Leftist feminists organized to transform class politics and the public sphere itself. They envisioned a public that welcomed the full participation of all people of India in its economic, cultural, and political life.

These three stands of the Indian women's movement—social reformism, nationalism, and leftism—jostled for space within the All India Women's Conference in the 1930s and 1940s. While they shared some overlapping concerns, activists within the AIWC did not fully agree on how to pursue their founding goals of women's education and rights. Nationalist feminists within the AIWC relied on a strong nation-state and the stability of dominant social norms to transition to independent governance. Leftist feminists aspired to harness the instability of independence mass movements to dismantle old social hierarchies of caste, class, and gender. The sexual politics of women's activism in the 1940s exposed critical differences between leftist and nationalist feminists within the AIWC. Even the most sincere appeals to a secular and cross-political unity could not paper over these differences.

Social Reform Feminism

Indian social reform feminism began in the mid-nineteenth century when Christian British colonial officials and men from the educated Muslim and Hindu Indian elite challenged gendered, hierarchal religious practices and social relations. Social reform movements focused predominantly on improving the conditions of Indian women's lives as wives, widows, and daughters. While often characterized simply as a means to justify colonial rule through the British "civilizing mission," social reformism failed to monopolize Indian women's issues. Historians such as Padma Anagol caution us to remember that even early in the social reform movement, Indian women enthusiastically supported their campaigns.[17] Due to the active participation of Indian women, social reform feminism had gained significant traction by the twentieth century as both an international and national movement. Moreover, it began to undermine rather than shore up the legitimacy of English rule over India.

Opposition to the AIWC's social reformist politics was fierce. The heightened sexual politics of women's education and health access dogged its work. During the second year of the All India Women's Conference, in 1928, the Begum of Bhopal agreed to take the post as president and attended the organization's meetings. The begum had been hugely influential in her support for women's education during the late nineteenth and early twentieth century, but the lessons she had learned about educated women's respectability sounded outmoded by the 1920s.[18] Kamaladevi Chattopadhyay, a prominent nationalist activist, was the general secretary who ran the AIWC alongside the begum during its first four years. She recounted members' mischievous response to the begum's horror of dance in an unpublished memoir. Chattopadhyay wrote, "We had been on the significant role of dancing in education. When this was mentioned the President interrupted sharply, raising her arm in protest. 'I can't have dance in any form discussed or approved in this session while I preside.'"[19] At the beginning of the twentieth century, social reformists, including the Begum of Bhopal, had to fight stereotypes of educated women as women without honor or morals. Dancing, as the profession of courtesans and sex workers, became the brush to tarnish early women's schools like the Women's College of Aligarh Muslim University.[20] Thus, for the begum, dancing in women's schools was a stereotype to be thoroughly shunned. For the active members of AIWC in the 1920s, however, fear of dancing was an antiquated joke.

In Chattopadhyay's account, the begum's objections did not impede the position of the AIWC:

> Zimha Lazarus, Principal of Women's College in Bangalore was on her feet advocating this forbidden form. She was charming and humorous with a very agile and resourceful brain. With hardly a pause, she nodded acceptance of the Chair's ruling, but went on with her speech advocating movements, rhythm, music, speaking with speed and blurring occasionally over d-a-n-c-e, which only a discerning ear could catch. So the resolution was passed, with small changes to make it less blatant and hurt the old lady's confirmed susceptibilities.[21]

In Chattopadhyay's recounting, the political edge of the AIWC's agenda for women's social reform took an easy precedence over the older, progressivist gender order represented by the begum. Definitions within the AIWC of acceptable politics for a women's organization faced new challenges in the 1930s with the intensity of the anticolonial movements—some nonviolent, others violent—all of which had prominent women activists. The AIWC's campaigns began to widen the boundaries of a gender-mixed public sphere from women's education to women's active involvement in governance and oppositional politics.

Nationalist Feminism

Nationalist feminists within the AIWC sought to make anticolonial activism an acceptable politics for women.[22] First, they lifted the ban on members' participation in politics in the early 1930s.[23] Second, they encouraged women from all political parties to join and participate. Mrinalini Sinha discusses the Child Marriage Restraint Act, or Sarda Act, passed in 1929 as the turning point for the development of nationalist feminism as distinct from social reform feminism.[24] In many ways, the Sarda Act was a classic social reform law that raised women's age of consent for marriage. It was not part of any of the religious personal laws and was the first civil piece of legislation that addressed women's rights. Its civil and thus universal character marks a radical break from other social reform campaigns. For opponents, it undermined the power of the religious personal laws that governed women by their religious affiliation and gave religious authorities free rein over legislation regarding marriage, women's property rights, and other issues considered familial in nature.

Sinha argues that the terrain for women's activism shifted social reform feminism itself because women were no longer only objects to be protected by law but were now also its activist subjects fighting to protect themselves. She writes, "The unprecedented involvement of women and of women's organizations in the debates surrounding the Sarda Act underwrote a crucial political development: the construction of women as *both* subjects *and* the objects of social reform in

India."[25] The universalized category of citizen that included Indian women and Indian men allowed the emergence of a distinctly nationalist feminism during the twentieth century. But there were limits to the nationalist feminist subject set by the nation-state. Gandhi invoked a nation that transcended other group boundaries, bringing all women into one political community, a unity that took the place of rather than eradicated other community strictures. Thus, the dominant Gandhian vision for nationalist feminism imagined a community where the nation-state provided women the defining location for their active citizenship. However, this protective and patriarchal role for the postcolonial nation-state "trumped the recognition of women's autonomy" as citizens or activists.[26]

Leftist Feminism

Through the AIWC, nationalists such as Sarojini Naidu were allied to women such as Kalpana Datta Joshi, a revolutionary terrorist who participated in the Chittagong Armory raid in 1930. Joshi gained her fame as an anticolonial terrorist in the Meerut Conspiracy Case in the 1930s. She also took an active role in organizing working-class women in the nationalist movement. Joshi joined the Communist Party in the 1940s after her release from prison and worked actively in MARS, the AIWC, and the CPI in the northern city of Chittagong, one of India's largest military bases during World War II.[27] Both strands in the AIWC—a nationalist feminist movement and a mass-based leftist women's movement—actively supported the reform of the Hindu personal laws and were fiercely anticolonial. Their strategies for effecting this change were quite different. Nationalist feminists sought to mobilize, educate, and provide for the masses of women. Leftist feminist sought to organize these peasant masses. Communist advocates of a mass-based women's movement sought to create a movement led and peopled by rural, peasant, working-class, and middle-class women.

Soma Marik posits a valuable insight about how communist women's activism differed from that of bourgeois nationalist women.[28] Marik describes the CPI's "stress on individualism" for women comrades combined with an equally strong emphasis on the collectivity of class politics.[29] She cites her 2001 interview with a powerful communist leader, Bani Dasgupta, who described her communist subjectivity in the following language: "We were taught that first comes our independent existence. To retain your independent existence you must learn to stand straight. You must learn to fend for yourself, to take on social responsibilities."[30] The nation-state did not provide the platform for communist women's activism; instead, individual women had to take on that responsibility for themselves. Leftist feminism demanded women's autonomy from statist, communal, and familial norms. Only then could leftist feminists join the collectivity of class politics—a collectivity that demanded an adherence to common ideals but did not promise protection or safety for that class-based loyalty.

Dasgupta became a powerful force in the communist women's movement and traveled widely as the secretary of the Women's International Democratic Federation to support the Afro-Asian women's movement in the 1950s and 1960s. She gained her independence and the skills to shoulder "social responsibilities" through the CPI. In stark contrast to nationalist women's location within the patriarchal fold of the nation-state, individuality outside of a statist patriarchy was, for communist women, the necessary precursor to the gendered class politics of Indian communism. What did self-reliance and standing straight mean for Bengali peasant women who negotiated norms of respectability differently from middle-class women in rural towns and localities? How did these gendered and classed lessons converge for peasant women in rural areas? Communist leaders in the Indian women's movement like Dasgupta, Manikuntala Sen, and Renu Chakravartty all provide personal narratives about joining the communist movement as uppercaste, middle-class, or elite Bengali women. They describe the sexual politics of renouncing respectable forms of women's seclusion from public life in order to become activists. For peasant women, sexual politics revolved around the right to live without sexual coercion and to claim their own bodily autonomy in a regime where large landowners had the first and final say over their sexual availability.

Organizing Rural Women and the Bengal Famine

At least three and a half million people died of starvation and disease during the Bengal famine between 1943 and 1945. Ten million people left their land in search of food. Over nine hundred thousand families sold off their land holdings, and 50 to 80 percent of small landholders and sharecroppers sold off their plough cattle. Potters, basket weavers, and people from fishing communities fared even worse and were the first to lose the tools of their trade.[31] These losses to the rural poor meant that 40 percent of the population in rural areas became landless as a result of the famine. Middle and large landholders (called *jotedars* and *zamindars*, respectively) gained in all of these transactions, with the jotedars who lived in rural areas and also acted as moneylenders reaping the largest share of the spoils.[32] Even after the immediate food shortage subsided in 1944, the devastation continued for those people stripped of the tools of their livelihood and their land.

During the famine, peasant women faced a complete reordering of daily life as the ideologies of hierarchical care that supported the status quo in rural areas lay in tatters.[33] The famine, in the context of the war and heightened nationalist movement, also undermined women's long-standing social constraints like purdah and other forms of women's seclusion from public life. Men abandoned or migrated away from their families in search of work first. They were also among the first to die of malnutrition. Women who lost their husbands and extended families had to seek food and work for themselves and their children. During the war, the greatest call for women's work was sex work to service the men in the military along the India-Burma front and construction work to maintain roads and infrastructure for the military.[34] Mostly poor Muslim and Dalit (oppressed caste) peasant women migrated to cities, like Comilla, Chittagong, and Kolkata, and entered brothels or worked off the streets. There is no record of whether any of these women were able to return to their localities when the famine subsided two years later. However, records of MARS and AIWC campaigns for dispossessed women's work training and homes documented the widespread displacement of women from their original families well after the famine ended.[35]

In May 1942, leftist women's groups created the coalitional Mahila Atma Raksha Samiti as a mass women's group to lead the fight against fascism, colonialism, and deprivation. In part, it formed in response to a Soviet-led appeal in September 1941 to unite women internationally against fascism.[36] Its members were largely middle class, came from a range of political parties, and numbered roughly two thousand. MARS activists had already begun organizing among women in Kolkata's slums when the first famine victims reached the cities of Bengal late in 1942. By early 1943, communist and noncommunist members of MARS fanned out from the cities to provide food relief and build shelters for dispossessed women and children in the countryside. By 1944, just two years later, MARS had 43,500 members, including many rural women, quickly becoming the largest peasant women's group in India.[37] It led a coalitional campaign that linked rural organizing by communist and nationalist women in a united effort to fight starvation and sex trafficking of dispossessed women and girls. They investigated women's reports of rape in peasant insurgencies against Indian landlords and British colonial officials. Additionally, they sought restitution of women into work and homes to provide new lives for women pushed into unpaid or low-paid sex work by the famine. Their organizing methods allowed leftist women's groups to build a mass movement of peasant and working-poor women.

The name Mahila Atma Raksha Samiti, or the Women's Self-Defense Committee, held complicated echoes of anticolonial and communal movements of the early twentieth century. "Self-defense" in these movements could signify religiously bigoted and sexist assumptions.[38] The targets of violent self-defense were often Muslims. Hindu men defended Hindu women's honor from Muslim men. Self-defense as deployed by nationalists sought an independent India defended by its Indian citizens. For nationalist feminists, Indian women were part of its defending citizenry. In the context of leftist feminist groups of the early 1940s, "self-defense" had a nationalist resonance but included another meaning, that of women actively defending their own rights and lives. Yet the complicated politics of honor in relation to sexualized violence against women and self-defense by women instigated the new political forms and strategies fostered by MARS during the famine and after.

The Soviet internationalist call for women's antifascist groups echoed a demand for the self-defense of women's honor by women. The English-language pamphlet "To Women the World Over" carried speeches from the women's antifascist conference held in Moscow filled with gruesome stories of German soldiers' rape of girls and women in Germany and on the battlefronts in Hungary and the Soviet Union.[39] Conference speakers described German soldiers' actions using the terms of women's sexual honor: "These villains have not only dishonored hundreds of thousands of women and girls; they have even infected them with foul diseases. How many Polish and Serbian women and girls they have driven into brothels; how many lives they have ruined; for many suicides they have caused in Poland, which they have drenched with blood!"[40] In the Indian context, the self-defense of women's honor shifted to the meaning implied by the intended audience of the Soviet pamphlet "women the world over"—that is, women's defense of their own honor against rape and sexual violence by a fascist enemy. Yet the earlier masculinist echoes of passive women "dishonored" by acts of wartime rape remain in the call to action. The verb "dishonor" as a synonym for rape locates the violent act of rape through its *effect* on the bodies of women raped. "Dishonor" does not apply to the men who raped. The abjection caused by rape and forced prostitution, however, is for women to avenge.

Historian Soma Marik's interviews with communist women leaders from this time add another facet to women's fight for social, or class-based goals. "The demand for women's self-defense was posed as a part of the defense against fascism. As Bani Dasgupta's interview makes clear, women also had to learn to fend for themselves and self-defense was linked to social goals. Notwithstanding persistent talks about honor, the crucial shift was in the insistence that women had to learn to fend for themselves and this defense was linked to 'social' (class) goals."[41] Marik emphasizes a radical shift away from two primary discursive fields of women's defense. First, it departed from the communalist "defense of women" discourse that mobilized a vulnerable and inert Hindu woman who needed to be defended from Muslim attack. It also broke from an emerging discourse of social reform movements and nationalism that articulated a secular woman who acted within a masculinist protective state. Self-defense in the communist discursive frame provided the women the independence necessary to achieve the greater ends of class struggle. "Women standing straight" in the leftist discourse of women's self-defense did not simply protect the honor of their community or nation-state; rather, independence allowed them to fight for greater class and social goals.[42]

Women's self-defense invoked a radical call to action, and MARS combined its internationalism and nationalism with local campaigns for women's self-defense. Antifascist solidarity with their nationalist and secularist campaign for the release of Indian independence leaders formed the backbone of their educational work among poor women. But these larger goals needed the traction of successful local reforms to better people's daily lives. In these first months, members focused their work in Kolkata to facilitate the fair distribution of subsidized food and cloth. Manikuntala Sen, a member of the CPI since the late 1930s, was a founding member of MARS. She recounted touring Bengal at this time "preaching anti-fascism, making speeches, and establishing *mahila samitis* (women's groups)."[43] Most MARS members, however, did not tour Bengal and had little contact with rural women. The MARS groups established in the countryside were few and isolated, mainly linked to locations in northern and eastern Bengal that had *nari samitis* (women's groups) that were part of active communist and peasant organizing efforts. The famine that spread across Bengal in the early months of 1943 changed MARS completely.

In the first months of MARS, members like Manikuntala Sen, Ela Reid, and Renu Chakravartty ran self-defense and first-aid classes for middle-class urban women to prepare for a military attack on the city. Their international antifascist demand sought the defense of India from attack by fascist military forces, a daunting task since the most highly trained Indian troops were stationed in the Mediterranean, with troops in Bengal almost wholly underresourced by the British, who feared an internal uprising.[44] Japanese forces occupied Burma in 1942, amassed their forces along the border with Bengal, and began bombing raids of Kolkata and the Bengali countryside the same year. The Arakan front, as the border between India and Burma was called, made Bengal the station for hundreds of thousands of troops from Australia, England, North Africa, and India who had no modern weaponry and little training.[45] British fears that if effective weapons were brought into India, those weapons would be used against them took precedence over the threat of invasion by the Japanese.[46] American and Chinese forces joined the battle after the Japanese successes in Burma, and US troops built a military infrastructure within Bengal.

MARS and its coalition partners demanded the release of imprisoned Indian independence activists, many of whom were national leaders from the major anti-colonial political parties. Alongside many other Indian parties and organizations, they argued that these imprisoned leaders were needed to lead India's self-defense against fascist aggression. Manikuntala Sen recounted the importance of anti-communalism, the support for a polity that gave minority religions in India equal access to rights and dignity, to their national platform. They sought the "uniting [of] the Hindus and the Muslims and people of all denominations, the Congress, the non-Congress, for the prisoners' release campaign."[47] To demand the release of all political prisoners imagined an independent Indian nation that was both secular and multireligious.

By the beginning of 1943, the conditions of the Bengal famine worsened. MARS's objectives had morphed into what Renu Chakravartty, another communist founder of MARS, defined as "defense of the people from starvation and death."[48] Manikuntala Sen described the work by MARS members in Kolkata:

> Dividing time into shifts, some of us would stay near the queues. Procurers from the sex trade would hover around young women who had to be safeguarded. Some women would give birth while they waited and they would have to be looked after. Sometimes a woman would remain in the queue with a dead child in her lap, refusing to let go of her place; there were many such incredible sights. Day and night, our workers didn't have a spare moment.[49]

Large landowners hoarded grain as prices for rice and wheat tripled and quadrupled in the almost empty markets. The Japanese occupation of Burma shut down Burma's rice exports to neighboring countries. In 1941, Bengal imported 296,000 tons of rice, yet by 1942 the flow had reversed to an exported 185,000 tons of rice.[50] The reason for rice shortages in Bengal was twofold. First, they did not have access to the usual suppliers of imported rice, and second, during the war the British diverted Bengal's rice to its troops. The British government bought up food staples across Bengal at sharply higher prices to feed to soldiers along the frontlines of India, and exported the rest to troops around the world. The famine gained international coverage by the summer of 1943, when the British-controlled press finally began to report on the crisis. "Mass of Walking Skeletons; Conditions in Rural Bengal," read one early headline on the front page of the *Hindustan Times*.[51] Still, Churchill turned down relief food supplies offered from the United States, citing the dangerous waters in the Bay of Bengal. His response to a plea from the government in Delhi for food supplies was to ask why Gandhi hadn't died yet.[52]

During the famine, middle-class MARS activists in the countryside felt first-hand the long-standing sexual vulnerability of rural, landless, *adivasi* (indigenous), and Dalit women at the hands of jotedar and zamindar landholders.[53] MARS led the fight against widespread trafficking of women and children mostly as sex workers for the military, large landholders, and moneylenders. MARS, alongside the AIWC and other allied women's groups, sought the criminalization of trafficking and fought for women's self-sufficiency through jobs and housing for trafficked women.[54] Through these goals, MARS leaders sought to build self-respect, economic self-sufficiency, and even social respect for trafficked women. They countered the dominant terms of middle-class charity and short-term government relief. In the process, they created networks of rural women organizers where few had existed before.

Rural MARS groups took up the crises of the colonial power's exploitative and neglectful governance. They started canteens for the starving and homes for destitute women and children, providing relief with their social reformist and nationalist feminist allies. MARS also built the sinews for a rural mass movement of peasant women. They held organizing schools for middle-class and peasant women that lasted from a week to a month to train new members about how to hold regular meetings, form demands, and run campaigns.[55] Antifascism among peasant women during the war in Bengal and Burma along the Arakan front meant a fight against the traffickers of women, often landholders and moneylenders, as well as the hundreds of thousands of Allied soldiers stationed in Bengal.[56] Members of MARS held an open rally in May 1944 that demanded "stringent measures for punishing those who traded in women's flesh and also measures for the rehabilitation of such women in society."[57] Kanak Mukherjee, a communist and founding member of MARS, traveled the breadth of rural Bengal and wrote frequently about peasant women during the famine. In 1944, she raised the alarm when the paltry government food and work relief ended almost as soon as it began. Her article, "Our Famine-Homeless Sisters' Plight: Bengal Government's Work Houses Closing Down," reported that the government workhouses were merely food relief kitchens serving food rather than providing work training to women.[58] She emphasized the real demand of jobs for the 6.5 million displaced and starving peasant women.

On January 6, 1945, MARS convened a coalition meeting to end women's prostitution due to famine conditions. They partnered with the AIWC and ten additional women's organizations. Nationalist feminists used starkly different language from leftist feminists. Sarojini Naidu spoke to the meeting using the unambiguous language of women's honor. "As long as one woman is defiled, as long as a man's lust devours another woman, as long as the stronger sex has the power to get hold of hundreds of shelterless women in their clutches, no woman's honor is safe."[59] The strongly moral tones of women's weakness and vulnerability in Naidu's speech reframed common notions of women's honor by focusing on the actions of men who "defiled" and "devoured" women. While women's honor should be kept safe, Naidu argued, she did not use the loss of honor to indelibly mark the women themselves as outside moral and social redemption. Naidu sought to arouse national sympathy for women who turned themselves and their children to sex work during the famine and to place the onus of shame on the men who exploited their vulnerability. Her condemnation of starving women's turn to sex work, however, still used the dominant framework of shame and honor.

Leftist feminists deployed language of a gendered political economy to describe women's famine-based sex work. In December 1945, at the AIWC national conference, Renu Chakravartty submitted her report about the new, endemic quality of trafficking in Bengal after the famine. She listed "economic stress and food shortage" as a primary reason for husbands selling their wives to traffickers and women selling themselves. She added two additional factors rarely mentioned in mainstream reports about the vast increase in prostitution. "A large percentage of the peasantry sold their lands and the poorest classes sold their implements of production, such as fishing nets, handlooms etc. in order to buy food, and were therefore left without any means or equipment for earning their livelihood."[60] She provided a materialist analysis of those who turned to sex work for survival. Dalit and adivasi women relied on fishing, handicrafts, and sharecropping, working in conditions of the greatest insecurity for the lowest wages. She ended by explaining, "The presence of a large army always tends to encourage immoral traffic."[61] She gave three suggestions for the AIWC's future work: first, create places to rebuild the tools of trade, such as looms and fishing nets; second, gather information about and prosecute abuses in government-run homes; and, third, demand the "enactment of a law by which traffickers can be promptly and heavily punished."[62] Strikingly, in this report she did not attempt to explain or excuse women's actions but rather explained the social and political context for those actions. Even in her use of "immoral traffic," a common term about women's sexual honor, Chakravartty referred to sex trafficking of women rather than women's sex work. Women's economic self-sufficiency was a key demand in the MARS campaign against sex trafficking. They sought women's access to paid work other than sex work, primarily through home-based labor in the handicraft industry—a goal that supported notions of women's honor.[63]

Women's honor and their loss of honor was deemphasized through these framings, even as they displaced women as actors securing their own futures. "Poor peasant women," wrote oral historian Adrienne Cooper, "were involved with MARS generally as recipients of charity or mobilized to support the *kisan sabhas* in demonstrations or at meetings. . . . Most women faced opposition from family, village or community for even minor involvement in such activities, because in itself this challenged women's traditional roles."[64] MARS's campaigns for economic independence still centered rural women in nationalist women's movements during the famine. Yet the MARS conference statement in 1944 demanded no less than their full participation: "To stop the rot in society and to re-establish the shelterless and destitute women in social life is one of the prime tasks in defense of the dignity of the women of Bengal."[65]

Communists in the AIWC and the Cold War

The end of the Second World War in the colonies of Europe and Japan did not ease Asian battles. The British, Australian, North African, and American troops stationed in Bengal since 1942 mostly departed by 1946. Indian "self-defense" groups during the Second World War solidified into an overwhelming resistance to British colonialism. Even the British knew their colonial control of India was over. For a brief window, the communists and anticolonial nationalist women's movement in

India stood politically united, but their ties were strained over whether the masses of Indian women should actively join an independent nation-state. The dominant Indian Congress Party and to a lesser degree the Muslim League refused to cede meaningful power to the largely illiterate rural masses of people or their demands. Abani Lahiri was a central peasant organizer during the Tebhaga movement and a Communist Party member. He remarked in his memoir that "the influence of feudal elements on the national movement in our country not only failed to attract the peasants to the common national platform, it pushed them away."[66]

When British-controlled troops moved from India to fight the communist-led, anticolonial insurgency in Malaya, ties of pan-Asian solidarity gained traction. The AIWC's journal *Roshni* published an appeal by the Singapore Women's Federation seeking pan-Asian solidarity in their shared anticolonial struggles. It began, "The people of India and Malaya have suffered severe oppression and are fighting for the ideals of human dignity and political liberty. We have to join hands together to break the chain of oppression and to be able to effectuate our ideals on a brighter road."[67] The anticolonial women's movement in India was a fierce, vocal, and united force against Indian troops fighting to maintain imperial rule in Asia. They also stood firmly against the Indian colonial forces that provided military support to the Dutch in Indonesia and the French in Vietnam. Colonial imperialism was the enemy of anticolonial nationalist movements, and they framed this enemy as a fascist ideological force.

For the antifascist united front of MARS and the leftist women's movement in Asia more widely, the pan-Asian women's movement strengthened an anti-imperialist alliance with women's groups in Europe, the United States, and the USSR through a common rejection of fascism.[68] Leftist and anticolonial women's groups celebrated the inauguration of the WIDF in Paris, France, at the end of 1945. Four women from the Indian women's movement attended this opening conference: Vidya Kanuga (later known as Vidya Munsi), a member of the All India Students Federation who later joined the Communist Party; Ela Reid, a politically nonaffiliated American woman who was a founding member of MARS; Jai Kishore Handoo, a member of the Women's Committee of India League in London (affiliated with the Congress Party) authorized to represent the AIWC; and Roshan Barber from the India League's London Office.

In particular, Reid and Handoo fought to widen the ethics of antifascism at the meeting to include the ongoing struggles against colonialism. Handoo addressed European women directly in the discussions "to mobilize public opinion in favor of freedom and democracy, and to proclaim your desire to see established in all colonial countries, especially in India . . . personally struggling, suffering imprisonment, machine gun fire by air, whipping and other humiliations too numerous to enumerate here."[69] The fall of Germany, Italy, and Japan in 1945 did not herald the defeat of fascism, Indian delegates argued. Fascism lived in the imperial subjugation of peoples across the globe. After debate among participants, WIDF members agreed to condemn imperialism as a founding tenet.

Avabai Mehta celebrated the WIDF's embrace of anticolonialism in "International Contacts of the AIWC," written for the AIWC's journal *Roshni*. She contrasted the 1945 board meeting held by the International Alliance of Women

(IAW) to the WIDF's founding meeting unfavorably due to the IAW's "timidity to endorse the AIWC resolution for the liberation of all peoples of the world."[70] Handoo was also the AIWC's representative at the IAW conference held in Geneva, Switzerland. Kamaladevi Chattopadhyay wrote a letter that clearly stated the AIWC position: "A termination of the war will not bring peace unless it leads to the abolition of imperialism and liberates all enslaved countries including India."[71] Yet even with Chattopadhyay's written endorsement to IAW leadership, Handoo failed to gain an explicit condemnation of colonialism. In the face of this intransigence, the AIWC still faced pressure from the IAW to repudiate leftist international groups, particularly the WIDF.

The president of the IAW, Margaret Corbett Ashby, also attended the founding conference of the WIDF in 1945. In a typed note she judged the conference "a disappointment because the communists over-played their hand."[72] She wrote a deeply unfavorable assessment of the conference, a copy of which she sent to Hansa Mehta as the president of the AIWC. Ashby argued that the WIDF's conference focus on antifascism produced a fleeting united front among the delegates from over thirty-five countries. "If you are flattened under an immense weight, unable to move or speak and past breathing, and then some large person removes the weight, grips your arm, stands you on your feet and with still fast grip walks you along, you are only conscious of freedom and release."[73] She predicted a swift end to this unity created by the fear of fascism's resurgence once their gratitude to the Soviet Union's Red Army abated. To the IAW chapters and groups affiliated with the IAW, she advocated a strategic solidarity. "I suggest that the alliance must continue as a feminist organization on friendly terms with this new organization which has reached masses of women we failed to arouse."[74] While not a mass organization, the AIWC was one anticolonial women's group publicly unimpressed with the IAW position on colonialism. Nevertheless, AIWC maintained old ties with the alliance and also sent delegates to WIDF meetings for two years.

Ashby waited less than a year after the 1945 Geneva board meeting to invite Mehta to join the IAW's executive committee. Her goal was the same: to reach out to, in her words, the "masses of women we failed to arouse." In a handwritten letter addressed to Mehta, Ashby wrote of Mehta's importance as the IAW attempted to build a constellation of pan-Asian women's support, using an oblique reference to women's centrality in the same anticolonial movements the IAW refused to support. "We do need you badly to keep us in touch not only with India but also with the other countries of Asia where the women are becoming increasingly aware of their citizen responsibilities."[75] Ashby was more blunt about her need for an Asian leader in the women's movement to advocate for the IAW across Asia. She wrote, "We do feel it would be of far greater influence if you could sign letters asking the women's associations to join up rather than if they get only Dr. Rydh's signature or mine."[76] Francisca de Haan has reminded scholars of the anticommunist stakes of international organizations like the IAW in the Cold War.[77] Rather than being politically neutral, the IAW saw its role as shaping the wider international women's movement toward Euro-American capitalist interests and away from communist ones.

The anticommunism within the AIWC, however, did not mirror the IAW's, which refused to condemn colonialism after the war ended. Instead, communist women in the AIWC forged a political platform that was too confrontational of elitist positions within the Indian women's movement within the Indian nationalist movement. The distrust of communism in the AIWC was not simply about abstract principles, nor was it uniform. For example, communist members such as Romesh Perin Chandra in the Punjab, as well as Renu Chakravartty in Bengal and Hajrah Begum Ahmad in Uttar Pradesh, worked alongside noncommunist women to found regional leftist yet politically nonaffiliated united front groups such as MARS and the Women's Self-Defense League of Punjab. Even as they organized regional antifascist women's groups, they continued to work actively to organize women into the AIWC and to tie the AIWC to area relief work. One rare example of the linkages between these groups occurred in 1944. Rameshwari Nehru, who was also the first cousin of India's first prime minister, Jawaharlal Nehru, gave her support to the Women's Self-Defense League of Punjab, which had one thousand working-class and peasant members and politics much closer to those of MARS in Bengal, to merge with AIWC.[78] In Punjab, at least, the leadership of the AIWC was not threatened by including working-class and peasant women as equal members of the organization.

Sometimes the activities of regional leftist women's groups overlapped in contentious ways with the AIWC. During the early months of 1947, a flurry of antagonistic letters by Kalpana Datta Joshi, a prominent member of the CPI, and Nellie Sen Gupta, a powerful member of the Congress Party and first president of MARS, were sent from Chittagong in the eastern part of Bengal to Indira Maydeo, the general secretary of the AIWC. Between March and July 1947, Joshi and Gupta debated whether Joshi's leadership of the AIWC could be distinguished from her work in MARS and the Communist Party.[79] By the end of the year, a letter from Nellie Sen Gupta and Asoka Gupta settled the matter, and Joshi was out. They took over as the new AIWC leaders of the renamed Chattagram Sahar Nari Sammelan branch.[80] Joshi left the AIWC soon afterward to concentrate on organizing women into MARS, the CPI, and the peasant movement.

The debate over the role of communist women in the AIWC became increasingly virulent as India's independence neared. In January 1946, an office holder and member of the Standing Committee from New Delhi named Kitty Shiva Rao wrote to Raj Kumari Amrit Kaur, a revered figure in the Congress Party and former president of the AIWC. Rao sent a copy of the letter to Hansa Mehta as the AIWC's current president. "The reason why I am writing this letter to you is, that I feel extremely disturbed and apprehensive with regard to the trend of things in the Conference concerning the Communist problem," she wrote.[81] She described her particular discomfort with Hajrah Begum's role as editor of the AIWC's Hindi-Urdu magazine, *Roshni*. "However many promises these people may give, surely their first loyalty is to their party and a magazine must be a sore temptation for propaganda purposes."[82]

Women like Hajrah Begum Ahmad, who was a long-term office holder for the AIWC and a member of the Communist Party, destabilized the founding tenets of the AIWC as a social reform organization. Hajrah Begum and other communist members pushed the AIWC to confront abuses by princely powers like the Nizam of Hyderabad and large landholding zamindars. They sought to sharpen the AIWC's class politics in favor of the poor and working class, not simply to highlight the group's nationalist bona fides. As editor of *Roshni*, Ahmad published accounts of peasant and working-class campaigns against large landholders and princes in states like Andhra, Maharashtra, Bengal, and the Punjab. However, these reports could not be used to depose Hajrah Begum as editor, though her open support and involvement raised Rao's hackles.

In the AIWC, support for poor women's movements congealed in the campaign to widen the group's membership by lowering dues so that all women could join. Only a few weeks before Rao's letter, Hansa Mehta was included in a conversation as the incoming president of the AIWC by Dr. K. Atchamamba. Atchamamba was a communist member of the AIWC who organized an AIWC club with twenty-five thousand members in Bezwada, Andhra. She addressed her letter to Kulsum Sayani, the general secretary of the AIWC. Atchamamba wrote, "We appreciate what you say regarding the enrolment of new members to our Sandham on the present basis. . . . But unfortunately there is no change in the attitude of Srimati Konda Parvati. She is still of the view that our Sangham is not affiliated in spite of the resolution of the S. C. [Standing Committee]."[83] The large number of new members enrolled by communists threatened the old order within the AIWC. These women were largely illiterate and poor, drawn into the nationalist cause through regional issues of exploitation around land and livelihood.

Atchamamba directly answered the anticommunism of Parvati's refusal to admit the group into the AIWC. "Our anxiety is not to 'capture' any organization, or even secure any positions or offices in any of the committees," she wrote. "We are anxious to work as a part of the All-India and the Provincial organization which is necessary for building up a strong all-India-wide women's organization."[84] Atchamamba reiterated the importance of a secular united front that the AIWC represented in the eyes of communist women. They organized as communists and focused their work among middle-class, working-class, and rural women. They sought to widen the AIWC's mission to be for all women of India, not just an elite few. Yet communist women also knew that admitting large numbers of peasant and working-class women would change the character and content of the AIWC's politics. Kitty Rao's description of this membership fight in the state of Andhra does not directly mention the Nizam of Hyderabad, nor his use of rape, burnings, and violent intimidation against the people under his control. Instead, Rao focuses on the number of women who joined the AIWC unit. "The first number mentioned, I believe, was 19,000, then it came to 10,000 and when the Sural S. C. questioned this figure they finally enrolled 2,500."[85] In Rao's telling of the membership struggle, those numbers were evidence that communists had taken over the AIWC. The loss of more open membership policies became a turning point for most of the group's leftist members.

Hajrah Begum remembered the conflict in blunt terms. AIWC members, she said, "did not care for the common people."[86] Manikuntala Sen in her memoir gave another reason for the closed doors of the AIWC. "They thought that if we opened the association to ordinary women, their leadership would be threatened, and were suspicious that perhaps we would try to turn the association into a Communist one."[87] The mass politics of communism was embedded in debates about increasing or limiting the number of members in the AIWC since its communist members actively pushed for lower dues and more members. Those numbers, whether of dues or of members, implicitly raised much more substantive issues of poor women's politics. Fairer wages, child care, access to property, dowry eradication, and the right to better lives were all communist issues in the 1940s; they were also largely peasant women's issues.

Hansa Mehta's measured response to Rao urged her to watch Hajrah Begum's actions as the *Roshni* editor, and only to remove her from the post if she put what Mehta called "objectionable materials" into the magazine. She also reiterated her commitment to an inclusive AIWC:

> We must have faith in our colleagues until they have betrayed it. The AIWC is neither for the Congress women nor for the Communists. We wish to unite all women on certain common issues viz on problems that affect women, their status and position in society. I believe the time has come when we must define it clearly. I would, therefore, not like the AIWC to be made into a political cock pit and forget the real issue.[88]

During the tumultuous year of her presidency, Mehta persevered in her assessment. Her advice to the incoming president, Dhavanti Rama Rao, in her speech at the AIWC conference held in December 1946 reiterated her advice: "The duty of our movement," she said, "is to unite the women of India, and through them the women of the world. . . . I hope our new President will see that this our little boat does not founder on the rocks of this party or that party, that it does not founder on the rocks of disunity; I hope this Conference will remain a uniting force and show what the women of the world can do to bring about peace and unity."[89]

The symbolic issue was the cost of AIWC membership—but the symbolism held a real significance.[90] With more affordable dues, the AIWC could become a mass-based rather than an elite women's organization. In December 1945, at the Hyderabad conference, the AIWC finally endorsed the independence movement in India and anticolonial movements around the world.[91] State feminists and communist women gained a long-shared goal in shifting the organization toward an overtly political stance. Yet the class character of these politics was not wholly aligned. By early 1947, the AIWC decided to sever all ties to the WIDF. According to Hajrah Begum, AIWC's leadership worried that joining the WIDF would "support world communist women's movement. So they did not agree, then we decided to affiliate on our own."[92] The AIWC's turn away from a mass-based, peasant women's movement was not absolute. In April 1947, Kamaladevi Chattopadhyay published an article in *Roshni* that said the AIWC must "build membership among rural, peasant and poor women," and "rebuild society, not focus on preventive measures."[93]

Anticommunism solidified within the AIWC by 1948, though its own reckoning of this shift is ambivalent. An editorial in *Roshni* described the turn somberly: "Three months ago provincial governments started the roundup of communist workers and although some of them were our members we deliberately did not comment on the governments' action as we were not aware of the full scope of their complicity in subversive actions, especially these days when anything which threatens the stability of our administration has to be viewed very seriously indeed."[94] The alliance between leftist and nationalist members within the AIWC faced an abrupt end even before India's formal independence. The conflict cannot be framed abstractly as communism versus nationalism, however. Instead, the coalitional politics within the big tent of the AIWC shattered over the admission of working-class and peasant women as activists on their own terms. The class politics of gender, rather than capitalism versus socialism, split the organization's cross-political unity. MARS joined the leftist internationalist group WIDF, and the AIWC ultimately joined the IAW. In international Cold War terms, their politics were oppositional—communist versus anticommunist—but their history of overlapping membership and political collaboration in the anticolonial movement tell a more complicated story.

Peasant Women's Subjectivity and the Tebhaga Movement, 1946–1947

The archival traces of peasant women's organizing in India are relatively scant: eyewitness accounts by sympathizers and activists, interviews, secondhand reports, movement songs, and the few demands that remain in the public record. Peasant women's militancy in the eastern state of Bengal was only one epicenter of the radical peasant women's movement in India. The activism of Bengali peasant women gained coherence and visibility during the Tebhaga fight (a name that translates to "Two-Thirds"), which lasted for a little over two years between 1946 and 1948 on the cusp of Indian independence.[95] The Tebhaga movement refers to the farmers' central demand: that sharecroppers and tenant farmers should own a greater share of their crops—that is, two-thirds instead of the customary one-half (or less). Peasant women who were involved in Tebhaga struggles across Bengal are remembered as the most daring activists; they were frequently shot, beaten, or raped for their militancy.[96] In the autonomous, peasant-controlled zones of Bengal that emerged during Tebhaga, these women also sought equality within their relationships with peasant men through demands for shared access to land, wages, and crops harvested, and for the right to familial relationships free from violence.[97] As yet, we have no histories that explore how peasant women's activism in Bengal shifted so radically over the ten years between 1936 and 1946. We do have testimonies about social changes toward greater gender equity wrought by their activism during Tebhaga.[98]

In Bengal, the AIWC-supported and MARS-run campaign against sex trafficking in the context of the Bengal famine portended the ripple effects in cultural and political movements to come. Perhaps most well-known in the radical politics of postwar Bengal, the Tebhaga movement emerged on the heels of the Bengal famine. Procommunist peasant activists, large numbers of them women, fought to keep two-thirds rather than only one-half of the grain crop for tenants and sharecroppers who worked the land. One enthusiastic observer, a Kolkata university student named Somnath Hore, recounted a speech by a peasant organizer named Dinesha. "No use creeping into your shells like tortoises every time you see a rich man. Start walking with your heads held high. The rich say that we are dancing like whores to the refrains of tebhaga. What I want to know is, who made whores of us anyway? And having turned us into whores, why does it hurt them to see us dance? Let the rich say what they want, we are going to harvest the rice and have the tebhaga."[99] Dinesha's recounted speech rejects the usual language of a woman's and her community's dishonor embodied by the whore. Instead, the whore embodies a consequence of power relations that beggars the many in the interests of the powerful few. His speech usurps the image of the dance girl's performance as a prostituted form of entertainment, one bought and paid for by rich men. "Why," he asks rhetorically, "does it hurt them to see us dance?" He turns the common sexualized and misogynist slur of feminizing anticommunism on its head. The peasants' dance is the dance of revolutionary change, one that tramples on traditions of rural power. Rather than accepting the normative relations of hierarchy and control, the dance girl is the peasant rebel who must dance to change the system. Dishonor and the embodied vulnerability of womanhood could now be configured as a weapon for the Tebhaga movement rather than being solely a source of shame or dishonor for women and their communities.

This story about a speech given during the Tebhaga movement in Dinajpur, one of its most militant localities in Bengal, allows a glimpse into how radically social mores for women's behavior were changing after the end of the Second World War, after the abatement of the Bengal famine and on the cusp of the Cold War between the Soviet Union and Euro-America. Adrienne Cooper collected an impressive number of interviews with women and men active in the Tebhaga movement during the 1980s. She noted a sea change in peasant women's organizing before and after the famine—from a relative passivity in MARS campaigns to the frontlines of the Tebhaga struggle. "At *tebhaga* meetings, women were encouraged to participate in the movement. . . . Poor peasant women participated in meetings and demonstrations, were in delegations to landlords and occasionally members of *tebhaga* committees. . . . However, women's militancy was remembered mostly because of their actions to resist arrests, when they displayed incredible courage, initiative and heroism in rescuing people."[100] In this context, the demands by women active in autonomous peasant zones called *tebhaga elaka* that emerged from *tebhaga* antilandlord struggles gain clarity. Women used social boycotts to punish violent men and to demand an equal share of their crops.

A leading communist organizer in the peasant movement, Albani Lahiri recounted in his memoir that the most active women during the Tebhaga movement came from adivasi and Dalit households—the same landless households hardest hit by the Bengal famine, the same women and girls most likely to be trafficked into the war-fueled sex industry.[101] Yet they were not alone as leaders; even some women from peasant families who owned small amounts of land participated actively in Tebhaga. Peasant women practiced courage in their fight against landowners and their homegrown armies. They became integral forces in a collectivity with other landless sharecroppers, tenants, and small landowning farmers, a radical formation in itself since it overturned respectability norms of gender segregation for women in public spaces. That women's roles have emerged in the record of Tebhaga, particularly their demands within their localities' gendered social orders and intimate relationships, is also remarkable. For peasant women's actions to gain historical visibility requires a cross-gender examination of normative gendered roles of leadership, honor, hierarchy, and respect. For peasant women, famine was not the precondition for their activism. Mass starvation itself did not foster the communist insistence on women's independent ability, in Dasgupta's words, to "stand straight." Instead, peasant women's self-defense against the political and social orders that produced and fueled the famine provided that necessary lesson.

Peasant women successfully resisted the British practices of punitive taxation on grain and land. They combated landowners' total control over landless and land-poor people's lives. They refused to cede their sexual and bodily autonomy to upper-caste men or their families. Marik notes a related transformation for middle-class activist women in MARS, "the mass recruitment during the famine and the transformation of the girls from women who had come forward for social welfare work into militant cadres."[102] Peasant women's activism did not mirror middle-class, urban women's experiences exactly. Their fight against sexual and economic exploitation faced different contours of power and privilege than those faced by middle-class women. Peasant women in the hot Cold War of Asia and Africa exposed the sexual politics of colonial and feudal complicity in the colonies. In no small part, they built women's pan-Asian, anti-imperialist solidarity through their collective refusal of these embodied systems of exploitation.

Notes

1. For regional examples, see Anthony Short, *The Communist Insurrection in Malaya, 1948–1960* (New York: Crane, Russak, 1975); Caroline Elkins, *Imperial Ambitions: The Untold Story of Britain's Gulag in Kenya* (New York: Henry Holt, 2005).

2. Carolien Stolte, "'Enough of the Great Napoleons!' Raja Mahendra Pratap's Pan-Asian projects (1929–1939)," *Modern Asian Studies* 46, no. 2 (2012): 403–23; Anna Belagurova, "The Chinese International of Nationalities: The Chinese Communist Party, the Comintern, and the foundation of the Malayan National Communist Party, 1923–1939," *Journal of Global History* 9 (2014): 447–70.

3. Gyanendra Pandey, *The Ascendancy of Congress in Uttar Pradesh: Class, Community and Nation in Northern India, 1920–1940* (London: Anthem, 1978); Ranajit Guha, *Elementary Aspects of Peasant Insurgency in Colonial India* (New Delhi: Oxford University Press, 1983); David Hardiman, *Peasant Nationalists of Gujarat, 1917–1934* (New Delhi: Oxford University Press, 1981).

4. In India, peasant women joined internationalist communist parties through anticasteist movements in the south and in Maharashtra, peasant movements in Andhra, Bengal, and Punjab, and leftist campaigns linked to the anticolonial women's movement.

5. See "Among Kisan Women," *People's War* 3, no. 46 (May 13, 1945): 2. This article detailed peasant women's participation in the AIKS conference in Netrakona, Bengal, April 7–9, 1945. Their leadership in the All India Kisan Sabha and even in the Bengal Provincial Kisan Sabha, however, was still negligible.

6. Aparna Basu and Bharati Ray, *Women's Struggle: A History of the All India Women's Conference, 1927–2002* (New Delhi: Manohar, 2003).

7. Cited in Renu Chakravartty, *Communists in the Indian Women's Movement, 1940–1950* (New Delhi: People's Publishing House, 1980), 70.

8. Ibid.

9. "Annual Report of the Member-in-charge of Social Section," Hansa Mehta papers, subject file 7, Nehru Memorial Museum and Library (hereafter NMML), New Delhi, India.

10. "18th Conference in Hyderabad," *Roshni* 1, no. 1 (February 1946): 21.

11. "Resolutions Passed by the Standing Committee of the All-India Women's Conference, at their meeting in Bombay on the 29th and 30th May 1943," Renuka Ray papers, folder 7, NMML.

12. Chakravartty, *Communists in the Indian Women's Movement*, 200.

13. Adrienne Cooper, *Sharecropping and Sharecroppers' Struggles in Bengal, 1930–1950* (Calcutta: K. P. Bagchi, 1988).

14. Peter Custers, *Women in the Tebhaga Uprising: Rural Poor Women and Revolutionary Leadership (1946–47)* (Calcutta: Naya Prokash, 1987), 22–25.

15. Elisabeth Armstrong, "Before Bandung: The Anti-Imperialist Women's Movement in Asia and the Women's International Democratic Federation," *Signs* 41, no. 2 (2016): 1–27.

16. Mrinalini Sinha, *Specters of Mother India: The Global Restructuring of an Empire.* (Durham, NC: Duke University Press, 2007).

17. Padma Anagol's study of Indian women's writing in Marathi journals shows that "nineteenth-century Indian feminists embraced and utilized the rhetoric of the 'civilizing mission' with alacrity." Padma Anagol, "Feminist Inheritances and Foremothers: The Beginnings of Feminism in Modern India," *Women's History Review* 19, no. 4 (September 2010): 533.

18. In the founding of Aligarh's premier women's college, then called the Muslim Girls' School and Hostel, the fight to create a girl's boarding school faced rumors that it taught music and dance to produce *nautch* girls for men's entertainment. See Rakhshanda Jalil, *A Rebel and Her Cause: The Life and Work of Rashid Jahan* (New Delhi: Women Unlimited, 2014), 17.

19. Kamala Chattopadhyay, "Some Reminiscences of the 1929 European Tour of the IAW in Berlin," n.d., Speeches and Writings, Kamala Chattopadhyay papers, NMML.

20. Jalil, *A Rebel and Her Cause*, 17.

21. Chattopadhyay, "Some Reminiscences."

22. Suruchi Thapar-Bjorkert, *Women in the National Movement: Unseen Faces, Unheard Voices, 1930–42* (New Delhi: Sage, 2006).

23. Radha Kumar, *The History of Doing: An Illustrated Account of Movements for Women's Rights and Feminism in India, 1800–1990* (New York: Verso, 1993), 68–69.

24. Sinha, *Specters of Mother India*.

25. Ibid., 155.

26. Ibid., 235.

27. Geraldine Forbes, *Women in Modern India* (Cambridge: Cambridge University Press, 1988). Kalpana Datta Joshi joined MARS in 1943 and was also an officeholder of AIWC in the 1940s.

28. Soma Marik, "Breaking through a Double Invisibility: The Communist Women of Bengal, 1939–1948," *Critical Asian Studies* 45, no. 1 (2013): 79–118.

29. Marik, "Breaking Through," 92.

30. Ibid.

31. Madhusree Mukerjee, *Churchill's Secret War: The British Empire and the Ravaging of India during World War II* (Chennai: Tranquebar, 2010), 66–67.

32. Cooper, *Sharecropping and Sharecroppers' Struggles in Bengal*, 133.

33. Asok Majumdar, *The Tebhaga Movement: Politics of Peasant Protest in Bengal, 1946–1950* (New Delhi: Aakhar, 2011), 225.

34. Yasmin Khan, "Sex in an Imperial War Zone: Transnational Encounters in Second World War India," *History Workshop Journal* 73, no. 1 (2012): 240–58.

35. Chakravartty, *Communists in the Indian Women's Movement*.

36. Gargi Chakravartty, "Emergence of Mahila Atma Raksha Samiti in the Forties—Calcutta Chapter," in *Calcutta: The Stormy Decades*, ed. Tanika Sarkar and Sekhar Bandyopadhyay (New Delhi: Social Science Press, 2015), 179.

37. Ibid.

38. Samita Sen, "Honor and Resistance: Gender, Community and Class in Bengal, 1920–40." in *Bengal: Communities, Development and States*, ed. Sekhar Bandyopadhyay, Ahijit Dasgupta, and Willem can Schendel (Delhi: Manohar, 1994), 209–54.

39. *To Women the World Over! Report of the Women's Anti-Fascist Meeting Held in Moscow on September 7, 1941* (Moscow: Foreign Languages Publishing House, 1941).

40. Ibid, 53–54.

41. Marik, "Breaking through a Double Invisibility," 103.

42. Ibid.

43. Manikuntala Sen, *In Search of Freedom: An Unfinished Journey* (Calcutta: Stree, 2001), 66.

44. Yasmin Khan, *The Raj at War: A People's History of India's Second World War* (Gurgaon, Haryana: Random House India, 2015).

45. Ibid.

46. Mukerjee, *Churchill's Secret War*, 59–61.

47. Sen, *In Search of Freedom*, 77.

48. Chakravartty, *Communists in the Indian Women's Movement*, 23.

49. Manikuntala, *In Search of Freedom*, 71.

50. Mukerjee, *Churchill's Secret War*, 68

51. "Mass of Walking Skeletons; Conditions in Rural Bengal," *Hindustan Times*, November 6, 1943.

52. Mukerjee, *Churchill's Secret War*, 235.

53. Majumdar, *Tebhaga Movement*, 224.

54. Chakravarty, "Emergence of Mahila Atma Raksha Samiti," 192.

55. Sunil Sen, *The Working Women and Popular Movements in Bengal from the Gandhi Era to the Present Day* (Calcutta: K. P. Bagchi, 1945), 31–33.

56. Chakravartty, *Communists in the Indian Women's Movement*, 41.

57. Ibid, 55.

58. Kanak Mukherjee, "Our Famine-Homeless Sisters' Plight: Bengal Government's Work Houses Closing Down," *People's War*, September 1944, 9.

59. Quoted in Chakravartty, *Communists in the Indian Women's Movement*, 69.

60. AIWC, "Annual Report of Member-in-Charge of Social Section, 1945," Hansa Mehta papers, subject file 7, NMML.

61. Ibid.

62. Ibid.

63. Cooper, *Sharecropping and Sharecroppers' Struggles in Bengal*, 270–72.

64. Ibid, 270.

65. Conference statement cited in Chakravartty, *Communists in the Indian Women's Movement*, 55.

66. Abani Lahiri, *Postwar Revolt of the Rural Poor in Bengal: Memoirs of a Communist Activist* (Calcutta: Seagull Books, 2001), 78.

67. "Singapore Women's Federation," *Roshni* 1, no. 5 (June 1946): 55.

68. Armstrong, "Before Bandung."

69. WIDF, *Congres International des Femmes*, WIDF Collection, Atria Institute on Gender Equality and Women's History, Amsterdam, Netherlands.

70. Avabai Mehta, "International Contacts of the AIWC," *Roshni* 1, no. 3 (April 1946): 49.

71. Quoted in the anonymous report, "18th Conference in Hyderabad," *Roshni* 1, no. 1 (February 1946): 28.

72. Margaret Corbett Ashby, "Report on Paris Conference, November 26th, 1945," Hansa Mehta Papers, subject file 7, NMML.

73. Ibid.

74. Ibid.

75. Letter to Hansa Mehta from Margaret Corbett Ashby, September 7, 1946, Hansa Mehta papers, subject file 6, NMML.

76. Ibid.

77. Francisca de Haan, "Continuing Cold War Paradigms in Western Historiography of Transnational Women's Organizations: The Case of the Women's International Democratic Women's Association," *Women's History Review* 19, no. 4 (2010): 547–73.

78. Hajrah Begum Ahmad interview, 1994, Oral History Project, NMML, New Delhi, India.

79. Letters to Indira Maydeo, general secretary of AIWC, from both Nellie Sen Gupta and Kalpana Joshi, March 15, 1947, July 26, 1947, and July 31, 1947, AIWC Branch reports, file 65, NMML.

80. Letter signed by Nellie Sen Gupta and Asoka Gupta, December 22, 1947, AIWC Branch reports, file 65, NMML.

81. Letter to Raj Kumari from Kitty Shiva Rao, January 3, 1946, Hansa Mehta papers, subject file 6, NMML.

82. Ibid.

83. Letter to Kulsum Sayani from K. Atchamamba, June 16, 1945, Hansa Mehta papers, subject file 7, NMML.

84. Ibid.

85. Ibid.

86. Hajrah Begum Ahmad interview, 1994, NMML.

87. Sen, *In Search of Freedom*, 56.

88. Letter to Kitty Shiva Rao from Hansa Mehta, January 16, 1946, Hansa Mehta papers, subject file 6, NMML.

89. Hansa Mehta, "Address by Mrs. Hansa Mehta on Handing over the Post of President to Lady Rama Rao at the Opening Session on Saturday, 28th December, 1946," Hansa Mehta papers, Second Installment, Speeches and Articles, 4, NMML.

90. Leftist members sought to lower dues from 3 rupees to 4 annas (one quarter of a rupee).

91. "All India Women's Conference Meets: Demands Immediate Indian Freedom," *People's War* 4, no. 31 (January 27, 1946): 10, 12.

92. Ahmad interview, 1994, NMML.

93. Kamaladevi Chattopadhyay, "The Task before the All India Women's Conference," *Roshni* 2, no. 3 (April 1947): 52.

94. "Civil Liberties in Danger," *Roshni* 3, no. 6 (July 1948): 3.

95. Custers, *Women in the Tebhaga Uprising*.

96. Lahiri, *Postwar Revolt of the Rural Poor in Bengal*.

97. Cooper, *Sharecropping and Sharecroppers' Struggles in Bengal*, 270–72; Majumdar, *Tebhaga Movement*, 224–25.
98. Sen, *The Working Women and Popular Movements in Bengal*, 41.
99. Somnath Hore, *Tebhaga: An Artist's Diary and Sketchbook*, trans. Somnath Zuthi (Calcutta: Seagull Books, 1990).
100. Cooper, *Sharecropping and Sharecroppers' Struggles in Bengal*, 270–71.
101. Lahiri, *Postwar Revolt of the Rural Poor in Bengal*.
102. Marik, "Breaking Through," 98.

References

Archives

Atria Institute on Gender Equality and Women's History, Amsterdam, Netherlands
Nehru Memorial Museum and Library, New Delhi, India

Periodicals

The Hindustan Times
People's War
Roshni

Selected Published Works

Armstrong, Elisabeth. "Before Bandung: The Anti-Imperialist Women's Movement in Asia and the Women's International Democratic Federation," *Signs* 41, no. 2 (2016): 1–27.

Cooper, Adrienne. *Sharecropping and Sharecroppers' Struggles in Bengal, 1930–1950.* Calcutta: K. P. Bagchi, 1988.

Chakravartty, Renu. *Communists in the Indian Women's Movement, 1940–1950.* New Delhi: People's Publishing, 1980.

Custers, Peter. *Women in the Tebhaga Uprising: Rural Poor Women and Revolutionary Leadership (1946–47).* Calcutta: Naya Prokash, 1987.

Lahiri, Abani. *Postwar Revolt of the Rural Poor in Bengal: Memoirs of a Communist Activist.* Calcutta: Seagull Books, 2001.

Majumdar, Asok. *The Tebhaga Movement: Politics of Peasant Protest in Bengal, 1946–1950.* New Delhi: Aakhar Books, 2011.

Marik, Soma. "Breaking through a Double Invisibility: The Communist Women of Bengal, 1939–1948." *Critical Asian Studies* 45, no. 1 (2013): 79–118.

Mukerjee, Madhusree. *Churchill's Secret War: The British Empire and the Ravaging of India during World War II.* Chennai: Tranquebar, 2010.

Sen, Manikuntala. *In Search of Freedom: An Unfinished Journey.* Calcutta: Stree, 2001.

Sinha, Mrinalini. *Specters of Mother India: The Global Restructuring of an Empire.* Durham, NC: Duke University Press, 2007.

CHAPTER 7

The Medicalization of Childhood in Mexico during the Early Cold War, 1945–1960

Nichole Sanders

While the shift from sentimental to scientific motherhood started before the Mexican Revolution (1910–1917), the role of science and, more importantly, the privileging of the medical and scientific role of motherhood over the social intensified after World War II. The historiography of Mexico has focused on this period as one of political and economic consolidation—historians and political scientists have called it "the Mexican Miracle." The Mexican economy grew on average 6 percent per annum, and the Partido Revolucionario Institucional (PRI) established itself as the dominant political party. Scholars have debated how much control the PRI actually exercised, and historians are now beginning to examine Mexico's role in the Cold War. Diplomatic historians of the Cold War in Latin America, until recently, largely focused on Cuba—the Cuban Revolution, the Bay of Pigs, and the Missile Crisis. They have also explored how US intervention in Latin American politics shaped the region geopolitically. Historians have examined the US-backed military coups in Guatemala and other countries in Central America as well as in Chile, Argentina, and Brazil.

More recently, labor and cultural historians have looked at the interplay between international and local politics, as well as the interaction of international politics with other domestic actors, to see what impact these actions have had on the daily lives of those who have lived through the events. While it is impossible to discount the rivalry between the USSR and the United States, these more recent works have shown that, oftentimes, local actors took advantage of Cold War foreign policy to further their own agendas. Mexico, however, is one country that is often overlooked in the historiography of Cold War Latin America. As historian Gilbert Joseph notes:

> The Mexican case not only points up oft-ignored, highly ambivalent relationships between Cold War allies but also showcases pivotal cultural and social issues, thereby moving the narrative away from its prevailing emphasis on diplomatic

confrontation and military intervention. That Mexico's experience has thus far received so little treatment in Cold War Studies is astonishing; not only is Mexico (with Brazil) one of Latin America's two "middle powers," but it is the southern neighbor of the hemisphere's Cold War hegemon.[1]

Scholars may have overlooked Mexico as a case study because of the complexities of Mexican-US relations. Mexico had always had a complicated relationship with its northern neighbor, and this relationship did not become any simpler after 1945. From the postrevolutionary controversies surrounding the Bucareli Treaty, to the expropriation of the oil industry, to post–World War II Mexican support of Guatemala's Arbenz administration and recognition of the Castro government, the postrevolutionary Mexican government often used foreign policy as a means to assert independence from US political and economic hegemony while formally remaining an ally of the United States. Yet at the same time the United States has been Mexico's largest trading partner, and the United States has always had substantial investments in the Mexican economy. And as Gilbert Joseph notes, the countries share a border surrounding which there have been historic tensions. Indeed, in many ways, US Cold War demands made ties even more difficult.

This chapter sheds light on the role that one Mexican government agency played during the Cold War, demonstrating how social welfare reformers interacted with the global maternal-child welfare community and how those interactions shaped Mexican social policy and influenced gender roles. Two major postwar entities promoted maternal-child health and welfare in Latin America—the Organization of American States (OAS), through the Pan American Child Congresses, and UNICEF. These agencies, shaped by US Cold War demands, shifted global maternal-child welfare policy toward medical interventions, rural health, and economic development within the context of the promotion of democracy. Mexican reformers, as an integral part of this community of reformers, implemented these policies in Mexico as well. We can see though an examination of these policies and their implementation in Mexico the interplay between the local context and the Cold War demands of international maternal-child welfare agencies. Mexican reformers applied these policies, especially the rural policies, to Mexico in order to modernize their country economically by promoting the health and welfare of children—what they considered to be the "wealth" of the country. Thus, domestic actors took advantage of global Cold War trends in order to further their own economic development goals—creating a rural export economy as well as reinforcing programs in urban areas to create what they considered to be ideal workers. For Mexican maternal-child welfare advocates, these programs had little to do with stopping communism or promoting democracy—the stated goals of the OAS in particular. Creating these programs, however, did give the Mexican government access to development funds for which they may not have otherwise been eligible. This chapter therefore highlights the interplay between local actors and larger transnational actors in the Cold War fight against communism. In the case of Mexico, one domestic agency was able to take advantage of international programs that were conceived to fight communism, using them to further their own goal of a modern Mexico.

One consequence of the adaptation of these programs was the erosion of women's political and social power.

Over the course of the twentieth century, children, globally as well as in Mexico, became increasingly important to the social welfare and reform community. In the 1930s, welfare advocates emphasized the "mother-child dyad" and put educational programs into place to train mothers in puericulture and other scientific child-raising techniques.[2] By the end of the 1940s, however, public health and welfare advocates began to shift discussions toward children and state-provided legal protections of children. The social role of mothers diminished. Mothers were still important, but their role became more strictly defined in a biomedical rather than public or social sense. They needed to receive prenatal and postnatal care, but the priority of such care was to preserve the health of the child. Mothers' role in educating and socializing their offspring diminished. Therefore, as the available medical interventions for children increased in the 1940s and 1950s, mothers played a less significant role in raising Mexico's children—a role that had been privileged in the late nineteenth and earlier twentieth century through the discourse of sentimental motherhood. If, under sentimental motherhood, a mother was seen as the primary and most important agent in a child's care and upbringing, scientific motherhood in Mexico saw children's care as a partnership between mothers and the state. As childhood became more and more scrutinized by the medical and welfare community, however, this relationship became more and more unequal. Mothers needed to receive appropriate medical care in order to produce healthy citizens, but the state's experts would make sure through state agencies that children were effectively raised. Increased medicalization of childhood, therefore, effectively depoliticized motherhood by negating the centrality of mothers to the rearing of Mexican children. Ironically, this happened as women got the vote in Mexico and more women of all classes entered the workforce.[3]

This chapter will examine how the increasing importance of children to the state and the transnational community simultaneously diminished women's social importance as mothers. Despite a long tradition of seeing mothers as integral to the education of future citizens, by the early Cold War mothers were seen as less necessary to the creation and rearing of future citizens. The Mexican state expanded welfare, education, and health services for children during this period and also increased programs that focused on maternal prenatal and postnatal care. By placing increased emphasis on the "child" part of the mother-child dyad, mothers became less essential to the national project. Reformers began to view childhood as its own category, with its own problems and "expert" solutions.

Sociologists Joseph Scheneider and Peter Conrad argue that "the effect of medicalizing public problems is their depoliticization. By removing the problems as ones on which honest and reasonable people might differ and in presenting one definition as inherently and 'really' preferential, the medicalization of social problems depoliticizes them and diminishes the recognition of moral choices that they represent."[4] Thus, the medicalization of childhood in Mexico served two purposes. Children became a separate medical category, though pediatrics, and a separate developmental category, through psychology. The monitoring of childhood therefore came under the purview of experts—doctors, social workers, and educators—

who were trained to interact and monitor this important social category.[5] Doctors, social workers, and teachers would provide the necessary education. All mothers really needed to do was submit to the medical community by visiting doctors for prenatal and postnatal care and by continuing to bring their children in for regular medical checkups.

Feminist groups had long argued that motherhood was key to gaining suffrage—that motherhood was the defining feature of women's citizenship.[6] This view saw women as guardian angels of the home, providing their children with the ideal home life and raising good future citizens. However, even as women gained the vote, their ability to argue that motherhood was political diminished. As women stepped onto the national political stage, the medical and reform community simultaneously moved to limit the social capital derived from their status as mothers. Mothers had to remain healthy and to help keep their children healthy, but mothers no longer held primacy in the education of their children. Mothers would work with the state, but the state, through its network of medical and social reformers, would take the lead. Maternal-child welfare advocates included doctors, nurses, social workers, and other health-care workers and volunteers. This chapter concentrates on the programs provided by the Secretaría de Salubridad y Asistencia (Secretary of Health and Welfare, or SSA) and the transnational rhetoric of the reform community through UNICEF and the Pan American Child Congresses (formally part of the OAS after 1948). While these were not the only organizations dedicated to maternal-child welfare, they can be seen as representative of the discourses promoted by other state agencies that worked with children.

Transnational Maternal-Child Health and Welfare

The two main postwar international influences on Mexican maternal-child welfare were the Pan American Child Congresses and UNICEF. The first Pan American Child Congress met in 1916 in Argentina. Physicians, nurses, social workers, teachers, feminists, and other child reform advocates attended these conferences, which, as historian Donna Guy has noted, often served as a way for the professionals in the host country to lobby for greater government spending for mothers and children.[7] Mexico hosted the seventh Pan American Child Conference in 1935, and, in order to begin implementing the reforms discussed, the Mexican government responded by creating the Secretary of Public Welfare in 1937, which merged with the Mexico City Department of Public Health in 1943 to become the Ministry of Health and Welfare.

These congresses were not without controversy before World War II. Early conferences had been principally organized by feminists, and the goals of these feminists were roundly critiqued by male physicians who believed that the organizers did not have any business discussing the health of children. Only with the participation of the American reformer Kathryn Lenroot did Latin American physicians begin to welcome professional women such as social workers and nurses. It was Katherine Lenroot and other women who pushed the conference in the 1920s and 1930s to think of child welfare in terms of the mother-child dyad. Social workers argued that the state should work in partnership with mothers to raise healthy and productive citizens. In contrast, the physicians argued for a biomedical approach to treating childhood disease. Male physicians were less inclined to view motherhood as having a social significance and saw the family as a unit being made healthy through the work of the male middle-class physician.[8]

In Mexico, the biomedical approach coexisted with a sociobiological approach through the 1940s, although the ascendancy of physicians in the 1940s pushed the focus toward biomedical solutions. Even the women in charge of maternal-child welfare programs usually had medical degrees.[9] Maternal training programs continued to exist, but mothers were seen as needing to be trained by professionals. Moreover, after World War II this training began to stress biomedical interventions more than social education.

The eighth Pan American Congress had been held in Washington, DC, and focused on war-related child welfare issues. In 1948 the Pan American Child Congresses officially became part of the OAS, which was created after World War II and approved by the United Nations as part of a hemispheric vision for peace and security. Its goals were to protect the Western Hemisphere from conflict and to protect the self-determination of nations (goals that were often in conflict, especially in light of US Cold War policy). The United States, on the other hand, viewed the OAS as a way to protect Latin America from communism.[10] Latin American nations were often frustrated with what they saw as unilateral actions taken by the United States (such as the 1954 coup in Guatemala). While some nations argued that a stronger OAS could protect Latin America from US actions, countries such as Mexico argued against strengthening the OAS for fear that the United States would be able to use the organization to further undermine national sovereignty.[11] Latin American nations were also unhappy with the economic aid provided to the region by the United States and with the OAS's emphasis on agrarian reform to create export markets.[12] They protested the fact that in order to receive aid, they had to conform to US policies. Despite the protests, however, the United States dominated the OAS with its objective to contain communism.

The ninth Pan American Child Congress, held in 1948 in Caracas, Venezuela, reflected international postwar maternal-child welfare trends, as well as overarching OAS goals for the region. These developments included a heavy shift away from the social motherhood promoted in the 1930s toward public health issues, particularly those affecting rural areas. Reformers recommended government-run health services, preventative disease programs (especially vaccinations and the prevention of tuberculosis), and more government attention to child nutrition. Where possible, reformers argued, these public health services should be created at the local level, particularly in the countryside.[13] The delegates also argued for the implementation of a Children's Code. This code would reflect the major concerns of the reform movement. For example, it promoted a "democratic attitude" and freedom of religion. It also called for the establishment of juvenile courts, child psychiatry agencies, and programs for neglected children. In addition, the congress issued a declaration on preschool-aged children, calling for a "progressive education" managed by the state and run on appropriate "psycho-biologic principles." This education would ensure that children had access to health care and proper nutrition, and would train mothers to be "competent."[14]

By the ninth congress it was clear that while delegates viewed mothers as important in child welfare, their role had diminished. With mothers no longer part of a dyad, welfare professionals advocated state intervention at an increasingly early age in order to protect children. This transition would be complete by the late 1950s, when the eleventh Pan American Child Congress took abandoned children as its theme. Mothers were no longer in the picture. By the early 1960s, the OAS shifted its emphasis explicitly toward improving regional standards of living and promoting democracy.

The other major postwar influence on international maternal-child welfare was UNICEF. The UN created the United Nations Relief and Rehabilitation Administration (UNRRA) in 1941 and 1942 to provide relief for Europe, and it began operations in 1944. By 1946 UNRRA had moved essential supplies such as basic foodstuffs, clothing, materials for shelter, medical and dental supplies and equipment, vaccines, hospital equipment, seeds, fertilizer, and agricultural equipment to over twenty countries, including countries in the soon-to-be Eastern Bloc.[15] UNRRA fell victim to Cold War politics, as the United States objected to the provision of relief to communist nations. Therefore, in 1946, the United Nations dismantled UNRRA and created the United Nations International Children's Emergency Fund (UNICEF). This fund was intended to be temporary, caring for children affected by the war in Europe.[16]

UNICEF's first priority was Europe's postwar famine. UNICEF organized relief aid according to a model it would use globally in the future. The agency delivered rations to organizations such as schools or clinics that were under the government's supervision. UNICEF therefore took the role of advisor and supplier, but it was up to each country to distribute the goods according to its own priorities. Often governments did this in conjunction with local committees. Organizers created UNICEF to partner with governments, and this is how UNICEF would later function in Latin America.[17]

During the immediate postwar years, the largest proportion of UNICEF assistance to medical programs went to maternal and child health. UNICEF provided equipment, such as baby scales, thermometers, lab supplies, incubators, oxygen tents, and other supplies and training. Yet UNICEF's disease campaigns, such as their International Tuberculosis Campaign, attracted the most notice. As Maggie Black has noted, "The success of the disease campaigns was a harbinger of a new era in international public health."[18] UNICEF's focus on disease eradication shaped the way that national health and welfare organizations created programs in their own countries.

After UNICEF established successful programs in Europe, it turned its attention to the countries most affected by the war in Asia. Asia presented a special challenge for UNICEF. In Europe the goal had been to repair the damage to infrastructure caused by the war and to get the population back on its feet. It became quickly apparent that in Asia, however, this task would be nearly impossible, since little infrastructure had existed before the war and the poverty endemic to the region was on a scale far more dramatic than in Europe. UNICEF simply did not have the funds to rebuild Asia. Officials studied the situation and decided to focus on disease prevention in Asia, since this could be done without an infrastructure and more cheaply, but would still provide large numbers of people with an improved quality of life. Therefore, although UNICEF did promote nutrition and maternal-child care programs in Asia, they focused primarily on disease.[19]

From 1946 to 1950, the "emergency needs approach" focused on providing children in Europe and Asia food, clothing, and health-care necessities. UNICEF distributed clothing to five million children in twelve countries, vaccinated eight million against tuberculosis, rebuilt milk processing and distribution facilities, and provided daily meals to millions of children in Europe. During the period from 1951 to 1960, UNICEF expanded its emergency services to include longer-term programming. Focusing on the health of children, UNICEF campaigned against tuberculosis, yaws, leprosy, and malaria; promoted sanitation and public health; and encouraged maternal and child health-care education. UNICEF helped countries produce and distribute low-cost, high-protein foods and fostered programs to educate people in their use in order to raise the nutritional profile of children. To provide for children's social welfare, UNICEF helped create informal neighborhood centers to train mothers in child-rearing and home improvement.[20]

UNICEF's approach to maternal-child welfare had been shaped by the exigencies of the Cold War. Their goal in Europe and Asia had been to help children in order to stave off communist threats in the immediate postwar years. Their funds had always been limited, largely because of US concerns over their programs in Eastern Europe. In fact, the United States had not supported UNICEF's transition to being a formal UN agency because it operated in these countries. Therefore, in order to help the most children possible, the organization focused its limited funds on children's health through vaccinations and other public health campaigns. UNICEF began implementing programs in Latin America in 1949 and came to Mexico in 1954. While UNICEF did not negate the importance of mothers, educating mothers was of secondary importance to the organization, which sought to help children within a context of "nurturing the values of democracy."[21] This shift toward the child can be seen in the programs advocated by the postwar Pan American Child Congresses as well. Delegates argued for a biomedical approach to protecting children, and the biosocial approach of the 1930s fell out of favor.

Mexican Health and Welfare Policy

The postrevolutionary government agency tasked with creating and implementing health and welfare policy until the early 1960s was the Secretaría de Salubridad y Asistencia (SSA), or Ministry of Health and Welfare. The Manuel Ávila Camacho administration (1940–1946) merged the Mexico City Department of Health with the former federal agency, the Secretaría de Asistencia Pública (SAP), or Ministry of Public Assistance, in 1943, creating a ministry dedicated to the health and welfare of poor Mexican families.

Under the direction of SAP, maternal-child welfare in Mexico was conducted largely through urban programs, with the broad goal of alleviating class-based poverty. Welfare reformers critiqued capitalism and hoped to "reintegrate" the poorest members of society into the economic system. These goals were similar to the goals of the 1930s "socialist education" projects, which sought to "modernize" rural peasants and urban poor. In cities, particularly Mexico City, SAP constructed mother's centers designed in large part to train mothers to raise their children in the most "modern" and "scientific" fashion. Each center had medical personnel to monitor and offer prenatal and postnatal care, but centers also provided programs for mothers to help them educate their children to be better citizens and to successfully navigate an urban setting. These programs largely mirrored the proposals of the seventh Pan American Child Congress, which is not surprising because, as host of the congress, Mexico's delegation was the largest. SAP considered mothers to be an equal part of the mother-child dyad, and they believed that mothers, in partnership with the state through SAP, would raise model citizens, seen as the wealth of a developing Mexico.

By the late 1930s, programs shifted away from an emphasis on the poor as a class. Reformers began to see the family as their most important focus, and they specifically targeted mothers and children within the family. SAP expanded programming throughout cities, building more mother-child centers, day cares, dining halls, and health clinics. SAP workers continued to educate mothers, but less to integrate poor mothers into the economy and more to monitor their health to make sure their babies and children were healthy. As one doctor argued, "Tender female brains need to assimilate the elements of a childcare [*puericultura*] that will mitigate fateful damage and achieve a new mentality—new mothers of the future, including those who are now fit, must take conscious, voluntary steps to submit to the saving standards of childcare."[22] In order to take advantage of the programs, mothers needed to submit to surveillance by SAP workers. If they wanted to, for example, take advantage of the dining hall, they had to brush their teeth and wash their hands in front of workers to make sure they were practicing appropriate hygiene. The increased monitoring dovetailed with the renewed emphasis on mothers and children. But now, mothers were no longer equal partners with the state but rather biomedical entities that had to be scrutinized by SAP workers to ensure they were performing their tasks as mothers correctly. The 1940s therefore saw a shift in the focus of the SSA; in the 1930s SAP had emphasized class uplift, and now it privileged the protection of the family, especially mothers and children within the family. As a SSA report noted, "The state's concern is to assure the conservation of the family and to prevent its disintegration. We are increasing technical and social programs for the protection of childhood."[23] SSA child welfare activists wanted to protect the Mexican family and saw mothers and children as the most vulnerable members of the family.[24] Reformers linked the health of the family to the health of the nation, and increasingly began to see this in medical and scientific, rather than social, terms.

In order preserve the health of mothers and children, in the early 1940s SSA targeted services toward mothers. Many of these services had been designed to teach mothers puericulture, or the scientific theory of child-rearing—that is, how to raise children according to the most "modern" scientific techniques. However, after WWII, following international trends, health services expanded and were designed to target pregnant women specifically. One report noted, "Social Services have been established to put pregnant women in contact with doctors in maternal-child welfare centers, in order to teach them the reasons behind the new methods for taking care of and protecting their children."[25] In some cases, the services were reorganized to be more efficient, another report stated, "We have reorganized these official establishments to use their own resources more efficiently, we've reduced the amount of time each mother is seen, and improved service. We have increased control and vigilance over the pregnant women so that they may enjoy earlier and more frequent consultations."[26] The newfound efficiency allowed for greater monitoring of pregnant women.

SSA also created new centers designed to protect children and to offer mothers prenatal and postnatal care. One of these centers, El Centro Materno-Infantil Gral. Maximino Ávila Camacho, was named after President Ávila Camacho's brother.[27] Its stated mission was as follows:

> First: To provide hygienic safeguards and medical assistance to children from conception through adolescence. Second: To provide hygienic safeguards and medical assistance to mothers. Third: Educational and social assistance to all preschool children according to SSA regulations. Fourth: social welfare to deserving families with children. Fifth: Sanitary precautions for the areas surrounding the center. Sixth: Technical training for medical and social service personnel.[28]

The clinic provided vaccinations; offered prenatal and postnatal care; delivered babies; supplied day-care services, a lactation room, and a dining hall; trained doctors, nurses, and day-care teachers; furnished sanitation, personal hygiene, and mental hygiene programs; and provided OB-GYN services. The center also coordinated campaigns against venereal diseases and tuberculosis, and participated in medical and scientific studies.[29]

Thus, new welfare centers created in the late 1940s and 1950s served less as places to educate poor mothers about how to raise their children and more as places for mothers and their children to receive health care. The clinic's goals were in line with the goals of most international child welfare agencies, and they reflect the ascendance of the biomedical approach. The programs focused on the health of children primarily and on the education of mothers secondarily. Even the day-care services, which on first glance seem like a boon for working mothers, actually reflect the mistrust the medical community had for mothers of young children. The ninth Pan American Child Congress had called for a progressive preschool education, and the expansion of day-care services in Mexico reflected the desire of the reform community to ensure that children were properly taken care of.

As services for women shifted toward prenatal and postnatal care, reformers no longer saw women as responsible for socializing children to become productive citizens. Mothers were to provide a healthy and happy start in life:

> All this is achieved by moral preparation and training of women in the different lessons, which she chooses. We are pleased, therefore that she is learning, achieving in this way, and training to adequately fulfill her noble mission as a

mother or simply as a housewife; thus achieving a clean and tidy home, providing proper nutrition and physical development of the family, turning her home into a welcoming place that is full of happiness. The woman, in this environment, raises her moral and cultural level, developing and dignifying her own personality.[30]

Mothers were to be trained for a moral mission, but the mission was now to fulfill the need for a clean, ordered, hygienic house. She was to provide the necessary nutritious meals for the physical development of her family and keep her home full of happiness. In this manner she could be a good mother. By tending to the health of her family she would elevate herself.

In order to help women accomplish these goals, SSA sponsored mother's clubs that were associated with maternal-child welfare centers. One mother's club offered the following classes: literacy, nutrition, dressmaking, needlework, pastry making, English, home economics, needlework, beading, toy making, artificial flowers, beauty, typing, embroidery by machine, and first aid. The clubs also offered mothers access to radio, television, and social activities.[31] Some classes, such as typing or English, were designed to help women find work if necessary, but many of the classes were to help mothers in the home or to give mothers remunerated employment that could be done in the home. The classes that directly pertained to motherhood were associated with health, such as diet, first aid, and economic cooking. In this way, SSA could be assured that mothers were properly looking after the health of their children.

Fathers, especially those fathers who abandoned their families, were a particular target as well. "In such cases, where the child will benefit, Legal Aid concentrates its efforts exhausting all legal remedies at its disposal, to force fathers to provide alimony. If Legal Aid cannot persuade the father that his attitude is unjust, then we will take him to court and have his wages garnished."[32] Interestingly, while the father is chastised for his physical absence, his salary is to be garnished to make sure his children have food. As Sandra Aguilar-Rodríguez has shown, experts by the 1950s began promoting improved nutrition.[33] This was part of the medicalization of childhood: improved nutrition would aid in the physical development of the child and could be monitored and regulated through dining halls and mother-child centers.

By the end of the 1940s, SSA programming turned to the countryside, where the agency created rural welfare centers to complement the welfare centers already in existence in the cities. Like the urban centers, these centers provided medical care and educational programs for mothers. Following transnational maternal-child welfare recommendations, welfare centers offered recreational facilities as well as day care and medical care. Often, these would be the sites of vaccination and other sanitation and public health campaigns. Health and welfare for mothers and children were also linked to issues of national development. According to an SSA official:

> Our country, like other developing countries, does not have the economic ability to resolve through assistance the problems that face our families, when these problems reach such heights and their demands remain unsatisfied. Because

of this, the SSA needs to adopt a policy of selecting services, placing priority on the emergency situations of our many working-class families, with low and insufficient salaries—we need to focus on families that can be rehabilitated—this should be considered an investment in the national economy.[34]

Investing in the health of children was seen as a way to develop the national economy. The emphasis on rural areas dovetailed with Mexico's increasing emphasis on development. SSA began cooperating with UNICEF in 1954, promoting a three-prong action plan that included the World Health Organization. The projects funded by UNICEF in the countryside focused on maternal-child health and vaccination campaigns.[35] As the 1950s progressed, new urban and rural programs reflected the emphasis on biomedical health rather than biosocial roles.

Mexican maternal-child welfare policy both influenced and was shaped by transnational maternal-child welfare discourses. Mexican reformers had their greatest influence in the 1930s, as social workers promoted the mother-child dyad and encouraged mothers to work in partnership with the state, through SAP, to raise healthy children. As medical doctors began to gain ascendancy in the Mexican welfare agency, as in the Pan American Child Congresses and UNICEF, a biomedical approach to maternal-child welfare took over. Mexican doctors had been trained in eugenics, and the combination of their medical and eugenic training privileged the physical health of the mother over her social role. Eugenics became linked to twentieth-century state formation all over Latin America. Mexico was no exception, and the welfare advocates who worked with children through SSA tended to have a background that favored eugenics as a model for racial improvement and social and economic progress.[36] Eugenicists strove to recreate the Mexican family as the base of a new modern and developed Mexico. They saw the state as the means though which a modern Mexico could be guaranteed. Thus, the intervention of the government into the Mexican family through education, health, and welfare programs is an important part of postrevolutionary state formation.

Mothers and children, therefore, became of increasing concern to reformers. They believed that if children were the wealth of the nation, then mothers had to be scientifically trained to make sure this wealth was harnessed properly. This idea of republican motherhood dates back to at least the nineteenth century. However, postrevolutionary Mexico created something new by wedding science and medicine to the social role of motherhood through eugenics. Thus, mothers were important not only because they raised and educated children but because their health directly impacted the health of their children. The postrevolutionary state saw overseeing the health of the Mexican family as its obligation. Monitoring mothers became central to this goal. In particular, by the 1940s and 1950s, monitoring mothers' health became the key. As SSA stated in a report to the president, "The development of the Mexican family rests on the protection of motherhood and childhood. The Mexican government, through multiple programs offered by SSA, seeks to improve conditions for mothers and children, specifically through focusing on their health."[37] Reformers saw the nuclear family as the strength of Mexico: "The Program of Social Welfare has created special legal aid programs to preserve and integrate the family, to defend the home and the family economy . . . and the general needs of the community."[38] A strong nuclear family, with the father providing economically for his family and with the mother looking after the health of the children, would aid in Mexico's overall economic development.

Mortality statistics, especially child mortality, were among the most important indicators that reformers used to show progress in uplifting society. Welfare advocates used reductions in mortality as proof that their programs were working. Reports made to the president from SSA highlighted these successes:

> It is rarely possible to register such a significant reduction in mortality as has happened during this administration, in spite of the fact that the country went through difficult circumstances because of the disorders caused by the World War, which started in 1939 and ended in 1945. The lowering of the infant mortality rate, translated in terms of lives saved, was 253,000 over six years. Infant mortality in 1940 was 125 deaths per 1,000 births and dropped to 105 deaths per 1,000 births in 1946. It is the duty of the state and society to create the conditions that offer improved life expectancies for children.[39]

Improving statistics helped to prove that modernization was taking place—indeed, as Michael Ervin and others have shown, the ability to keep statistics and monitor the population through statistics was an important marker of national success.[40] SSA kept careful records of their efforts in order to document their achievements. This allowed them to justify government funding and to showcase Mexico's improvements to the international health and welfare community.

The Mexican government never dedicated a large percentage to its federal budget to health and welfare spending. SSA relied heavily on partnerships to finance its programs. In the cities, much of its money came from the fundraising efforts of local women's organizations.[41] In the countryside, however, the Mexican government relied on partnerships with international entities such as UNICEF and the World Health Organization. In order to be eligible for these funds, SSA had to implement "approved" policies. While Mexican reformers did not couch their rhetoric in terms of anticommunism, they did see these programs as being the most scientific and modern way to develop their economy. Over and over again, SSA policy makers linked the health of children and the Mexican family to the health of the country. In Mexico, what was seen by international agencies as programs to defend vulnerable populations against the "attractions" of communism was seen by Mexicans as an opportunity to modernize their country and become part of the developed world. In Mexico, the domestic welfare community took advantage of international trends to promote their own development agenda.

Maternalism in Mexico

This shift from social motherhood to biological motherhood occurred at the same time that many feminists were using maternalism as a strategy to gain suffrage in Mexico. Maternalism, as defined by Seth Koven and Sonya Michel, "exalted women's capacity to mother and applied to society as a whole the values they attached to that role: care, nurturance, and morality."[42] According to many maternalists, women deserved the vote because of the importance of their social role as mother. This role grew out of nineteenth-century conceptions of sentimental motherhood, the idea that women should remain "guardian angels of the home" and that any activities that took them outside the home should be philanthropic in nature and serve as extensions of their domestic role—such as promoting child education, health, and welfare.[43]

In the 1940s, feminists used a variety of arguments to persuade the government to grant women suffrage—one of which was maternalism. Ana Lau discusses two women's organizations that were active in the 1940s and 1950s, the Ateneo Mexicano de Mujeres and the Alianza de Mujeres de México. As Lau notes, women in the Ateneo promoted the idea that the ideal woman and citizen was a homemaker and caretaker of children. Mexican maternalists argued that this made their political and administrative work "respectable," as the purpose of seeking suffrage was to allow women to participate in the resolution of problems affecting the country, family, and children. According to Lau, this allowed feminists to argue that women were to be guardians of the homeland, family, and children, without compromising their traditional role. These two organizations saw motherhood as the key to women's citizenship. Their ability to care for, educate, and nurture their families is what would allow them to effectively participate in politics.[44] As Sarah Buck notes, other women organized to promote child welfare and to celebrate the mother—establishing Mother's Day and other celebrations.[45] Women continued to promote a sentimental view of motherhood, one they now linked to citizenship. Lau notes that the Alianza was linked to the PRI; this new form of women's citizenship is what the prevailing political party chose to promote.

With the economic growth of the 1940s, 1950s, and 1960s also came an increase in the number of women working in Mexico. The percentage of "economically active" women increased from 1.45 percent to 5.11 percent of the economically active population in Mexico between 1930 and 1970, and jumped from 6.7 percent to 8.09 percent in Mexico City during the same period.[46] These numbers are very narrowly defined and include neither informal sector labor nor part-time work that many mothers would have engaged in. However, it is clear that to the "experts" the number of working mothers was growing. This also created anxiety among those in the reform community, many of whom felt that children would be better served by stay-at-home mothers.

Conclusion

Historian Judith Bennett argues that many seeming contradictions in women's history can be explained by the concept of a patriarchal equilibrium. She argues that if we take a longer view of history, we see far more continuities than ruptures in patriarchal oppression. Bennett's research about women who brewed ale in medieval England shows that "brewsters faced a host of institutions that worked, at least in part, to subjugate women to men. As a result, changes which undermined the forces of patriarchy in one sector were subtly countered by forces in other sectors. . . . Put more abstractly, what happened is this: an economic change that may have advantaged women was countered effectively by responses rooted in ideology, law, politics and family."[47] As Elizabeth Dore puts it, during the nineteenth century women took two steps forward and one step back.[48]

As women began to make greater political gains based on sentimental ideas of motherhood and as more mothers began to work outside the home, other sectors in Mexican society worked to curtail women's political and economic gain. If women had power because they were mothers, then the "experts" would rewrite expectations of motherhood to remove any influence they would have over children. Child-rearing and educating would be done by the state, through their phalanx of state agencies and experts (many of whom, ironically, were women). Medicalizing childhood effectively removed room for debate—this was no longer a moral issue, but one that could be best served by medicine.

Historian Diego Armus has pointed out that looking at how international trends in health intersect with local realities can provide important insights.[49] The Pan American Child Congress held in Washington, DC, in 1942 took as its focus programs for children uprooted by the war, particularly orphans and refugees.[50] In quite literal terms the international reform community sought to protect children who had no parents by implementing programs designed by specialists to replace parents with the state. These programs included nutrition and medical care, as well as supervised recreational programs and guaranteed access to education. It was perhaps this shift, which occurred as a result of the war, that persuaded reformers that they were better suited to care for children than mothers themselves. In addition, the creation of UNICEF also shifted attention away from the social role of mothers and toward medical interventions. After World War II, international maternal-child welfare agencies reflected the Cold War priorities of rebuilding Europe and Asia, in part to combat the attractions of communism. Additionally, practical realities in Asia, for example, made disease prevention an efficient choice for agencies like UNICEF, since they lacked the money to build an infrastructure that had never existed. Mexico did not have to rebuild after the war, but its poverty and lack of development meant that Mexican reformers were eager to implement these policies: they would use the programs and the funding to create a strong and modern Mexico. The Mexican desire to modernize dovetailed handily with the major international agencies' desire to fight communism.

How did these practices, formed as a response to Cold War contingencies, play out in Mexico, a country that had not experienced the devastation of World War II? How did Cold War politics affect maternal-child welfare policies? The main result of implementing policies that focused on children was the domestic containment of motherhood. Feminists had been organizing to demand suffrage since before the Revolution, and women were finally allowed to vote in municipal elections in 1947 and federal elections in 1953 (although the first presidential election in which they could vote did not take place until 1958). In large part, according to Ana Lau and Sarah Buck, they were able to achieve suffrage because of maternalist arguments made in the 1940s. Thus, as Mexican women began to achieve political parity, other discourses moved to curtail that parity, as Bennett shows. By the early Cold War period in Mexico more women worked outside the home, went to school, and participated politically. Yet their social significance as mothers was curtailed. For the maternal-child welfare community, mothers became biomedical entities that had to be monitored and surveilled in order to protect children.

As Alan McPherson argues, "The paradox holds that the more historians find out about the Cold War in the hemisphere, the more the Cold War itself fades into the background."[51] Yet because of the shifts in international health and welfare policy as a result of the Cold War, important shifts occurred in Mexico as well. International policies, especially policies advocated by postwar agencies such as UNICEF and the OAS, changed the relationship of the mother to the state in Mexico. The implementation of these new policies had important gendered effects. When we examine the Cold War through the lens of mothers' bodies, we can see that it allowed the state more control over the physical body and health of the mother, even as women's political and social power was constrained.

Notes

1. Gilbert M. Joseph, "What We Now Know and Should Know: Bringing Latin America More Meaningfully into Cold War Studies," in *In From the Cold: Latin America's New Encounter with the Cold War*, ed. Gilbert M. Joseph and Daniela Spenser (Durham, NC: Duke University Press), 8.

2. The term "mother-child dyad" was used to define what reformers saw as a unique and special bond that existed between a mother and her child. They argued that this bond made them one entity rather than two individuals.

3. Childhood as a category has recently begun to receive more attention from historians. Historians in Latin America have begun to write histories of children and childhood as a social category. In Mexico, children and childhood have been explored more often as part of women's and family history. This is particularly true of the history of children in the twentieth century. Historians such as Mary Kay Vaughan, Ana Lau, Sarah Buck, and Jocelyn Olcott have explored the relationship of the state to mothers and the privileging of a particular kind of motherhood. Ana Lau and Sarah Buck argue that mothers themselves used maternalism, an ideology that maintained that women should be granted political rights based on their social status as mothers, in the 1940s as a way to gain suffrage. For maternalists, mothers' social role as educators and caretakers of children led them to merit equal political rights. Historians have also explored the intersections of motherhood and the social reform movement, particularly through the relationship between women and eugenic thought. Alexandra Minna Stern examined the development of eugenics in Mexico and how eugenicists sought to rewrite power in the Mexican family, especially vis-à-vis mothers and their children. Katherine Bliss has written extensively about social reformers and prostitution. The medical community in particular was concerned about the diseases they believed prostitutes to spread and the impact of these diseases on the health of Mexican families. Historians such as Ann Blum have looked more specifically at children through the lens of the social welfare movement. Blum argues that orphans were a particular concern for reformers. Blum also examines the connection between children and the medical community through a discussion of hospitalism, a disorder in which children in large orphanages failed to thrive. Doctors were dismayed to observe that despite employing the latest medical

and scientific advances in childrearing, children seemed listless and only improved after spending time with their families. Eileen Ford also examines the construction of childhood as a social category after the Revolution. As Ford notes, after 1940 the number of children exploded and childhood as an idealized experience was seen as a right for children of all classes, not just the elite. Looking at constructions of childhood, according to Ford, gives us a window, therefore, into how civil society functioned during this period. See Pablo Rodríguez and María Emma Manarelli, eds., *Historia de la infancia en América Latina* (Bogota: Universidad Externado de Colombia, 2007); Tobias Hecht, ed., *Minor Omissions: Children in Latin American History and Society* (Madison: University of Wisconsin Press, 2002); Sarah Buck, "Activists and Mothers: Feminist and Maternalist Politics in Mexico, 1923–1953" (PhD diss., Rutgers University, 2002); Jocelyn Olcott, "'Worthy Wives and Mothers': State-Sponsored Women's Organizing in Postrevolutionary Mexico," *Journal of Women's History* 13, no. 4 (2002): 106–31; Ana Lau, "Expresiones politicas femeninas en Mexico del siglo XX: el Ateneo Mexicano de Mujeres y La Alianza de Mujeres de Mexico (1934–1953)," in *Orden Social e identidad de género Mexico, siglos XIX y XX*, ed. Maria Teresa Fernandez Aceves, Carmen Ramos Escandon, and Susie Porter, (Mexico: CIESAS, 2006), 93–124; Mary Kay Vaughan, "Modernizing Patriarchy: State Policies, Rural Households, and Women in Mexico, 1930–1940," in *Hidden Histories of Gender and the State in Latin America*, ed. Elizabeth Dore and Maxine Molyneaux (Durham, NC: Duke University Press, 2000); Alexandra Minna Stern, "Responsible Mothers and Normal Children: Eugenics, Nationalism, and Welfare in Post-revolutionary Mexico, 1920–1940," *Journal of Historical Sociology* 12, no. 4 (December 1999): 369–97; Katherine Bliss, *Compromised Positions: Prostitution, Public Health and Gender Politics in Revolutionary Mexico City* (University Park: Pennsylvania State University Press, 2001); Ann Blum, "Dying of Sadness: Hospitalism and Child Welfare in Mexico City, 1920–1940," in *Disease in the History of Modern Latin America: From Malaria to AIDS*, ed. Diego Armus (Durham, NC: Duke University Press, 2003), 209–36; Eileen Ford, "Children of the Mexican Miracle: Childhood and Modernity in Mexico City, 1940–1968" (PhD diss., University of Illinois at Urbana-Champaign, 2008).

4. Joseph Gusfield, foreword to *Deviance and Medicalization: From Badness to Sickness*, by Peter Conrad and Joseph W. Schneider (Philadelphia: Temple University Press, 1992), viii.
5. Nichole Sanders, *Gender and Welfare in Mexico: The Consolidation of a Postrevolutionary State* (University Park: Penn State University Press, 2011).
6. Not all women's organizations made this argument, but a significant number, especially by the 1940s, did.
7. Donna Guy, "The Pan-American Child Congresses, 1916 to 1942: Panamericanism, Child Reform, and the Welfare State in Latin America," in *White Slavery and Mothers Alive and Dead: The Troubled Meeting of Sex, Gender, Public Health, and Progress in Latin America*, (Lincoln: University of Nebraska Press, 2000), 38–39.
8. Guy, *White Slavery and Mothers*, 62–63.
9. See Sanders, *Gender and Welfare*, 91–98.
10. Barbara Lee Bloom, *The Organization of American States* (New York: Chelsea House, 2008), 17.
11. Ibid., 29–34.
12. O. Carlos Stoetzer, *The Organization of American States* (Westport, CT: Praeger, 1993), 135–40.

13. "Final Act of the Ninth Pan American Child Congress: Caracas, Venezuela, January 5–10, 1948" (Washington, DC: Pan American Union, 1948), 11–13.

14. "Final Act," 14–25, 28–32.

15. Maggie Black, *The Children and the Nations: The Story of UNICEF* (New York: UNICEF, 1986), 2–3.

16. Ibid., 4–8, 33.

17. Ibid., 45.

18. Ibid., 50–55.

19. Ibid., 70.

20. "United Nation Children's Fund—History Organization," Nobelprize.org, *www .nobelprize.org/nobel_prizes/peace/laureates/1965/unicef-history.html.*

21. Richard Jolly, *UNICEF: Global Governance That Works* (New York: Routledge, 2014), 20.

22. Federico Villaseñor, "Formemos Futuras Madres," *Vida*, January 1942.

23. "Resumen Sintético de las Actividades de la Secretaria de Salubridad y Asistencia durante el sexenio 1940–46," AGN/SSA/Oficialía Mayor, vol. 4, exp. 03/803.1/2, p. 4.

24. Nichole Sanders, "Improving Mothers: Poverty, the Family, and 'Modern' Social Assistance in Mexico, 1937–1950," in *The Women's Revolution: Women and Womanhood in Mexico, 1910–1953*, ed. Patience Schell and Stephanie Mitchell (Lanham, MD: Rowman and Littlefield, 2006).

25. "Punto IX: Protección de la Niñez, a la maternidad y a las clases débiles," AGN/SSA/ Oficialía Mayor, vol. 4, exp. 03/803.1, p. 55–56.

26. Ibid., 55–56.

27. Antonio Candaño, director del Centro Materno Infantil Gral. Maximino Ávila Camacho, "Informe sintético," July 1951, AGN/SSA/Oficialía Mayor, vol. 4, exp. 03/803.1/1.

28. Ibid.

29. Ibid.

30. "Síntesis del informe de las actividades realizadas por la Dirección General de Asistencia Social Durante el periodo comprendido entre el lo de septiembre de 1953 al 31 agosto de 1954," AGN/SSA/Oficialía Mayor, vol. 3, exp. 803.1, 6–7.

31. "Dirección General de Asistencia Social: Aspecto administrivo de las actividades realizadas por la Dirección General de Asistencia Social Durante el periodo comprendido entre el lo de septiembre de 1954 al 31 agosto de 1955," AGN/SSA/ Oficialía Mayor, vol. 7, exp. 803.1, p. 7.

32. "Dirección General de Asistencia Social," 20–21.

33. Sandra Aguilar-Rodríguez, "Cooking Modernity: Nutrition Policies, Class and Gender in 1940s and 1950s Mexico City," *Americas* 64, no. 2 (October 2007): 177–205.

34. "Secretaria de Salubridad y Asistencia: Dirección General de Asistencia Social: Síntesis e información de las actividades realizadas durante el periodo comprendido entre el 1º de septiembre de 1956 al 31 de agosto de 1957," AGN/SSA/Oficialía Mayor, vol. 10, exp. 03/803.1/1, p. 4.

35. "Dirección Gral. De Hig. y Asistencia Materno Infantil: Informe de las labores desarrolladas durante el tercer trimestre del ano 1957," AGN/SSA/Oficialía Mayor, vol. 8, exp. 803.1, p. 4.

36. Sanders, *Gender and Welfare*; Beatriz Urías Horcasitas *Historias Secretas del Racismo en Mexico (1920–1950)* (Mexico: Tusquets Editores, 2007).

37. "Dirección Gral. De Hig. y Asistencia Materno Infantil: Informe sinóptico de las labores técnicas y administrativas realizadas en el periodo comprendido entre el 1º de

septiembre de 1955 al 31 de agosto de 1956," AGN/SSA/Oficialía Mayor, vol. 8, exp. 803.1, p. 1.

38. "Secretaria de Salubridad y Asistencia: Dirección General de Asistencia Social: Síntesis e información," 13.

39. "Resumen Sintético de las Actividades de la Secretaria de Salubridad y Asistencia," 2–3.

40. Michael Ervin, "The 1930 Agrarian Census in Mexico: Agronomists, Middle Politics, and the Negotiation of Data Collection," *Hispanic American Historical Review* 87, no. 3 (2007): 537–70.

41. Sanders, *Gender and Welfare.*

42. Seth Koven and Sonya Michel, eds., *Mothers of a New World: Maternalist Politics and the Origins of the Welfare States* (New York: Routledge, 1993), 4.

43. Carmen Ramos Escandón, "Señoritas porfirianas, mujer e ideología en el México progresista, 1880–1910," in *Presencia y transparencia: La mujer en la historia de México*, ed. Carmen Ramos Escandón et al. (Mexico City: El Colegio de México, PIEM, 1987), 154–56.

44. Ana Lau, "Expresiones politicas femeninas en Mexico del siglo XX: El Ateneo Mexicano de Mujeres y La Alianza de Mujeres de Mexico (1934–1953)," in *Orden Social e identidad de genero Mexico, siglos XIX y XX*, ed. Maria Teresa Fernandez Aceves, Carmen Ramos Escandon, and Susie Porter (Mexico City: CIESAS, 2006), 11, 104.

45. Sarah Buck, "Activists and Mothers: Feminist and Maternalist Politics in Mexico, 1923-1953" (PhD diss., Rutgers University, 2002).

46. Statistics compiled by me from Instituto Nacional de Estadística y Geografía, *Estadísticas Historicas* (CD-ROM). INEGI does not define what specific occupations "count" as economically active. My assumption is that the category is defined very narrowly, thereby missing a lot of work in the informal sector.

47. Judith Bennett, *History Matters: Patriarchy and the Challenge of Feminism* (Philadelphia: University of Pennsylvania Press, 2006), 77–78.

48. Elizabeth Dore, "One Step Forward, Two Steps Back: Gender and the State in the Long Nineteenth Century," in Dore and Molyneaux, *Hidden Histories of Gender and the State in Latin America.*

49. Diego Armus, "Disease in the Historiography of Modern Latin America," in Armus, *Disease in the History of Modern Latin America: From Malaria to AIDS*, 9–10.

50. Sanders, *Gender and Welfare*, 39–43.

51. Alan McPherson, "The Paradox of Latin American Cold War Studies," in *Beyond the Eagle's Shadow: New Histories of Latin America's Cold War*, ed. Virginia Garrard-Burnett, Mark Atwood Lawrence, Julio E. Moreno (Albuquerque: University of New Mexico Press, 2013), 308.

References

Archives

Secretaría de Salubridad y Asistencia in the Archivo General de la Nación (National Archives of Mexico), Mexico City, Mexico

Selected Published Works

Black, Maggie. *The Children and the Nations: The Story of UNICEF.* New York: UNICEF, 1986.

Bloom, Barbara Lee. *The Organization of American States.* New York: Chelsea House, 2008.

Conrad, Peter, and Joseph W. Schneider. *Deviance and Medicalization: From Badness to Sickness.* Philadelphia: Temple University Press, 1992.

Guy, Donna. "The Pan-American Child Congresses, 1916 to 1942: Panamericanism, Child Reform, and the Welfare State in Latin America." In *White Slavery and Mothers Alive and Dead: The Troubled Meeting of Sex, Gender, Public Health, and Progress in Latin America*, edited by Donna Guy. Lincoln: University of Nebraska Press, 2000.

Jolly, Richard. *UNICEF: Global Governance That Works.* New York: Routledge, 2014.

Joseph, Gilbert M. "What We Now Know and Should Know: Bringing Latin America More Meaningfully into Cold War Studies." In *In From the Cold: Latin America's New Encounter with the Cold War*, edited by Gilbert M. Joseph and Daniela Spenser. Durham, NC: Duke University Press, 2008.

Lau, Ana. "Expresiones politicas femeninas en Mexico del siglo XX: El Ateneo Mexicano de Mujeres y La Alianza de Mujeres de Mexico (1934–1953)." In *Orden Social e identidad de genero Mexico, sigklos XIX y XX*, edited by Maria Teresa Fernandez Aceves, Carmen Ramos Escandon, and Susie Porter. Mexico City: CIESAS, 2006.

McPherson, Alan. "The Paradox of Latin American Cold War Studies." In *Beyond the Eagle's Shadow: New Histories of Latin America's Cold War*, edited by Virginia Garrard-Burnett, Mark Atwood Lawrence, Julio E. Moreno. Albuquerque: University of New Mexico Press, 2013.

Sanders, Nichole. *Gender and Welfare in Mexico: The Consolidation of a Postrevolutionary State.* University Park, PA: Penn State University Press, 2011.

Stoetzer, Carlos O. *The Organization of American States.* Westport, CT: Praeger, 1993.

CHAPTER 8

Africa's Kitchen Debate

Ghanaian Domestic Space in the Age of the Cold War

Jeffrey S. Ahlman

In a 1964 article written for the Ghanaian state-run monthly *The Ghanaian*, journalist Kate Sey asked the seemingly innocuous question: "Why is it that a lot of modern housewives are going in for gas-stoves[?]"[1] Framing her question around what she saw as a recent abundance of magazine and newspaper advertisements promoting such appliances, Sey presented a relatively straightforward answer to her query: the appliance and others like it, such as the refrigerator and electric iron, provided women the power of time. "If we thoroughly understand and thoroughly manage [it]," Sey insisted in reference to the stove, "a gas stove can be a great saving of time, labour, and expense."[2] Here, Sey echoed many of the nineteenth- and early-twentieth-century American and European advocates of gas and, later, electric stoves, who, in the appliance's infancy, promoted the modern stove's efficiency, beauty, and ease.[3] As Sey turned to the stove itself, she devoted the rest of her article to a tutorial on the proper maintenance and use of this amenity and icon of the modern kitchen. In doing so, Sey emphasized features including the stove's cleanliness, the absence of smoke and dust from the stove's flame, the cook's ability to regulate temperatures, and the appliance's baking capabilities. As a result, Sey advised her audience that a "gas stove is especially useful in flats where ladies and bachelors very often have to do all their own work or a greater part of it themselves."[4]

The venue in which Sey's article appeared is almost as important as the article itself. As a state-run magazine in the mid-1960s, *The Ghanaian* represented the voice of the pan-Africanist and socialist state of the ruling Convention People's Party (CPP) and its president, Kwame Nkrumah. Unlike most other state- and party-run magazines and newspapers, however, *The Ghanaian* aimed to cultivate an audience of middle-class and elite women. During its heyday between 1961 and 1966, for instance, nearly every issue of the magazine featured a woman or group of women on its cover. At the same time, the magazine's editors and writers took a clear interest in issues that they saw as uniquely affecting women, including domestic labor, marriage, romance, and the home. Such articles accompanied much more conventional CPP discussions of the need for and benefits of increased productivity, a collectivist approach to labor, socialism at home and abroad, news of Nkrumah's travels and accomplishments, and current events in Ghana and Africa more broadly. In many ways, *The Ghanaian* represented a pan-Africanist and socialist *Redbook*—the popular women's magazine so commonly featured on American supermarket shelves—with its eclectic mix of politics and "women's stories."[5]

More broadly, *The Ghanaian* served as perhaps the most prominent venue through which the CPP reframed issues perceived to be of unique concern to women—including modern appliances, cleanliness, and even the architectural layout of the home—through the lens of emerging transnational debates over Cold War domestic space. Outside of Africa, the politics of mid-twentieth-century domestic space have proved central to the growing cultural history of the Cold War in Europe and the United States, with scholars of both the United States and the Eastern Bloc connecting them to everything from the exercise of "soft power" to expositions on socialist and capitalist progress.[6] Africa, however, has largely remained absent from these historical and historiographical debates. This is in spite of the fact that the reconfiguration of the African domestic sphere stood at the center of many newly independent African governments' understandings of the modernization and nation-building processes of the early postcolonial era. The result has been a general blindness to a set of continental and transnational debates in which domestic space came to provide a site through which politicians, journalists, and others could define and negotiate the changing social and gender dynamics of their new nations within the evolving local and international contexts of decolonization and the Cold War.

Adopting Ghana as its primary site of analysis, this chapter interrogates the CPP press's construction of the modern Ghanaian domestic sphere for its national and international audiences in the first years of Ghanaian self-rule. As the first sub-Saharan country to emerge from European colonial rule, Ghana represented the future of Africa for many inside and outside of the country. Seeking to reap the benefits of the international prestige that followed the country's independence, the government of Kwame Nkrumah, Ghana's first prime minister (and, after 1960, president), embarked upon an extensive program of political and social transformation. Decolonization, Nkrumah argued, was not just a process of political liberation; it was one of social, cultural, and economic revolution in which every aspect of Ghanaian life was to be imbued with what his government presented as the values and mores of a burgeoning postcolonial, nonaligned, and socialist state.

As a result, in the pages of party- and state-run publications like *The Ghanaian*, the home and particularly the kitchen became key sites through which the Nkrumah government constructed and negotiated the gender dynamics of its envisioned postcolonial ideal. On one level, the kitchen stood in as a medium through which to talk about the new opportunities and possibilities brought forth by self-rule. Not only was greater access to modern consumer goods promised, but so too were a range of social and economic benefits stemming from the expansion of modern architecture and interior design, the redistribution of female labor, and the introduction of new technology into Ghanaian daily life. At the same time, the debates surrounding the modern Ghanaian kitchen also signaled a broader cultivation of the rationalized, scientifically minded worldview the CPP aimed to cultivate in its citizenry's day-to-day interactions with the world. Here, issues of Ghanaian and socialist womanhood, labor, and domesticity collided with idealized and aspirational domestic spheres rooted in a seeming bourgeois modernity of cleanliness, consumerism, and technology. The result was a political and social environment whereby local and continental debates over midcentury Ghanaian domestic space functioned as spaces to exhibit more foundational debates over postcolonial modernity, independence, womanhood, and Cold War nonalignment.

Defining the Domestic in Twentieth-Century Africa

In 1957, when Ghana became independent, the cultural politics of domestic space were increasingly becoming a central feature of the burgeoning Cold War in the Global North. For the United States, the modern kitchen became a site through which to extol the virtues of a consumption-oriented society. As historian Greg Castillo has shown, as early as the immediate postwar years, American propaganda experts isolated the so-called fat kitchen out as a visual example of what capitalist democracy and economics had to offer.[7] Focused primarily on American-German relations in the postwar rebuilding of West Germany, Castillo traces American efforts to reorient a postwar asceticism in Western Europe with exhibitions of "technology-laden dream kitchens" featuring everything from electric washing machines and ranges to refrigerators and deep freezes.[8] The goal of such showcases of American domestic space was only in part to create a market for American goods in Western Europe. More importantly, Castillo suggests, the market itself was to be a cultural and ideological tool. Engagement with American consumer goods—buying, selling, or even just gazing at them—was seen as part of a broader process of political and cultural realignment in Western Europe and West Germany specifically, one that aimed both to erase the horrors of the war and wartime technologies and to center the home as the site for postwar technological innovation, stability, and accumulation.[9]

In Africa, questions of domesticity and domestic space had long framed the Global North's engagements with the continent's peoples. Beginning in many places as early as the mid-nineteenth century, domestic science and training programs aimed to take the continent's young people—especially girls—and train them in running a modern household. Such training was highly gendered and generational as mission and, later, colonial educational officials constructed curricula that emphasized such domestic skills as cooking, cleaning, sewing, and washing clothes, among others. As historian LaRay Denzer has shown in western Nigeria specifically, in mission settings many girls received this training alongside boys who obtained agricultural and other vocational training. This system envisioned dual-gender cohorts of young men and women each trained in the proper etiquette, norms, and mores of a modern, Christian colonial domesticity.[10] In other settings, young women and men coupled training in such professions as nursing and midwifery with ritualized exhibitions of proper dining and service techniques. Such activities, Nancy Rose Hunt insists in her discussion of the early-twentieth-century Congo, were instrumental in the construction of both African and European colonial-era gender ideologies.[11]

In the Gold Coast (preindependence Ghana), domesticity regimes permeated the mission and colonial educational systems. In doing so, Gold Coast girls and young women joined their Nigerian and Congolese compatriots, among others, in learning the skills necessary for being a good housewife and mother. As elsewhere, colonial curricula emphasized personal skills like needlework, basket weaving, and sewing in conjunction with such domestic necessities as cooking, cleaning, and laundering—skills that broadly fell under the rubric of "housecraft." Accompanying this instruction was a further emphasis on etiquette and "good behavior." Through such training, anthropologist Takyiwaa Manuh and others argue, missions in particular aspired to cultivate a desirable pool of educated, marriageable women for the colony's rising class of professional men.[12] Because, among British colonies, the Gold Coast had one of the highest proportions of educated professionals (each of whom demanded an equally respectable wife), Gold Coast missions and schools had little choice but to help secure an ample pool of socially and domestically qualified women—something that many regularly lamented was in short supply and needed consistent attention. To this end, prominent Gold Coast journalist Mabel Dove proclaimed in 1933, "The school girl of the past may be fittingly said to have been fully decorated with modesty and reserve, a quality which we are striving so much to get back to today." According to Dove, for these schoolgirls of the past, "Domesticity was their strong point."[13]

Outside the schools, home, child care, and cooking demonstrations further positioned issues of domesticity and domestic space at the center of colonial understandings of African womanhood. By the 1950s and early 1960s, baby shows and home presentations that had begun in the Gold Coast as early as the 1920s and 1930s had grown into major national and international functions as the colony transitioned into self-rule.[14] For instance, a 1956 ideal home exhibition organized by the socially active Federation of Gold Coast Women offered tutorials in proper home management as well as in the correct use and maintenance of household appliances. Attendees to the event also gained insight into areas of home design, decorating, and cleaning.[15] As historian Bianca Murillo has argued in her analysis of the event, the exhibition promised to provide Gold Coasters of all classes with a lesson in the benefits of the modern lifestyle. Moreover, this lesson was not to be limited only to those who attended. Rather, upon leaving the showcase, attendees were to educate and encourage their friends and neighbors in how to integrate this domestic modernity into their daily lives, in turn creating a cascading effect of modernizing homes throughout the emergent nation.[16]

After independence, the CPP government of Nkrumah continued promoting a modernized domesticity in the country as the government and party both hosted their own events, which promised "to help boast [*sic*] up womanhood in Ghanaian society."[17] Ideals of order, cleanliness, and hygiene dominated these events. In the government's "baby shows," for instance, demonstrations of child-care techniques ranging from antenatal care to breastfeeding and toilet training methods accompanied pageants aimed at honoring the healthiest and happiest babies.[18] Likewise, clean home competitions sought to promote a similar ideal. As the organizers of one 1962 event explained, the objective of such an event was to "stimulate . . . interest in improving the standard of living in the home and thus minimise as much as possible those environmental and other factors which are harmful to the health of the people."[19] As a result, over the course of a week, judges traveled to various contestants' homes and evaluated the homemaker on criteria of cleanliness and hygiene, with special attention paid to the contestants' kitchens, living quarters, bathrooms and toilets, and other spaces of modern living. Moreover, contestants were to be divided based on social class ("Upper," "Middle," and "Lower") so as to ensure equitable judgment, with a total of seventy-two houses in the country's second-largest city (Kumasi) set for inspection.[20] Further complementing such contests in the first years of self-rule were weekend courses and seminars, run by organizations including the more radically minded Ghana Women's League, which combined training in health and "mothercraft" with citizenship exercises, discussions over the role of women in the trade union movement, and participation in local and national service projects.[21]

Postcolonial Domesticity and the Cold War Kitchen

As Murillo has shown, the ideal home exhibitions of the 1950s and 1960s offered Ghanaians a glimpse into what she describes as a "stereotypical middle-class" life. A romanticized familial model of a housewife and male breadwinner stood at the foundation of this idealized domestic sphere as many of the exhibitions, in her words, "stress[ed] above all a woman's importance as wife, housekeeper and caregiver and a man's authority as head of household."[22] Real and imagined consumption proved central to this social ideal. Men, and husbands in particular, were to supply the women in their lives with the means through which to purchase the goods and resources necessary for running a modern household. Women themselves, if they worked (and most did), were often seen as doing so outside of the formal economy, with most using their incomes to ensure economic independence apart from their husbands' support.[23] Women's broader activities, particularly for middle-class and elite women, were additionally envisioned as including participation in voluntary, charitable, and community improvement organizations, whereby their labor in these venues became acts of leisure and, in many cases, was understood as reinforcing male authority in the household.[24] Such an emphasis carried both political and social undertones as it joined broader debates in the country over marriage law, polygamy, and the relationship of the Ghanaian familial structure to an imagined Western nuclear family ideal.[25]

The contradictions between the bourgeois, consumption-oriented domesticity of the ideal home exhibits, cleanliness competitions, and baby shows, on the one hand, and the Nkrumah government's increasingly radical pan-Africanist and socialist ideology, on the other, were evident. From the CPP's earliest days in the late 1940s, Nkrumah and the burgeoning party had positioned the Gold Coast at the epicenter of Africa's emergent anticolonial politics. By the country's 1957 independence, a wide network of scholars, journalists, and activists both inside and outside of Ghana, had begun to promote the Ghanaian path to self-rule and postcolonial development as the African path. Or, as the prominent African American novelist Richard Wright argued in a 1957 essay, Ghana was to be "a kind of pilot project of the new Africa."[26] Nkrumah himself furthered such sentiments at the country's independence festivities with his famed insistence that Ghana's "independence is meaningless unless it is linked up with the total liberation of the African continent."[27] By the early 1960s, through a series of pan-African and anti-imperial conferences in Accra, along with the creation of scholarship and housing programs for African anticolonial expatriates and exiles in the country, Nkrumah's Ghana had in turn emerged as what one South African freedom fighter described as the "Mecca of Pan-Africanism."[28]

Key to Nkrumah's and the CPP's vision for Ghana and Africa more broadly was not only the socialist reconstruction of the country and continent as a whole, but also the infusion of a global socialist ethos into the two intersecting populaces. Work regimes, for instance, emphasized communal and collective labor, with one journalist for *The Ghanaian* proclaiming in 1965, "For now in Ghana, working for the state is working for ourselves."[29] Meanwhile, on the job, workers endured insistent demands for increased productivity and self-sacrifice. In state- and party-run institutions, administrators and supervisors further insisted that their employees serve as living examples of the idealized pan-African and socialist citizens envisioned in the party's rhetoric and ideology. The result for many workers was a day-to-day work environment governed by an overarching culture of discipline and surveillance.[30] Youth organizations such as the Ghanaian Builders Brigade and the Ghana Young Pioneers, meanwhile, sought to further cultivate the CPP's pan-African and socialist ethos through a sometimes-rigid focus on the disciplining, regimentation, and ideological education of the country's young men, women, and schoolchildren.[31]

For Nkrumah and the CPP, such a regime was a necessary manifestation of the Cold War and the perceived neocolonial atmosphere Ghana entered in 1957. If colonialism was a system designed to ensure the direct exploitation of African resources and labor for European gains, as Nkrumah would argue throughout much of the first decade of self-rule, the Cold War was a conflict centered on how to manipulate, both directly and indirectly, the continent's resources and people for future capitalist gain.[32] As elsewhere, socialism was to be a path to national and continental self-reliance and cooperative development. Similar to Julius Nyerere's Tanzania, the idioms of self-reliance underpinning Nkrumah-era Ghanaian socialism "could," as historian Priya Lal has argued in reference to Tanzania specifically, "be understood [either] as a literal developmental strategy or an idealized developmental outcome," depending on the context.[33] However, in contrast to the villagization schemes put forward by Nyerere in Tanzania, programs of rapid industrialization, technological and infrastructural development, mechanized agriculture, and centralized production were the hallmarks of Nkrumah-era socialism. As a result, the goal for Nkrumah was a uniquely pan-African political, social, and cultural modernity built from the industrial and technological artifice that guided the Global North's success.

Inside the CPP, the question of technological innovation was ultimately a cultural and ideological one, and the domestic sphere represented one of the most intimate arenas through which to disseminate this message. As portrayed by the party's and government's various publications, the "traditional" Gold Coast/Ghanaian kitchen was a space rife for modernization—if it could be considered a space within a westernized conception of the "home" at all. Even in the early twenty-first century, much of Ghana's cooking takes place in open-air cooking spaces outside of an individual's living quarters. Such practices were even more prevalent in the mid-twentieth century. In villages, one 1955 report on childhood nutrition explained, women often built clay hearths at the center of their compounds; it was here—not inside their individual living quarters—that most of the family's cooking took place.[34] Even in Accra, the country's capital and most modernized city, not much was different. As Ioné Acquah noted in her 1958 social survey of the city, nearly all of the city's cooking was "carried on in the open compound."[35] Likewise, in the Western Region industrial cities of Sekondi and Takoradi, sociologist K. A. Busia noted tendencies toward communal, open-air kitchens. However, for Busia, such practices were indicative of the increasingly unsanitary and congested nature of Gold Coast urban life.[36]

The modern kitchen, in contrast, was to be part of the interior of the home itself, featuring space for food preparation, cooking, and storage. As one 1957 article written for the Department of Social Welfare and Community Development suggested, such delineated cooking and food storage spaces were central to the health of the nation. Through the creation and proper maintenance—that is, detailed cleaning—of such domestic space, Ghanaians could eradicate "the spread of diseases such as . . . gastro-intestinal infections and helminths [intestinal worms]." Additionally, the department combined discussions of diligent hand-washing practices with reflections on the need for proper shelves, tables, floors, and utensils in all kitchens.[37] Government-run mass education programs linked demonstrations of model kitchens, smokeless stoves, and food storage devices to lectures on everything from health and cleanliness to proper hostessing techniques and etiquette.[38] Other programs and especially press accounts presented the modern kitchen as a space designed for the preservation of women's time and energy, while still others sought to reassure Ghana's women that it did not take much money to create an "ideal kitchen."[39] Meanwhile, architects commissioned with designing homes for the country's various resettlement and development projects debated how to integrate the modernity and convenience of indoor, demarcated kitchen spaces into the cultural and economic milieus of Ghanaian rural and urban life.[40]

Even more importantly, the modern kitchen and the home more broadly carried significant ideological meaning for the CPP, particularly as they related to the future of Ghanaian womanhood in the early Cold War era. Internationally, the 1959 "kitchen debate," which famously featured the Soviet premier Nikita Khrushchev and the US vice president Richard Nixon debating the personal and technological virtues of the "Miracle Kitchen" at the American National Exhibition in Moscow, brought this seemingly innocuous domestic space into the center of the Cold War. At the heart of the Khrushchev-Nixon debate was the question of the modern woman. For Nixon, set on highlighting the ease and seamlessness of the American kitchen, the Moscow display kitchen revealed a life in which American women were no longer burdened by the tediousness of domestic labor.[41] The implication was that American women would now enjoy greater freedoms for leisure and consumption. The ultimate goal of such a kitchen design, Nixon thus assured the Soviet premier, was to create a social and cultural sphere for women structured around choice: women would now have the freedom to choose not only what to buy for their homes but also what to do with the time these purchases gave them.[42]

In his debates with Nixon, however, Khrushchev dismissed his American counterpart's rosy picture of women's liberation through consumerism. Moreover, he openly questioned the social utility of a society rooted in a consumerist ethos that necessarily cultivated such a short attention span, whereby engineers, builders, and manufacturers were incentivized to build homes and other goods with such shoddiness as to ensure their short life spans.[43] At least some of the Soviet public who took in the exhibition also appeared to question the logic and principles underpinning the American displays. As one man explained to the Soviet *Izvestia*, "Well there are many interesting things here. I liked, for instance, . . . the geodesic dome with its frame and prefabricated aluminum pipe. . . . My wife would probably have liked the kitchen utensils best, and my son the shallow transistor television set. . . . But frankly, I expected more and, if you'll pardon my saying so, I'm a little disappointed."[44] Issues of durability, dependability, and collective benefit thus grounded the Soviet critique of the American exhibit. Technologies purportedly designed to liberate women from the monotony of housework may appear shiny and glamorous, but, as one group of exhibition goers further implied, they were also quite shallow. As they commented on the event, they asked: "Is it possible to consider kitchens and cosmetics as a cult of man?"[45] As such, within the Soviet Union, many visitors and public commenters read the "Miracle Kitchen" of the American National Exhibition as little more than a showcase of the capitalist fetishization of that which was new and glitzy, albeit ticky-tacky.

The Soviet kitchen, by contrast, highlighted the intersection of technology and socialist womanhood. Whereas the American kitchen was to free women from the monotony of domestic labor for the benefit of their leisure, the rationality, organization, technologies, and efficiency of the Soviet kitchen was to shepherd the country's women, to paraphrase Lenin, from the confinement of domestic enslavement.[46] The Soviet goal was thus to create a domestic space that would further open Soviet women to the possibilities of public life, possibilities necessarily tied to the continued expansion and celebration of socialist production.[47] As Khrushchev himself insisted during his debate with Nixon, Soviet women had access to many, if not all, of the same appliances as their American counterparts. But, as Soviet historian Susan Reid has shown, the social and cultural framework underpinning the use and functionality of these appliances was different in the Soviet context.[48] As Reid explains, within Soviet discourse household appliances were not seen as consumer goods; rather, they were machines foundationally connected to the broader scientific and technological revolution taking place within the Eastern Bloc. Moreover, through their use of these technologies, Soviet women not only partook in the appliances' benefits within the home but also intended to utilize the items to free themselves from the home so that they could, according to Reid, "become fully-rounded, cultured individuals, fit for communism."[49]

In newly independent Ghana, the intersecting ideals of socialist womanhood, scientific and technological innovation, and national production that drove Soviet and other Eastern Bloc reflections on the kitchen inspired similar debates. The early 1960s in particular was a time during which Nkrumah and the CPP increasingly looked to the Soviet Union as a model for how to rapidly build a modern industrial society. Stories of Soviet cities, industries, reservoirs, and construction projects, including home building, regularly peppered the pages of the CPP press during the period, with one article in the CPP-run *Evening News*, for instance, describing Siberia as a "wonderland of technological construction and human progress."[50] Moreover, the February 1962 visit of Soviet cosmonaut Yuri Gagarin was a national event in Ghana as schoolchildren, workers, party members, diplomats, and others packed the streets of Accra to greet the Soviet space-age hero.[51] Additional *Evening News* reports similarly fixated on the Soviet space program as they covered the day-to-day activities of Soviet cosmonauts during their orbits around the earth.[52] Furthermore, the July 1962 opening of the Soviet Trade and Industrial Exhibition in Accra provided the country's residents with a firsthand glimpse at the promise of socialist industrial and technological development with displays of everything from a "giant model" of *Sputnik* to refrigerators, washing machines, and other domestic appliances.[53]

As with the Soviet kitchen, the Ghanaian Cold War kitchen was to be more than a space of domesticity. It was also to be a mechanism for women's (at least partial) liberation from the home. As Kate Sey argued in her 1964 eulogy to the gas stove, such modern consumer amenities freed Ghana's modernizing women from unneeded wastages of "time, labour, and expense" in their domestic tasks—energy and wealth that they could then presumably reinvest in the country's postcolonial nation-building project.[54] As the article directly following Sey's piece—an article titled "Woman's Role outside the Kitchen"—explained, "Not long ago the kitchen was thought to be the only place for a woman. But with the coming of western civilization and hence education it has been realized that a woman has a place—in fact places outside the home."[55] In rural areas, the article suggested, women played active roles as everything from farmers and fishmongers to the ubiquitous petty traders, while others specialized in skills such as sewing and other professionalized craftwork. If we make the direct connection to Sey's article above, so-called modern women were to use the labor freedoms gained from their stoves and other appliances to take up active roles in the formal labor force as, according to the article, "female receptionists, clerical assistants, [and] private secretaries, etc." Others used their freedoms to participate in fields ranging from nursing to politics, while still others made inroads as students in the country's most prestigious institutions of higher education.[56]

Kate Sey, for her part, actively promoted such ideas. Writing in an April 1964 issue of *The Ghanaian*, Sey openly confronted the conventional expectations of the country's women with visions of new possibilities unleashed by Nkrumah's nation-building project. "Hitherto," she wrote with a good amount of hyperbole, "almost the only prospect open to our women, was marriage—a life-time of drudgery perhaps, and of subjugation to a husband who was lord and master of all he surveyed." "But today," she insisted, "the picture is different. The running of [the] home is now combined with office and factory work."[57] Even more importantly, she argued, women now had the time and skill to pursue work in fields previously "looked upon or classified as exclusively man's [sic] jobs," including "meteorology, radiography, journalism and others, in all of which the women are as good and capable as their male counterparts."[58] In a sense, Sey and others suggested, the changing nature of the postcolonial domestic sphere provided the country's women the space and opportunity to explore these extradomestic ideals and thus to play an increasingly active role in the country's political, social, and technological development.

Education, Science, and Generational Domesticity

Politically and intellectually, the imagery of the modern kitchen provided the CPP with the means by which to explore the broader social and ideological intersections between postcolonial womanhood and Cold War science and technology. Going back as far as the late 1940s and early 1950s, education stood at the center of all of these debates for the CPP. As early as 1951 and 1952, for instance, the CPP rooted its social policy in educational expansion as it introduced fee-free primary education into the colony. The result over the ensuing decade was an exponential growth in the number of students at all levels of Gold Coast preuniversity education.[59] Moreover, the colony's girls and young women were perhaps the greatest beneficiaries of the CPP's educational initiatives as they joined the colony's (and later country's) schools in numbers that eventually rivaled their male peers, especially at the primary level. By 1958, for instance, more than a third of all primary school students and approximately a quarter of middle school students were girls. By the end of the 1960s, those numbers would jump to just under 45 percent of primary school students and more than 35 percent of middle schoolers.[60]

Just as importantly, as historian Jonathan Zimmerman has shown, an attempted curricular revolution accompanied the country's enrollment boom, with scientific and technological education taking center stage. In an attempt to move away from the more traditional model of rote education, CPP party and government officials promoted an educational model founded upon what Zimmerman describes as a scientific, explorative, and discovery-oriented learning experience. The program, according to Zimmerman, was thus to be "child-centered . . . not teacher-centered; active, not passive; grounded in experience, not simply in books; and focused on the community, not just the school."[61] As a result, over the course of the first decade of self-rule, the CPP government imported teachers and education specialists from the United States, Canada, and elsewhere, as it sought to promote and build its envisioned curriculum in the nation's schools. These expatriate teachers and specialists in turn helped train local teachers, held "refresher courses," and helped develop the infrastructure and intellectual know-how required for the Nkrumah government's resource- and time-intensive curricular revolution.[62]

Intellectually, the sciences—with their broadly positivist and often-technocratic rationality—most closely captured the ideological spirit of development and progress advanced by the CPP. Moreover, the overwhelmingly masculine demographics of most scientific fields—not just in Ghana, but globally—provided the CPP with an opening through which to frame its country's envisioned scientific revolution as more than just an educational and technological transformation. Instead, debates over science education were linked to those of the modern kitchen in that they both became part of a broader discourse of social revolution tied to local and international idioms of gender equity and women's liberation from the home.

As a result, schoolchildren—and girls in particular—who showed unique scientific acumen regularly received national attention and praise in the Ghanaian press. In April 1957, for instance, a Ms. Amelia Addae graced the front page of the party-run *Evening News*. For the CPP, Addae, whose academic success had earned her the opportunity to travel to the United States for advanced training in lab work, provided the party with a face for the celebration of CPP-led female academic and scientific achievement.[63] Seven years later, Letitia Obeng received similar praise in *The Ghanaian* as the magazine highlighted Ghanaian women's achievements with a prominent photograph of the distinguished scientist at work at the Ghana Academy of Sciences.[64] Moreover, after the 1961 inauguration of the CPP's preeminent youth organization, the Ghana Young Pioneers, select groups of students—young men and women alike—traveled to the Soviet Union and other Eastern Bloc countries, where they toured what was promoted by the party and their host countries as the world's most cutting-edge research and industrial facilities.[65]

However, the CPP's female journalists, most notably writing in *The Ghanaian*, took the narratives surrounding girls' scientific education and achievement and directly connected them to the party's wider discourse on modernized domesticity. If the modern home—replete with its order, technology, and rationalism—was to be the mechanism through which to recalibrate women's work in the home, then entrance into scientific fields was to serve as a pathway for the country's women into a range of new careers and areas of expertise central to the nation-building project. Moreover, the country's mothers had a special obligation. As both women and mothers, many of the party's female writers insisted, these women had a responsibility to explore the sciences themselves so as to serve as models for their daughters both inside and outside the home, demonstrating for the next generation what it meant to be a complete, modern woman in the post-colonial era. As columnist Josephine Sappor explained in a 1961 issue of *The Ghanaian*, technical fields including physiotherapy, radiography, meteorology, and medical lab work—along with artistic ones such as ceramics, dress design, architecture, and drama—all proved fertile ground for women in the country's professional job market.[66] Perhaps arguing the narrative of generational diffusion more prominently than any of her contemporaries, Sappor insisted that the goal for Ghana's women could not just be greater participation in the country's scientific professions. Rather, it had to be to provide a blueprint for a lifestyle that blended Ghanaian women's domestic obligations as wives and mothers with an assorted array of outside interests, ambitions, and advanced careers. Only through such modeling, she argued, could the country's mothers truly begin to impart to their young daughters ideals of modern womanhood that extended beyond the home.[67]

Gender and the Limits of Domestic Liberation

The underlying theme of Sappor's and her colleagues' writings was an assertion of the Ghanaian woman's and—to a different extent—girl's right to shape her place in the emergent country and to do so both independent of and in the context of the home. As in the Soviet Union and Eastern Bloc more broadly, liberation from the tedium of the domestic labor of the home did not imply an end to women's obligations at home. Instead, it reframed these obligations in a way that signaled a broader sharing of interests and obligations to the nation. Education and employment in scientific and technological fields were in turn to signal Ghanaian women's entrance into the new knowledge market of the modern world. Through the sciences, an individual not only gained expertise in particular subjects tied to the technological and industrial development envisioned for the country but, at the same time, also gained a new way of thinking explicitly linked to the logic, reasoning, mathematical, and problem-solving skills of a rationalized modern world.

For the CPP as a whole, the narratives surrounding the domestic emancipation of the country's women and the scientific education of its young women and girls were at their foundation ideological. At their most basic level, they were to refute the political and social confinement presumably imposed on the country's women by the supposed backwardness of "tradition" and colonial domesticity. Science was thus to be one path for the country's women out of the real and figurative kitchen and into the modern world of postcolonial nation-building. Politics, health care, and academia, among others, were to serve as other pathways. Yet, the sciences in particular were to carry with them the epistemological transformation demanded of self-rule as they signified the necessary ontological break between the past and the future required of the emergent state. For as one columnist for the *Evening News* explained in early 1962, "In considering the emancipation of women in Ghana, . . . the problem is not one of a fight for civil rights and liberties but rather one of an awakening of aspirations for higher attainment in the academic, social and political roles of the nation."[68] Put another way, the question for Ghana's modern women was thus how to think bigger and to be more ambitious as they pursued a life in service to the postcolonial nation.

At the same time, the Ghanaian focus on women's domestic emancipation and scientific education had broader Cold War implications. The world Nkrumah and the CPP imagined was one necessarily constructed out of the legacy of imperial rule, and colonial domesticity regimes were in turn part and parcel of the exploitative and extractive nature of the colonial project itself. By supposedly excising women from the public sphere, "tradition" and colonial domesticity bifurcated the population, leading to further dependency and stagnation, party ideology argued. If independence was to be a moment of national reawakening and redefinition, the transition to self-rule was also to be a period of new vulnerability tied to the potential for the neocolonial intrusions of the Cold War on an envisioned independent Africa. As a result, debates over women's domestic liberation or of women taking, to quote Nkrumah, "their places side by side with men" were just as much about national and continental security as they were about new opportunities for women and pathways to greater gender equity.[69] As party activist and national secretary of the National Council of Ghana Women, Margaret Martei advised her audience during a 1962 speech, they were now "women of the modern atomic age," and they carried the national and domestic responsibilities of this designation.[70]

However, as I have shown elsewhere, the realities for women on the ground seldom aligned with the idealized visions put forward by the party's leaders or even its female writers.[71] In terms of employment, opportunities for women grew exponentially during the late 1950s and early 1960s as the generation of Ghanaian young women who reaped the benefits of the educational expansion of the early 1950s came of age in the newly independent country.[72] On the job, though, these women often faced regular opposition to their presence, even in key party and government institutions where male administrators and managers singled out their female employees for ridicule and punishment for everything from perceived indiscipline and inefficiency on the job to their perceived inability to balance their obligations at work with those at home.[73] Such sentiments also made their way into the party apparatus itself as male leaders chastised the party's female activists for their apparent increasing indiscipline, irrationality, and "fuss[iness]" in the postindependence years, even while they praised the party's women's organizations for their accomplishments.[74] Additionally, the CPP had very little to say about those young women who, by means of education and class position, did not fit into the party's vision for the country's modernizing ideal. These included not only traders, but also the often nonliterate "small girls" and, for that matter, "small boys" who worked in the service of many of the country's elite and middle-class households.[75]

At the same time, the emerging emancipatory narratives of women's domestic liberation that marked the early 1960s competed with the similarly powerful, hypermasculinized imagery of the Ghanaian postcolonial nation-building project. Here, party and government publications, including the The Ghanaian, suggested, muscular men laboring in the country's docks, harbors, and construction sites exemplified nation-building as they literally built the infrastructure of the modern nation. In many cases, this also included building the homes and kitchens that were to serve as Ghanaian women's domestic emancipation. As a result, many of the country's women faced often-discordant expectations and opportunities in their efforts to balance the realities of life in a country that saw itself as at the political and social nexus of the global Cold War and African decolonization. As elsewhere, decolonization and socialism were to be pathways to a particular kind of postcolonial modernity, one intimately rooted in the creation of an industrial society free of foreign subversion and dependency and capable of asserting itself internationally independent of both the East and West. This meant that women and others who experienced the often conflicting nature of life in the highly ideological postcolonial state encountered both messages publicly celebrating women's domestic liberation and gender equity and equally public denunciations of the ways in which many women sought to take advantage of these opportunities.[76]

Conclusion

As historians Shane Hamilton and Sarah Phillips have argued, the famed 1959 Moscow kitchen debate between Khrushchev and Nixon helped reframe the battleground of the Cold War in both the capitalist and socialist blocs. As they note, the impromptu event "revealed that the cold war was not just a geopolitical confrontation between two nuclear-armed superpowers. It was also a battle for the hearts, the minds, and—perhaps most importantly—the stomachs of citizens in the cold war world."[77] The stakes for both the Soviet Union and the United States were ideological in that each superpower used the imagery of the modernized, rational, and technological kitchen to capture the social and economic successes of their respective socialist and capitalist worldviews and policies. The kitchen specifically, they and others suggest, was universal and essential in peoples' lives. At a minimum, everyone had to eat, and the process of adequately storing and preparing the food for one's family was a time- and labor-intensive process. It was also one that, in both countries, disproportionately fell on women. As a result, by focusing their debate on the kitchen, Nixon, Khrushchev, and others in the Soviet Union and the United States placed women, their domestic labor, and their opportunities inside and outside the home at the center of the Cold War's broader ideological struggle.

The kitchen debates that arose in the Ghanaian press in the early 1960s in turn followed those christened by the United States and the Soviet Union at the 1959 Moscow exhibition. In its most idealized iterations, the modern kitchen promised new modes of comfort and ease of work for the Ghanaian household. As a result, it foretold a future linked both to the availability of bourgeois consumer goods and to the rationalized, ordered, and technologically minded modernity many within the CPP believed would be required for the country's and continent's rapid postcolonial development. At their most basic levels, party and government publications insisted that colonial and "traditional" domesticity regimes had stunted the political and social development of the country's female citizenry by confining the country's women to the home and in turn removing them from the political, social, and cultural work required to forge a modern nation. The modern kitchen in Ghana thus emerged as a key symbol of postcolonial nonalignment that extended beyond the international and diplomatic sphere. Nonalignment here was a social phenomenon, one necessarily tied to the active construction of a politically, socially, and economically independent postcolonial society freed from the constraints and subversion of the broader Cold War.

Notes

During the essay's development, Bianca Murillo kindly helped me think through many of the issues addressed in it. Similarly, Philip Muehlenbeck and the essay's two anonymous readers enriched the text with their constructive comments and suggestions. Versions of this essay were previously presented at the 2015 Annual Meeting of the Society for Historians of American Foreign Relations and the Five Colleges History Seminar.

1. Kate Sey, "A Modern Amenity—The Gas Stove," *The Ghanaian*, September 1964.
2. Ibid.
3. See, for instance, Jane Busch, "Cooking Competition: Technology on the Domestic Market in the 1930s," *Technology and Culture* 24, no. 2 (1983): 222–45; Priscilla J. Brewer, "'We Have Got a Very Good Cooking Stove': Advertising, Design, and Consumer Response to the Cookstove, 1815–1880," *Winterthur Portfolio* 25, no. 1 (1990): 35–54; Howell J. Harris, "Inventing the U. S. Stove Industry, c. 1815–1875: Making and Selling the First Universal Consumer Durable," *Business History Review* 82, no. 4 (2008): 701–33; Harris, "'The Stove Trade Needs Change Continually': Designing the First Mass-Market Consumer Durable, ca. 1810–1930," *Winterthur Portfolio* 43, no. 4 (2009): 365–406.
4. Sey, "A Modern Amenity."
5. For a brief survey of *Redbook*'s history, see Victoria Goff, "Redbook," in *Women's Periodicals in the United States: Consumer Magazines*, ed. Kathleen L. Endres and Therese L. Lueck (Westport, CT: Greenwood, 1995), 297–310.
6. See, for instance, Susan E. Reid, "The Khrushchev Kitchen: Domesticating the Scientific-Technological Revolution," *Journal of Contemporary History* 40, no. 2 (2005): 289–316; Paul Betts, "Building Socialism at Home: The Case of East German Interiors," in *Socialist Modern: East German Everyday Culture and Politics*, ed. Katherine Pence and Paul Betts (Ann Arbor: University of Michigan Press, 2008); Greg Castillo, *Cold War on the Home Front: The Soft Power of Midcentury Design* (Minneapolis: University of Minnesota Press, 2010).
7. Greg Castillo, "The American 'Fat Kitchen' in Europe: Postwar Domestic Modernity and Marshall Plan Strategies of Enchantment," in *Cold War Kitchen: Americanization, Technology, and European Users*, ed. Ruth Oldenziel and Karin Zachmann (Cambridge, MA: MIT Press, 2009), 33–58. Also see Castillo, "Domesticating the Cold War: Household Consumption as Propaganda in Marshall Plan Germany," *Journal of Contemporary History* 40, no. 2 (2005): 261–88.
8. Castillo, "The American 'Fat Kitchen' in Europe," 38–40.
9. Ibid., 44–52.
10. LaRay Denzer, "Domestic Science Training in Colonial Yorubaland, Nigeria," in *African Encounters with Domesticity*, ed. Karen Tranberg Hansen (New Brunswick, NJ: Rutgers University Press, 1992), 116–42.
11. Nancy Rose Hunt, *A Colonial Lexicon: Of Birth Ritual, Medicalization, and Mobility in the Congo* (Durham, NC: Duke University Press, 1999), esp. ch. 3. Also, see Hunt, "Colonial Fairy Tales and the Knife and Fork Doctrine in the Heart of Africa," in Hansen, *African Encounters with Domesticity*, 143–71.
12. Takyiwaa Manuh, "Women and Their Organizations during the Convention People's Party Period," in *The Life and Work of Kwame Nkrumah: Papers of a Symposium Organized by the Institute of African Studies, University of Ghana, Legon*, ed. Kwame Arhin (Trenton, NJ: Africa World Press, 1993), 104. Also, see C. K. Graham, *The History of Education in Ghana* (London: Frank Cass, 1972), ch. 5.
13. Mabel Dove, *Selected Writings of a Pioneer West African Feminist*, ed. Stephanie Newell and Audrey Gadzekpo (Nottingham, UK: Trent Editions, 2004), 31. Dove's article was originally published under the pseudonym "Marjorie Mensah" in the *Times of West Africa* (Accra) on September 25, 1933.
14. On the early history of Gold Coast "baby shows" and "home exhibitions," see Jean Allman, "Making Mothers: Missionaries, Medical Officers and Women's Work in

Colonial Asante, 1924–1945," *History Workshop* 38 (1994): 23–47; and Allman and Victoria Tashjian, *"I Will Not Eat Stone": A Women's History of Colonial Asante* (Portsmouth, NH: Heinemann, 2000), ch. 5.

15. Bianca Murillo, "Ideal Homes and the Gender Politics of Consumerism in Postcolonial Ghana, 1960–1970," *Gender and History* 21, no. 3 (2009): 563–64.

16. Ibid., 564.

17. Susana Halm to District Commissioner (Sekondi), "Proposed 'Baby Show' Competition," Takoradi, October 12, 1963, Public Records and Archives Administration Department (hereafter, PRAAD)-Sekondi, Western Regional Archives (hereafter, WRG) 8/1/189.

18. "Suggested Programme Contents: National Health Week—November 3–9, 1963," PRAAD-Kumasi, Ashanti Regional Archives (hereafter, ARG) 17/5/7.

19. Secretary of Central Planning Committee for Health Education to National Organizer of the Ghana Young Pioneers, "National Health Week," Accra, January 22, 1962, PRAAD-Kumasi, ARG 17/5/7.

20. National Health Week, 1962, Subcommittee for Clean Homes Competition, Minutes, February 24, 1962, PRAAD-Kumasi, ARG 17/5/7.

21. "Aims and Objectives of the Ghana Women's League," appendix to Women's Africa Committee, "Informal Report Prepared by Elizabeth Hunting Wheeler for the Pre-Conference Briefing Session (Conference: Ghana Federation of Women, in Accra, July 15–25)," July 12, 1960, Smith College (SC), Sophia Smith Collection (SSC), Countries Collection (MS 445), box 13, folder 9.

22. Murillo, "Ideal Homes and the Gender Politics of Consumerism," 560.

23. On the economics and familial politics of Ghanaian women's labor outside the home, see, for instance, Claire C. Robertson, *Sharing the Same Bowl: A Socioeconomic History of Women and Class in Accra, Ghana* (Ann Arbor: University of Michigan Press, 1984); Christine Oppong and Katharine Adu, *Seven Roles of Women: Impact of Education, Migration, and Employment on Ghanaian Mothers* (Geneva: International Labour Office, 1987); and Gracia Clark, *Onions Are My Husband: Survival and Accumulation by West African Market Women* (Chicago: University of Chicago Press, 1994).

24. See, for instance, longtime CPP opponent Nancy Tsiboe's representation of the mission of her "Happy Home Institutes," in Jessie Ash Arndt, "Ghanaian Voices Hope: Founder of Happy Home Institutes," *Christian Science Monitor*[?], [n.d.], SC, SSC, Countries Collection (MS 445), box 13, folder 9.

25. "There Would Be No Question of Illegitimate Children, They Would All Have Rights," *Evening News*, May 26, 1962; Convention People's Party, *Programme for Work and Happiness for All* (Accra: Central Committee of the Convention People's Party, [1962]), 34–35; O. Owusu-Afriyie, *Parliamentary Debates*, April 1, 1963, vol. 31, cols. 576–580; Lucia Mercilene, "A Women's Eye-View of the Maintenance of Children Bill," *The Ghanaian*, June 1963. Also, see Stephan F. Miescher, *Making Men in Ghana* (Bloomington: Indiana University Press, 2005), ch. 5.

26. Richard Wright, "The Birth of a Man and the Birth of a Nation," unpublished ms., [1957?], Yale University Beinecke Rare Book and Manuscript Library (hereafter, Beinecke Library), Richard Wright Papers (hereafter, Wright Papers), box 5, folder 81.

27. Kwame Nkrumah, speech at the independence of Ghana, March 6, 1957, excerpted in Nkrumah, *I Speak of Freedom: A Statement of African Ideology* (New York: Frederick A. Praeger, 1961), 107.

28. Peter Molotsi, quoted in Luli Callinicos, *Oliver Tambo: Beyond the Engeli Mountains* (Cape Town: David Philip, 2004), 264. I explore the themes of this and the two subsequent paragraphs in much greater depth in several of my other essays and in my forthcoming book. See, for instance, Jeffrey S. Ahlman, "The Algerian Question in Nkrumah's Ghana, 1958–1960: Debating 'Violence' and 'Nonviolence' in African Decolonization," *Africa Today* 57, no. 2 (2010): 67–84; Ahlman, "Road to Ghana: Nkrumah, Southern Africa, and the Eclipse of a Decolonizing Africa," *Kronos: Southern African Histories* 37 (2011): 26–43; Ahlman, "Managing the Pan-African Workplace: Discipline, Ideology, and the Cultural Politics of the Ghanaian Bureau of African Affairs, 1959–1966," *Ghana Studies* 15/16 (2012/2013): 337–71; Ahlman, *Living with Nkrumahism: Nation, State, and Pan-Africanism in Ghana* (Athens: Ohio University Press, forthcoming).

29. E. B. Mac-Hardjor, "Increased Productivity: What It Means for Our Prosperity," *The Ghanaian*, January 1965.

30. Ahlman, "Managing the Pan-African Workplace."

31. Cati Coe, *Dilemmas of Culture in African Schools: Youth, Nationalism, and the Transformation of Knowledge* (Chicago: University of Chicago Press, 2005), 65–70; Ahlman, "A New Type of Citizen: Youth, Gender, and Generation in the Ghanaian Builders Brigade," *Journal of African History* 53, no. 1 (2012): 87–105; Ahlman, *Living with Nkrumahism*, esp. ch. 3.

32. See, for instance, Kwame Nkrumah, *Africa Must Unite* (London: Panaf, 1963); and Nkrumah, *Neo-Colonialism: The Last Stage of Imperialism* (London: Thomas Nelson, 1965). For Nkrumah's analysis of colonialism specifically, see Nkrumah, *Towards Colonial Freedom: Africa and the Struggle against World Imperialism* (London: Farleigh, 1947).

33. Priya Lal, "Self-Reliance and the State: The Multiple Meanings of Development in Early Post-Colonial Tanzania," *Africa* 82, no. 2 (2012): 212.

34. Faye Woodard Grant, *The Nutrition and Health of Children in the Gold Coast* (Chicago: University of Chicago Press, 1955), 6.

35. Ioné Acquah, *Accra Survey: A Social Survey of the Capital of Ghana, Formerly Called the Gold Coast, Undertaken for the West African Institute of Social and Economic Research, 1953–1956* (London: University of London Press, 1958), 47.

36. K. A. Busia, *Report on a Social Survey of Sekondi-Takoradi* (London: Crown Agents for the Colony on behalf of the Government of the Gold Coast, 1950), ch. 1.

37. Department of Social Welfare and Community Development, "Cleanliness in the Home," *Advance*, April 1957.

38. Department of Social Welfare and Community Development (Ghana), *Mass Education Women's Work Handbook*, [1964?], SC, SSC, Countries Collection (MS 445), box 13, folder 9.

39. "Ideas for Ideal Homes," *The Ghanaian*, September 1958; "The Ideal Kitchen," *Evening News*, January 19, 1961.

40. Volta River Preparatory Commission Ajena Township, *Final Report*, March 1956, Princeton University Archives (PUA), W. Arthur Lewis Papers (Lewis Papers), box 22, folder 1; "Housing the People at Little Cost," *Evening News*, July 24, 1961. On the tenuousness of these debates at both the planning and local levels, see, specifically, Jordan E. Shapiro, "Settling Refugees, Unsettling the Nation: Ghana's Volta River Project Scheme and the Ambiguities of Development Planning, 1952–1970" (PhD diss., University of Michigan, 2003), 233–55; Stephan F. Miescher, "Building the

City of the Future: Visions and Experiences of Modernity in Ghana's Akosombo Township," *Journal of African History* 53, no. 3 (2012): 371–76; Miescher, "'No One Should Be Worse Off': The Akosombo Dam, Modernization, and the Experience of Resettlement in Ghana," in *Modernization as Spectacle in Africa*, ed. Peter J. Bloom, Stephan F. Miescher, and Takyiwaa Manuh (Bloomington: Indiana University Press, 2014), 193, 196, and 187–197.

41. "The Two Worlds: A Day-Long Battle," *New York Times*, July 25, 1959, reproduced in Shane Hamilton and Sarah Phillips, eds., *The Kitchen Debate and Cold War Consumer Politics: A Brief History with Documents* (Boston: Bedford/St. Martins, 2014), 43–51.

42. "Two Worlds."

43. Ibid.; Ye. Litoshko, "A Talk to the Point," *Pravda*, July 25, 1959, in Hamilton and Phillips, *Kitchen Debate and Cold War Consumer Politics*, 51–54.

44. V. Osipov, "First Day, First Impressions," *Izvestia*, July 26, 1959, in Hamilton and Phillips, *Kitchen Debate and Cold War Consumer Politics*, 55.

45. "Unfavorable Comments on Exhibition," n.d., in Hamilton and Phillips, *Kitchen Debate and Cold War Consumer Politics*, 65.

46. Lenin, cited in Reid, "Khrushchev Kitchen," 291.

47. Reid, "Khrushchev Kitchen."

48. "Two Worlds"; Reid, "Khrushchev Kitchen"; Reid, "'Our Kitchen Is Just as Good': Soviet Responses to the American Kitchen," in Oldenziel and Zachmann, *Cold War Kitchen*, 83–112.

49. Reid, "Khrushchev Kitchen," 313.

50. "Soviet Union: A Giant in Industrial and Technological Might," *Evening News*, October 14, 1961. See also "Mighty Construction Proceeds in Once Neglected Siberia," *Evening News*, August 21, 1961; "Russia Has World's Biggest Reservoir," *Evening News*, October 3, 1961; "A Typical Russia Town, What It Enjoys," *Evening News*, October 25, 1961.

51. AmEmbassy, Accra, to Department of State, Washington, "Soviet Astronaut Gagarin's Visit to Ghana," February 13, 1962, in *Confidential U. S. State Department Central Files, Ghana 1960–January 1963: Internal and Foreign Affairs* (hereafter, *U. S. Confidential State Department Files, Ghana*), reel 4. See also Yuri Gagarin, "Africa Cannot Fail Us," *Ghanaian Times*, February 5, 1962; and "Akwaaba Yuri," *Ghanaian Times*, February 6, 1962.

52. "Soviet Spacemen Descending Today," *Evening News*, August 13, 1962.

53. "A Guide to the Soviet Exhibition," *Evening News*, January 10, 1962. See also "Osagyefo Opens Giant Soviet Exhibition," *Evening News*, January 10, 1962; and "Over 100,000 View Soviet Industrial Fair," *Evening News*, July 14, 1962.

54. Sey, "Modern Amenity."

55. A Correspondent, "Woman's Role outside the Kitchen," *The Ghanaian*, September 1964.

56. Ibid.

57. Kate Sey, "Women in Ghanaian Society: They Have Equal Opportunities with Men," *The Ghanaian*, April 1964.

58. Ibid.

59. On the CPP's late colonial educational program, see Gold Coast, *Accelerated Development Plan for Education, 1951* (Accra: Government Printer, 1951); and Gold Coast, *Progress in Education in the Gold Coast* (Accra: Government Printer, 1953). For a discussion of the political and ideological agenda underpinning the CPP's educational policy, see Ahlman, *Living with Nkrumahism*, ch. 2.

60. Miranda Greenstreet, "Employment of Women in Ghana," *International Labour Review* 103, no. 2 (1971): 126.

61. Jonathan Zimmerman, "'Money, Materials, and Manpower': Ghanaian In-Service Teacher Education and the Political Economy of Failure, 1961–1971," *History of Education Quarterly* 51, no. 1 (2011): 3.

62. Ibid.

63. "A Studious Girl," *Evening News*, April 9, 1957.

64. Sey, "Women in Ghanaian Society."

65. Interview: Lawrence Bessah, Shama, Western Region, July 5, 2008; Z. B. Shardow to Secretary of the Cabinet, "Appeal on 59 U. S. S. R. Scholarships to Ghana Young Pioneers for Various Courses in Youth Work," Accra, December 12 1962, PRAAD-Accra, Record Group (hereafter, RG) 3/1/590; J. B. Elliot to Shardow, "Training in the Soviet Union," Moscow, July 26, 1962, PRAAD-Accra, RG 3/1/590.

66. Josephine Sappor, "Careers for Ghana Women: Candid and Explicit Evaluation and Suggestions," *The Ghanaian*, September 1961.

67. Ibid.

68. Victoria Nyarku, "The Role of Women in Ghana," *Evening News*, January 27, 1962.

69. Kwame Nkrumah, "To the Students of Women's Training College," in *Selected Speeches of Kwame Nkrumah*, vol. 1, ed. Samuel Obeng (Accra: Afram, 1979), 196.

70. Margaret Martei, "National Council of Ghana Women Preamble," [1962], PRAAD-Sekondi, WRG 8/1/189.

71. See, for instance, Ahlman, "Managing the Pan-African Workplace"; Ahlman, *Living with Nkrumahism*, ch. 5.

72. Greenstreet, "Employment of Women in Ghana," 222.

73. Ahlman, "Managing the Pan-African Workplace," 356–62.

74. Minutes of the First Conference of Ashanti Regional Executive—NCGW, held on Sunday, July 8, 1963, PRAAD-Kumasi, ARG 17/9/5.

75. On the role of child domestic labor in mid-century Ghanaian households, see Busia, *Report on the Social Survey of Sekondi-Takoradi*, 34–37; and Acquah, *Accra Survey*, 74–77.

76. More broadly, see Ahlman, *Living with Nkrumahism*, ch. 5.

77. Shane Hamilton and Sarah Phillips, "Introduction: The Kitchen Debate in Historical Context," in Hamilton and Phillips, *Kitchen Debate and Cold War Consumer Politics*, 1.

References

Archives

Princeton University Archives, Princeton, New Jersey
Public Records and Archives Administration Department–Accra, Ghana
Public Records and Archives Administration Department–Kumasi, Ghana
Public Records and Archives Administration Department–Sekondi, Ghana
Smith College, Sophia Smith Collection, Northampton, Massachusetts
Yale University Beinecke Rare Book and Manuscript Library, New Haven, Connecticut

Periodicals

Advance
Ghanaian Times

The Evening News
The Ghanaian
New York Times
Times of West Africa

Selected Published Works

Acquah, Ioné. *Accra Survey: A Social Survey of the Capital of Ghana, Formerly Called the Gold Coast, Undertaken for the West African Institute of Social and Economic Research, 1953–1956*. London: University of London Press, 1958.

Ahlman, Jeffrey S. "The Algerian Question in Nkrumah's Ghana, 1958–1960: Debating 'Violence' and 'Nonviolence' in African Decolonization." *Africa Today* 57, no. 2 (2010): 67–84.

———. *Living with Nkrumahism: Nation, State, and Pan-Africanism in Ghana*. Athens: Ohio University Press, forthcoming.

———. "Managing the Pan-African Workplace: Discipline, Ideology, and the Cultural Politics of the Ghanaian Bureau of African Affairs, 1959–1966." *Ghana Studies* 15/16 (2012/2013): 337–71.

———. "A New Type of Citizen: Youth, Gender, and Generation in the Ghanaian Builders Brigade." *Journal of African History* 53, no. 1 (2012): 87–105.

———. "Road to Ghana: Nkrumah, Southern Africa, and the Eclipse of a Decolonizing Africa." *Kronos: Southern African Histories* 37 (2011): 26–43.

Allman, Jean, and Victoria Tashjian. *"I Will Not Eat Stone": A Women's History of Colonial Asante*. Portsmouth, NH: Heinemann, 2000.

Busia, K. A. *Report on a Social Survey of Sekondi-Takoradi*. London: Crown Agents for the Colony on behalf of the Government of the Gold Coast, 1950.

Castillo, Greg. "The American 'Fat Kitchen' in Europe: Postwar Domestic Modernity and Marshall Plan Strategies of Enchantment." In *Cold War Kitchen: Americanization, Technology, and European Users*, edited by Ruth Oldenziel and Karin Zachmann. Cambridge: MIT Press, 2009.

———. *Cold War on the Home Front: The Soft Power of Midcentury Design*. Minneapolis: University of Minnesota Press, 2010.

———. "Domesticating the Cold War: Household Consumption as Propaganda in Marshall Plan Germany." *Journal of Contemporary History* 40, no. 2 (2005): 261–88.

Convention People's Party. *Programme for Work and Happiness for All*. Accra: Central Committee of the Convention People's Party, [1962].

Dove, Mabel. *Selected Writings of a Pioneer West African Feminist*. Edited by Stephanie Newell and Audrey Gadzekpo. Nottingham, UK: Trent Editions, 2004.

Gold Coast. *Accelerated Development Plan for Education, 1951*. Accra: Government Printer, 1951.

———. *Progress in Education in the Gold Coast*. Accra: Government Printer, 1953.

Greenstreet, Miranda. "Employment of Women in Ghana." *International Labour Review* 103, no. 2 (1971): 117–29.

Hamilton, Shane, and Sara Phillips, eds. *The Kitchen Debate and Cold War Consumer Politics: A Brief History with Documents*. Boston: Bedford/St. Martins, 2014.

Hunt, Nancy Rose. *A Colonial Lexicon: Of Birth Ritual, Medicalization, and Mobility in the Congo*. Durham, NC: Duke University Press, 1999.

Lal, Priya. "Self-Reliance and the State: The Multiple Meanings of Development in Early Post-Colonial Tanzania." *Africa* 82, no. 2 (2012): 212–34.

Manuh, Takyiwaa. "Women and Their Organizations during the Convention People's Party Period." In *The Life and Work of Kwame Nkrumah: Papers of a Symposium Organized by the Institute of African Studies, University of Ghana*, edited by Kwame Arhin. Trenton, NJ: Africa World Press, 1993.

Miescher, Stephan F. "Building the City of the Future: Visions and Experiences of Modernity in Ghana's Akosombo Township." *Journal of African History* 53, no. 3 (2012): 367–90.

———. *Making Men in Ghana*. Bloomington: Indiana University Press, 2005.

———. "'No One Should Be Worse Off': The Akosombo Dam, Modernization, and the Experience of Resettlement in Ghana." In *Modernization as Spectacle in Africa*, edited by Peter J. Bloom, Stephan F. Miescher, and Takyiwaa Manuh. Bloomington: Indiana University Press, 2014.

Murillo, Bianca. "Ideal Homes and the Gender Politics of Consumerism in Postcolonial Ghana, 1960–1970." *Gender and History* 21, no. 3 (2009): 560–75.

Reid, Susan E. "The Khrushchev Kitchen: Domesticating the Scientific-Technological Revolution." *Journal of Contemporary History* 40, no. 2 (2005): 289–316.

———. "'Our Kitchen Is Just as Good': Soviet Responses to the American Kitchen." In *Cold War Kitchen: Americanization, Technology, and European Users*, edited by Ruth Oldenziel and Karin Zachmann. Cambridge: MIT Press, 2009.

Zimmerman, Jonathan. "'Money, Materials, and Manpower': Ghanaian In-Service Teacher Education and the Political Economy of Failure, 1961–1971." *History of Education Quarterly* 51, no. 1 (2011): 1–27.

CHAPTER 9

Mobilizing Women?

State Feminisms in Communist Czechoslovakia and Socialist Egypt

May Hawas and Philip E. Muehlenbeck

In the early years of the Cold War, socialist governments that espoused support for sexual equality came to power in both Czechoslovakia (1948) and Egypt (1952). Under the Communist Party of Czechoslovakia (Komunistická strana Československa, or KSČ) in Czechoslovakia and under Gamal Abdel Nasser's regime in Egypt, women's rights were publicly supported and greatly expanded. Both regimes passed new laws to ensure voting rights, equal educational and employment opportunities, government-paid maternity leave, subsidized day care, and other rights for women.

Having passed such progressive legislation, both regimes proclaimed the "woman question" to have been "solved" by socialism, yet many sexually based inequalities remained in both societies and went largely ignored. Moreover, both regimes effectively hijacked women's movements, putting the organizations under direct governmental control and guiding their agendas and activities. Both governments crushed all autonomous political movements and politically silenced feminist leaders who did not accept the dictates of the new state feminism. While select women who supported the regimes, such as Aziza Hussein and Julie Prokopová, were allowed the scope for public work in their countries, women continued to hold only a small fraction of midlevel political positions and remained largely absent from the upper echelons of power. Meanwhile, feminist leaders who opposed the new state-led women's movements found themselves in perilous predicaments. In Czechoslovakia, the show trial of Milada Horáková resulted in her execution for treason, and in Egypt Doria Shafik was placed under house arrest for fifteen years until she fell to her death from her apartment balcony.

Czechoslovakia and Egypt provide illuminating case studies in how two socialist states—one from the "Second World" and the other from the "Third

World"—dealt with feminist issues. In both countries the governments' expansion of women's rights had more to do with the pursuit of economic modernization than with the expansion of women's civil rights. On the one hand, both governments supported women's empowerment, albeit mainly as a means to add women to the workforce rather than because of an altruistic desire for gender equality. On the other hand, each government was deeply invested in protecting women's difference—particularly as mothers—in order to further state demographic goals. The experience of feminists in Czechoslovakia and Egypt was not unique— similar state feminist projects took place in all corners of the world: Cuba, India, Senegal, China, the Soviet Union, Vietnam, and elsewhere. State feminism was used primarily as a method for mobilizing support for the regime. While Egypt and Czechoslovakia will forever be linked in the annals of Cold War history as a result of their arms deal in 1955, this chapter, based on a reading of the Czech national archives and the Egyptian women's cultural press, focuses on the way that both regimes used their state-led women's organizations in support of their demographic goals—to increase the birthrate in the case of Czechoslovakia and to limit the birthrate in the case of Egypt.[1]

The Women's Movement in Egypt, 1919–1952

Starting in the late nineteenth century and developing rapidly in the early and mid-twentieth, the Egyptian feminist movement was part and parcel of the call for Egypt's political liberation and national sovereignty. The demand for women's rights often manifested in the argument about what form the Egyptian state should take. Despite being momentarily united at various moments, such as in the uprisings against British rule, women's political groups and activist communities in Egypt, from philanthropist organizations to Leftist and Islamist political parties, differed on which fundamental constitutional tenets would set Egypt on the "right track."

In this context, overpopulation and the concurrent responsibility of women-citizens have been essential to the development of Egypt's economic policies (and, subsequently, its political independence).[2] From early on, women's organizations in Egypt figured centrally in the process of demographic management. Women activists, civil workers, intellectuals, and public figures, often working through civil institutions spearheaded by women, such as NGOs, social organizations, and the press, took up the demographic debate along with the complex issues with which it intersected, such as nation-building and citizenship, modernization and industrial progress, and the improvement of public health.

Since political resistance in Egypt, like elsewhere, has never been insular, feminist discourse moved between local and global platforms, working for reform on the national level while agitating on an international level against such issues as imperialism, racism, and slavery. The Egyptian Feminist Union (EFU), which had been the leading, although by no means sole, women's political organization in Egypt from 1923 onward, sought tricontinental—regional and international—ties. While advocating for universal suffrage, for example, the EFU linked itself to the International Alliance of Women (IAW). Realizing that European feminism came with its own forms of imperialism that dismissed or neglected the colonized context, Egyptian feminists through the EFU called for a "third way" anti-imperialism inspired by Leftist discourses, and eventually affiliated themselves to the Women's International Democratic Federation (WIDF). The EFU also initiated unions for regional pan-Arab cooperation, such as on the issue of Palestine, which manifested in the inauguration of the Arab Feminist Union in 1945.

On the local level the EFU also took the lead in trying to create an infrastructure for social service in loco parentis. Initiatives for social reform were popularly instigated and staffed by women because social work was one way by which they carved out socially acceptable roles for themselves in the public sphere and were also spurred in part by charitable religious obligations.[3] For the improvement of public health the EFU spearheaded a series of medical dispensaries during the early twentieth century such as al-Baghālah dispensary in Sayyidah Zaynab, which, powered by voluntary and paid workers, offered basic hygiene and health instruction as well as specialized health examinations and treatment for poor women and children. Dispensaries were also launched to deal with wide-ranging health issues from tuberculosis to infant mortality. As early as 1924 the EFU and other women's organizations called for the creation of supervised children's parks and day-care centers in urban quarters and, later, around the country. By 1937 women's political lobbying for reform extended to the countryside, and feminists at the EFU called on leading women, large landowners, and the government to create infrastructural services for the people of rural Egypt. Workers at the EFU called to provide fresh water, build educational facilities, and open a cooperative bank for peasants, also urging the government to sell state-owned land to peasants at a reduced cost.[4] By taking such communal projects and institutionalizing them within the centralized state, Gamal Abdel Nasser's government would later create its trademark reputation as the prime actor working for reform at a grassroots level.

The EFU also helped instigate a mobile dispensary-clinic model to address health and reproductive matters in both urban and rural areas. This clinic would be used so expansively in the Nasser period that it became an iconic representative of the family-planning program of the 1960s. Yet as early as 1937 feminists "were asking the government to send mobile health units equipped with doctors, nurses, midwives, and medical supplies to the villages" with the aim of including "basic instruction in hygiene and health, and in new techniques of childbirth and childcare."[5] Dispensary units offered infertility treatment in addition to contraceptives. Contraceptives were not publicly promoted or encouraged and were offered primarily to married women who could show their husband's consent and specify some economic or health reason. Meanwhile, even a decade before the family-planning program had been set up, some women's magazines, targeting audiences more literate and urban than those reached by the dispensary units, recommended the use of "natural" means of birth control, such the Knaus-Ogino method, to address the problem of overpopulation.[6]

The Women's Movement in Czechoslovakia, 1920–1948

Czechoslovak women had long been some of the most 'liberated' in the world in terms of voting rights, educational opportunities, and political and civic activism.[7] After its creation from the ashes of World War I, Czechoslovakia's first constitution, ratified in February 1920, granted women full voting rights, abolished discrimination in employment and education, and guaranteed six weeks of maternity leave for new mothers. Such constitutional rights were provided by Czechoslovakia decades earlier than 90 percent of the world's other nation-states. Despite this enlightened legislation, sex discrimination remained commonplace. For example, during the Great Depression—when unemployment rates in Czechoslovakia reached over 21 percent—women were typically the first to lose their jobs. Furthermore, employers could legally use policies of unequal pay for equal work, and women's wages were often 50 to 60 percent less than those earned by men.[8]

As a result of such inequalities Františka Plamínková founded the country's first national women's movement, the National Council of Women (NCW), in 1923. The NCW served as an umbrella organization coordinating the activities of more than sixty women's associations across Bohemia, Moravia, and Slovakia with a combined membership of over three hundred thousand. Under Plamínková's leadership, the NCW established working groups focusing on social issues affecting women and launched projects designed to improve women's position within the legal, social, economic, and cultural spheres of Czechoslovak society. Plamínková also became a prominent international figure, becoming vice president of both the International Woman Suffrage Alliance and the International Council of Women, and in the process helped integrate Czechoslovak women into the international women's movement. In 1925 Plamínková was elected to the Czechoslovak National Assembly, where she advocated not only for women's rights but also against the perils of German Nazism. In September 1938 she sent an open letter to Adolf Hitler to protest his threats against Czechoslovakia. Her letter obviously did not deter Hitler, and six months later Nazi Germany occupied all of Czechoslovakia. During the Nazi occupation, the Czechoslovak women's movement was forced to move underground, but Plamínková continued her work on behalf of Czechoslovak nationalism and the international women's movement until she was arrested by the Nazis and executed in June 1942.[9]

Following WWII, Milada Horáková, a former colleague of Plamínková who herself had spent five years in a Nazi prison during the war, sought to resuscitate the NCW, but the application to renew the organization's registration was denied by the communist-controlled Ministry of the Interior.[10] With revival of the NCW thus blocked, Horáková founded a new organization, the Council of Czechoslovak Women (CCW). Horáková gained prominence as an elected member of the National Assembly and, building on the legacy of the NCW, turned the CCW into a powerful national organization.

Because they constituted a majority of the electorate, female voters were heavily courted during Czechoslovakia's 1946 parliamentary elections, with each of the major political parties claiming to be the true champion of women's rights. As a member of the National Socialist Party Horáková stumped for that party, but the Communist Party of Czechoslovakia (KSČ) recruited the most female members and, as a result, won the election with 38 percent of the vote (the National Socialist Party finished second with 18.3 percent of the vote).[11] Additionally, half of the women elected to the National Assembly during the election were representatives of the KSČ.[12] Over the next several years the KSČ continued to attract women to its party and by May 1947 boasted over 446,000 female members (30.5 percent of its overall membership). To put this figure into perspective, the entire membership of the National Socialist Party was just under 600,000 at this time.[13] This partisan competition for the allegiance of Czechoslovak women created a debilitating fissure in the women's movement between supporters of the KSČ and anticommunists, creating conditions in which Czechoslovak women spent more time fighting their political opponents than unifying for women's rights.

The Expansion of Women's Rights under Socialist Regimes

In January 1948 the KSČ-controlled Ministry of the Interior purged the Czechoslovak security forces and filled its ranks with Communist Party members. The noncommunist members of the coalition government attempted to force new elections by resigning from their cabinet positions in protest, but this backfired: it allowed the KSČ to fill the power vacuum and eventually led to the communists taking complete political control of Czechoslovakia. Initially, the communist takeover appeared to portend a bright future for Czechoslovak women. Upon taking power the KSČ almost immediately enacted legislation that the Czechoslovak women's movement had long been fighting to obtain. Seeking to construct a new social and political order, the communists created a new constitution in May 1948. Guided by Marxist-Leninist ideology and Soviet tutelage, the KSČ government sought to establish legal principles of equality between the sexes in order to fully incorporate Czechoslovak women into the process of building a socialist society. The new constitution prohibited discrimination against women in all aspects of social and civil life (such as employment and education) and declared the state's obligation to assist women with their maternal responsibilities.[14] Under the KSČ, women were now guaranteed equal pay for equal work, and the state established day-care centers, cafeterias, and laundromats to assist families with their work-life balance (although these services were slow to actually appear, in part because of a lack of funding but mostly because there were no independent women's organizations to lobby for them).

The KSČ government launched an ambitious Soviet-inspired industrial plan featuring a labor-intensive strategy for economic development. This necessitated an increase in the nation's labor force, and, as a result, the number of women employed outside of the home grew dramatically. The percentage of women in the workforce increased from 38 percent in 1948 to 71 percent in 1960 and 85 percent by 1970.[15] By the 1960s, 97 percent of women between the ages of fifteen to fifty-four who were deemed able to work were employed—giving Czechoslovakia the highest rate of female employment in the world.[16] While women accounted for only 22 percent of the country's labor force in 1945, this had grown to 48 percent by 1975—which ranked third in the world behind only the Soviet Union and East Germany. By comparison, the percentage of women in Western workforces during this period ranged from 18 to 38 percent.[17] Moreover, even these statistics are misleading because many women in the West worked part-time jobs (approximately 25 percent in the United States), while in Czechoslovakia nearly 90 percent of female workers were employed in full-time jobs.[18]

The Czechoslovak women's movement had been fighting for such economic opportunities for decades—and they became a reality almost overnight once the communists came to power. The communists claimed that employment outside the home was a precondition for women's liberation and gender equality. But there was a downside to such change, as women were now obliged to work. Those who preferred to stay home but were unable to justify unemployment because of motherhood, disability, or illness were at best labeled as parasites and at worst faced punishment. The government also used moral and financial incentives to encourage women to join the labor force—most notably by creating a wage structure in which two incomes (of both wife and husband) were necessary in order for a family to achieve a comfortable lifestyle and by granting employed women preferential access to scarce and rationed goods. Furthermore, while women eventually accounted for 48 percent of the country's workforce, Czechoslovak women faced stiff inequalities in career advancement and only accounted for 5 percent of managerial positions.[19] Therefore, while new laws in theory ensured women received equal pay for equal work, women were rarely actually doing equal work. As a result, women on average received one-third less income than men, a ratio that held steady throughout the communist period, even after the number of female university graduates reached parity with the number of university-educated men.[20]

KSČ policies also expanded educational opportunities for women as the number of female university students in Czechoslovakia rose from 10,148 in 1945 to 48,927 in 1975—an almost quintuple increase in a span of only thirty years. During this period the female proportion of university students in Czechoslovakia increased from 18.5 percent to 41.0 percent.[21] While female university graduates were still heavily concentrated in traditionally feminine fields such as education, women were also twice as likely to be doctors or engineers in communist Czechoslovakia as they were in the United States or Western Europe.[22]

Just as the communist political system allowed women to make marked improvement in employment and education, it also led to a dramatic increase in female political representation. In the mid-1960s women constituted approximately 31 percent of all elected political representatives in Czechoslovakia and 22 percent of the National Assembly—among the highest levels of female political participation in the world at a time when women accounted for only 2.6 percent of the members of the United States Congress.[23] When the KSČ took power in 1948, Czechoslovakia already had the highest percentage of women serving as national legislators in the world, yet under communist rule the number tripled in just fifteen years.[24]

In Egypt women enjoyed a similar, if less spectacular, expansion of their educational, employment, and political rights. The 1952 Egyptian revolution dispossessed King Farouk, ending a 350-year-old monarchy, and instated the military rule of the Free Officers, which was later presided over by Gamal Abdel Nasser. New laws were designed to increase the penetration of women in the workplace, as early feminists had always demanded, and the laws were announced in the fiery, all-citizens-on-deck oratory of Nasser's socialist republic. Such laws included government-paid maternity leave, the abolition of formal gender discrimination in hiring, and the explosive expansion of women's access to higher and professional education. Under a law that implemented six years of compulsory free education to all Egyptian children, the number of girls enrolled in primary school increased by 170 percent between 1953 and 1971. Over the same period, female enrollment in secondary schools increased by 631 percent and the proportion of female university students increased from 7.5 percent to 40 percent.[25] Likewise, from 1961 to 1969, women's participation in the Egyptian labor force increased by 31.1 percent (although it remained a relatively low 10 percent of the overall total), and the state guaranteed women equal pay for equal work.[26] Women's access to public office also expanded, if tentatively, particularly in the fields of journalism, education, and social affairs. Additionally, more women, such as Aziza Hussein, were officially selected as diplomatic representatives for Egypt and the Middle East in international meetings and conferences. The 1956 Constitution gave women the right to vote, and in 1957 two women were elected to the National Assembly.

These statistics are not a true reflection of the political influence women had in communist Czechoslovakia or socialist Egypt, however, because effective political power in these countries did not lie in the National Assembly but rather within the upper echelons of the ruling party. The number of women in various bodies within the Czechoslovak political system dwindled at each subsequent level of the hierarchy. While women made up 40 percent of trade union leadership at the local level, they accounted for 37 percent of the membership in the county national committees, 28 percent in district national committees, 22 percent in the National Assembly, and only 11 percent in the Central Committee of the KSČ. Additionally, the proportion of female members in the Communist Party of Czechoslovakia peaked in 1949 at 33 percent and dipped to about 27 percent throughout the 1950s and 1960s.[27] The political participation of Egyptian women was even lower. For example, in 1957 5.5 million men had registered to vote but only 144,000 women had. A decade later, in 1967, only 11.5 percent of eligible male voters abstained from voting, but 77 percent of potential female voters refrained from doing so.[28] Moreover, neither state had a female head of state, and only a handful of women ever occupied posts in government ministries. In Czechoslovakia no more than two (of twenty-four) ministerial posts were ever held by women at the same time, and in Nasser's Egypt only one government ministry was ever headed by a woman. Furthermore, these were seemingly token appointments overseeing "female concerns": the only ministries women led were the Ministry of Food and the Ministry of Consumer Affairs in Czechoslovakia and the Ministry of Social Affairs in Egypt.[29]

In single-party authoritarian oligarchies such as Czechoslovakia and Egypt, female participation in the lower levels of the political system had limited impact and was essentially symbolic. While the governments in both countries passed legislation to foster gender equality and made concerted efforts to increase occupational, educational, and political opportunities for women, inequalities remained, and both societies remained patriarchal at their cores.

The KSČ and the Czechoslovak Women's Movement

The communists viewed all independent organizations, such as the CCW, as foreign elements that might undermine the KSČ's authority. As a result, shortly after the KSČ's seizure of the government, communist members of the CCW gained control of the organization and began to purge it by expelling members who opposed the communist takeover—including Horáková, who also resigned from her position in the National Assembly in order to take part in the anticommunist movement. The CCW was renamed the Council of Women (CW) and lost any semblance of autonomy from the KSČ government. Women from other mass trade union, youth, and agricultural associations were given automatic membership in the CW, which gave the CW more than 2.5 million members almost overnight. The KSČ boasted that this impressive membership figure demonstrated women's approval of both their regime and the CW, despite the fact that the vast majority of the CW's members had not actively joined the organization.[30]

The communists went further than simply taking control of Horáková's organization, however. In September 1949 Horáková was arrested by the secret police and faced a show trial for treason. The former leader of the Czechoslovak women's movement was sentenced to death and was executed by hanging on June 27, 1950.[31] Marie Švermová, a member of the KSČ Central Committee who led a campaign encouraging women to sign a resolution calling for Horáková's death, would later herself be expelled from the Communist Party and imprisoned from 1954 to 1956. The fates of Horáková and Švermová exemplify the danger women activists faced if they ran afoul of the new government.

In March 1950 the Council of Women merged with the leading women's organization in Slovakia (Živena—Union of Slovak Women) to create a new organization called the Czechoslovak Women's Union (CWU). Unlike the CW, the membership of the CWU was not as broad (having only 115,000 members in comparison to the CW's 2.5 million).[32] Women's equality, which had previously been the top priority of the pre-1948 Czechoslovak women's movements such as the Council of Czechoslovak Women, was explicitly left out of the CWU's objectives. Instead, the organization's planning documents list its three primary tasks as organizing women to take part in socialist state building, defending the state against "hostile elements and ideological direction," and "mobilizing women to actively fight for [world] peace."[33] Its charter also proclaimed that the organization should encourage women "to train their children spirited patriotism and international solidarity with the working people of the world" and "teach them to love and be devoted to the first worker of the republic, President Klement Gottwald, and our best friend and ally, the Soviet Union."[34] Such an orientation shows that the CWU's primary purpose was to coordinate the support of women for the domestic and foreign policies of the KSČ rather than to establish and ensure women's equality.

The CWU's subservient relationship to the KSČ was codified in law through the Act on Volunteer Organizations of 1951, which required that the organization's objectives, activities, and staffing all be approved at the highest levels of the Communist Party.[35] The CWU also differed from previous Czechoslovak women's associations because its predecessors had been financed through membership dues, donations, and public funding, but as a state institution the CWU was financed directly by the KSČ government.[36] The CWU was largely funded from the budget of the Ministry of Information, which in itself indicates that the communists viewed the organization's role mostly as propagandistic.

Like the CW, the CWU proved to be short lived. Communist leaders were unhappy with the constant attempts of noncommunist members (who constituted about 60 percent of the CWU's membership) to inject more feminist objectives into the union's activities.[37] KSČ leaders even began to question the need for a women's organization. One party leader referred to the organization as "a relic from a capitalist society in which individual segments of the population who felt their interests threatened defended themselves in so-called interest groups."[38] In line with Marxist doctrine, which placed class interests above all else, the KSČ leadership declared that the basic problems of female equality had now been solved by their progressive legislation. Under socialism, it was claimed, there was no need for women to lobby for their own interests because they were now fully emancipated; as a result, the discussion of women's issues was no longer necessary.[39] "There is no communism in our skirts and trousers" is how one KSČ member put it.[40] Using this rationale in early 1952, the government disbanded the CWU and replaced it with the Czechoslovak Women's Committee, which lasted from 1952 to 1967.

Unlike the CW or CWU, the Women's Committee was not a broad-based membership organization but rather a small group of eighty prominent women from within the Communist Party. For example, its president, Anežka Hodinová-Spurná, and vice president, Julie Prokopová, were both members of the Central Committee of the KSČ. The committee had no autonomy of its own, and, according to historian Alena Heitlinger, its recommendations on domestic issues were "either ignored by the authorities or politely received but rarely implemented."[41] Instead, its role was merely symbolic with its main tasks being to represent Czechoslovak women at international forums such as the Women's International Democratic Federation and to publish two women's magazines, *Vlasta* (in Czech) and *Slovenka* (in Slovak), which the KSČ used as vehicles to disseminate its propaganda.[42]

Under the communists the membership of women's organizations in Czechoslovakia dwindled from nearly half a million prior to the communist coup of 1948 to only eighty by 1952. Moreover, the purpose of the movement had been changed from fighting for women's equality to serving as a conduit for propaganda and political mobilization of women to encourage them to play a role in building a communist society. By the early 1950s the term "women's movement" rarely appeared in government documents or public pronouncements, having been replaced by "work among women."[43] The once-influential Czechoslovak women's movement—which had in effect decided the outcome of the country's 1946 parliamentary elections—had, in the words of historian Denisa Nečasová, become "toothless" (*bezzube*) by 1952.[44]

The Nasser Regime and the Egyptian Women's Movement

The relation between the Nasser regime and independent women's activism in Egypt was similarly uneasy. Although the reforms of the Nasser period (1952–1968) echoed much of what Egyptian feminists had been calling for the previous half century, these various debates, particularly on the issue of overpopulation, would be subsumed within the discourses, objectives, and ideals of Egyptian Arab socialism. Laws passed under Nasser actually represented the culmination of decades of raging debates about women's social and political roles. Many of the "third way" international ties, for example, clinched by Nasser's government during the militant aggressions and stalemates of the Cold War expanded the international links that had been forged by women's civil organizations before the 1950s to create political platforms for women's empowerment through regional (particularly Arab) and international solidarity. Moreover, many of the reform measures implemented in the Nasser period continued social initiatives launched by feminist organizations in the first half of the twentieth century to address the lack of social services provided for the poor, especially in rural areas.

Although the Ministry of Social Affairs had been created in 1939 to assume responsibility for the services provided by women's philanthropic associations, the state's outreach at this time remained tentative. Even after women's organizations became supervised and regulated by the ministry, the ventures for social work in the 1930s and 1940s remained open for participation and largely self-financing. Thus, when it came in the late 1950s and 1960s, the strong centralization of power and assertive assumption of responsibility for public affairs by the state appeared to be a portent of good fortune for the women's movement. After decades of political lobbying and intense social work by feminists, Egypt's new revolutionary state would finally take on its shoulders the responsibility of resolving women's issues that had been at the forefront of political debate for decades, particularly suffrage, equal employment, improvement of women's and children's health, regulation of fertility, and the reform of common laws regulating family affairs.

With the heralding of industry as the means to a new economy and the proclamation of gender equality as a constitutional act in 1956, "state feminism" was born.[45] Although socialist state feminisms used different policies to address specific local needs, representatives of state feminism worldwide asserted the universality of their libertarian objectives, often in solidarity with and in pointed comparison to contemporaneous state projects in other socialist countries.[46] As Arab socialism grew, the "new woman" motif recognizable in the party discourses of many socialist regimes of the 1960s, including Czechoslovakia, was lodged firmly at the center of Egyptian nationalist discourse. Women, set alongside men as the nation's citizens, were portrayed as able laborers, professionals, peasants, and industrious homemakers, albeit not always as politicians and public figures. A mode of public address was gradually institutionalized through which women were urgently called upon to take their place as enfranchised political citizens in order to build, develop, and manufacture the nation.

By 1952 the women's movement in Egypt had already matured, and splintered, into groups with intersecting political allegiances, all with claims on the nation-state. Nasser's regime hijacked the women's movement by putting all its organizations under direct governmental control and monitoring the activities of individuals. An iconic moment in 1956 symbolized the problematic nature of state feminism: in the same year that Egyptian women were given the right to vote, the EFU, like other independent organizations with political purposes, had to "self-destruct as a feminist organization."[47] For the state and its institutions to work democratically requires civil workers, journalists, philanthropists, the intelligentsia and other nonstate actors; Nasser's regime, like the regime in Czechoslovakia, condoned none of these. Rather than strengthen the women's organized, if fragmented, networks, Nasser's state allowed the voice of only one strain—the one falling in line with "national development"—to grow. Thus, at the same time as the Nasser government invested on an unprecedented scale in a popular-based, state-sponsored education system, and even as it supported women's entry into the workforce and made vital the role of female citizens in building the nation, the government crushed all autonomous political movements and silenced feminist leaders who did not accept its dictates.

A vast crackdown on autonomous elements of society was set in motion to eliminate political opposition, bolstered by the increasing domination of military-owned industry and the establishment of a powerful secret police apparatus. This definitively culminated with the nationalization of the media, film industry, and publishing houses in 1960; or, in the terms of the day: the ownership of the press was transferred to the Arab Socialist Union, putting the press in the hands and service of "the people." [48] By 1959 some feminists critical of the regime, such as Inji Aflatun, had been sent to jail; others, such as Doria Shafik, were placed under house arrest.[49] Still others, such as Saiza (or Ceza) Nabarawi, would reroute their activism to venues outside of Egypt.[50] Other feminists gradually became public voices representing state feminism and eventually gained for themselves, rightly or wrongly, the reputation of being part of the state's drive to mobilize women for its own (gradually suspected) purposes. Names from the prerevolutionary generation, for example, include Suhayr al-Qalamawi—the first woman to receive a doctorate of Arab and Islamic studies, a professor at Cairo University, and eventual head of the state's publishing association. Ḥawwā' Idrīs continued to operate the EFU-established day-care center "Dār al-ḥadānah" for working mothers, responding to their expanding needs for child care that the socialist state still failed to meet.[51] Meanwhile, Amina el Said assumed editorship of *Ḥawwā'* (1954–1969), the only women's magazine allowed in the Nasser period, and helped mobilize women for national campaigns (although she also managed to maintain the call for reform of common laws unfair to women).[52]

With the consolidation of the state system, by 1964 women's associations had to be registered with the Ministry of Social Affairs for close monitoring. The state chose which women's organizations would represent the nation's women and then made those groups into the women's branches of the state's political organizations. Thus, for example, al-Ittiḥād al-nisā'i al-'arabi al-'ām, or the General Arab Feminist Union, would later be renamed the General Arab Women's Union: "What had been born out of independent feminist activism in the mid-1940s had come by the 1950s and 1960s to be harnessed by states to serve their purposes."[53] Yet even the activities of women condoned by the regime were controlled. In order to attend meetings of the Arab Feminist Union abroad, for example, delegates had to present their male guardian's written permission to travel before obtaining exit and entry visas. In this way the state could control the mobility of individual women.

The result was that during the 1960s and onward, writing proliferated (due to the increased levels of literacy made a constitutional mandate in 1923 and vigorously implemented in 1953), but the voices were fewer.[54] Women's organizations, assemblies, and the women's press, which had been responsible for much of the political activity in Egypt for a half century despite the attempted crackdowns of various regimes, were now curtailed. From the 1960s onward, documented manifestations of organized public activity in opposition to the government are scarce, but government-approved brochures, pamphlets, conference proceedings, statistical surveys, and the like, outlining the role and status of the "new revolutionary Egyptian woman" are abundant.

Egypt's National Family Planning Program

Along with participating in the working and professional middle class, women were given the responsibility of controlling the number of mouths the state had to feed. By 1960 Egypt's population stood at twenty-six million and was growing at an annual rate of 2.34 percent, a dramatic increase over the 1.41 percent growth rate recorded in the 1947 census.[55] Since the most populous country in the Arab world had to produce enough to feed itself and increase its gross domestic product (GDP), and since the state had taken upon its shoulders the burden of feeding the many mouths of its citizens, decreasing the birth rate was imperative. As the state-run media urged the new woman to use birth control, research and statistical offices on population control and family regulation monitored and studied the situation. In 1953 the National Commission for Population was launched, and eight family-planning clinics were opened for field study.[56] To carry out the family-planning campaign, the idea of a mobile clinic dispensary in rural areas, which had been introduced by women's philanthropic organizations in the 1930s with the aim of providing basic medical services, fighting epidemics, and encouraging hygienic practices, emerged again. This time the units also gave out free contraception, with an emphasis on oral contraceptives.

In order to address the overpopulation problem, and taking into account measures favored by international demographic and development theories, the Nasser regime again drew on prerevolutionary discourses linking reform of motherhood to social welfare. The Nasser-era authorities promoted the family-planning project as one of its strategies for social development, a step toward the ultimate aim of providing a decent standard of living for Egyptians.[57] Family planning laid out new conceptions of citizenship and civic responsibility for women. By carrying the burden of large-scale social transformations, however, the state also authorized for itself unprecedented control over the transformation of individual behavior and the medical management of individual bodies.

In 1962 Egypt's National Family Planning Program was announced. In 1966, after four years of planning, 1,991 clinics were set up inside government health bureaus, rural health units, maternal and child health clinics, and outpatient departments of major hospitals. The clinics were open half the week to supply contraception to Egyptian women. Mainly staffed by nurses from the Ministry of Public Health, the staff of each clinic also included a member from the Ministry of Social Affairs whose job was to keep statistics of patients. By 1968, the number of clinics had grown to 2,631 and the number of women patients to over 230,000.[58] Clinics targeted urban working women and rural women as sources of health risk, unrestricted fertility, and the subsequent stalling of the nation's modernization.

The short-term goal of these mobile health units was to lower population numbers; the longer-term and more important goal was to create productive healthy families. Still drawing on prerevolutionary aims of progress and modernization, the campaign for family planning now featured a social engineering discourse about the duties and obligations of the Arab-socialist state and Arab-socialist citizen. This, in turn, allowed a whole range of state reconstructions of Egyptian family life. "The management of reproduction, like the inclusion of courses in personal hygiene in the newly expanded public school system, the subsidizing of household appliances like refrigerators, and the licensing of village midwives, was an attempt to create new sorts of families as a means to creating a [new] modern society."[59] In the state-controlled media, cartoons and articles, pamphlets and conferences, films and literature, and radio interviews and political speeches all drove the point home each day: the modern family used planning, the modern woman did not give in to her husband's unceasing demands, and the nuclear family that limited the number of children to two or three would find the wherewithal to provide for children's education, health, and professional training under the aegis of a watchful state. The modern woman in the Nasser period was the socialist woman, and the inevitability of progress promised by the revolution was presented in "glossy photos appearing in newspapers, magazines, textbooks, and state-authored pamphlets of 'the Egyptian woman' working in factories and offices, going to school, waiting to obtain birth control from state family-planning clinics, and presiding over her kitchen, which featured the latest in Egyptian-manufactured domestic appliances."[60]

Meanwhile, voluntary family-planning initiatives were also harnessed to the state's family-planning program. The General Family Planning Association (GFPA) had grown from the efforts of voluntary groups led mainly by women who promoted family-planning ideas and services. By the late 1960s, the General Family Planning Association operated around most of Egypt and supervised several hundred family-planning clinics under the aegis of the state.[61] In 1964 the Joint Committee for Family Planning was founded to facilitate (and monitor) the various volunteer groups working to provide services, sponsor research, and publicize information on family planning.[62] The committee was eventually replaced in 1965 by the Supreme Council for Family Planning, which reported to the prime minister or the minister of health and was served by members from the Ministry of Health, the Ministry of Social Welfare, the Ministry of Higher Education, the state cabinet, local administrations, and the Central Agency for Public Mobilization and Statistics.[63]

Like others of its kind, the Egyptian family-planning program primarily targeted women, and not only by asserting the importance of women's sexual self-control. Oral contraceptives were by far the most popular method of birth control during this period because of being easily prescribed, while male methods such as condoms were scarcely discussed. Men were not addressed directly as active, responsible partners. More commonly, slapstick satire in the media mocked men who linked manhood to fatherhood for being provincial. The media asserted instead that manhood was more properly defined as the ability to provide the benefits of modern living, including education and health care, for the whole family.

Rural families in particular were depicted as impediments to the success of state development programs. Such communities were criticized for the prevalence of early marriage among them, and for holding such beliefs as preferring male children, seeing large families as indicators of men's virility and women's health, placing an inflated importance on extended kinship networks, and believing that having a large number of children would provide wealth for the family by increasing its labor capacity. Popular media stressed lower-class women's inability to exercise reproductive agency and advocated family planning for the rural population as a way to improve the status of all men and women.

In its early phases, family planning, like state feminism itself, projected a dual—sometimes contradictory—construction of women as both objects and agents of national transformation, integral to the building of a postindependence Arab socialist Egypt. The direct address to Egyptian women to regulate reproduction in the 1960s constructed images of women, on one hand, as citizens responsible for their own well-being and the nation's welfare and, on the other hand, as sites of contestation, subjects of blame and subalternity who needed to be properly guided by agents of development and state planners to become mature citizens.[64] For both opponents and advocates, religious and secular figures, state actors and feminist activists, the discussion did not foreground the emancipation of women's bodies as such, but took for granted that the choice to use contraception should be considered within the paradigms of marital, heterosexual relations in the interest of the health of the family and the nation.[65] Family planning on the side of state *or* citizen—whether couched in discourses of social engineering or of gender empowerment—was more properly a nationalist issue tied to the goals of progress and modernization. Even as the means used to persuade women (who are still the foremost target of population control programs) to have fewer children have notably changed over the past five decades, from promoting the use of contraceptives to improving economic conditions for the rural population and widening employment chances for women, the long-term goal of "motherhood reform" has often been economic self-sufficiency and national progress.

By the early 1970s, the family-planning program was generally understood to have been a failure, with poor administration, poorly trained clinicians, and a population indifferent or even hostile to government intervention. There have been many attempts to understand why, although there are no easy answers, for Egyptian family planning in the Nasser era clearly lay at the intersection of issues of citizenship and social welfare which were extended to rural segments previously excluded from these spheres. It is nominally true that various societal groups opposed the family-planning program outright, such as those who feared contraception would undermine the religious purpose of marriage to bring up children and those who feared it would promote sexual licentiousness by allowing women more freedom. The historian Laura Bier notes, however, that even the more thorough research on these programs does not adequately consider issues of women's motivation and agency (or "rights" and "choice"). Bier stresses that scholars do not properly take into account the local complexities faced by women in making reproductive decisions. In the Egyptian context this could be seen in the program administrators' lack of understanding of the rural population's actual conditions and, subsequently, the misinterpretation (willful or otherwise) by village audiences of the state's messages.[66] Egyptian women thus responded to the program in unexpected ways, located as these women were in complexities of class, religion, location, and personal circumstance.

Equally importantly, however, the Egyptian family-planning program remained through the 1960s and 1970s a clinic-based program for providing oral contraceptives. It lacked an adequate number of personnel, particularly trained personnel, as well as sufficient follow-up and outreach. By the early 1980s, participation rates remained lower than desired, and discontinuation rates remained high.[67] By all accounts this was to change from the 1980s onward, with Egypt lauded as a more successful case among countries working on population control, although there is some controversy about whether this is due to increasing rural poverty or to successful population control strategies.[68]

The Czechoslovak Economic and Demographic Crisis and the Cold War

As in Egypt, the KSČ was gravely concerned about the country's demographic future, but in Czechoslovakia the fear centered on the nation's population decline. From the end of World War II until 1960 the Czechoslovak economy grew at an impressive average of 8 percent per year, and its annual industrial output increased fourfold.[69] Such growth resulted in substantial increases in the living standards of the population and gave Prague the means to pursue a Cold War policy of increasing its influence in Africa and elsewhere in the developing world through foreign aid programs and the expansion of its diplomatic network. In an attempt to attain middle-power status, Czechoslovakia sought to develop both economic and diplomatic relations with nearly every independent state on the African continent. During this period Czechoslovakia operated more embassies in Africa than did the Soviet Union. Prague gave significant military aid to newly established national armies of independent African states as well as to national liberation movements still fighting against European colonialism. From 1954 to 1968 Czechoslovakia was a major, perhaps even the leading, exporter of small arms to Africa, sending over $249 million in military aid to the continent.[70] During those same years, Czechoslovakia dedicated a greater percentage of its GDP to bilateral economic assistance to Africa than did the United States and devoted more than twice as much of its GDP to Africa as did the Soviet Union.[71] Prague's per-capita involvement in Africa during these years was likely unsurpassed by any other state, making Czechoslovakia an important ally for the Soviet Union in the global Cold War—but this was only possible because of its strong economy.[72] Beginning in 1960, the Czechoslovak economy started to become less efficient. Greater decline took place in 1961 and 1962, and by 1963 it was experiencing a negative growth rate of 3 percent, leading to what economists have labeled an "inverted economic miracle."[73] This economic decline affected Czechoslovak foreign policy by forcing the KSČ to dramatically reduce its foreign aid commitments.

At the same time Czechoslovakia also experienced a sharp decline in its birthrate. In 1955 Czechoslovakia had one of Europe's highest birthrates, but a decade later Hungary, East Germany, and Belgium were the only countries on the continent with a lower birthrate.[74] KSČ demographers understood that there was a direct correlation between Czechoslovakia's decreasing birthrate and a high percentage of women employed in full-time jobs. Facing the double burden of full-time employment outside of the house and almost complete responsibility for housekeeping after work, overworked Czechoslovak women in the mid- to late 1950s had become less inclined to have large families, prompting government officials to fear a looming population crisis. The country's demographic crisis was exacerbated by the fact that over two million ethnic Germans had been expelled from the country after World War II.

The KSČ faced a quandary. On one hand, its labor-intensive faltering economy relied heavily on female labor, so much so that women accounted for approximately half of Czechoslovakia's labor force and represented 80 percent of the total increase of the country's workers since 1948.[75] On the other hand, if Czechoslovak women focused on work at the expense of having children, that would worsen the demographic crisis, thus diminishing the country's future labor pool. This dilemma was further aggravated by the fact that the response of Western countries, who often responded to declining birthrates by importing migrant labor from other countries, was not a realistic possibility behind the Iron Curtain in communist Czechoslovakia—leaving increased fertility as the only viable option for population growth.

This demographic problem was one of the major issues discussed at the KSČ's Twelfth Congress of the Party in December 1962 at which party leaders voted to establish a new organization—the State Population Commission. Established as an advisory body and research arm of the government, the State Population Commission comprised thirty-four members nominated by government ministries, universities, and social science research and medical institutes. The main tasks of the commission were to investigate the causes of the birthrate decline, to recommend policies that might reverse the negative demographic trend, and to develop educational programs and political propaganda to encourage families to have more children.[76]

The State Population Commission conducted a series of surveys into the social and practical aspects of female employment with a particular emphasis on its relationship to the declining birthrate. It identified a housing shortage, the insufficient availability of services, and the exceptionally high level of female employment as the primary factors that negatively influenced the country's birthrate. For example, only 12 percent of young married couples had their own apartments. The vast majority lived with their parents, and many lived separately from each other (each living with their own parents). This resulted in many couples waiting until they had their own living space before having children.[77] The housing shortage was also viewed as playing a large role in the decrease in marriages and increase in divorces.[78] A scarcity of availability of day-care providers also inhibited working women from having children. Yet, the commission identified the high percentage of women working full-time jobs as the biggest hurdle impeding the country's birthrate. Many Czechoslovak women considered employment outside of the house as more of a "necessary evil" than an opportunity, as almost 80 percent told government researchers that their primary reason for working was the need for two incomes to support a family.[79] This convinced the Czechoslovak government that many women would be happy to work less and have more children if they could afford to do so.

On the recommendation of the State Population Commission the government passed a law that provided paid maternity leave for six months, with additional unpaid leave until the child's first birthday, and invested additional funds to increase state-provided child services as a means to encourage Czechoslovak women to take time off work in order to have children. In 1967 paid maternity leave was further extended from twenty-two to twenty-six weeks for married women and to thirty-five weeks for unmarried women. The State Planning Commission determined that the average number of children per family would need to increase from 1.9 to 2.5 in order to sustain Czechoslovakia's existing population of fourteen to fifteen million. But surveys of young couples conducted in 1959 and 1963 revealed that the planned family average would be only 2.2 children.[80] Therefore, it was decided that the state needed to launch a propaganda campaign designed to encourage couples to have three or more children in order to raise the average number of offspring per family.

Beginning in 1963, the KSČ directed media outlets such as the national television and radio stations, newspapers, and journals, to influence the public (especially young people) toward pronatalism. Mass media was asked to emphasize that children strengthened the love between spouses and made life happier, and that a continuation of current negative demographic trends would adversely affect national economic development and by extension an individual's living standards. Media was asked to promote the idea that having three children was the ideal family size, to warn against the dangers of abortion, and to tout the progress in social services that the state provided in order to lessen the demands of work and parenthood. The State Planning Commission was tasked with overseeing this effort and produced a television series entitled *Family and Society* and a radio program named *Intimate Conversations*, both of which aired in 1963.[81] Czechoslovakia's main daily newspaper, *Rudé Právo* (Red Right), and *Vlasta* (the official magazine of the Women's Committee, which had the nation's second-largest circulation behind *Rudé Právo*) also published op-eds and news stories with a pronatalist bent. This propaganda campaign led scholar John Besemeres to label Czechoslovakia the most pronatalist country in Eastern Europe, explaining that it maintained "the most elaborate, all-persuasive and obtrusive media campaign on behalf of increased fecundity."[82]

Another way the government chose to attack the demographic crisis was to restrict women's access to abortions. The KSČ legalized abortion in 1957, and less than a year later Czechoslovak women were averaging 25.8 abortions for every 100 births, and the average increased to 42.8 per 100 in 1961. The combination of natural miscarriage and abortion meant that the approximately 422,000 pregnancies in Czechoslovakia in 1961 resulted in only 218,378 live births.[83] In response, several propopulation changes were introduced in the early 1960s in order to limit the accessibility of abortion. In 1961 the prospective father was allowed to block a potential abortion; in 1962 women seeking abortions were required first to appear before an abortion committee to explain their reasons for ending their pregnancy; in 1963 a fee for abortions (which had previously been free) began to be assessed and a law restricting women to one abortion every six months began to be more strictly enforced.[84]

The Czechoslovak Women's Committee was neither informed nor consulted by the State Planning Commission for any of its projects despite these issues having direct relevance to women. The issue was almost exclusively discussed by male Communist Party bureaucrats with very little input from individual women and no involvement from the women's movement. In the hundreds of pages of reports, memos, and recommendations that the State Planning Commission produced discussing the demographic crisis, the Women's Committee was not mentioned a single time.[85] Sixteen different government departments were tasked with various responsibilities for improving the country's birthrate, but the Czechoslovak Women's Committee had no role whatsoever. The women's movement did not even have a seat at the table of such discussions.[86] Its only involvement with this issue was to run pronatalist articles in its publications.

The Czechoslovak government made a concerted effort to revive its economy while simultaneously increasing the birthrate through state intervention to assist women in balancing their work and family lives. Eventually Czechoslovakia would spend more than 10 percent of its annual budget on funding for kindergartens, subsidized day care, tax and rent reductions based on the number of children a family had, paid maternity leave, and other incentives geared toward increasing the birthrate—far exceeding the level of equivalent expenditures of any other country in the world.[87] To cite only one quantitative example, the number of day-care centers and kindergartens in the country had increased from twenty-five hundred in 1936 to sixty-seven thousand in 1967, a dramatic increase no doubt, but this still left nearly 90 percent of children under the age of three without a place in day care.[88] Therefore, despite a massive amount of state assistance, government intervention was never comprehensive enough to meet the regime's goals. In 1963 and 1964 minimal gains were made in the birthrate (24,000 more births than in 1962), but in 1965 the decline returned and even intensified. By 1967 Czechoslovakia had the fewest number of births (216,000) in its history.[89] Recognizing that it had failed to fix its demographic crisis, the Czechoslovak government abolished the State Planning Commission in July 1970.[90] In large part because of the country's demographic and economic crises and the economic toll they took, Czechoslovak foreign policy would never return to its activism of the 1950s and early 1960s.

When the KSČ came to power in 1948 it immediately made the Czechoslovak women's movement subservient to its control. Political scientist Sharon Wolchik has noted that from the mid-1960s onward, the KSČ's policy toward women was "determined largely by its impact on the birthrate."[91] KSČ officials believed that birthrates were susceptible to government influence and therefore enacted policies that sought to encourage fertility. Women were not consulted about these policies in any meaningful way. Instead, the women's movement was used solely as an outlet to promote the virtue of women taking time off work to have children before returning to the labor force once the children had reached school age.

Conclusion

In both communist Czechoslovakia and Nasserist Egypt socialist regimes reduced the structural basis of gender inequality and allowed women to become more independent and publicly active than they had ever been before. Many women supported the socialist regimes because of the progressive legislation the governments had enacted. When the communists came to power in Czechoslovakia in 1948 and the Free Officers came to power in Egypt in 1952, however, the two revolutions ended the autonomy of feminist groups working within the public sphere and civil society. All independent political organizations were disbanded and prohibited. In their place state-run organizations for mass mobilization were established. The socialist governments in Prague and Cairo channeled the women's movements in their countries toward fulfilling the political objectives of the state. No political activism outside of the structures created by the governments were allowed because the regimes feared that a flourishing civil society could foster opposition movements that might topple them from power.

The opposition between the work of feminists in civil society and the trajectory of state feminism places the debates on population control in both countries within particular gender paradigms. Devoid of effective women's participation, such state policies are entwined in larger, complex political issues, seem to be always about something else besides women. Debates about the authority ceded to the state for the construction and control of individual bodies through development programs, which became apparent across the globe during the Cold War through population management programs, have remained contentious. This antagonism is visible in anger toward the First World's perceived manipulation of the Third World through development aid, in fear and phobias expressed publicly in North America and Europe toward "communist contamination" and "immigration threats," and in local resentment toward, and active resistance of, the state's control of private bodies and individual freedom.

Notes

1. For an overview of the 1955 arms deal between Czechoslovakia and Egypt as well as a history of the bilateral relations between these two countries during this time, see Philip E. Muehlenbeck, *Czechoslovakia in Africa, 1945–1968* (New York: Palgrave Macmillan, 2015).
2. See, for example, a roundtable event attended by various university faculty and local experts, and covered by *al-Hilāl* magazine in June 1950, entitled "Mushkilat tandhīm

al-nasl" [The Problem of Birth Control]. Six guest speakers discussed whether expansion in agriculture and industry was enough to solve the overpopulation problem in Egypt? See *al-Hilāl* 6, no. 58 (June 1950): 114–19.

3. See Zahia Marzūk's "al-misriyya fi-l maydān al-ijtimā 'i" [Egyptian women in the social sphere], *al-Hilāl* 9, no. 58 (September 1950), 146–47, in which she defines "social work."

4. See Margot Badran, *Feminists, Islam, and Nation: Gender and the Making of Modern Egypt* (Princeton: Princeton University Press, 1995); and Beth Baron, "The Origins of Family Planning: Aziza Hussein, American Experts, and the Egyptian State," *Journal of Middle East Women's Studies* 4, no. 3 (Fall 2008): 31–57.

5. Badran, *Feminists, Islam, and Nation*, 160.

6. See "Bint al-Nīl tuquaddima lakī ṭarīqat taḥdīd al-nasl: al-ṭarīqah al-ṣiḥiyya l-il ṭabīb al-'ālamiy Ojino" [*Bint al-Nīl* presents to you a healthy method for birth control from the world-renowned doctor, Ogino], *Bint al-Nīl* [Daughter of the Nile], no. 98 (December 1953): 24.

7. Phyllis H. Raabe, "The Structure of Employment and Careers as a Work-Family Problem: The Case of Communist Czechoslovakia," in *Women, Work, and Society*, ed. Marie Čermáková, Working Paper 95, no. 4 (Prague: Institute of Sociology of the Academy of Sciences of the Czech Republic, 1995), 59.

8. Alena Heitlinger, *Women and State Socialism: Sex Inequality in the Soviet Union and Czechoslovakia* (Montreal: McGill-Queen's University Press, 1979), 135.

9. Soňa Hendrychová, "Františka Plaminkova," in *A Biographical Dictionary of Women's Movements and Feminisms: Central, Eastern, and South Eastern Europe, 19th and 20th Centuries*, ed. Francisca de Haan, Krassimira Daskalova, and Anna Loutfi (Budapest: Central European University Press, 2006), 438–39.

10. From April 1945 to February 1948 the Czechoslovak Republic ruled a democratic Czechoslovakia through a coalition government of the Czechoslovak Social Democratic Party, the Czechoslovak National Social Party, and the Communist Party of Czechoslovakia (KSČ). Václav Nosek of the KSČ held the position of minister of the interior, which allowed the KSČ to have disproportionate influence over the ministry.

11. Melissa Feinberg, "Battling for Peace: The Transformation of the Women's Movement in Cold War Czechoslovakia and Eastern Europe," in *Women and Gender in Postwar Europe: From Cold War to European Union*, ed. Joanna Regulska and Bonnie G. Smith (New York: Routledge, 2012), 19–21. For Czechoslovakia's 1946 parliamentary election results, see Paul Zinner, *Communist Strategy and Tactics in Czechoslovakia* (Westport, CT: Greenwood, 1975), 258.

12. Melissa Feinberg, *Elusive Equality: Gender, Citizenship, and the Limits of Democracy in Czechoslovakia, 1918–1950* (Pittsburgh: University of Pittsburgh Press, 2006), 220.

13. Ibid., 202–3.

14. Sharon L. Wolchik, "The Status of Women in a Socialist Order: Czechoslovakia, 1948–78," *Slavic Review* 38, no. 4 (1979): 583.

15. Heitlinger, *Women and State Socialism*, 148.

16. Jiřina Šiklová, "Inhibition Factors of Feminism in the Czech Republic after the 1989 Revolution," in Čermáková, *Women, Work, and Society*, 35.

17. Ibid. For female workplace participation in the West, see Heitlinger, *Women and State Socialism*, 147–48, 586; and Patricia Voydanoff, *Work and Family Life* (Newbury Park, CA: Sage, 1987).

18. Raabe, "Structure of Employment and Careers," 59.

19. Heitlinger, *Women and State Socialism*, 158.

20. Ibid., 66, 154.

21. Wolchik, "Status of Women in a Socialist Order," 584–85.

22. Sharon Wolchik, "Ideology and Equality: The Status of Women in Eastern and Western Europe," *Comparative Political Studies* 13, no. 4 (January 1981): 451.

23. Heitlinger, *Women and State Socialism*, 159. For historical data on the number of women in the United States Congress, see Rutgers University, Center for American Women and Politics, "Historical Information about Women in Congress," *www.cawp. rutgers.edu/history-women-us-congress.*

24. Wolchik, "Ideology and Equality," 459; and Wolchik, "Status of Women in a Socialist Order," 593.

25. Selma Botman, *Engendering Citizenship in Egypt* (New York: Columbia University Press, 1999), 56.

26. Laura Bier, *Revolutionary Womanhood: Feminisms, Modernity, and State in Nasser's Egypt* (Stanford: Stanford University Press, 2011), 68.

27. Wolchik, "Ideology and Equality," 592.

28. Botman, *Engendering Citizenship in Egypt*, 55.

29. Heitlinger, *Women and State Socialism*, 159–60.

30. Denisa Nečasová, "Women's Organizations in the Czech Lands, 1948–89," in *The Politics of Gender and Culture under State Socialism: An Expropriated Voice*, ed. Hana Havelková and Libora Oates-Indruchová (New York: Routledge, 2014), 62.

31. Dana Musilová, "Milada Horáková," in de Haan, Daskalova, and Loutfi, *A Biographical Dictionary of Women's Movements and Feminisms*, 180.

32. "Personnel Problems in the Czechoslovak Women's Union," December 12, 1951, Records of the Central Committee of the Communist Party of Czechoslovakia, 1945–1989, Women's Commission, 1945–1954, unit 64, NA-UV KSČ/AUML 22, box 2, National Archives of the Czech Republic, Prague (hereafter, NAP).

33. Draft organizational rules for the Czechoslovak Women's Union, [undated, but late 1949], Records of the Central Committee of the Communist Party of Czechoslovakia, 1945–1989, Women's Commission, 1945–1954, unit 64, NA-UV KSČ/AUML 22, box 2, NAP.

34. Proposed organizational order of the Czechoslovak Women's Union, [undated, but late 1949], Records of the Central Committee of the Communist Party of Czechoslovakia, 1945–1989, Women's Commission, 1945–1954, unit 64, NA-UV KSČ/AUML 22, box 2, NAP.

35. Nečasová, "Women's Organizations in the Czech Lands," 58.

36. Ibid., 62.

37. Denisa Nečasová, *Buduj Vlast—Posílíš Mír!: Ženské hnutí v českých zemích 1945–1955* [Build up your country—to strengthen peace!: The women's movement in the Czech lands, 1945–1955] (Brno: Matice moravská, 2011), 297.

38. Quoted in Nečasová, "Women's Organizations in the Czech Lands," 63.

39. Department of Mass Organizations, meeting minutes, November 8, 1951, Records of the Central Committee of the Communist Party of Czechoslovakia, 1945–1989, Department of Mass Organizations, unit 14, NA-UV KSČ/AUML 19, box 3, NAP.

40. Nečasová, "Women's Organizations in the Czech Lands," 61.

41. Heitlinger, *Women and State Socialism*, 68.

42. Ibid., 68.

43. Nečasová, "Women's Organizations in the Czech Lands," 69.

44. Nečasová, *Buduj Vlast—Posíliš Mír!*, 177.

45. Mervat F. Hatem, "Egypt's Economic and Political Liberalization and the Decline of State Feminism," *International Journal of the Middle East Studies* 24, no. 2 (May 1992): 231–51; Mervat F. Hatem, "The Paradoxes of State Feminism," in *Women and Politics Worldwide*, ed. Barbara Nelson and Najma Chowdhury (New Haven: Yale University Press, 1994); Dorothy E. McBride and Amy G. Mazur, *State Feminism: Innovation in Comparative Research* (Philadelphia: Temple University Press, 2010).

46. See Bonnie G. Smith, *Global Feminisms since 1945* (London: Routledge, 2000); and Kumari Jayawardena, *Feminism and Nationalism in the Third World* (London: Zed, 1994).

47. Badran, *Feminists, Islam, and Nation*, 219. Renaming itself the Huda Shaarawy Association, it focused on social service under government control.

48. See Yehyā Abu Bakr, "Kalimat al-ḥaq shiʿār al-iʿlām al-thawriy" (The word of truth is the motto of revolutionary media), *Al-Majallah al-masriyyah l'il ulūm al-siyāsiyyah* [Egyptian Political Science Review] 3 (July 1963): 27–34. Abu Bakr denounces "the enemies of the state" (oppositional media) that spread political falsehood and created national enmity. He defines the role of the centralized state-approved media as the propagation of "truth" for the sake of developmental goals such as democracy, progress, and modernization.

49. See Doria Shafik's editorials from 1952 to 1957 in the magazine *Bint al-Nīl* (Daughter of the Nile), the mouthpiece for her organization (launched in 1948). Shafik's editorials start by embracing the 1952 coup in patriotic celebration of the Egyptian blow to world imperialism, and offer a call to arms for women to stand firm in their support of the coup (June 1953, no. 91, 3). Subsequent editorials, however, question the position taken by the revolutionary leaders on the Egyptian women's movement. Not one year later, Shafik's editorials would critique the revolutionary leaders' neglect of women's affairs (August 1953, no. 94, 3), warning that national liberation would never happen if women were not granted equal political rights to men, and vowing that Egyptian women would not accept being silent observers in the new political era (March 1953, no. 88, 3). With her utter dedication to the call for civil liberties and admirable ability to mobilize women in public hunger strikes and street protest, Shafik quickly became a thorn in the side of the Nasser government. Yet the fragmentation of nonstate actors made it easy for the state to incite hostility toward such figures. Outspoken, often critical, and always fashionably dressed (often with an eye on the international media), Shafik had not always been popular with other women, and reporters supporting the regime continued to critique her even after her arrest and silence, thus implicitly defining "acceptable" (state) feminism, which was patriotic and representative of the state's needs. (See Fawziyyah Saʿīd's running criticism in one issue after another of *Ākhir sāʿah* [The last hour], for example, of "Hollywood-oriented, elegantly-dressed feminists.")

50. Nabarawi became an active member in the WIDF in 1953. She spoke out against imperialism and for peace, nonalignment, and the Palestinian cause until her death in 1985.

51. See Asma Ḥalīm's article "Al-Marʾah ʿalā ard al-thawrah" [Women in the land of the revolution] in *al-Talīʿah* [The forefront] 10 (October 1965): 10–25, on what would be later called the "double burden." Ḥalīm remonstrates that without resources like childcare centers, working women spend all day out of the house only to continue working when they reach home, in an endless cycle of stress.

52. One of the most prolific feminist writers of the past century and a long-standing

representative for Egyptian women at the UN and other international bodies, Amīna al-Saʿīd was perhaps the most famous female Egyptian public figure during the Cold War. Much of her writing crystallized the intricate relation between the Egyptian women's movement and developmental goals. Often speaking about social conditions and the need for improvement, al-Saʿīd, for various reasons, was one of the few feminist figures who managed to stay on the right side of Nasser's government. Her running social commentary in newspapers and magazines often called for an increase in work and productivity, spoke of the importance of education for women, asserted that healthy and self-sufficient families lay at the heart of a productive, self-sufficient nation, and defined population increase as one of the biggest problems facing modern Egypt. All this may have increased her scope for social work under the Nasser regime. Although she wrote for most of the Egyptian press at one time or another, see, as one example, her regular articles in the monthly magazine *al-Hilāl* during the years 1950 to 1965.

53. Badran, *Feminists, Islam, and Nation*, 250.

54. Bier, *Revolutionary Womanhood.*

55. Ibid., 125.

56. Mary Taylor Hassouna, "Assessment of Family Planning Service Delivery in Egypt," *Studies in Family Planning* 11, no. 5 (May 1980): 159–66. The National Commission for Population was placed under the auspices of the Ministry of Social Affairs in 1958 and became known as the Egyptian Association for Population Studies. Meanwhile, centralized initiatives for statistical research were launched in all fields related to developmental goals, and they answered to the related ministries such as agriculture, industry, education, and communications. Hassan Husayn, "Taṭawwur al-khadamāt al-iḥsaʾiyyah f-il jumhuriyyah al-ʿarabiyyah al-muttahidah fī ʿahd al-thawrah" [Developing statistical services in the United Arab Republic in the era of the revolution], *Al-Majallah al-masriyyah lil ʿulūm al-siyāsiyyah* 28 (July 1963): 191–93.

57. Mohamad Talʾat ʿIsah, "Dawr al-muwāṭin fī mujtamaʿnā al-jadīd" [Citizens' roles in our new society], *Al-Majallah al-masriyyah lil ʿulūm al-siyāsiyyah* 29 (August 1963): 11–24. ʿIsah first stresses the vital educational or didactic role of the media in clarifying the "role of citizens in our new society" (13) and "crystallizing the goals of Arab socialism for the sake of building a society of industry and equal opportunity, a society of production and service provision" (14). Toward this end, "the family should be an effective tool for socialist upbringing and the creation of a virtuous moral and ethical ethos through the use of family planning which helps raise the general living standards of society as a whole, and the living standards of families (especially those of workers and peasants)" (15).

58. Bier, *Revolutionary Womanhood*, 129.

59. Ibid, 130.

60. Ibid., 3. See also, on the image of the socialist woman in the media, Soha Abdel Kader, *Egyptian Women in a Changing Society, 1899–1987* (Boulder, CO: Lynne Rienner, 1987), especially 104–19.

61. By the end of the Nasser era in 1967, GFPA centers had risen to 446, and government health units came to 2,900, in all but one city of Egypt. Hassouna, "Assessment of Family Planning Service Delivery in Egypt," 160.

62. Ibid, 159.

63. Ibid, 160.

64. Kamran Asdar Ali, *Planning the Family in Egypt: New Bodies, New Selves* (Cairo: American University in Cairo Press, 2002).

65. Bier, *Revolutionary Womanhood*, 135.

66. Ibid.

67. Hassouna, "Assessment of Family Planning Service Delivery in Egypt," 166.

68. Warren C. Robinson and Fatma H. El-Zanaty, *The Demographic Revolution in Modern Egypt* (Lanham, MD: Lexington, 2006).

69. Alexandre Teles Carreira, "The Reforms of 1964–1968 in Czechoslovakia and the Issue of the Autonomy for Enterprises," OK Economics, econc10.bu.edu/economic_systems/Economics/Economic_History/Czechoslovakia/czechoslovakia.htm; and Colleen Feehan, "The 'Inverted Economic Miracle': Recession in Czechoslovakia, 1962–63," OK Economics, econc10.bu.edu/economic_systems/NatIdentity/EE/Czechoslovakia/Recession%200f%201962-1963.htm.

70. "SIPRI Arms Transfer Database," Stockholm International Peace Research Institute, www.sipri.org/databases/armstransfers.

71. Data analysis by author. From 1954 to 1968 the United States gave $31.725 billion in bilateral economic assistance to Africa. In comparison, the Soviet Union spent $5.585 billion and Czechoslovakia $1.129 billion. Czechoslovakia devoted 0.1090 percent of its GDP to Africa; in comparison, the United States spent 0.0949 percent and the Soviet Union spent 0.0417 percent. For data on Czechoslovak and Soviet economic aid to Africa, see Christopher Stevens, *The Soviet Union and Black Africa* (London: Macmillan, 1976), 69. For data on United States economic aid to Africa, see "Foreign Aid Explorer," USAID, *explorer.usaid.gov*. For data on each country's GDP during 1954 to 1968, see "Maddison Project," *www.ggdc.net/maddison/maddison-project/home.htm*.

72. For an overview of Czechoslovak policy toward Africa, see Muehlenbeck, *Czechoslovakia in Africa*.

73. George Feiwel, *New Economic Patterns in Czechoslovakia* (New York: Praeger, 1968), 60, 75–77.

74. Letter from Prime Minister Oldřich Černík to the Ministers of Finance and of Labor and Social Affairs, July 17, 1968, Records of the State Population Commission, ÚPV, Office of the President of Government—Normal Registry—1967, box 247, sv. 843, ar. j. 8, b. 247, NAP.

75. Heitlinger, *Women and State Socialism*, 587.

76. Government Resolution of the Republic of Czechoslovakia, December 19, 1962, resolution number 1157, Documents of the Communist Party of Czechoslovakia, ÚV ČSR / ČR-RŽP, Usneseni vlady CSR ze dne19.12.1962 c. 1157, NAP.

77. Report from the State Population Commission, "Appraisal of Population Development in CSSR," October 15, 1964, Documents from the State Population Commission ÚPV, Office of the President of Government—Normal Registry, box 220, sv. 843, ar. j. 1, b. 6, NAP.

78. Report on Population Development in Czechoslovakia after 1962 sent by the minister of health to Vaclav Dolejsi, head of the Statistical Department, February 20, 1962, Documents from the State Population Commission ÚPV, Office of the President of Government—Normal Registry, box 220, sv. 843, ar. j. 1, b. 6, NAP.

79. Report from the State Population Commission, "Appraisal of Population Development in CSSR."

80. Ibid.

81. Alena Heitlinger, "Pro-natalist Population Policies in Czechoslovakia," *Population Studies* 30, no. 1 (1976): 131–32.

82. John F. Besemeres, *Socialist Population Politics: The Political Implications of Demographic Trends in the USSR and Eastern Europe* (White Plains, NY: M. E. Sharpe, 1980), 263.

83. Report from the State Population Commission, "Appraisal of Population Development in CSSR."

84. Barbara Havelková, "The Three Stages of Gender Law," in *The Politics of Gender Culture under State Socialism: An Expropriated Voice*, ed. Hana Havelková and Libora Oates-Indruchová (New York: Routledge, 2014), 41.

85. See documents from the State Population Commission ÚPV, Office of the President of Government—Normal Registry, box 220, sv. 843, ar. j. 1, b. 6, NAP.

86. For a discussion of the role each government department was assigned to play in increasing the birthrate, see Government Resolution of the Republic of Czechoslovakia, August 21, 1961, resolution number 710, Documents of the Communist Party of Czechoslovakia, ÚV ČSR/ ČR-RŽP, Usneseni vlady CSR ze dne 21.8.1961 c. 710, NAP.

87. Havelková, "The Three Stages of Gender Law," 47.

88. Ibid., 37; and undated report from the State Population Commission, Records of the State Population Commission, ÚPV, Office of the President of Government—Normal Registry—1967, box 247, sv. 843, ar. j. 8, b. 247, NAP.

89. Letter from Prime Minister Oldřich Černík to the Ministers of Finance and of Labor and Social Affairs, July 17, 1968.

90. Government Resolution of the Republic of Czechoslovakia, July 2, 1970, resolution number 148, Documents of the Communist Party of Czechoslovakia, ÚV ČSR / ČR-RŽP, Usneseni vlady CSR ze dne 2.7.1970 c. 148, NAP.

91. Wolchik, "The Status of Women in a Socialist Order," 599.

References

Archives

National Archives of the Czech Republic, Prague, Czech Republic

Periodicals

al-Hilāl [The Crescent]
Bint al-Nīl [Daughter of the Nile]
al-Majallah al-masriyyah l'il ʿulūm al-siyāsiyyah [Egyptian Political Science Review]
Ākhir sāʿah [The Last Hour]
al-Talīʿah [The Forefront]

Selected Published Works

Ali, Kamran Asdar. *Planning the Family in Egypt: New Bodies, New Selves*. Cairo: American University in Cairo Press, 2002.

Badran, Margot. *Feminists, Islam, and Nation: Gender and the Making of Modern Egypt*. Princeton: Princeton University Press, 1995.

Bier, Laura. *Revolutionary Womanhood: Feminisms, Modernity, and the State in Nasser's Egypt*. Stanford: Stanford University Press, 2011.

Botman, Selma. *Engendering Citizenship in Egypt*. New York: Columbia University Press, 1999.

Feinberg, Melissa. *Elusive Equality: Gender, Citizenship, and the Limits of Democracy in Czechoslovakia, 1918–1950*. Pittsburgh, PA: University of Pittsburgh Press, 2006.

Hassouna, Mary Taylor. "Assessment of Family Planning Service Delivery in Egypt" *Studies in Family Planning* 11, no. 5 (May 1980): 159–66.

Hatem, Mervat F. "Egypt's Economic and Political Liberalization and the Decline of State Feminism." *International Journal of Middle East Studies* 24, no. 2 (May 1992): 231–51.

———. "The Paradoxes of State Feminism." In *Women and Politics Worldwide*, edited by Barbara Nelson and Najma Chowdhury. New Haven: Yale University Press, 1994.

Heitlinger, Alina. "Pro-natalist Population Policies in Czechoslovakia." *Population Studies* 30, no. 1 (March 1976): 123–35.

———. *Women and State Socialism: Sex Inequality in the Soviet Union and Czechoslovakia.* Montreal: McGill-Queen's University, 1979.

Nečasová, Denisa. *Buduj Vlast—Posíliš Mír!: Ženské hnutí v českých zemích 1945–1955* [Build up your country—to strengthen peace! The women's movement in the Czech lands, 1945–1955]. Brno, Czech Republic: Matice moravská, 2011.

———. "Women's Organizations in the Czech Lands, 1948–89." In *The Politics of Gender Culture under State Socialism: An Expropriated Voice*, edited by Hana Havelková and Libora Oates-Indruchová. New York: Routledge, 2014.

Raabe, Phyllis H. "The Structure of Employment and Careers as a Work-Family Problem: The Case of Communist Czechoslovakia." In *Women, Work, and Society*, edited by Marie Čermáková. Working Paper 95, no. 4. Prague: Institute of Sociology of the Academy of Sciences of the Czech Republic, 1995.

Wolchik, Sharon. "Ideology and Equality: The Status of Women in Eastern and Western Europe." *Comparative Political Studies* 13, no. 4 (January 1981): 445–76.

———. "The Status of Women in a Socialist Order: Czechoslovakia, 1948–78." *Slavic Review* 38, no. 4 (1979): 583–602.

CHAPTER 10

A Vietnamese Woman Directs the War Story

Duc Hoan, 1937–2003

Karen Turner

War is terrible for everyone, on all sides. In Vietnam, the sacrifices of ordinary people have been ignored. I want to tell their stories. That is why I make my films." War veteran, actress, producer, and director Duc Hoan, affectionately known in Hanoi intellectual circles as the "elder stateswoman" of Vietnamese film, viewed herself as a critic who drew on her own experiences to explore the themes of war and loss that dominated her work. Despite her popularity among Hanoi intellectuals of the war generation, however, Duc Hoan was never granted the official recognition her films deserve, in part because she challenged postwar masculine ideals of service and in part because she refused to shape her films and performances according to rigid dichotomies of heroes and traitors. When she died in 2003 at age sixty-six, official obituaries erased her military experience in two wars and her twenty-year directing career to focus on her role as an ingénue whose "beautiful young face and sparkling eyes" captivated audiences in her first film, *The Story of A Phu* (*Vo cong A Phu*), released in 1960.[1]

Duc Hoan's life history would be interesting if only because she was one of the few women anywhere in the world to gain the credibility and muster the resources to shape narratives of war. But the value of her story rests as well in her experiences as a witness to Vietnam's struggle for independence from French colonialism, the war Vietnamese call the "American War," postwar reconstruction, isolation from the United States and its allies after 1975, and the economic reforms (*doi moi*) that brought the nation into the global marketplace after the mid-1980s. It is important at the outset to note that while an examination of Duc Hoan's life and art can offer invaluable information about gender relations and artistic expression during these tumultuous years, and although she was sensitive to problems facing ordinary people, she enjoyed advantages and experiences that were not available to most of her peers, as I will discuss in more detail later in the chapter. Her early life was troubled by the influence of a strict Confucian father, but she did not have to resort to manual labor or a trade to earn a living. She was educated in French schools that made her aware of her subaltern status, but her learning also enabled her to escape an oppressive home life to work as a village teacher in the areas controlled by the Viet Minh. Her high-profile service in the Viet Minh armies was unusual as well, for most women who supported the anticolonial wars after 1945 operated as guerrilla fighters or as faceless laborers (*dan cong*) who hauled supplies to the remote border areas. Hidden from the history of this final battle, these women—estimated at about one hundred thousand strong—played an important role in the final Viet Minh victory against the French.[2]

After the United States began an air war against North Vietnam in 1965, Duc Hoan's education and expertise enabled her to work in a relatively privileged position as director of a theater troupe to raise the spirits of the men and women stationed on the Ho Chi Minh Trail. At that time, the ten thousand miles of pathways and roads that made up the trail were considered by both sides to be the key to winning the war, for the trail was the only route that the northern armies could use to send men and materiel to the southern battlefields. The trail was sheltered by jungles and mountains that shielded the military base camps, but it also housed wild animals and plants—and exposure to malaria-bearing mosquitoes—that posed dangers to the soldiers and volunteers.[3] While Duc Hoan did witness and share some of the hardships endured by the young people she met, she did not suffer the long-term deprivations that marked the lives of the thousands of women who joined the Volunteer Youth Brigades in their late teens and early twenties. These women's service helped tip the balance from defeat to victory, for they took on backbreaking and dangerous tasks in some of the most heavily bombarded sites and remained in the field in some cases for as long as six or seven years; then they returned home too sick or too old to marry and bear children. Duc Hoan was aware of her good fortune, proud of her young husband and healthy son and daughter, and mindful that she had escaped physical and mental trauma. Yet, although she was freer than most women to chart her personal destiny, her art was shaped by the tension between socialist promises of emancipation for women and the lived experiences of women of all classes. Her films display great sympathy for women and men trapped in traditional networks of family and social expectations in the context of revolution and war. While it is true that the Vietnamese experience shaped her stories, her need to "shadowbox" with the censors, as David Marr so aptly terms the interplay of power and resistance between Vietnamese media intellectuals and bureaucrats since the French colonial era, resonates with that of filmmakers in any society that subordinates art to didactic forces.[4]

Indeed, Duc Hoan's history exemplifies the liminal position of the intellectual in Vietnam, for she derived benefits from state-funded media enterprises and called herself a patriot, but at the same time chafed at what she viewed as officialdom's unrealistic and rigid interpretations of social problems. Duc Hoan's formative years in film were spent under the tutelage of Soviet filmmakers, and she attended to socialist realism's dictate to create characters caught up in historical movements. But her films also explored the ways that individuals conducted their personal lives in times of national crisis and rejected simple solutions to complex problems. Her characters made choices, choices that often offended the censors, and a hallmark of her craft rested in her ability to transmit messages about shared social problems so subtly that her films were never banned. Her professional history demonstrates the truth of David Marr's conclusion that although the Vietnamese state closely monitors the media, state controls have never been absolute.[5]

Duc Hoan's life story and body of work raises interesting questions. How did firsthand experience with war affect her representations of gender issues, and how does her gender explain her interpretations of war? Who were her intended spectators? How did she use the cinematic apparatus to negotiate between state censors and her own sense of justice? In addressing some of these questions, I have found very helpful those critics who apply Mikhail Bakhtin's writings on dialogism to film.[6] Bakhtin's understanding of the interplay between language, power, and interpretation that characterizes the works of intellectuals who create within an oppressive state apparatus helps to explain Duc Hoan's multiple voices. Akin to intellectuals in other socialist states, she viewed herself as both a privileged subject and vulnerable object in ideological power struggles.[7] A product of the socialist revolution that promised domestic liberation for women, an employee of the state her entire professional life, and a self-described patriot to the core, she nonetheless believed her duty rested in speaking back to state agendas when they ignored human dilemmas. Benedict Kerkvliet's observation that the state's firm grasp on the media does not prevent debate within its own artistic community rings true in Duc Hoan's case.[8]

Dramatic events in Vietnam's history touched Duc Hoan personally, and like many elites of her generation, at times she related her life story not as a personal narrative but as part of a nationwide struggle for survival against all odds. In the "French" time, she told me in an interview, the soul of Vietnam was wounded by a century of colonial domination that began in the mid-nineteenth century and ended at the historic battle of Dienbienphu in 1954. She cherished the ideal of family life, but understood that leaving her traditional Confucian family liberated her, just as Ho Chi Minh's revolution promised women emancipation from colonial dominance and Confucian patriarchy:

> I left my home to join the anti-French resistance when I was ten. Bigger than other girls of my age, I was able to convince the authorities for a time that I was old enough. Why did I, a sheltered, bourgeois girl, take such a chance with my life? Because I hated the way my French Catholic school teachers looked down on the Vietnamese students. Because when the French took over Hanoi in 1946, my family had to leave the city to hide in the countryside. Because after my mother died, home had no meaning for me anymore. You see, I was the youngest of six daughters and my father followed the traditional Confucian ways. In 1948, at age 60, he remarried a young woman and had a son, and after that, my sisters and I were pretty much on our own. After all, as the old saying goes, "A hundred girls aren't worth a single testicle." I knew my sisters would marry and I did not want to burden them. So for all of these reasons, it was easy for me to follow Ho Chi Minh.[9]

Duc Hoan's personal liberation mirrors the experience of other young female intellectuals, who enjoyed new opportunities with the establishment of liberated zones controlled by the Viet Minh forces that offered an alternative community.[10] Revolutionary elites there trained Duc Hoan to teach in village schools, to speak Chinese, and to serve in an artillery unit in the final victory.

Duc Hoan laughingly told me how the French had unwittingly radicalized their Vietnamese students by teaching them about liberty and equality, but that, in the end, she didn't need the French to alert her to the fact that women could participate in national liberation:

> Stories about Vietnam's founding mothers, the Trung Sisters who fought the Chinese in the first century, and Lady Trieu, the peasant girl with huge breasts who rode into battle on an elephant to expel the Chinese, were sung by our mothers as lullabies. We took the fact that women always fought when the country was in danger for granted. Our heroines were never successful at gaining power in the long run, but neither were they crazy women like Joan of Arc. Why would a woman want to dress up like a man when her feminine beauty is her greatest asset? I also admired Russian women heroines, like Alexandra Kollantai, and I knew about women fighters there.[11]

Travel outside her urban environment when she taught in village schools and worked in literacy campaigns in the countryside in the Third Interzone in the North allowed her to observe the hardships suffered by rural women. But she also noted their relative freedom. Village moral codes were strict and transgressions against the interests of the patriarchal family punished severely, but household survival hinged on sending women out to the fields and markets to produce and sell their goods. Always sad about the family she lost, she also appreciated the camaraderie she shared with teachers and comrades in the field and the generosity of the farmers who shared their food in hard times. "They were the most beautiful human relationships I have ever had. We were like a big family and still get together whenever we can."[12] When the military needed her, she joined the Viet Minh army in 1953 to become an interpreter for Vietnamese units sent to south China for training. She told me ruefully—in Chinese, our common language—that Viet Minh commanders could send her so far from home, in the company of men, because she had no family to worry about her reputation.

Military service offered Duc Hoan the key to legitimacy as a critic of the regime later in life, for in Vietnam, as in most nations after a war, veterans have a higher claim to narrate war than civilians who remain as voyeurs. Her service in the historic battles at Dienbienphu earned Duc Hoan a place in history, but she refused to claim any glory for her actions. "I joined the E367 Artillery Unit, but I was no different from other men and women. I learned to shoot a gun and how to jump out of the line of fire."[13] When the Vietnamese made one of their first feature films, a reenactment of the famous battle, Duc Hoan was involved. Some of the French captives were used as extras, and she recalled how she pitied these defeated, gaunt men who once seemed so powerful and fearsome. War as the great equalizer that diminishes all of its participants would become one of the enduring themes of her films.

Art and Nationalism

After independence in 1954 and before the escalation of the US war in 1965, Vietnam enjoyed a period of peace that allowed young people "to learn about literature and love and life," an old army veteran told me in Hanoi as he explained the disruptions the US war brought to the lives of youth.[14] During this time, Duc Hoan was noticed by a Russian theater expert she called Vaxilliev, who trained her for her first acting role because he was captivated by the unique beauty of this former artillery woman—according to a report written much later.[15] Duc Hoan recalled that her role in this film, *The Story of A Phu* (*Vo Cong A Phu*) was filmed in a Potemkin village decorated with fake flowers and populated with citified actors. The government bore the cost, she told me, because the state deemed important the film's message that minority women suffered abuse that would be eliminated by socialist policies. *A Phu* became a success, in part because Vietnamese film was a novelty at this time and in part because it traveled to places its intended spectators could easily reach—village marketplaces and fields.[16] Duc Hoan had enjoyed life in the countryside during her stint as a teacher for the Viet Minh, but by her own account, life in the mountains proved more traumatic than the fighting at Dienbienphu or the frightful bombing of the North during the American War. The burial customs practiced by the minority people offended her, she said, and she shivered when she recalled funerals in which rice was placed in the mouth of the corpse and consumed by relatives when it fell out. "I spent all my time worrying that someone would die while I was there."[17] In this case, she echoed a persistent hegemonic message that the minority peoples were indeed backward and in need of reform and that the Viet majority, now backed by socialist policies that endeavored to raise the lives of all citizens, naturally deserved to take a leading role in this effort.[18]

As an actress, she was feted by Eastern Bloc film festivals. For example, in the *Newsletter of the Afro-Asian Film Festival*, which documented events at the festival held in Indonesia in 1964, her photo was captioned to emphasize her beauty. She was deemed "one of the most charming and attractive stars that has graced our festival." The authors of this newsletter railed against First World producers who operated with bigger budgets but did not understand their African and Asian subjects: "Who knows Afro-Asians better than Afro-Asians themselves?" Technology was not the key to honest representations, it declared: "Only Afro-Asian artists can truthfully and with revolutionary objectivity depict what is Afro-Asian. . . . Our considered contention is that we would rather have a piece of art that might not be technically 99% perfect but politically impregnated with the revolutionary zeal and depiction of Afro-Asian life."[19] This event brought Duc Hoan in touch with other socialist filmmakers and reinforced her commitment to use film to serve her people and country.

She was in step with the times. By 1960, all media and print productions had been firmly placed under control of the state in Vietnam. For the fledgling film industry, this meant that Party committees within film units informed directors of current political agendas and the Ministry of Culture controlled permissions, equipment, and regulations. Those artists willing to work within the system traded their loyalty to party policies for housing, health-care benefits, and the chance to receive overseas training.[20] Intellectuals such as Duc Hoan became cultural workers in this system, and she expressed gratitude for the policies that allowed her to gain professional expertise abroad. On the other hand, she disliked the puritanical views of the uneducated cadre who promoted proletarian values rather than artistic merit.

The impact of the American War would dominate Duc Hoan's midlife as a film producer and director, but she missed direct participation in the very fiercest years of the war. In 1965, just as the United States escalated the air war against the North, she was assigned to work in a government coal mine as an administrative secretary, and in 1967 she left for the Soviet Union. She returned in 1972 to witness the Christmas bombings of Hanoi and Haiphong, the first time that B-52s were used against major urban areas. A proud Hanoian to the core, she told me that the psychic scars from those days mirrored the physical destruction of segments of her beloved city. To keep up morale in the face of this violence both in the cities and along the strategic Ho Chi Minh Trail, the government in the North enlisted theater troupes and accomplished musicians to travel with the soldiers. Duc Hoan walked down the trail with a set designer for her film studio and spent the final years of the war in four heavily bombed villages in Quang Binh Province, near the hotly contested sites along the border between North and South Vietnam. As director of a theater troupe charged with bolstering the morale of soldiers and local militia under constant fire, she was well funded for the only time in her artistic career. She recalls that the troupe enjoyed German cosmetics and well-made costumes. She repeated a theme that would come up again and again in her work: "In the most sad, violent times, people need relief from their sadness." War is not simply about grim determination: "When the US aircraft came to bomb us, we had a sense of helplessness. There was nothing most of us could do when the bombs fell and they seemed to fall randomly."[21] She repeated a saying that I had heard from others who witnessed the air attacks: "A B-52 trying to aim a bomb is like a stork trying to shit into a test tube." This sense that there was no way to prepare to escape the bombs added to the psychological problems that plagued city dwellers. Duc Hoan added, "Our leaders felt it worthwhile to invest in art to encourage the spirit of the people fighting the war and to remember that life goes on after people come out of their bomb shelters."[22]

Women on the Margins

Duc Hoan eventually learned to work with sound recording and by the end of the war began to direct her own films for the Hanoi-based Vietnam Feature Film Studio, founded in 1959. "Now I had some influence over how the stories were told."[23] Her first film, produced just after the end of the war, focused on women who crossed the boundaries between the familiar lowlands and the unknown world of the jungle when they went out to defend the Ho Chi Minh Trail. *From a Jungle (Tu mot canh rung)* depicts the lives, loves, and struggles of youth volunteers. Produced in 1977 and released in 1978, only three years after the war's end, this film offended the censors by challenging the party line that war was a heroic enterprise with no room for personal emotions. Duc Hoan was determined to bring to the screen the realities of life for young people charged with important duties but released from the strictures of family and community. "I wanted to show the young women as full of life, able to laugh, love and have fun but yet act with competence equal to the men."[24]

The techniques that Duc Hoan used to critique the orthodox combat genre, which focused on hardship, sacrifice, and unsentimental male heroics, can best be appreciated in a Vietnamese context. Simply placing women on the battlefield was not as radical a departure in Vietnam as in other countries, for in Vietnamese history women fighters were identified with the founding and endurance of the Vietnamese nation.[25] As Jeanine Basinger has observed of US films about women in combat, women rarely serve as heroes, but when they do, certain rules must be followed: defiance of conventional roles and a view of life as disposable for the larger good, competence in a man's world, and the ability to maintain healthy relationships with fellow soldiers.[26] Interestingly, Duc Hoan's female characters follow this paradigm. She based them on real women she had encountered on the trail, where she developed a particular admiration for the female liaison agents who guided soldiers on the march to the South through the dense jungles: "These women worked in isolation and they held the fates of the soldiers they led in their hands, because only they knew their assigned 50 kilometers of the Trail and if they led a group into ambush, everyone would be killed. These were the quiet ones, the ones who did not act with violence."[27]

Duc Hoan's multiple interpretive positions complicated what seems on the surface to be a simple film about love and war. She was not averse to shaping her story to inspire young people to work hard and cooperate, qualities the government wanted to encourage in the postwar reconstruction period. In the film a young country bumpkin, unruly and cynical at first, learns about discipline and camaraderie from his more experienced peers. Duc Hoan shows how the war reversed traditional gender roles. Men and women work as equals in the service of the soldiers and trucks that supplied the southern front. Men cry over lost friends, and frightened women and men hold hands as they form human borders to guide trucks through the night in jungles without roads. In this early film, she conforms to the official view of the South as a corrupt place, juxtaposing sets showing clean-living young northern soldiers working for a noble cause with glimpses of a decadent Saigonese officer who keeps a young woman as his concubine. But she does not portray the northern soldiers as mere tools of the state. The film pokes fun at the prudish and suspicious male political commissars charged with preaching party doctrine to keep young people in line. Not only was their task impossible, but it was also unnecessary because, as the film demonstrated, these youth held to their own moral values. Duc Hoan, proud to be known as a sophisticated Hanoian herself, identified the urban men and women as far more interesting characters than the unsophisticated party men of humble, often rural, origins. In an interview in the Vietnamese journal *Cinematographic Magazine*, published in Hanoi in 1988, she was celebrated as a "native Hanoian" who used Hanoi as a stage for her stories.[28] This identification with urban culture limited Duc Hoan's vision because far more volunteers and soldiers came from villages in the North than from its cities. Indeed, rural women have always worked in the fields and on the roads, and so their presence on the Ho Chi Minh Trail was not so startling as the appearance of "Hanoi maidens" who had to learn to endure hardship and deprivation taken for granted as part of daily life by their sisters in the countryside.

At a time when the entire nation was recovering from thirty years of war and every family was mourning their dead, Duc Hoan spoke for youth: "Old people only want to think of sadness in war. But young people want to live. They were so young, and they had their love lives."[29] Her target audience was not the young but the elders, the nervous party and army commissars and parents who sent their young women so far from supervision. At this time, only selected documentary war footage was available for narrative film, so these re-creations extend a particular power over spectators. Duc Hoan understood that when the nation sent its young women to war, it placed the nation's future at risk and shared a universal worry: if the war tainted its young, who would reproduce a new generation of soldiers and citizens, and how would society reintegrate women who had broken taboos when they took on roles such as burying the dead? We know from field records that Ho Chi Minh himself was so worried about women in the field that he sent mental health workers to check up on them, and ordered field commanders to give them the best of the meager supplies for personal hygiene.[30] In some ways, Duc Hoan seemed to be teasing her conservative spectators when she allowed them to enter the world created by youngsters in the jungle. On the one hand, she wanted to reassure the elders that boundaries between sexual love and friendship were not violated, that the pure young virgins who went to war would come home in the same state. The film moves back and forth between scenes of youthful play and dogged duty, and in one almost carnivalesque sequence men and women engage in a water fight that seems to verge out of control. But one theme remains constant: young women worked with men as equals without losing their feminine appeal.

Duc Hoan did not always resist dominant cultural and political dictates when shaping her stories about love, revolution, and war. She came of age during a time when Vietnamese intellectuals questioned the oppression of individuals under the old "feudal" system and saw as necessary for modernity the freedom to choose a romantic partner rather than to follow the wishes of the extended family. French-educated intellectuals like Duc Hoan were also exposed through their study of literature to French romanticism that celebrated individual freedom.[31] As we have seen, in her own life she liberated herself from her Confucian family because she understood that she would never find fulfillment or happiness within that system and also because the revolution offered new opportunities for some women. She followed her heart at least in her second marriage, to a man fifteen years her junior, an unusual arrangement for a woman of any generation in Vietnam. Her depictions of love among the characters in her films also defy conventional and political norms, for she was always concerned with the ways that individuals responded to situations. At first glance, her portraits of the young men and women creating their own space for free relations deep in the jungle might seem sanitized because they are void of sexual tensions. Other sources, however, suggest that "revolutionary love" is not simply an impossible ideal. Oral histories and a recently discovered war diary, written by a young doctor in the throes of war—and thus not tainted by postwar culture or expectations—indicate that young men and women could have close, platonic friendships based on a common spirit of fighting for a greater good and the sheer need to survive. The diary of Dang Thuy Tran, a Hanoi-educated doctor who at the age of twenty-four volunteered to work in one of the most dangerous areas along the Ho Chi Minh Trail, focuses on anger toward the American enemy and documents daily life on the run as she moves her hospitals and patients to temporary safety.[32] But her emotional life is richly recorded as well: she longs for the safety of home, broods about a man who seemed not to share her romantic feelings, and expresses deep affection for the young soldiers who came to her jungle hospital. She places these relationships in kinship terms in which she cares for them as if they were younger brothers. The diary's portrait of young people creating their own networks of support in the midst of violence and death echoes in many ways Duc Hoan's postwar reconstructions in film.

But one topic seems off-limits: the problem of sexual assault within the communist armies. Diaries by men who witnessed the courage of young women on the trail mention their beauty, but usually not in sexualized terms. In fact, the men often worried about the future for these young women, whose ravaged bodies bore the imprint of hardship. It is only in postwar fiction that northern writers have touched on rape and sexual relations, but even in these representations of wartime life, rarely is the thorny problem of sexual aggression among the ranks taken up.[33] Evidence from other wars is instructive, for some female soldiers who fought with the Russian communist armies in World War II testified that "today it seems impossible to think of a million women with the front line troops without a great deal of sex going on. But then we weren't like that. The conditions were hardly conducive to sex anyway. We were filthy, exhausted, and hungry."[34] When I was in Hanoi in 1996, I interviewed a military historian and asked him about sex within the military; he dismissed my query by accusing me of acting like a typical American obsessed with sex. In time, I think, Vietnamese authors will deal with issues of sexual violence during the war, but they may be reluctant to do so because such information would add to the stigma already attached to women who served.

War and the Family

"Wars have their endings inside families," the feminist writer Cynthia Enloe so wisely remarked in an article about representations of women in postwar Vietnam.[35] Duc Hoan realistically addressed a very sensitive problem in her second major film, *Love and Distance* (*Tinh yeu va khoang cach*), released in the early 1980s, which features a beautiful young wife looking forward to the homecoming of her soldier husband. But when he appears, mutilated and sick, she is repulsed. Duc Hoan sympathized with both sides of this terrible dilemma: "People did not want to face it. But it was a situation many families had to handle. Sick, angry husbands, wounded in mind and body, came home—sometimes after thirty years in the field if they had fought the French. Their war wounds hurt their families. We cannot blame the wives for their feelings."[36] The camera allows the spectator to see the point of view of the female character when it focuses on the male veteran's mutilated face. But the rejected man's reactions are portrayed as well. He turns inward, writing poetry and music about his idealistic phase as a young soldier setting out to save his nation and protect his family and his terrible disappointment at returning home maimed and rejected.

This film is important in a Vietnamese context not only for raising a touchy domestic issue but also for inverting the gender of the victim. Many male veterans who addressed the issue of rejection focused not on mutilated men but on malaria-ridden, prematurely aged women veterans with ruined bodies that repulse men. In the short story "A Blanket of Scraps," written by a male veteran in 1992, a woman who became ill while serving in the Volunteer Youth Brigades becomes a beggar, a childless woman, with no roots after the war.[37] When a widower she meets tries to make love to her, her disease-ridden, dried-up body renders him impotent. Duc Hoan told me she sympathized with women veterans but felt that more social problems resulted from the far more numerous wounded men returning home and the lack of medical or psychiatric facilities to help them and their families. Her film pleads for compassion for women who admire their wounded husbands but experience a very human distaste for the scars of war inscribed on their bodies.

Duc Hoan's most famous and controversial film, *Obsession* (*Am anh*), set and produced in the immediate aftermath of the end of the war bur only released in 1988, focuses on how actions taken during war affect the postwar family. The most fully developed character is a North Vietnamese Army regular who defects to the enemy. Duc Hoan explained why she made the film: "After the war, Vietnamese people on both sides needed to put the hatred out of their hearts and forgive each other for mistakes. War should never happen, but when it does, some people are forced to use guns. At the end of the day, even the victorious ones are victims, because they lose so much, sometimes their families, their sweethearts, their health."[38] Duc Hoan's own family had split because of political and pragmatic decisions, and she still mourned a sister she had not seen for over thirty years. In her family, only Duc Hoan followed the socialist revolution, but with an open mind and compassion for others who made different decisions. "We are a typical Vietnamese family, tied by emotions and memories, split apart by politics and war."[39]

The film focuses on two male leads, the deserter, Quang, who wins the woman, and Thuan, the stalwart soldier who loses her. With flashbacks that allow the viewer to witness both Thuan and Quang as young lovers smitten by the same woman, Hai, the film creates an emotional link between the despised deserter and the stalwart veteran. The film counters messages that the North drove home to their soldiers and citizens during the war and in the early years of reconstruction when survival literally hinged on morale: that personal life must take second place to the political goals set forth by the party, and that men could leave home for war without anxiety because a good socialist woman would never change allegiances once committed to a soldier. Duc Hoan faced a tough task by examining the motivations of a deserter:

> Everyone feared and hated deserters and so it was hard to paint Quang as a
> sympathetic character. The deserters were the most hard to forgive. We hated
> them more than the Americans because they knew so much and could betray so

many people. But we have to put ourselves in their position and remember the strong human will to survive. At the end of the war we had to find ways to bring everyone into the community.[40]

The terrible crime of military desertion is not the only breach of faith committed in the film. Through a series of flashbacks, viewers learn that the loyal Thuan and the confused Hai had become engaged before the war. But after Hai is alone, without word from her fiancé for years, she meets Quang in an isolated jungle station. Quang plays on her pity by telling her he is a musician, an unwilling recruit with no interest in war—in itself a subversive message. The seduction scene shows Hai protesting her love and loyalty to Thuan, while Quang physically and emotionally overpowers her—in fact, his actions border on rape. It seems that only if Hai were innocent of aggressive sexuality could she become a sympathetic character. In fact, Hai, the female lead, is denied any memory in flashbacks that would explain her actions. She seems subject to the forces of the men who love her.

Phan Thanh Hao—a journalist, interpreter, and friend of Duc Hoan and her family—explained the enduring interest in *Obsession* among Hanoi intellectuals when I interviewed her in 1997: "*Obsession* is unique because it was made only a short time after the war and it was the first time a woman director did anything on war. Only a woman could have understood the pain of the defector's wife back home—better for the family if he had been a war martyr or invalid."[41] Duc Hoan might have understood a woman's pain, but she also knew where the power rested in the postwar world; as a result, she aimed her call for forgiveness and reconciliation at a male audience. But she did not employ masculine symbols of war to captivate her male spectators: no flags, portraits of Ho Chi Minh, medals, or heroic music mark her sets. Personnel in the camp hospital who treat the mentally disturbed Quang after he breaks down display kindness toward him. In fact, because she could not afford to hire professional actors, Duc Hoan herself plays a sweet-natured nurse, adding to the power of her personal message about forgiveness. When she has Quang explain his actions by saying, "I was just afraid. I don't hate anyone," Duc Hoan encodes her most important message: individuals caught up in war suffer the same human frailties shared by those more fortunate, and the patriotic fervor of the war makers is not always powerful enough to influence individuals to act against their nature.

Women unable to marry because of war wounds were also victims of war, and Duc Hoan took up this problem in her last film, a television production called *Love Song by a River* (*Chuyen tinh ben song*), shown in 1991.[42] Two sisters, orphaned by war, share disappointment in love. One sister, married to a simple, rural man, loves a shallow party bureaucrat who pretends to be an artist. This sister takes up with a fast crowd of young people infatuated with Western ideas and clothes. When her husband finds her dancing to a disco tune, he beats her in anger. Meanwhile, the other sister, a former volunteer youth who is unmarried, watches the married couple and their child with envy, despite their domestic problems. One night the single sister begs a traveling medicine man to make love to her because she wants a child, even if she can never hope for marriage. In a fairly graphic bedroom scene, the camera focuses on their mutual victimization rather than their sexuality. He is maimed by war, a drunk who cannot forget the sound of bombs. She calls herself a "lame duck" as she pleads with him to ignore her mangled body so he can make love to her. When she does not become pregnant, she is deeply disappointed. The camera follows the lame sister as she looks longingly on her lucky married sister and the spurned husband who watches his wife's defection. Even when the husband eventually beats his wife in anger, he is shown as a sympathetic character, driven to excess by his helplessness.

Duc Hoan adapted the film from a short story by a village writer, changing the story because the original, about a mutilated woman veteran married to a medicine seller, had no social value. "I rewrote the story into a real situation. After the war so many women could only imagine love because they could never experience it."[43] Indeed, women who "ask for a child" outside of marriage became so numerous that with the urging of the Vietnam Women's Union, the government responded in 1986 by including in the revised marriage laws a provision allowing the children of single mothers rights to full citizenship.[44] Legal acceptance has not erased unease about women who reject the patriarchal family system in order to claim their right to motherhood. Duc Hoan's depiction of a woman so desperate that she would turn to a stranger for sex and a child speaks to this social problem but ignores another problem that worries Vietnamese women—the rising rates of domestic violence in Vietnamese postwar society.[45] When I asked Duc Hoan about the film's suggestion that an abusive man is better than no man at all, she pointed out that the married sister "needed to understand that her husband became angry with her because he loved her. She was lucky to have this man. Keeping her family together is her duty."[46] Duc Hoan made no apology for portraying married life with all its difficulties as far preferable to the single life for women. However, she never talked about the irony of her own situation: she divorced her first husband, a neglectful army veteran, and married a man fifteen years younger in her own quest for individual happiness. In *Love Song by a River*, she aimed her critical eye not at those who search for personal fulfillment but at the weak party functionary who seduces a young woman away from her simple, illiterate, but good-hearted husband. "Be satisfied with what you have, don't destroy it. Don't take after things that are modern or Western and think they are superior to your own culture"—this was her message, she said.

Negotiating the War Story

Love Song by a River, though sympathetic to women who defied pressure to conform to patriarchal ideals of marriage, was in line with other journalistic and media presentations in the 1990s. Duc Hoan's worry about the dangers of the market converged with widespread anxieties about "social evils," such as divorce, delinquency, and drug use, as the nation opened its borders to the world; those concerns were also shared by the older generation. By the mid-1990s evaluations of the negative aspects of the global marketplace that did not directly name high-ranking party members or policies could be tolerated and even encouraged by conservative officials wary of the turn toward capitalism.[47] Duc Hoan's view of the countryside shifted over rime: *From a Jungle* ridicules country bumpkins whereas *Love Song by a River* presents the countryside as a site of traditional values and stability. Duc Hoan recognized that her views had changed over time:

> When I made *From a Jungle* I was myself more influenced by the heroic mode at that time than I thought. I knew perfectly well that women suffered more than men. They risked their health when they worked in water for long periods of time. They were so malnourished that they didn't have their periods. Some women didn't have enough clothes and had to hide in caves when chemicals and fires destroyed their only garments and many lost their hair from malaria.[48]

What altered her memory? A series of documentaries produced in 1995 for television to commemorate the thirtieth anniversary of the end of the American War incorporated wartime archival footage that had been banned by the censors. Duc Hoan, like many viewers, was jarred by this footage. "When I saw the thin girls, their lips and eyes darkened by malaria, their shoulders slumping with fatigue, I regretted casting young, healthy women in the film in 1978. Yes, I used real women who had served as liaison agents, but we chose healthy women and we dressed them up."[49] Her goal at the time she made the film was to show that young people could enjoy love during the chaos of war, subverting the theme of heroic, unsentimental sacrifice that ruled the day in Hanoi. Later, when the full costs of war could not be ignored, she would regret her decision to focus on healthy young people.

As she constructed her films, Duc Hoan was guided not simply by official codes but rather by a form of self-censorship. As an intellectual who worked within the socialist system, she knew quite well how to work around policy shifts. When Hoan made *From a Jungle* she understood that sanctioned themes of heroic sacrifice were intended to mute postwar poverty and dislocation:

> The men in charge of images of war wanted to show films about bombs and violence, to show off Vietnamese men standing up heroically against the enemy. The Deputy Minister of Culture criticized the film for being too much like a poem. He ordered me to give up scenes about daily life in the secluded jungle stations, such as one in which I wanted to show two young people kissing. I had to compromise by showing the romantic scene reflected in a pool of water. But they didn't even like this because we let the camera linger too long on the reflection. I told them they should either trust me or get rid of me.[50]

She had high-enough status and support as a veteran of two wars to keep her important scenes in the final cut. Years later in an interview, her cameraman for *From a Jungle* told a newspaper in Vietnam about her clever handling of the now-famous "kissing scene." "It takes a woman to really know how to deal with love," he said.[51] More accurately, it took a member of the revolutionary generation with impeccable credentials to push the limits with the party watchdogs, especially during the period of tight censorship when the film was made and shown.

When examining the role of censorship in postcolonial Vietnam, we should acknowledge that state control did not begin with the revolutionary socialist governments. In Vietnam, cinema was first used by the French colonial government as a technique to rationalize their enterprise, forcing ambitious Vietnamese filmmakers to adhere to colonial ideology if they wanted to practice their trade. One of the few surveys of the film industry in Vietnam, written by John Charlot, traces the dance between artists and party bureaucrats after 1954 in the North. Much of his information squares with Duc Hoan's accounts.[52] Charlot contends that censorship is not simply a matter of draconian measures enacted by state functionaries. True, scripts must first satisfy officials in the Ministry of Culture, but everything depends on who is keeping watch at the time and how much power immediate bosses have to halt interference from higher-ups. Duc Hoan revered her supervisor, Tran Dac, the vice director of the Vietnam Feature Film School and himself an artist, for understanding her goals and serving as a buffer with the censors.

Thus, for Duc Hoan as for her comrades, censorship must be seen as a fluid site of negotiation rather than a stark confrontation with the state. As Marr points out, neither party functionaries nor ordinary spectators operate in a single interpretive mode, and much depends on personal power rather than rules.[53] Censorship in Vietnam can be imposed in many ways, such as withholding funds, delaying production, or banning films outright, but cinema in any society is subject to pressures to conform to certain themes, and that domination and resistance always remain in flux. As Jan Plamper notes in an article about censorship in the first two decades of Soviet power in Russia, a period generally believed to be one of total control:

> Censorship can be seen as one of the many "practices of cultural regulation,"
> a broadly defined rubric that is meant to accommodate market forces in the
> capitalist West, too. Once the nature of the interaction between censors and cultural
> producers is no longer determined a priori, once various practices of cultural
> regulation in different times and places open up for comparison, the historian's task
> becomes one of figuring out the commonalities and differences and ultimately the
> logic at work in each case.[54]

The censors in a socialist system are nearly always the first spectators that a filmmaker must satisfy, but government functionaries do not always have monolithic perspectives, especially about the war, because so many commissars in the art world are themselves former veterans who know firsthand how violence tests human emotions and actions. Duc Hoan's negotiation about the kissing scene in *From a Jungle* was unique for its time, but other directors continued to bargain with the censors to keep the scenes most essential to their messages. For example, the director Luu Trong Ninh had to agree to cut scenes in his 1992 film *Please Forgive Me* (*Hay tha thu cho em*), which centers on tensions between those in the older war generation who romanticize communal values and younger people who reject the postwar nation's poverty. The film was shown briefly then banned when the censors deemed four scenes offensive—one of them a clip in which a character notes that soldiers from the North as well as the South committed atrocities during the war. Luu Trang Ninh told *Far Eastern Economic Review* journalist Murray Hiebert that he funded the film himself, but would have to pay back his loans and would probably cave in to pressure. And he had obviously agreed to support the party line in general, perhaps as an additional token to "purchase" artistic license. "We haven't made enough preparation to enjoy real democracy, so I sympathize with what our leaders are doing. Otherwise the situation would veer out of control."[55]

As Vietnamese leaders prepared to reform the socialist economy into a more market-based system that exposed the nation to the outside world, a period of what Charlot calls "glasnost" pried open the film industry to some degree. Films such as Dang Nhat Minh's *The Young Woman on the River* (*Co gai tren song*, 1987) features a former South Vietnamese soldier as the hero who marries a prostitute whereas a weak northern party official betrays his lover. When censors objected to the sex scenes and the negative portrait of the communist official, the filmmaker agreed to cut the sex scenes because he considered the example of the heartless functionary a more important message. His decision was supported by his own supervisors when some officials in the Ministry of Culture protested.[56] Studies of other segments of Vietnamese society such as Ben Kerkvliet's work on resistance in the countryside confirm the widespread occurrence of what he terms "creeping pluralism."[57] But tolerance of multiple interpretations has not in fact stimulated a spate of innovative productions. Some filmmakers decry the market pressures that now force them to satisfy urban consumers as well as government functionaries. Some film critics also find that films made by Vietnamese filmmakers in the diaspora, such as Tony Bui's *Three Seasons*, diminish the agency of their female characters.[58]

When women represent the violated nation, individual women's stories become subsumed within nationalist representations. As historian Hue-Tam Ho Tai has suggested, during the war not only did women enter the military in large numbers, but the nation itself was feminized by foreign invaders who literally penetrated and violated the homeland.[59] And so it follows that a remasculinized vision of the nation would well serve a small nation entering a competitive international arena. In this milieu, film and fictional representations of women have shifted as well. The woman warrior who fought with men to save the nation now takes second place to the moral mother who replenishes and nurtures future citizens. But doubts about women's moral character surface in troubling ways, especially in fiction by male writers. One of the most popular post–reform era short stories, Nguyen Huy Thiep's "The General Retires," published in 1992, features a good, old-fashioned veteran army man whose daughter-in-law feeds aborted fetuses to the dogs she raises as a sideline. All of these productions warn that women are morally weak and susceptible to the ill effects of foreign influence. Men, embedded in kinship and community, have the means to resist these pressures and therefore must take the lead in the new world. For women who hope to compete as equals with men in a market economy, this revival of the more oppressive elements of traditional culture is bad news indeed.[60]

By the 1990s, Duc Hoan was, by her own account, marginalized in the film industry. However, she had been extraordinarily privileged to play any part at all in postwar productions because, as she pointed out, only one other woman veteran gained the right to direct films after the war. Yet she also acknowledged that compared with less-educated soldiers and ordinary citizens, she enjoyed a position that enabled her to participate in the business of constructing memory. Her life and productions demonstrate how the artist in a socialist regime works with multiple identities and subjectivities that display fluidity over time in response to shifting social pressures, statist values, and personal experiences.[61] Indeed, Duc Hoan exemplifies the Vietnamese intellectual whose standing allows for a fluid relationship between service and duty. During the wars, she supported the military needs of the state. After the French and American Wars, when the nation was no longer threatened by outside forces, she directed the camera toward internal social problems, supported by her own belief that human feelings always transcend politics. But she could never escape politics and had to carefully craft her films to remain true to her vision without being so offensive to current government campaigns that they would never reach her audiences.

Reflections

Duc Hoan died of cancer in Hanoi in March 2003. When evaluating her life and work, I suggest that her resistance to official policies cannot be labeled as "feminist" in the conventional Western sense because she valorized motherhood as a woman's natural right and supported marriage even when abusive for women. But Western readers must remember the environment that shaped her—a homeland that had been at war with outside invaders for over thirty years, a nation so decimated that family became the only bulwark against disaster after the war. Indeed, Duc Hoan's life and work offer a valuable perspective to challenge essentialist arguments about women's natural roles. Although she believed in biological destiny, in her own life she made choices that do not square with a scheme that sees women as natural peacemakers.[62] Moreover, like most Vietnamese women, she did not see a contradiction between maternal instincts and fighting for country. As many women told me in interviews in 1996 and 2000, taking up arms to save the nation was the only way to guarantee a peaceful future in which to raise children.

Like many other women, Duc Hoan proved as capable of aiding the war effort as working for reconciliation, as willing to present the male perspective as the female view to translate her messages effectively. But she never equated competent women with masculine traits. Literally "vetted" by dint of her military service to take an active role in representing stories of war, Duc Hoan never succumbed to pressure to adopt a male vision of the heroic side of war in order to prove her ability to function in a man's world. However, though she considered the problems of women in all of her films, she did not consistently privilege her female characters' point of view. Realistic about power dynamics, she aimed the camera at the male spectator when it suited her goals, for she knew full well that lasting peace hinged on helping men reconcile with former enemies and forgive vulnerable women who could not live up to officially promoted ideals. Ironically, however, Duc Hoan herself was remembered not for her talent as an interpreter of war and its residue but as a beautiful young actress in the service of the state.

Notes

The original version of this essay was published in *Cinema, Law, and the State in Asia*, ed. Corey K. Creekmur and Mark Sidel (New York: Palgrave Macmillan, 2007). I am grateful to the editors and to the publisher, Palgrave Macmillan, for permission to revise and republish it in this volume.

1. Unless otherwise stated, I obtained most of my information about Duc Hoan's personal life and career from many direct conversations with her in Hanoi in the spring of 1996 and the summer of 2000 as we watched her films together, toured her former film studio, and discussed her goals and techniques. Some portions of these interviews are recorded in a documentary film I produced with Phan Thanh Hao, *Hidden Warriors: Women on the Ho Chi Minh Trail*, released in 2004 and privately distributed by Karen Turner. I have also had help from her family and friends in Hanoi and the United States. Special thanks to Phan Thanh Hao for discussions and sources. To the best of my knowledge, no systematic treatment of her work yet exists and the exact dates of some of her films are not clear, but I have done my best to present a workable chronology. I base my observations about reactions to her death from on obituaries in Vietnamese publications. Most of them do not use Duc Hoan's name but instead the name of her character, My, in *The Story of A Phu*. See, for example, "Vinh biet co My," *Van hoc-Nghe thuat*, September 6, 2004. The official party newspaper, *Lao Dong*, titled its obituary "Co My, ngay ay da ra di" (Ms. My, those days are gone), a tribute to her role as My in 1960. It did also note her acting ability: "Duc Hoan was able to show the internal conflict of My, a girl with a strong character who overcome obstacles to reach happiness" (*Lao Dong*, April 4, 2003). But discussions of the films that she directed have been left out in most publications.

2. For a more complete account, see Karen Turner and Phan Thanh Hao, *Even the Women Must Fight: Memories of War from North Vietnam* (New York: John Wiley, 1998), 32–33; and Arlene Eisen, *Women and Revolution in Vietnam* (London: Zed, 1984). These numbers are clearly estimates. For a thorough account of women's participation in the south, see Sandra Taylor, *Vietnamese Women at War* (Lawrence: University of Kansas Press 1999).

3. For a complete history of the Ho Chi Minh Trail, see John Prados, *The Blood Road: The Ho Chi Minh Trail and the Vietnam War* (New York: John Wiley, 1999).

4. David Marr, "A Passion for Modernity: Intellectuals and the Media," in *Postwar Vietnam: Dynamics of a Transforming Society*, ed. Hy V. Luong (Lanham, MD: Rowman and Littlefield, 2003), 270.

5. Ibid., 257–95.

6. See Robert Stam, *Subversive Pleasures* (Baltimore: Johns Hopkins University Press, 1989).

7. Mikhael Bakhtin, *The Dialogical Imagination* (Austin: University of Texas Press, 1981). See also Stam, *Subversive Pleasures*.

8. Benedict J. Tria Kerkvliet, "Rural Society and State Relations" in *Vietnam's Rural Transformation*, ed. Benedict J. Tria Kerkvliet and Doug J. Porter (Boulder, CO: Westview, 1995). See also Lan Duong, "Manufacturing Authenticity: The Feminine Ideal in Tony Bui's Three Seasons," *Amerasia Journal* 31, no. 2 (2005): 1–18.

9. Interview with Duc Hoan, spring 1996, Hanoi. See note 1.

10. For another life history of an elite Vietnamese woman, see Mark Sidel's introduction to and translation of Le Thi, "Changing My Life: How I Came to the Vietnamese Revolution," *Signs* 23 (1998): 1017–30.

11. Interview with Duc Hoan, spring 1996, Hanoi.

12. Ibid.

13. Ibid.

14. Turner, *Even the Women Must Fight*, 120.

15. In *Cinematographic Magazine*, Hanoi, 1988.

16. Judith Mayne, "Paradoxes of Spectatorship," in *Ways of Seeing Film*, ed. Linda Williams (New Brunswick, NJ: Rutgers University Press, 1995).

17. Interview with Duc Hoan, spring, 1996, Hanoi.

18. For state relations with ethnic minorities, see A. Terry Rambo and Neil Jameison, "Upland Areas, Ethnic Minorities and Development," in Luong, *Postwar Vietnam*.

19. *Newsletter of the Afro-Asian Film Festival*, 1964. (Gelaro bung karno, Jakarta, Indonesia, 1964). I am grateful to Phan Than Hao for directing me to this publication.

20. For a discussion of the relation between artists and the socialist state, see Marr, "A Passion for Modernity," 272–73.

21. Interview with Duc Hoan, summer 2000, Hanoi.

22. Ibid.

23. Interview with Duc Hoan, spring 1996, Hanoi.

24. Ibid.

25. This long history of women as founders and protector of the nation is unique among national origin stories. See Turner, *Even the Women Must Fight*, 26–33. For a discussion of women and war in the West, see Margaret Higonnet, "Women in the Forbidden Zone: War, Women and Death," in *Death and Representation*, ed. Sarah Goodwin (Baltimore: Johns Hopkins University Press, 1992). A good source for comparing the ways that women have entered war and then are remembered is Gerard DeGroot and Corinna Benniston-Bird, eds., *A Soldier and a Woman: Sexual Integration in the Military* (London: Routledge, 2000).

26. See for example, Jeanine Basinger, *The World War II Combat Film: Anatomy of a Genre* (New York: Columbia University Press, 1986).

27. Interview with Duc Hoan, spring 1996, Hanoi.

28. *Cinematographic Magazine*.

29. Filmed interview with Duc Hoan, Hanoi, 2004, included in *Hidden Warriors: Women on the Ho Chi Minh Trail*, produced by Karen Turner and Phan Thanh Hao, directed by Karen Turner, 2004.

30. Turner, *Even the Women Must Fight*, 111.

31. For a useful discussion of changing conceptions about the correct nature of love as state priorities shifted in Vietnam, see Harriet Phinney, "Objects of Affection: Vietnamese Discourses on Love and Emancipation," *Positions: East Asia Cultures Critique* 16, no. 2 (2008): 329–58.

32. This remarkable source has captivated Vietnamese audiences and provides invaluable insight for historians trying to escape the lens of postwar memories. See Dang Thuy Tram, *Last Night I Dreamed of Peace*, trans. Andrew Lam (New York: Three Rivers, 2008).

33. Phan Thanh Hao and I discuss these issues in Turner, *Even the Women Must Fight*, especially in chapters 4 through 7.

34. See Shelley Saywell, *Women in War: From World War II to El Salvador* (New York: Penguin, 1986), 145. In general, comparisons between Soviet and Vietnamese militarized women and their postwar experiences are very useful. See, for example, essays in DeGroot and Bird, *A Soldier and a Woman*.

35. Cynthia Enloe, "Women after War: Puzzles and Warnings," in *Vietnam's Women in Transition*, ed. Kathleen Barry (London: Macmillan, 1996), 299–313.

36. Interview with Duc Hoan, spring 1996, Hanoi.

37. Ngo Ngoc Boi's short story, "The Blanket of Scraps," about a woman who is viewed as grotesque because of her physical condition is a revealing description of the ways that women veterans paid for their service. Ngo Ngoc Boi, "The Blanket of Scraps," in *Literature News: Nine Stories from the Viet Nam Writers Union Newspaper, Bao Van Nghe*, ed. Rosemary Nguyen (New Haven: Yale University Council on SE Asia Studies, 1997), 96–113.

38. Interview with Duc Hoan, summer 2000, Hanoi.

39. Interview with Duc Hoan, spring 1996, Hanoi.

40. Interviews with Duc Hoan, spring 1996 and summer 2000, Hanoi.

41. Interview with Duc Hoan, spring 1996, Hanoi.

42. See Phinney, "Objects of Affection," for a discussion of women who choose motherhood without husbands.

43. Interviews with Duc Hoan, spring 1996 and summer 2000, Hanoi.

44. See Tam Nguyen Thanh, "Remarks on Women Who Live without Husbands," in *Vietnam's Women in Transition*, ed. Kathleen Barry (New York, St. Martin's, 1996). Harriet Phinney's work places these decisions about marriage and motherhood in a broader context that extends beyond war veterans. See Phinney, "Objects of Affection."

45. Le Thi Quy has written several pieces about this problem. An accessible source is "Domestic Violence in Vietnam and Efforts to Curb It," in Barry, *Vietnam's Women in Transition*, 263–74.

46. Interviews with Duc Hoan, spring 1996 and summer 2000, Hanoi.

47. See Ashley Pettus, *Between Sacrifice and Desire: National Identity and the Governing of Femininity in Vietnam* (New York: Routledge: 2003), 116–17, for a useful discussion of how shifting government policies affect conceptions of women's roles.

48. Interviews with Duc Hoan, spring 1996 and summer 2000, Hanoi.

49. For a discussion of the ways that new materials reshape narratives of war, see Simona Monticelli, "National Identity and Representations of Italy at War: The Case of the Combat Film," *Modern Italy* 5 (2000): 133–46.

50. Interviews with Duc Hoan, spring 1996 and summer 2000, Hanoi.

51. *Cinematographic Magazine.*

52. John Charlot, "Vietnamese Cinema: First Views," *Journal of Southeast Asian Studies* 22 (1991): 33–62.

53. See Marr, "Passion for Modernity," 272.

54. Jan Plamper, "Abolishing Ambiguity: Soviet Censorship Practices in the 1930s," *Russian Review* 61 (2002): 2–204.

55. Murray Hiebert, "Luu Trong Ninh and Vietnam Film Censorship," *Far Eastern Economic Review*, July 22, 1993.

56. Kaneyoshi Takeshi, "Filmmaker Gives Voice to Common Folk: Dang Nhat Minh Known for Artistry, Keen Social Observation," Nikkei Net Interactive, *www.nni.nikkei. eo.jp/FRI NJKKEI/inasia/prizes/1999/99dang.html* (accessed August 21, 2006).

57. Kerkvliet, "Rural Society and State Relations."

58. Duong, "Manufacturing Authenticity."

59. For a very useful study of memory, see Hue-Tam Ho Tai, "Faces of Memory and Forgetting," in *The Country of Memory: Remaking the Past in Post-Socialist Vietnam*, ed. Hue-Tam Ho Tai (Berkeley: University of California Press, 2001).

60. Duong, "Manufacturing Authenticity," 211–20.
61. Stam, *Subversive Pleasures*.
62. Duc Hoan's choices—like those of many Vietnamese women who fought in many capacities, including becoming militarized, for a peaceful future in which to raise children—complicate Sarah Ruddick's work. See Ruddick, *Maternal Thinking: Toward a Politics of Peace* (Boston: Beacon, 1989).

References

Periodicals

Cinematographic Magazine
Far Eastern Economic Review
Lao Dong
Newsletter of the Afro-Asian Film Festival

Selected Published Works

Bakhtin, Mikhael. *The Dialogical Imagination*. Translated by Caryl Emerson and Michael Holquist. Austin: University of Texas Press, 1981.

Barry, Kathleen, ed. *Vietnam's Women in Transition*, London: Macmillan, 1996.

Kerkvliet, Benedict J. Tria. "Rural Society and State Relations." In *Vietnam's Rural Transformation*, edited by Benedict J. Tria Kerkvliet and Doug J. Porter, 65–96. Boulder, CO: Westview, 1995.

Marr, David. "A Passion for Modernity: Intellectuals and the Media." In *Postwar Vietnam: Dynamics of a Transforming Society*, edited by Hy V. Luong, 257–95. Lanham, MD: Rowman and Littlefield, 2003.

Ngo Phuong Lan. "The Changing Face of Vietnamese Cinema." In *The Mass Media in Vietnam*, edited by David G. Marr, 91–96. Canberra: Australian National University, 1998.

Phinney, Harriet. "Objects of Affection: Vietnamese Discourses on Love and Emancipation." *Positions: East Asia Cultures Critique* 16, no. 2 (2008): 329–58.

Stam, Robert. *Subversive Pleasures*. Baltimore: Johns Hopkins University Press, 1989.

Taylor, Sandra. *Vietnamese Women at War: Fighting for Ho Chi Minh and the Revolution*. Lawrence: University of Kansas Press, 1999.

Turner, Karen, with Phan Thanh Hao. *Even the Women Must Fight: Memories of War from North Vietnam*. New York: John Wiley, 1998.

CHAPTER 11

Global Feminism and Cold War Paradigms

Women's International NGOs and the United Nations, 1970–1985

Karen Garner

A s World War II ended, international actors faced new configurations of global power. A state of Cold War emerged as rivalries and confrontations between the "free world" led by the United States and other capitalist democracies and the "communist world" led by the Soviet Union and other socialist states overturned earlier visions of a collaborative "one world" community that idealistic internationalists had dreamed of during the world war. Cold War conflicts in Eastern Europe, Asia, Africa, the Middle East, and Latin America divided and sometimes immobilized the postwar global governance system, led by the United Nations (UN), an intergovernmental organization established in 1945. Not surprisingly, "international" women's organizations also acted according to their leaders' Cold War nationalist allegiances when they engaged in UN forums, which contradicted any of their claims to speak in a unitary voice.

This chapter examines the challenges that global feminists faced when advocating for and carrying out three important UN-sponsored world women's conferences: the first commemorated International Women's Year in 1975; the second and third, held in Copenhagen in 1980 and Nairobi in 1985, celebrated the UN Decade for Women. In addition, a fourth conference, the Women's International Democratic Federation World Congress for Women, was also held in 1975 to commemorate International Women's Year. Women within international women's nongovernmental organizations (NGOs) had to work with women and men in the UN Secretariat and with government delegates to these UN conferences at a time when Cold War geopolitics determined UN operations. Cold War geopolitics inspired heated debates among government delegates at the UN women's conferences and many disputes among feminist activists from "Western Bloc," "Eastern Bloc," and "Third World" nations regarding who had the right to speak for "women" at the conferences and concurrent NGO forums.[1] This chapter uses these imperfect terms as they were understood during the Cold War: the "Western Bloc" refers to the United States, its North Atlantic Treaty Organization (NATO) and Western European allies, Australia, and New Zealand; the "Eastern Bloc" refers to the Soviet Union and its Warsaw Pact allies, along with Yugoslavia and Albania; and the "Third World" refers to developing countries, generally located in the Southern Hemisphere, that were nonaligned with either the Western Bloc or Eastern Bloc.[2] As explained in the following account, even though Cold War–era politics as practiced at the UN did not serve *all* "women's interests" (and one could argue they did not serve *any* "women's interests"), they also largely determined the activism of women's NGOs from different global locations within UN forums. However, as this chapter also argues, in spite of their ongoing disagreements, feminist activists from the West, East, and Third World expanded their international contacts, forged networks that crossed political (if not ideological) divides, and paved the way for new forms of feminist cooperation in global governance forums after the Cold War ended.

Cold War Feminist Geopolitical Blocs as Defined in UN Forums

From the time of their founding in the West at the turn of the twentieth century, women's international NGOs strove to define a universal "global feminist" identity that would stand for women's freedom of choice and equality with men and would advocate on behalf of "women's interests" against multifarious structures of oppression. Prior to World War I, Western women's NGOs established chapters in colonies and countries around the world and collaborated with local women in various locations to envision and invent new gender power relations. After World War I ended, Western feminists launched international campaigns as members of a new "Liaison Committee of Women's International Organizations" to promote peace and disarmament, establish married women's nationality rights, and criminalize the cross-border trafficking of women and children and prostitution, among many other causes. They claimed to speak for the "voice of women" in the League of Nations and other international forums.[3] These Western women's organizations promoted a "liberal feminism" that emphasized individual rights for women guaranteed by modern liberal democratic states—such as property rights, voting rights, freedom of speech, freedom of religion, and freedom of association—and state intervention through labor laws, social services, and regulation of vital industries to curb corporate greed and to guarantee equal access and equal protections for all.[4] In order to continue their leading roles in the global governance system representing global women after World War II ended in 1945, these historically Western-led women's NGOs quickly forged a "consultative" status for themselves, observing government meetings, advising, and providing research data to the new United Nations Secretariat, specialized UN agencies associated with the Economic and Social Council (ECOSOC), and especially the UN Commission on the Status of Women (CSW).[5] Cold War–era Western women's NGOs generally supported an evolutionary approach to achieving equal rights with men through expanded educational opportunities for women and girls and through political, legal, and civil rights campaigns waged in UN forums.[6] By the 1970s, the following Western women's international NGOs were among the most active in establishing and promoting the UN International Women's Year, the UN Decade for Women, and NGO forums at UN conferences: the World Young Women's Christian Association, the International Alliance of Women (formerly the International Woman Suffrage Alliance), the International Council of Social Democratic Women, the International Council of Women, the International Federation of Business and Professional Women, the International Federation of University Women, the International Planned Parenthood Association, the Women's International League for Peace and Freedom, and the World Council of Catholic Women's Organizations.[7]

The Women's International Democratic Federation (WIDF), a new association of socialist women's organizations that "generally supported the Soviet Union" in Cold War geopolitical confrontations, formed in 1945.[8] The WIDF challenged the historic Western women's international NGOs for leadership of the global women's movement with their own visions of what was needed to gain freedom and equality. From its founding, the WIDF included forty-one socialist women's organizations based in countries around the world, including chapters in the Soviet Union, Eastern and Western Europe, North and South America, Africa, and Asia. By 1985, membership had expanded to 135 organizations from 117 countries.[9] However, because WIDF members generally advocated for the Soviet Union's foreign policy positions, Western governments monitored WIDF activities and deliberately mislabeled WIDF member organizations as "Soviet fronts" that disseminated Soviet propaganda.[10] After ECOSOC awarded consultative status to the WIDF and to Western women's NGOs, members of the WIDF often set themselves up as socialist counterpoints to Western liberal feminist organizations in UN forums and at the six WIDF World Congresses that were convened between 1945 and 1969.[11] For example, WIDF members advocated for immediate emancipation of women in societies around the globe to match the gender equality that women in states governed by socialist parties purportedly experienced.[12] They presented themselves in global forums as champions of "peace" through active pursuit of multilateral disarmament efforts, opposition to military pacts such as NATO and to the establishment of Western military bases in foreign countries, and support for détente in the 1970s; as advocates of "anticolonialism" through criticism of US foreign policy in Korea, Vietnam, Angola, the Middle East, and so on; and as more legitimate advocates of women's and children's social and economic welfare than Western feminist organizations with "bourgeois agendas."[13] Along with the WIDF, the International Federation of Women in Legal Careers, the Pan-African Women's Organization, the Afro-Asian People's Solidarity Organization, the Committee of the Bulgarian Women's Movement, and the Soviet Women's Committee of the All-Union Central Council of Trade Unions were among the most active socialist women's organizations participating in the UN International Women's Year and the Decade for Women global forums.[14] Indeed, "UN records clearly show that it was Eastern Bloc women, working with the WIDF . . . that pressed for the [commemoration of International Women's Year.]"[15] In 1972, the Romanian delegate to the Commission on the Status of Women, Florica Andrei, proposed an "International Women's Year"; the UN General Assembly accepted the proposal in December 1972 and named 1975 as IWY.[16]

Women from many newly independent Third World nations joined UN forums as representatives of their nations' governments as those nations formally became UN members during the 1960s.[17] These Third World women generally represented the Group of 77 (G-77) alliance of nonaligned developing nations that articulated an anticolonial critique of the world capitalist economy and of the foreign policies of wealthy, industrialized Western Bloc countries that exploited their natural resources and labor. Third World women also organized NGOs and challenged the Cold War paradigms that had shaped women's (and men's) participation at the UN.[18] They questioned East-West definitions of "feminist" issues and proposed new gender-conscious development theories that prioritized the expansion of women's roles in social and economic development initiatives.[19] In 1963, they allied with Eastern European delegates to the CSW to draft a resolution condemning all forms of discrimination against women that became the Declaration on the Elimination of Discrimination Against Women adopted by the UN General Assembly in 1967, and the Convention on the Elimination of All Forms of Discrimination Against Women with monitoring mechanisms adopted by the General Assembly in 1980. In these ways, they demonstrated that, in addition to their focus on global development, they also "embraced modern principles of gender equality and were prepared to combat customs and traditions that thwarted the advancement of women" in their own nations.[20] In the 1970s and 1980s, along with the Eastern and Western Bloc women's NGOs, they helped to define the IWY and Decade for Women themes of "equality, development, and peace," and they facilitated global feminist participation in the UN-sponsored International Women's Year conference held in Mexico City, the WIDF World Congress for Women held in East Berlin, and the UN Decade for Women conferences held in Copenhagen in 1980 and in Nairobi in 1985.[21]

Organizing International Women's Year Commemorations in a Cold War Context

When the UN Commission on the Status of Women met in 1972 and proposed to the General Assembly that 1975 be designated International Women's Year (IWY), its action was inspired by WIDF members and relied on the long-established women's NGOs that had consultative status with the UN to plan and rally international support for the year's activities.[22] In early 1974 two subcommittees of the Conference of NGOs in Consultative Relationship to the Economic and Social Council of the United Nations (CONGO) formed to plan NGO participation in International Women's Year events. These subcommittees were the CONGO Subcommittee on IWY, which was chaired by a US woman, Esther Hymer, of the International Federation of Business and Professional Women and met in New York, and the CONGO Subcommittee on the Status of Women, which was chaired by Iranian Shahnaz Alami of the WIDF and met in Geneva, Switzerland. The elected president of CONGO, another American woman, Rosalind Harris of The International Social Service NGO, was also based in New York.

The rival CONGO subcommittees operating in the two UN capitals, New York and Geneva, exhibited tensions that reflected both bureaucratic and East-West geopolitical rivalries within the UN system. One of the earliest conflicts focused on proposals for an IWY conference and its location. The WIDF had already been planning to host a World Congress for Women in East Berlin to coincide with the thirtieth anniversary of the federation's founding in October 1975, and Shahnaz Alami proposed that the WIDF World Congress also commemorate International Women's Year.[23] The WIDF's proposal raised red flags among Western women's NGOs and Western governments. Already in February 1974, Mary McGeachy Schuller, a Canadian woman retired from a career in the UN Secretariat and a member of the International Council of Women, was urging CONGO president Rosalind Harris to establish the primacy of the New York–based CONGO subcommittee to give it "its proper place and authority" to organize NGO participation during IWY.[24] In March 1974 the US delegate to the CSW, Pat Hutar, objected to holding the only IWY conference in a communist country and introduced a proposal to hold a separate UN-sponsored world women's conference in the Western Hemisphere. The Soviet delegate to the CSW, Tatiana Nikolaeva, rejected the US proposal and argued that a second conference would be costly and redundant. The US position prevailed, however, with strong support for a UN conference among the Western Bloc and Third World CSW delegates.[25] Following the request of the CSW, in May 1974 the UN General Assembly voted formally to hold an IWY world conference in Bogotá, Colombia.[26]

The New York–based subcommittee also supported holding a UN-sponsored conference in Bogotá (and the subsequent change in venue to Mexico City).[27] Meanwhile, the Geneva-based subcommittee expressed their objections to the location because of its distance from Europe, and the WIDF moved forward with its plans for a separate IWY World Congress. In April 1974 Harris stepped in to establish the chain of command regarding CONGO participation in International Women's Year and asserted the authority of the New York subcommittee to develop IWY activities, thus ensuring that Western NGOs would dominate the planning process.[28] When the UN General Assembly finalized the decision to hold a conference for IWY, CONGO resolved to sponsor an NGO forum to be held in conjunction with the government meetings and determined that the New York subcommittee would organize the official NGO forum, known as the "Tribune."[29]

From that point forward, the New York subcommittee and the WIDF each moved forward with planning their own IWY conference. Controversies did not surface again until late in 1974. Back in January 1974, the UN Secretariat had selected two women to plan and oversee UN-sponsored IWY programs.[30] Helvi Sipilä, a Finnish lawyer with a liberal feminist orientation who attached great importance to women's legal, educational, and economic rights, led the UN IWY planning. She was the highest-ranking female member of the UN Secretariat, serving as UN assistant secretary general and head of the Centre for Social Development and Humanitarian Affairs.[31] She was later named IWY conference general secretary.[32] Sipilä was assisted by Margaret K. Bruce, a British national employed in the UN Secretariat working on human rights issues since the UN's founding; she also served as deputy director of the UN Branch for the Promotion of Equality of Men and Women.[33]

The UN-sponsored IWY conference was set to take place in Mexico City in June and July 1975. By the time these decisions had been made in October 1974, there was not much time or money available for IWY conference preparations. The UN budget for the 1974–1975 fiscal year had already been approved, and it did not include provisions for the IWY conference. Moreover, the Commission on the Status of Women would not be involved in conference preparations.[34] Therefore, Sipilä and Bruce had to invite governments, organize the Mexico City meetings, and draft the conference document, the "World Plan of Action," that governments would consider and approve at the conference. Moreover, they had to raise money through voluntary contributions to cover all these activities.[35]

The tasks were daunting, and some of the actions that Sipilä subsequently took to carry out those tasks revealed that she did not necessarily recognize the conflicts between rival NGOs regarding the two global meetings, or between NGOs and government representatives who had differing goals and prioritized different issues in the conference treaty.

For example, by early October members of the Geneva subcommittee were objecting to being left out of the IWY Tribune planning process as the New York subcommittee began to organize.[36] To smooth over some of the tensions, in early November 1974 Rosalind Harris visited Geneva and met with Shahnaz Alami of the WIDF and other women's NGOs to assure them that their input would be incorporated into future Tribune planning. Harris also was surprised to learn that the WIDF was moving forward with its plans for a World Congress to be held in East Berlin in October 1975.[37] However, the WIDF Congress planning committee had previously met with Sipilä in Geneva in July 1974 and in Tihany, Hungary, in November 1974, and they understood that they had Sipilä's full support for their October 1975 IWY World Congress.[38] By November 1974, the WIDF also had statements of support for the IWY World Congress from world leaders such as "Indira Gandhi, Prime Minister of India, Soviet Cosmonaut Valentina Tereshkova, Jeanne Marin Cisse, permanent delegate to the UN from the Republic of Guinea, P. C. Terenzio, General Secretary of the Inter-parliamentary Union; Yassar Arafat, President of PLO," among others, which makes it clear that the WIDF had been widely publicizing plans for the conference.[39]

Following her November trip to Europe, Sipilä traveled in early December to Mexico City to confer with the Mexican government regarding UN conference arrangements. With the Mexican government's pledge to provide material and institutional support for the UN IWY conference and the concurrent NGO Tribune, Sipilä returned to New York and urged the subcommittee there to move forward with their plans for the Tribune.[40] As CONGO formed a Tribune planning committee, they selected US liberal feminist Mildred Persinger as committee chair. A New York–based representative of the World Young Women's Christian Association, Persinger had a decade-long resume of advocacy for women's rights in state, national, and international forums.[41] The Tribune committee comprised only a few individuals; all were Westerners and the majority were Americans.

The members represented the long-established NGOs with consultative status that had insider connections with the UN Secretariat and with their governments' UN delegations.[42]

In order to draft the conference treaty, or "World Plan of Action," that government delegates would review and amend in Mexico City, Sipilä and Bruce mined the statements that feminist activists had prepared for the 1974 UN World Population Conference and reports for previous CSW sessions on women's equal rights. In March 1975 they also formed an advisory committee with interested government representatives to review the draft conference document.[43] Women's organizations with membership in CONGO also sought to shape the UN conference document. Although their direct input into the document drafting process was limited, the long-established East-West women's organizations had laid the groundwork for International Women's Year during several decades of activism at the CSW and in other UN agencies and commissions. Their ideas infused the draft World Plan of Action, and they interjected themselves into UN conference preparations at every opportunity.

In early February 1975 World YWCA staff member Katherine Strong reported on a briefing that Helvi Sipilä had held for the Geneva subcommittee. At the briefing Sipilä summarized the IWY conference plans as NGO representatives quizzed her about the draft World Plan of Action and asked whether NGOs could review the draft before Sipilä presented it to her consultative committee of government representatives in March. According to Strong, Sipilä "obviously hasn't considered the question before and at first was quite negative. However, Mrs. Bruce was with her and whispered some suggestions, so she finally agreed that the draft which is now being worked on here in Geneva . . . will let some of us [NGO representatives] at least have it and can then send our reactions to Mrs. Sipilä before the meeting of the [government] Consultative Committee, which will be meeting in New York on March 3–14."[44]

At the end of February 1975, just prior to meeting with the government committee, Margaret Bruce briefed the New York–based subcommittee on the draft World Plan of Action. She invited comments from the NGOs before she met with the government consultative committee that included among its twenty-three members Princess Ashraf Pahlavi of Iran, Attorney General Pedro Ojeda Paullada of Mexico, Elizabeth Reid of Australia, and Leticia Shahani of the Philippines.[45] CONGO president Rosalind Harris sent a copy of the draft World Plan of Action to the Geneva-based subcommittee for their review and comments as well.[46] According to Marianne Huggard, an invited NGO observer at the government consultative committee sessions, government delegates voiced competing perspectives, and the draft World Plan of Action incorporated all their views. Huggard was a British woman who revealed her Western biases when she described the four major worldviews: "the African view with the major thrust on development, the Mexican emphasis on the Charter of Economic Rights and Duties of States, the Communist bloc concerned with Peace and the moderate view of the U. S. and Western Europeans."[47]

In the meantime, the Tribune organizing committee chaired by Mildred Persinger designed NGO meetings that would run concurrently with the UN government conference. Twenty-five panel sessions focusing on global women's roles and status would feature representative women who presented case studies describing specific "women and development," peace, and leadership projects that were operating in various parts of the world.[48] From their earliest meetings, the members of Persinger's committee were concerned about including activists from the developing world, and they "strongly encouraged" participating international NGOs to include members from Asian, African, and Latin American chapters to counterbalance the large number of women they expected from the United States and Canada.[49] Over half of the Tribune's $191,000 budget, approximately $100,000, was dedicated to funding travel for participants from developing countries.[50] These explicit and generous provisions can be interpreted as recognition by the committee that issues of fairness and inclusiveness were important and that without material support for travel costs, women from developing countries would be disadvantaged. The provisions also illuminate Cold War considerations: the Western-dominated committee specifically sought to build alliances with Third World women, most likely to counteract alliances between Third World and Eastern Bloc nations. Despite these efforts to broaden Tribune attendance, however, Western women's organizations retained the power to design the program.[51] Additionally, following Harris's guidelines, Persinger informed all attendees that the Tribune as a body would not adopt any formal "political" statements. If individual NGO activists produced such statements, they could circulate them and request signatures, but no single statement would speak for "the Tribune."[52] These arrangements angered many feminists who attended the Tribune, whether they came from the East, West, or the Third World, because they presumed "women's issues" were somehow separate from world "politics."

As events unfolded, Cold War conflicts impacted both the government conference and the NGO Tribune proceedings in Mexico City in June and July. Although the government delegates reached broad agreement on objectives to promote women's global advancement as specified in the World Plan of Action, they were divided along East-West and West–Third World lines on several political issues, including the proposed New International Economic Order (NIEO).[53] Formulated in 1973 by the G-77 developing countries at the UN, the NIEO called for substantial revisions of the post–World War II global economic order that the United States and Great Britain defined in the 1944 Bretton Woods Agreements. The NIEO outlined more equitable international trade policies regarding pricing, restoration of national controls over the sale of raw materials and commodities produced in developing nations, more liberal financing terms for economic development, and increased technology transfer from the developed Western nations to the underdeveloped Third World.[54] Third World nations supported by the Eastern Bloc pushed for the adoption of the NIEO throughout the 1970s and at the IWY conference. They asserted that the UN must address worldwide economic inequities in the distribution of wealth before inequalities between men and women could be resolved effectively within nations.[55] Third World nations also recognized and condemned systems of oppression that encompassed and transcended men's use of gender power to dominate women, including South Africa's policy of racial apartheid and Israel's Palestinian policy and Zionist ideology, which was defined as racism. More often than not, public debates among government delegates and demonstrations at the conference site—including a dramatic walkout staged by Asian and African nations when Leah Rabin, wife of the Israeli prime minister, rose to speak at the conference—focused on these geopolitical disputes rather than on expanding "women's power" vis-à-vis men.[56]

A second IWY conference document, "Declaration of Mexico on the Equality of Women and Their Contribution to Development and Peace," specifically addressed global power issues of the Cold War "neo-colonial" era that the Platform for Action avoided, including a call to "eliminate colonialism, neo-colonialism, imperialism, foreign domination and occupation, Zionism, *apartheid*, racial discrimination, the acquisition of land by force and the recognition of such acquisition, since such practices inflict incalculable suffering on women, men and children."[57] Government delegates approved thirty statements of principle enumerated in the Declaration of Mexico by a vote that exposed Cold War divisions. The majority, eighty-nine southern and Eastern Bloc nations, voted in favor of the declaration. The United States, Israel, and Denmark opposed the declaration because it equated Zionism with racism, and, by implication, the right of Israel to exist as a state was denied. Eighteen nations, most of them US allies in Western Europe, abstained from voting.[58]

The Mexico City meetings also fell short of the goals set by many feminist activists who believed that government delegates *and* the Tribune organizers ignored their perspectives and denied their voices.[59] For Western feminists who wanted to keep the focus on women's rights and status, the most distressing issue was that geopolitical issues dominated the government delegates' debates and the media coverage at the conference.[60] Consequently, on June 26 some two thousand activists organized a delegation, named themselves the "Voice of the United Women of the Tribune," and tried to present their "demands" for revisions of the World Plan of Action to the government delegates assembled at the UN conference site. The vocal activists denounced the governments for focusing their public statements on criticisms of Western imperialism, Zionism, and apartheid that seemed to ignore women.[61] The activist delegation called for revisions of the World Plan of Action to include statements about women's rights to control their own bodies, to access health care, and to participate in global development policy making and programming. They demanded funding to combat discrimination against women and the creation of a new UN Office for Women's Concerns headed by a high-ranking official that would monitor implementation of the World Plan of Action, investigate violations of women's rights, and analyze the gender impact of UN-sponsored development programs. Finally, they appealed for time to speak before the conference's general assembly.[62]

The well-known American feminist Betty Friedan, leader of the National Organization for Women (NOW), became a media-appointed spokeswoman for many of the Western feminist critics who attended the Mexico City meetings. Leading the feminist march to the UN conference site, Friedan called attention to herself and to the shortcomings of the IWY conference and the NGO Tribune using provocative rhetoric that the world press quoted widely, announcing, for example, that the IWY conference was merely "a callous manipulation of women by their governments."[63] Many Latin American feminists who attended the Tribune, how-ever, rejected Friedan's grandstanding and denied her the right to speak about their concerns. These women asserted that "their interests [Western feminist-defined women's issues] are not relevant to ours [Latin American women's con-cerns]. And besides, we were never involved in the statement."[64]

These criticisms were only one manifestation of fundamental divisions among the feminists who met in Mexico City. Feminists who represented vastly different global locations struggled to determine who had the authority to define "wom-en's issues" at the IWY meetings, and they continued to debate with one another throughout the UN Decade for Women. According to non-Western women, white Western women monopolized power and used it coercively in the international political arena. A group of Native American women published one such critique of white Western women's misuse of power at the IWY conference and Tribune. These Native American women argued that they had been denied access to the UN conference because the US government delegation did not represent their interests. They also argued that they had been denied a voice at the NGO Tri-bune because Mildred Persinger had organized the Tribune program as a series of planned panel sessions that did not allow for open discussion of systems of oppression that they asserted were most important to nonwhite, non-Western women, "such as, racism, imperialism, and colonialism."[65]

Socialist women from the Soviet Union and Eastern Europe who were well represented at the IWY Tribune in Mexico City actively disseminated their femi-nist "ideas about equality between women and men—both in international and national contexts" based on socialist theory.[66] These socialist women joined Third World feminists in criticizing the speeches of Western feminists, such as Betty Friedan. Socialist women asserted that Western women had little knowl-edge about the situation of women in Eastern Europe, who experienced a greater degree of gender equality in their countries than women living in Western capital-ist democracies.[67]

Eastern Bloc and Third World women energetically promoted their alternate feminist agendas throughout IWY, as recent published scholarship and primary documents make clear.[68] During IWY commemorations, their critiques of Western imperialism (exhibited by Western male-led governments and Western feminist-led women's organizations alike) gained momentum and shaped the ensuing UN Decade for Women conferences in Copenhagen and Nairobi.[69] In March 1975 an Afro-Asian Symposium on Social Development of Women held in Alexandria, Egypt, and organized by the Afro-Asia People's Solidarity Organization brought together women from Eastern European, African, and Asian nations in advance of the IWY UN conference and Tribune. As historian Kristen Ghodsee notes, the meeting was significant because

almost all the Eastern Bloc countries sent delegations to share their experiences and promote socialism as the ideal economic system to achieve development and national independence for women and men in Africa and Asia. Occurring as it did months before the Mexico City conference, it is important to note that the socialist countries emphasized that women's issues must be linked to the larger political issues of the day, encouraged the African and Asian delegates to embrace a language of global solidarity, and supported their demands for a New International Economic Order."[70]

Although Ghodsee noted that alliances between Third World and Eastern Bloc women were "always informed by the realities of superpower rivalry" and were "undoubtedly part of a larger Cold War [propaganda] campaign" waged by the Eastern Bloc women, they nonetheless also represented unified opposition to "American warmongering," racism, and colonialism.[71]

In addition to the Afro-Asian Symposium, the WIDF World Congress for International Women's Year was held from October 20 to October 24 in East Berlin. Nearly two thousand delegates from 141 countries gathered for plenary sessions and three days of planned discussions. Unlike the IWY Tribune panel sessions in Mexico City that had focused on such topics as "building a human community," "Third World craftswomen and development," "women across cultures," and "attitude formation and socialization processes," the World Congress emphasized current geopolitical issues and held sessions on "the progress of détente," "universal disarmament," "the historic victory of the heroic people of Vietnam and all the peoples of Indochina, the victories of Guinea-Bissau and the Cape Verde islands, Angola and Mozambique, Portugal and Greece," and "Israeli aggression against the Arab people," among others.[72] Countering the goals of the IWY Tribune organizers, WIDF Congress participants asserted that "women's problems" could not be discussed separately from the context of world conflicts and the widespread oppression, exploitation, and discrimination that the conflicts created and exposed.[73] Emphasizing their differences from Western feminists, Eastern Bloc women asserted that their World Congress was more inclusive of global women's perspectives than previous IWY gatherings. They claimed that because of "the fact that the Congress was held in a socialist country, the participants were able to appreciate the opportunities women have had to take part in the economic, political, social and cultural life of their society. This will give many women of the world added strength to continue the struggle for their rights."[74] Indeed, long-established Western women's international organizations were also represented among the participants, along with Eastern Bloc and Third World women. A French representative of the International Federation of University Women reported that the World Congress "offered the picture of a world other than the one we [usually] meet in our own international meetings. Not only were there participants from countries where we have no affiliates (North Korea, Cuba, Eastern European countries, etc.), but also the participants from countries where we have . . . associations were usually very different [ideologically and politically] from our members."[75]

Cold War Geopolitics Impact UN Decade for Women Conferences

In 1978 the UN General Assembly initiated the planning process for the second world women's conference called to "readjust programs for the second half of the Decade [for Women] in light of new data and research."[76] Responding to pressures from G-77 nations, the General Assembly named three additional conference subthemes—"education, health, and employment"—all related to the theme of development. Iran offered to host the mid-decade conference in Teheran. However, when the Islamist revolution overthrew Reza Shah Pahlavi's regime in 1979, Iran withdrew its offer, but not before Western feminist groups denounced the prospective host country for claiming to support women's rights while violating fundamental human rights.[77] After Iran's withdrawal, Denmark stepped in to host the conference and corresponding NGO forum in Copenhagen, and UN planning went forward. The UN General Assembly also passed a resolution stipulating that the secretary general of the 1980 conference must come from a developing nation, and Lucille Mair from Jamaica was selected to fulfill the role.[78]

Lucille Mair held strong political convictions that were drawn from her life experiences growing up in a Third World nation and serving in several posts in Michael Manley's democratic socialist government.[79] In addition to other diplomatic posts she held at the United Nations, Mair served as Jamaica's delegate to the Mexico City IWY conference and had been a vocal member within the G-77 coalition that had proposed the New International Economic Order. According to UN historian Devaki Jain, Mair "was in many ways as committed to Third World concerns as she was to those of women. She was able to link quite explicitly macro issues of imperialism and the 'violence of development' with the violence women face within more intimate spaces."[80] In an interview with the *New York Times* after she was named secretary general for the mid-decade conference, Mair openly acknowledged that she had been selected because she was a black woman from a developing nation. She accepted the post because she had a political agenda that she hoped to further. Mair told the *Times* reporter, "Third World women are acutely conscious of their condition. There comes a time when we need to put the problem in a global context. This is it."[81]

The preparatory committee headed by Lucille Mair was far more inclusive than the IWY conference committee led by Helvi Sipilä had been. Mair again relied on women's NGOs to mobilize support for the conference, and she included representatives of twenty-eight NGOs, along with government delegates and representatives from UN agencies, as official members of the organizing committee. With official representation on the conference organizing committee, women's NGOs had greater input into the content of the final conference documents than they had in Mexico City. Mair also included representatives on the organizing committee from the African National Congress, the Palestinian Liberation Organization (PLO), the Pan-African Congress, and patriotic front groups from Zimbabwe—all rival governing bodies that Western governments did not officially recognize.[82]

It was clear from the start of preparations for the conference that geopolitical issues such as the continuing Israeli-Palestinian conflict and South Africa's apartheid policy commanded the government delegates' attention. Recounting various Cold War–era conflicts underway in 1980 that provided the historical context for the mid-decade conference, British feminists Georgina Ashworth and Lucy Bonnerjea complained:

The Copenhagen conference took place a little over a year after the Conservative Party's election victory in Britain, and during the Republican nomination proceedings in the United States. The Olympic Games were taking place in Moscow at the time, without numerous Western athletes who had been pressed not to go in protest over the Soviet invasion of Afghanistan. A special session of the UN General Assembly was taking place on the question of Palestine, while Iran and Iraq were nurturing conflict against each other and against the West. So the 1980 Conference on Women became a political battleground. Every party accused the other of politicization, and it was true of all. Few governments delegations remembered, or chose to remind themselves when voting took place, that the subject and the object of the Conference was the removal of the subordination of women. Alliances and alignments in foreign policy determined the contributions made and the votes cast.[83]

Additionally, at conference preparatory meetings Western feminists condemned the practice of female circumcision in North African countries, naming the practice "female genital mutilation" and thus alienating African governments. These divisive issues also dominated conference and NGO forum sessions in Copenhagen.[84] For example, as the Israeli delegate spoke to the conference's general assembly, Palestinian activist Leila Khalid, whom the United States described as a "known hijacker and terrorist," led a walkout of government delegates from Arab nations, the Soviet Union, several Eastern Bloc nations, and the South African National Congress. These delegates staged another walkout in support of the Palestinian Liberation Organization when Jehan Sadat of Egypt addressed the conference assembly.[85] The PLO had denounced Egypt for recognizing the state of Israel, and the public demonstrations of support for the PLO again captured international press attention. Moreover, when the conference document, the Copenhagen Program of Action, officially recognized the legitimacy of the PLO's opposition to the state of Israel and explicitly named Zionism as a form of racism (just as the IWY Declaration of Mexico had), the United States, Australia, Canada, and Israel rejected the treaty and twenty-two nations allied with the United States abstained from voting.[86] Once again, the majority of nations approved the Program of Action. Eastern Bloc nations considered the passage of the conference treaty to be a triumph, not only because the treaty challenged US foreign policy but also because it included language that celebrated the status of women in socialist countries.[87] According to the United Nations' report on the conference proceedings:

> In the countries with centrally planned economies a further advancement of women took place in various fields. Women in those countries actively participated in social and economic development and in all other fields of public life of their countries, including in the active struggle for peace, disarmament, détente, and international cooperation. A high level of employment, health, education and political participation of women was achieved in countries with centrally planned economies, in which national mechanisms are already in existence with adequate financial allocations and sufficient skilled personnel.[88]

As Kristen Ghodsee has noted, "That the rest of the delegates in Copenhagen accepted this Soviet propaganda as truth attests to the power and persuasiveness of women from the Eastern Bloc countries."[89]

Nonetheless, some feminists have argued that, "despite the political static, the Copenhagen conference produced the best researched documents of the decade."[90] This was due to Lucille Mair's leadership during conference preparations. Mair recruited women scholars and development specialists from southern nations to draft sections of the Program of Action. The UN conference secretariat also organized regional meetings prior to the conference to gather input from women around the world in order to more accurately define global women's concerns. The practice of holding regional preparatory meetings was repeated for the 1985 conference in Nairobi as well.

The Copenhagen NGO forum organizing committee led by Elizabeth Palmer, an American woman recently retired from a career leading the World YWCA, facilitated the NGO forum, but she did not control the proceedings to the same degree as Mildred Persinger had in 1975. Palmer turned over the responsibility for organizing thematic workshops and panel sessions to specific NGOs, and so, for example, the Women's International League for Peace and Freedom selected and coordinated sessions related to the theme of peace. Other NGOs took charge of coordinating sessions focused on development, equality, education, employment, migrants and refugees, family, health, and racism and sexism.[91] By many accounts, the 1980 forum structure was more fluid and inclusive than the 1975 Tribune.[92] At the Copenhagen forum, nearly 175 meetings, panels, workshops, demonstrations, exhibits, performances, and films took place daily for ten days running from July 14 to July 24, using meeting rooms and a flexible-use open space.[93]

However, Palmer, like Persinger before her, determined that the NGO forum as a whole would not issue any sweeping political resolutions.[94] There were no scheduled plenary sessions during which the full contingent of NGO activists could meet as a group to discuss the concurrent government conference sessions or to formulate joint political statements.[95] These arrangements disappointed some forum participants, and they tried to correct this when they met in Copenhagen.[96] Sixty activists organized an impromptu plenary session to address the need for more communication between the forum and the UN conference sites and to seek more opportunities for NGOs without consultative status with ECOSOC to address conference delegates on substantive women's issues.[97] As a result of this meeting, several thousand NGO activists marched to the Bella Convention Centre to address government delegates at the UN conference site. Responding to a pressing conflict of the day, the activists declared their support for striking Bolivian miners who were being suppressed by government troops, an issue raised dramatically and persuasively by mine worker Domitila Barrios de Chúngara. They also directed global attention to women's rights and nuclear disarmament campaigns. As a result of their dramatic demonstration, Lucille Mair brought several of the demonstrators into the conference meeting to address the government delegates. This was a radical departure from established UN conference procedure. Women activists considered this concession "a major step in forging a greater role for civil society in global decision making."[98]

The increased attention that governments paid to women activists was not the only progressive achievement in Copenhagen. At their meetings NGO forum activists discussed many previously taboo topics including domestic violence, sexual abuse, female circumcision, contraception, and abortion. These ground-breaking discussions at the NGO forum also elicited government responses. One specific and immediate impact of these discussions was registered when the UN International Children's Emergency Fund (UNICEF) pledged to work with governments to eradicate female circumcision, emphasizing the dangers to girls' health.[99]

Both the long-established Eastern and Western Bloc NGOs and the more recently formed NGOs from Third World nations expanded their influence in planning for the Nairobi end-of-decade women's conference when the Commission on the Status of Women was designated as the official conference planning body within the UN. Unlike the first two world women's conferences in which the CSW played a limited role in preparations, the CSW, now chaired by the Nigerian delegate Olajumoke Oladayo Obafemi, called a special session to meet in Vienna in February 1983 to take charge of the planning process with assistance from the UN Secretariat. Leticia Ramos Shahani, the new assistant secretary general in charge of the Vienna-based Centre for Social Development and Humanitarian Affairs, had replaced Helvi Sipilä in 1981. Shahani, from the Philippines, had long associations with the CSW. She was named secretary general for the Nairobi conference and worked closely with the commission over the next two years to plan it.[100] Both the CSW and Shahani welcomed the input of international women's NGOs, and as UN conference plans were getting underway in 1983, the General Assembly formally invited NGOs to participate in UN conference preparatory meetings. This invitation, UN historian John Mathiason asserts, represented the UN's recognition of the integral role of NGOs in the Decade for Women and "set the stage, as well, for the NGO Forum that became famous at Nairobi."[101]

CONGO once again convened the NGO forum committee, with a much larger membership than the one formed to organize the IWY Tribune but with members still drawn from NGOs with consultative status at the UN.[102] The NGO forum planning committee faced many logistical difficulties associated with the greater number of expected participants (ultimately, fourteen thousand women attended the 1985 NGO forum) and with the location of the meetings in Nairobi, Kenya.[103] The UN decision to accept Kenya's offer to host the conference was based on political rather than practical considerations. African women and Third World feminists had attached great symbolic importance to hosting a world women's conference and NGO forum in an African nation. The local planning committee of Kenyan women asserted that the end-of-decade events would mark "the first time that women in the African region have undertaken to organize an international conference of major proportions. It is obvious that the success of the work of the Kenya NGO organizing committee in hosting the 1985 forum will boost the morale and the status of women throughout the developing world."[104] However, the Kenyan government and some of the more conservative African women's NGOs were anxious about "excited or extremist participants"—their code words for radical Western feminists, particularly those who were outspoken lesbians, who challenged African social norms and cultural practices. Kenyan president Daniel Toroitich arap Moi nearly canceled the NGO forum in the spring of 1985 rather than allow lesbian and other radical women to speak out freely at the forum sessions.[105] In their program negotiations with the New York–based forum organizing committee, the local Kenyan women's committee was also concerned with prioritizing the "Kenyan women's perspective" and the "African women's perspective" that defined economic development as the key to women's liberation.[106]

The UN Decade for Women conferences and forums exposed fundamental differences within the global women's movement but did not resolve them. In spite of these unresolved conflicts the Nairobi conference and 1985 NGO forum were still perceived as productive gatherings.[107] There was "talk, talk, talk," as feminists expressed their competing perspectives but no organized demonstrations or marches to the conference site as had occurred in Mexico City and Copenhagen.[108] These previous marches had, according to some critics, "little impact on the UN conference and only divisive repercussions for the forum."[109] At the UN conference in Nairobi political controversies that had played out over the UN Decade for Women were evident again. As in Mexico City and Copenhagen, the Israeli-Palestinian conflict, South African apartheid policy, and global inequities critiqued by Third World nations all caused heated debates among the government delegates. Nonetheless, the final conference document, "Forward Looking Strategies for the Advancement of Women to the Year 2000," was adopted by consensus. Government delegates agreed to compromises in the language so long as those changes did not prohibit them from signing the much-debated conference document; for instance, condemnations of Zionism were replaced by more widely acceptable language denouncing "all forms of racism and racial discrimination." The final document also "emphasized action over intention" and defined specific actions that governments should take to achieve women's equality and to recognize women's central role in furthering national development and achieving international peace.[110]

Conclusion

As the UN Decade for Women ended, contemporary feminist observers identified an "emergent global feminism" that resulted from the three world women's conferences and NGO forums, and especially from the Nairobi meetings. This approach had helped move the government delegations beyond Cold War–era politics in order to produce the Forward Looking Strategies document, which was seen as "an international working agenda for women."[111] In a less naive, or less optimistic, assessment based on several decades of experience, political scientist Amrita Basu asserted in 2010 that women's movements remain "primarily national rather than global but are more influenced by global forces than they were in the past." Yet Basu also has argued that international conferences like those sponsored by the United Nations during the Decade for Women are significant: they strengthen *national* women's movements because they increase opportunities for the exchange of ideas and strategies and for the development of competencies so that feminists can influence state policies, policies that continue to have the most immediate impact on women's lives.[112] Feminist movements throughout the world have been affected in varied ways by the neoliberal globalization of labor and commodity markets that has proceeded at hyperspeed since the end of the Cold War with the near-disappearance of an alternative socialist economic model and by the eruption of many "new" wars as the geopolitical landscape transformed with the collapse of the Soviet Union and the Warsaw Pact alliance in Eastern Europe. The "global feminist" movement is no more unified today than it was during the Cold War era. Nonetheless, the United Nations continues to provide important forums for international exchange among national feminist representatives, and, by providing material resources and visionary leadership, it has strengthened its bureaucratic offices that research and monitor women's human rights and socioeconomic status in countries around the world.

Notes

1. I discuss some of these difficulties in my previously published book *Shaping a Global Women's Agenda: Women's NGOs and Global Governance, 1925–85* (Manchester: Manchester University Press, 2010). I would like to thank Manchester University Press for permission to publish excerpts and revised versions of this text here. See also Mary E. Hawkesworth, *Globalization and Feminist Activism* (Lanham, MD: Rowman and Littlefield, 2006), 111–12, 118; Francisca de Haan, "Continuing Cold War Paradigms in Western Historiography of Transnational Women's Organizations: The Case of the Women's International Democratic Federation," *Women's History Review* 19, no. 4 (September 2010): 550–51.

2. Jocelyn Olcott notes the problems with these terms historically and contemporarily: "The politics of place highlighted the constant tug between nationalism and internationalism and the challenges of forging bonds of intellectual and political solidarity across the divide between, on the one hand, those areas dubbed Western, Northern, developed, industrialized or First World and, on the other, those areas dubbed non-Western, Southern, developing (or even, in some iterations, *under*developed), or Third World. These geopolitical designations vary by context, ideological orientation, and scholarly conversation and do not map unproblematically onto one another. Indeed, the question of *how* to map then without reifying or eliding meaningful differences of power and resources remains an unresolved question for students of transnational feminism." Jocelyn Olcott, "A Happier Marriage? Feminist History Takes the Transnational Turn," in *Making Women's Histories Beyond National Perspectives*, ed. Pamela S. Nadell and Kate Haulman (New York: New York University Press, 2013), 244.

3. "An Experiment in Cooperation, 1925–1945: The History of the Liaison Committee of Women's International Organisations" (Essex, England: W. Hart and Sons, Ltd., 1945), Mary A. Dingman Papers, Schlesinger Library, Radcliffe Institute, Harvard University, Cambridge, Massachusetts, box 1.

4. For a definition of "liberal feminism," see Rosemary Tong, *Feminist Thought: A Comprehensive Introduction* (Boulder, CO: Westview, 1989), 11–13.

5. Peter Willetts, "Consultative Status for NGOs at the United Nations," in *"The Conscience of the World": The Influence of Non-Governmental Organizations in the UN System*, ed. Peter Willetts (London: Hurst, 1996), 37–43.

6. Helen Laville, *Cold War Women: The International Activities of American*

Women's Organizations (New York: Palgrave, 2002), 116–17; Laura Reanda, "The Commission on the Status of Women," in *The United Nations and Human Rights: A Critical Appraisal*, ed. Philip Alston (Oxford: Oxford University Press, 1992), 282–83; "Statement of Working Party of Representatives of Women's International Organizations Present at the Third Session of the United Nations Commission on the Status of Women Held in Beirut, Lebanon, March 21–April 3, 1949," March 30, 1949, World Young Women's Christian Association Archives, Geneva, Switzerland (hereafter WYWCA).

7. Garner, *Shaping a Global Women's Agenda*, 11n1.

8. Francisca de Haan, "The Women's International Democratic Federation (WIDF): History, Main Agenda, and Contributions, 1945–1991," *Women and Social Movements, International*, document database, *wasi.alexanderstreet.com/help/view/ the_womens_international_democratic_federation_widf_history_main_agenda_and_ contributions_19451991*.

9. de Haan, "Continuing Cold War Paradigms," 550.

10. Ibid., 555–57; Laville, *Cold War Women*, 113–17; Melanie Ilic, "Soviet Women, Cultural Exchange and the Women's International Democratic Federation," in *Reassessing Cold War Europe*, ed. Sari Autio-Sarasmo and Katalin Miklossy (New York: Routledge, 2011), 160. See also Incoming Telegram United States (CSW) Delegation, New York Infotel No. 384 from Moscow, February 12, [1950], from the Secretary of State, Dorothy Kenyon Papers, Sophia Smith Collection, Smith College, box 53.

11. de Haan, "Women's International Democratic Federation (WIDF)"; Nitza Berkovitch, *From Motherhood to Citizenship: Women's Rights and International Organizations* (Baltimore, MD: Johns Hopkins University Press, 1999), 107–8.

12. Kamila Chylińska, "Political Activity of Women in Eastern Europe," *Annals of the Academy of Political and Social Science* 375 (January 1968): 68.

13. Kristen Ghodsee, "Rethinking State Socialist Mass Women's Organizations: The Committee of the Bulgarian Women's Movement and the United Nations Decade for Women, 1975–1985," *Journal of Women's History* 24, no. 4 (2012): 52; Melanie Ilic, "Soviet Women, Cultural Exchange and the Women's International Democratic Federation," 161–63; Fanny Edelman, WIDF general secretary, "Address to the 7th Congress," in the conference program for the Seventh WIDF Congress: International Women's Year—Equality, Development, Peace—Berlin, GDR, October 26, 1975, in *Women and Social Movements, International*.

14. World Congress for International Women's Year, "Bulletin" (Women's International Democratic Federation, 1974); Ghodsee, "Rethinking State Socialist Mass Women's Organizations," 49–73; Natalia Vishneva-Sarafanova, *Soviet Women's World: The United Nations Decade for Women, 1976–1985*, trans. Peter Tempest (Moscow: Novosti Press Agency Publishing House, 1983).

15. Ghodsee, "Rethinking State Socialist Mass Women's Organizations," 51. See also Hilkka Pietilä, *The Unfinished Story of Women and the United Nations* (New York: United Nations Non-Governmental Liaison Service, 2007), 39.

16. United Nations, *Meeting in Mexico: The Story of the World Conference of International Women's Year* (New York: United Nations, 1975), 17–18.

17. Lisa Baldez, *Defying Convention: U. S. Resistance to the UN Treaty on Women's Rights* (New York: Cambridge University Press, 2014), 14.

18. Ibid., 35; Devaki Jain, *Women, Development and the UN: A Sixty-Year Quest for Equality and Justice* (Bloomington: Indiana University Press, 2005), 24–25.

19. Jain, *Women, Development and the UN*, 44; Berkovitch, *From Motherhood to Citizenship*, 156–61; Pietilä, *Unfinished Story of Women and the United Nations*, 37.

20. Mary E. Hawkesworth, *Globalization and Feminist Activism* (Lanham, MD: Rowman and Littlefield, 2006), 113.

21. Garner, *Shaping a Global Women's Agenda*, 216; Hawkesworth, *Globalization and Feminist Activism*, 118–19. See also John R. Mathiason, *The Long March to Beijing: The United Nations and the Women's Revolution*, vol. 1: *The Vienna Period* (n.p., 2001), 35–36; United Nations, *Meeting in Mexico*, 17–18.

22. Arvonne S. Fraser, *The UN Decade for Women: Documents and Dialogue* (Boulder, CO: Westview, 1987), 1; Jane Connors, "NGOs and the Human Rights of Women at the United Nations," in Willetts, *The Conscience of the World*, 158–60; Arnold Whittick, *Woman into Citizen: The World Movement towards the Emancipation of Women in the Twentieth Century with Accounts of the Contributions of the International Alliance of Women, the League of Nations and the Relevant Organizations of the United Nations* (London: Athenaeum, 1979), 267; de Haan, "Women's International Democratic Federation (WIDF)"; Conference program, with speeches, for the Seventh WIDF Congress: International Women's Year—Equality, Development, Peace—Berlin, GDR, October 26, 1975, in *Women and Social Movements, International*.

23. NGO Subcommittee Committee on Status of Women (Geneva), meeting minutes, February 22, 1974, International Women's Tribune Centre Records, 1970–2000, Sophia Smith Collection (hereafter IWTC); NGO Subcommittee on International Women's Year (New York), March 6, 1974, IWTC, box 1; Alice Paquier to Mildred Jones, April 2, 1974, WYWCA World Consultants at UN and Specialized Agencies, 1973–1976, WYWCA.

24. Mary Craig Schuller-McGeachy, president, International Council of Women, to Rosalind Harris, International Social Service, New York, February 19, 1974, IWTC, box 1.

25. Baldez, *Defying Convention*, 74–75; Leticia Ramos Shahani, "The UN, Women and Development: The World Conferences on Women," in *Developing Power: How Women Transformed International Development*, ed. Arvonne S. Fraser and Irene Tinker (New York: Feminist Press, 2004), 30; Hawkesworth, *Globalization and Feminist Activism*, 118.

26. NGO Committee on International Women's Year, meeting minutes, May 15, 1974, IWTC, box 1.

27. NGO Committee on International Women's Year, meeting minutes, October 30, 1974, IWTC, box 1.

28. Rosalind Harris to Niall MacDermot, chair, NGO Committee on Human Rights (Geneva), April 4, 1974, IWTC, box 1.

29. NGO Committee on International Women's Year, meeting minutes, May 29, 1974, IWTC, box 1.

30. United Nations, "What Is International Women's Year?," [January 1974?], IWTC, box 1.

31. Fraser, *UN Decade for Women*, 22; Jain, *Women, Development and the UN*, 59–60.

32. NGO Committee on International Women's Year, meeting minutes, October 30, 1974, IWTC, box 1.

33. Mathiason, *Long March to Beijing*, 22.

34. During the 1970s the CSW no longer held annual sessions; it convened every other year and would not meet again until 1976.

35. Mathiason, *Long March to Beijing*, 37.
36. Alice Paquier to Mildred Jones, October 14, 1974, World Consultants at UN and Specialized Agencies, 1973–1976, WYWCA.
37. Alice Paquier to Mildred Jones, November 8, 1974, World Consultants at UN and Specialized Agencies, 1973–1976, WYWCA.
38. Dorothy R. Steffens, executive director, Women's International League for Peace and Freedom to Margaret K. Bruce, deputy director, Centre for Social Development and Humanitarian Affairs, IWY Secretariat, November 11, 1974, IWTC, box 2.
39. World Congress for Women, International Women's Year Bulletin, "Documents of the Meeting of International, Regional and National Organizations to Establish an International Preparatory Committee for the World Congress for International Women's Year, Tihany, Hungarian People's Republic, 4–5 November 1974," in *Women and Social Movements, International*.
40. Mildred Jones to Elizabeth Palmer, December 19, 1974, World Consultants at UN and Specialized Agencies, 1973–1976, WYWCA.
41. Garner, *Shaping a Global Women's Agenda*, 205–6.
42. IWY tribune organizing committee, January 29, 1975, IWTC, box 2. Led by Mildred Persinger of the World YWCA, the NGO tribune committee included Robert W. C. Brown of the International Association for Religious Freedom, Richard C. Fagley of the Committee of the Churches on International Affairs, Kay Fraleigh of the International Alliance of Women, Rosalind Harris of International Social Services and the president of CONGO, Harriet Hollister of the Friend's World Committee, Esther Hymer of the International Federation of Business and Professional Women, Mary McGeachy Schuller of the International Council of Women, Fanny Simon of the International Council of Social Democratic Women, Annabelle Wiener of the World Federation of UN Associations, and Page Wilson of the Population Crisis Committee.
43. Fraser, *UN Decade for Women*, 32.
44. Katherine Strong to Mildred Persinger and Mildred Jones, February 5, 1975, World Consultants at UN and Specialized Agencies, 1973–1976, WYWCA.
45. NGO Committee on International Women's Year, meeting minutes, February 26, 1975, IWTC, box 1.
46. Rosalind Harris to Shahnaz Alami, March 3, 1975, IWTC, box 1.
47. NGO Committee on International Women's Year, meeting minutes, March 19, 1975, IWTC, box 1.
48. "IWY Tribune, Organizing Committee, Tribune Schedule," June19–July 2, 1975, IWTC, box 2.
49. IWY tribune organizing committee meeting, [January 1975?], IWTC, box 2.
50. IWY tribune 1975 budget, January 1–August 15, 1975, IWTC, box 2.
51. IWY tribune organizing committee, March 13, 1975, IWTC, box 2.
52. "Guidelines for the Conduct of IWY Tribune Sessions," May 27, 1975, IWTC, box 2.
53. See Garner, *Shaping a Global Women's Agenda*, 225–26. The conference document proposed government action to increase women's political participation, expand education for women and girls, train and employ women in the formal economy, improve levels of health and nutrition for women, implement programs to benefit families, develop gender-conscious population policies, improve housing, and address other social issues affecting women. Governments also agreed to hold periodic reviews to mark progress on achieving World Plan of Action goals and to

establish two new UN offices: the International Research and Training Institute for the Advancement of Women (INSTRAW) and a UN Voluntary Fund (UNIFEM) specifically targeting women and development projects. Jain, *Women, Development and the UN*, 70.

54. Robert Looney, "The New International Economic Order," in *Routledge Encyclopedia of International Political Economy*, ed. R. J. B. Jones (London: Routledge, 2001), 1128–30, *faculty.nps.edu/relooney/NIEO.pdf*.

55. United Nations, *Report of the World Conference of the International Women's Year, Mexico City, June 19–July 2, 1975* (New York: United Nations, 1976); *www.un.org/womenwatch/daw/beijing/otherconferences/Mexico/Mexico%20conference%20report%20optimized.pdf*. See for example, the opening statement by Mexican President and Conference host Luis Echeverria on 124.

56. Virginia Allan, Margaret Galey, and Mildred Persinger, "World Conference of International Women's Year," in *Women, Politics and the United Nations*, ed. Anne Winslow (Westport, CT: Greenwood, 1995), 35–39; United Nations, *Meeting in Mexico*, 27–31. See also Judith Zinsser, "From Mexico to Copenhagen to Nairobi: The United Nations Decade for Women, 1975–1985," *Journal of World History* 13, no. 1 (Spring 2002): 139–68.

57. "The Declaration of Mexico on the Equality of Women and their Contribution to Development and Peace," United Nations Document E/conf.66/34, *un-documents.net/mex-dec.htm*.

58. Ibid., especially principles 24 and 26. See also United Nations, *Meeting in Mexico*, 27.

59. Press release, June 25, 1975, IWTC, box 1; "Tribune's Voice to Be Heard at Tlatelolco?," *Xilonen* (Mexico City), June 26, 1975, microfilm, IWTC.

60. Allan, Galey, and Persinger, "World Conference of International Women's Year," 35–39.

61. "Daniel in the Lioness's Den," *Xilonen* (Mexico City), June 23, 1975, on microfilm, IWTC; "Report on the World Conference on International Women's Year," *Congressional Record*, 94th Congress, 1st Session, 121:133 (September 11, 1975), S15823–S15829.

62. Press release, June 25, 1975, IWTC, box 1; "Tribune's Voice to Be Heard in Tlatelolco?"

63. United Press International, "Women," press release, June 26, 1975, Barbara McClure White Papers, Schlesinger Library, Radcliffe Institute, Harvard University, Cambridge, Massachusetts (hereafter BMW), box 1.

64. Ibid. See also Domatilla Barrios de Chungara's critiques of Betty Friedan and Western feminism's relevance for Latin American women noted in Olcott, "A Happier Marriage?," 244n40.

65. "Native American Women Denied a Voice at International Women's Year Conference," *AKWESASNE Notes*, Early Autumn 1975, 33, IWTC, box 3.

66. Raluca Maria Popa, "Translating Equality between Women and Men across Cold War Divides: Women Activists from Hungary and Romania and the Creation of International Women's Year," in *Gender Politics and Everyday Life in State Socialist Eastern and Central Europe*, ed. Shana Penn and Jill Massino (New York: Palgrave MacMillan, 2009), 62–67.

67. Ibid.

68. See for example: de Haan, "Continuing Cold War Paradigms"; de Haan, "Women's International Democratic Federation (WIDF)"; Ghodsee, "Rethinking State Socialist

Mass Women's Organizations"; Ilic, "Soviet Women, Cultural Exchange and the Women's International Democratic Federation"; and Popa, "Translating Equality between Women and Men across Cold War Divides."

69. Kristen Ghodsee, "Revisiting the United Nations Decade for Women: Brief Reflections on Feminism, Capitalism and Cold War Politics in the Early Years of the International Women's Movement," *Women's Studies International Forum* 33 (2010): 5–8.

70. Ghodsee, "Rethinking State Socialist Mass Women's Organizations," 56.

71. Ibid., 59–60.

72. "Tribune Organizing Committee, Tribune Schedule," June 19–July 2, 1975, IWTC, box 2. Other panel sessions at the Mexico City Tribune included "Law and the Status of Women," Agriculture and Rural Development," "Health and Nutrition," Education," "Women at Work," "Population," "Women and Environment: Urbanization," "Women in Public Life," "The Family," and "Peace and Disarmament."

73. Fanny Edelman, "Address to the 7th Congress."

74. Ibid.

75. Alice Paquier, "World Congress for International Women's Year, Berlin, GDR, 20–24 October 1975," International Women's Year, WYWCA.

76. Fraser, *UN Decade for Women*, 69.

77. Joan Kelly, "Comment on the 1980 International Women's Decade Conference in Iran," *Signs* 4, no. 2 (Winter 1978): 388.

78. Mathiason, *Long March to Beijing*, 46–48.

79. Peggy Antrobus, "A Caribbean Journey: Defending Feminist Politics," in Fraser and Tinker, *Developing Power*, 139.

80. Jain, *Women, Development and the UN*, 89.

81. Fraser, *UN Decade for Women*, 71.

82. Planning committee for the world conference of the UN Decade for Women, meeting minutes, July 4, 1979, NGO Forum, Copenhagen, July 1980, WYWCA.

83. Georgina Ashworth and Lucy Bonnerjea, eds., *The Invisible Decade: UK Women and the UN Decade 1976–1985* (Aldershot: Gower, 1985), 2.

84. Fraser, *UN Decade for Women*, 75–78; United Nations, "Preparatory Committee for World Conference of Decade for Women Discusses Effects of Apartheid on Women in Southern Africa," press release, April 14, 1980, IWTC, box 1; United Nations, "Preparatory Committee for World Conference of Decade for Women Discusses Effects of Israeli Occupation on Palestinian Women," press release, April 14, 1980, IWTC, box 1.

85. Maureen T. Whalen et al., *Report of the United States Delegation to the World Conference of the United Nations Decade for Women: Equality, Development and Peace, July 14–30, 1980* (Washington, DC: United States Department of State, 1980), 103, *babel.hathitrust.org/cgi/pt?id=mdp.39015034240989;view=1up;seq=1*.

86. Irene Tinker, "A Feminist View of Copenhagen," *Signs* 6 (Spring 1981): 531 and 534; Ghodsee, "Rethinking State Socialist Mass Women's Organizations," 62. See also Ashworth and Bonnerjea, *Invisible Decade*, 2–3: "The long term interests of women in the Western alliance were relegated to the side-lines by their own governments."

87. Whalen, *Report of the United States Delegation*, 3, 106, and 116.

88. Ghodsee, "Revisiting the United Nations Decade for Women," 7.

89. Ibid.

90. Fraser and Tinker, *Developing Power*, xxiv.

91. "Planning Committee Assignments at NGO Forum," July 14–24, 1980, IWTC, box 4.
92. Fraser, *UN Decade for Women*, 145–46.
93. Anne Walker, "Vivencia! At the NGO Forum," April 9, 1980, IWTC, box 5.
94. Preregistration brochure, c. 1980, WYWCA; Meeting minutes, January 31, 1980, NGO Forum, Copenhagen, July 1980, WYWCA.
95. "It's Ideas That Matter Says Elizabeth Palmer," *Forum 80 Newsletter*, July 17, 1980, microfilm, IWTC.
96. J. Patricia Morrison, International Section Program Department, "[Evaluation] Mid-Decade Forum for Women, Copenhagen, 14–24 July 1980," NGO Forum, Copenhagen, July 1980, WYWCA.
97. "Call for NGO Plenary," *Forum 80 Newsletter*, July 17, 1980, IWTC; and "NGO Plenary Makes an Action Plan," *Forum 80 Newsletter*, July 18, 1980, microfilm, IWTC.
98. Anne Walker, "The International Women's Tribune Centre," in Fraser and Tinker, *Developing Power*, 94.
99. Fraser, *UN Decade for Women*, 151.
100. Garner, *Shaping a Global Women's Agenda*, 270; Fraser, *UN Decade for Women*, 159.
101. Mathiason, *Long March to Beijing*, 51 and 53.
102. Sixty-four CONGO member organizations volunteered to serve on the Forum 1985 planning body, although a steering committee composed of twenty-two women formed its coordinating and decision-making body. Altogether, the final Forum 1985 report noted, "The Planning Network involved some 378 persons, although even that large number included few Third World women." "Summary of the Meeting of the Planning Committee for NGO Activities in Relation to the 1985 Conference on the Decade for Women," September 19, 1983, IWTC, box 11; "Update on Activities of the NGO Planning Committee," July 1984, IWTC, box 7; *Forum '85 NGO Planning Committee Final Report: Nairobi, Kenya*, [December 1985?], IWTC, box 15.
103. These included the challenge of raising over $1.2 million to cover forum expenses and travel expenses for women from developing countries. *Forum '85 NGO Planning Committee Final Report: Nairobi, Kenya.*
104. "The Kenya Organizing Committee for the Activities of the 1985 World Conference of the UN Decade for Women: Project Proposal for the Funding of the Committee's Activities in Organizing and Hosting the NGO Forum 1985," IWTC, box 11.
105. Alice Paquier, International Federation of University Women in Geneva, to Nita Barrow, Virginia Hazzard, Alba Zizzamia, and carbon-copied to Edith Ballantyne, October 18, 1983, IWTC, box 7; Carole Seymour Jones, *Journey of Faith: The History of the World YWCA, 1945–1994* (London: Allison and Busby, 1994), 320–21.
106. Minutes of the fourth meeting of the NGO Planning Committee, June 11, 1984, IWTC, box 11; NGO Forum, Nairobi, preconference consultation, Vienna, October 22–24, 1984, IWTC, box 8.
107. Ghodsee, "Revisiting the United Nations Decade for Women," 9.
108. Irene Tinker, "Reflections on Forum 85 in Nairobi, Kenya: Voices from the International Women's Studies Community," *Signs* 11 (Spring 1986): 587.
109. Ibid.
110. Zinsser, "From Mexico to Copenhagen to Nairobi," 158–64; Leticia Ramos Shahani, "The UN, Women and Development: The World Conferences on Women," in Fraser and Tinker, *Developing Power*, 34.
111. Jean F. O'Barr, "Reflections on Forum 85 in Nairobi, Kenya: Voices from the

International Women's Studies Community," *Signs* 11 (Spring 1986): 585. See also Ghodsee, "Revisiting the United Nations Decade for Women," 9.

112. Amrita Basu, "Introduction," in *Women's Movements in the Global Era: The Power of Local Feminisms*, ed. Amrita Basu (Boulder, CO: Westview, 2010), 11–14.

References

Archives

Arthur and Elizabeth Schlesinger Library on the History of Women in America, Cambridge, Massachusetts

Sophia Smith Collection, Smith College, Northampton, Massachusetts

World Young Women's Christian Association Archives, Geneva, Switzerland

Selected Published Works

Ashworth, Georgina, and Lucy Bonnerjea, eds. *The Invisible Decade: UK Women and the UN Decade 1976–1985.* Aldershot: Gower, 1985.

Baldez, Lisa. *Defying Convention: U. S. Resistance to the UN Treaty on Women's Rights.* New York: Cambridge University Press, 2104.

Basu, Amrita, ed. *Women's Movements in the Global Era: The Power of Local Feminisms.* Boulder, CO: Westview, 2010.

Berkovitch, Nitza. *From Motherhood to Citizenship: Women's Rights and International Organizations.* Baltimore, MD: Johns Hopkins University Press, 1999.

"The Declaration of Mexico on the Equality of Women and their Contribution to Development and Peace." United Nations Document E/conf.66/34. *un-documents.net/ mex-dec.htm.*

de Haan, Francisca. "Continuing Cold War Paradigms in Western Historiography of Transnational Women's Organizations: The Case of the Women's International Democratic Federation." *Women's History Review* 19, no. 4 (September 2010): 547–73.

———. "The Women's International Democratic Federation (WIDF): History, Main Agenda, and Contributions, 1945–1991." *Women and Social Movements International,* document database. Alexander Street Press, 2011. *wasi.alexanderstreet.com/help/view/ the_womens_international_democratic_federation_widf_history_main_agenda_and_ contributions_19451991.*

Fraser, Arvonne S. *The UN Decade for Women: Documents and Dialogue.* Boulder, CO: Westview, 1987.

Fraser, Arvonne S., and Irene Tinker, eds. *Developing Power: How Women Transformed International Development.* New York: Feminist Press, 2004.

Garner, Karen. *Shaping a Global Women's Agenda: Women's NGOs and Global Governance, 1925–85.* Manchester: Manchester University Press, 2010.

Ghodsee, Kristen. "Rethinking State Socialist Mass Women's Organizations: The Committee of the Bulgarian Women's Movement and the United Nations Decade for Women, 1975–1985." *Journal of Women's History* 24, no. 4 (2012): 49–73.

———. "Revisiting the United Nations Decade for Women: Brief Reflections on Feminism, Capitalism and Cold War Politics in the Early Years of the International Women's Movement." *Women's Studies International Forum* 33 (2010): 3–12.

Hawkesworth, Mary E. *Globalization and Feminist Activism*. Lanham, MD: Rowman and Littlefield, 2006.

Jain, Devaki. *Women, Development and the UN: A Sixty-Year Quest for Equality and Justice*. Bloomington: Indiana University Press, 2005.

Laville, Helen. *Cold War Women: The International Activities of American Women's Organizations*. New York: Palgrave, 2002.

Mathiason, John R. *The Long March to Beijing: The United Nations and the Women's Revolution*. Vol. 1, *The Vienna Period, the United Nations and the Women's Revolution*. Published by author, 2001.

Pietilä, Hilkka. *The Unfinished Story of Women and the United Nations*. New York: United Nations Non-governmental Liaison Service, 2007.

"Report on the World Conference on International Women's Year." *Congressional Record*, 94th Congress, 1st Session, 121:133. September 11, 1975. S15823–S15829.

Tinker, Irene. "International Notes: A Feminist View of Copenhagen." *Signs* 6 (Spring 1981): 531–37.

——. "Reflections on Forum 85 in Nairobi, Kenya: Voices from the International Women's Studies Community." *Signs* 11 (Spring 1986): 586–89.

United Nations. *Meeting in Mexico: The Story of the World Conference of International Women's Year*. New York: United Nations, 1975.

——. *Report of the World Conference of the International Women's Year, Mexico City, 19 June–2 July 1975*. New York: United Nations, 1976. *www.un.org/womenwatch/daw /beijing/otherconferences/Mexico/Mexico%20conference%20report%20optimized.pdf*.

Vishneva-Sarafanova, Natalia. *Soviet Women's World: The United Nations Decade for Women, 1976–1985*. Translated by Peter Tempest. Moscow: Novosti Press Agency Publishing House, 1983.

Whalen, Maureen T., et al. *Report of the United States Delegation to the World Conference of the United Nations Decade for Women: Equality, Development and Peace, July 14–30, 1980*. Washington, DC: United States Department of State, 1980. *babel.hathitrust.org /cgi/pt?id=mdp.39015034240989;view=1up;seq=1*.

Women and Social Movements International document database. Alexander Street Press, 2011.

Zinsser, Judith. "From Mexico to Copenhagen to Nairobi: The United Nations Decade for Women, 1975–1985." *Journal of World History* 13, no. 1 (Spring 2002): 139–68.

PART III

Masculinities

CHAPTER 12

"Men of the World" or "Uniformed Boys"?

Hegemonic Masculinity and the British Army in the Era of the Korean War

Grace Huxford

The Korean War is sometimes referred to as "the forgotten war."[1] The unclear war aims of the conflict and the inconclusive end to hostilities in 1953 meant that the war slipped into obscurity: although it was the first United Nations (UN) war and arguably the first "hot" war of the Cold War, it has been neither praised nor vilified to any great extent.[2] Its obscurity is even more profound in the United Kingdom. Although Britain had the second-largest national contingent of troops, few history books, novels, or films mark the British contribution to the UN force, which had pledged support to the Republic of Korea following the invasion of the south by the communist North Korean People's Army on June 25, 1950. By 1951, the British had contributed twelve thousand troops to the mission in Korea. However, coming just five years after the end of the Second World War, Korea was largely eclipsed by this earlier conflict within the British imagination. In the Second World War Britain had "stood alone" in 1940 and triumphed in a worthy fight between good and evil—ideals that appealed to the British public and politicians in the second half of the twentieth century as Britain declined both economically and internationally.[3] Korea, by contrast, served no such purpose, either at the time or afterward. Subsequently, in the UK today many Korean War veterans describe themselves as forgotten by British popular culture and memory.

Historians too have neglected the significance of the Korean War to British social history and the history of Britain in the Cold War. Large-scale histories of the postwar period make only passing references to it.[4] Yet despite the dearth of academic work focusing on the Korean War, it was important in a multitude of ways: it prompted heated discussion over the place of rearmament within the postwar Labour government led by Prime Minister Clement Attlee; it caused Britain to reanalyze its role in the world and in relation to the United States, the British Commonwealth, and its dwindling imperial commitments; and it caused Britain to articulate its opposition to communist regimes and to reiterate its democratic credentials. Less obviously, Korea also coincided with shifts in generational relationships, as a younger generation of servicemen (many of whom had been too young to serve in the Second World War) came to terms with their own, and their parents,' military experience. Although some historians see the 1950s as a "domestic decade" for Britain (particularly compared with its international involvement in the 1940s), it was actually a time of mass mobilization.[5] From 1948, the British government had introduced peacetime conscription for all young men (aged eighteen to twenty-six), and in October 1950 this was extended to two years. This conscription had a profound impact on a generation of young men, many of whom went to serve in Korea (if aged over nineteen), and in turn caused wider debates about military service and—importantly—what it meant to be a British *man* during the early years of the Cold War.

The meaning of masculinity was intensely debated within British society in the 1950s. As historian Richard Vinen recently argued, national service conscription "involved competing and conflicting notions of what adult masculinity might involve."[6] For instance, in 1950, shortly after Attlee's commitment of British forces to the UN mission in Korea, the War Office sponsored the production of a Crown Film Unit film entitled *Men of the World* (1950).[7] Amid aerial shots of exotic locations including Libya, Singapore, and Malta, the film focused on the character of the British soldier and his suitability to act as a policeman in the postwar world, from the markets of Libya to the jungles of Malaya. The film's narrator intones: "The British soldier. All around the globe you'll find him. From Gibraltar to Hong Kong. Everywhere he stands against the threatening years, staunch symbol of our common will to order. . . . Citizen in his sense of the responsibilities of freedom. Soldier in his acceptance of the disciplines of duty. Truly a man of the world."[8] The soldier was still regarded as a frontline defender, even with the indistinct battle lines of the Cold War.[9] Against this new international political background, *Men of the World* nevertheless echoed tropes from an imagined (and idealized) imperial past: though engaged in the complex process of "seeking a role" in the postwar period, the "ubiquitous British soldier" still policed local bazaars and British Army officers still formed exclusive polo clubs across the world.[10] He was depicted as both an adventurer and symbol of martial masculinity.[11]

Yet at the same time, Britain's position in the Cold War brought this representation of masculinity into doubt. Speaking in the House of Commons in 1951, Conservative politician Walter Bromley-Davenport noted that "boys have fought like men" in Korea, but he called for the government to "let them grow up a bit before they encounter the enemy."[12] Similarly, in *A Brave New World Revisited* (1959), English writer Aldous Huxley stated that much of the dystopian future he had imagined in his 1931 novel *A Brave New World* had come true, where "endless columns of uniformed boys, white, black, brown, yellow, march obediently towards the common grave."[13] Several important questions therefore emerge from this debate: Did the Cold War herald a new "hegemonic masculinity" for the British?[14] Or were older traditions of masculinity of more comfort and utility to the British state—and soldier—in these new "threatening years"?

Through the case study of British servicemen in the Korean War, this chapter explores the multiple and often conflicting definitions of manhood that British military men and commentators used to describe servicemen in the 1950s. I argue that British servicemen often criticized or underplayed their role in Korea, especially when they compared it with their fathers' experiences in the Second World War. Following the work of Vinen and others, I contend that the Second World War was used as a measure of masculinity against which their own experiences in Korea were compared, not altogether favorably. A particular definition of masculinity had become hegemonic in the 1950s, but the actual experiences of men in Korea sometimes sat uncomfortably outside this. In response, men from a variety of social backgrounds endeavored to reconcile their inability to fulfill particular hegemonic notions of masculinity. The chapter also addresses the context and significance of the Cold War in greater detail, noting that the menace of communism failed to produce an appealing definition of manhood in 1950s Britain.

In making this argument, I also seek to understand the theoretical utility of the contentious concept of "hegemonic masculinity" in Cold War history, a concept typically associated with the Australian sociologist of masculinity R. W. Connell. By defending the ever-broadening analytical focus of Cold War historiography beyond its traditionally US-centric parameters, I highlight the role of hegemony in both contemporary gender relations *and* present-day history writing. In other words, we cannot question the hegemony of US-centered Cold War history without also acknowledging the impact of hegemony on identity politics for the people who lived through the conflict. This chapter goes some way in addressing the lived experience of men who fought in the Korean War by drawing on letters, diaries, and the seldom-used battle experience questionnaire filled out by British officers, as well as parliamentary debates, fiction, and commentary. The focus here on masculinity is deliberate but not unproblematic: discussions over male duties and roles may have captivated policy makers and military officials, but the definition of femininity at the time was equally important. Therefore, it is also vital to analyze characterizations of femininity and their relation to particular constructions of masculinity. Femininity and masculinity are inexorably connected, particularly in the case of hegemonic masculinities. Overall, therefore, this small case study aims to show the complex and overlapping ways gender identity was conceptualized within Cold War British culture and society.

Britain, National Service, and the Korean War

The British role in Korea was highly complex, complicated by wars of decolonization and Cold War politics. Among its many interventions in the 1950s, the British Army fought communist guerrillas in Malaya, suppressed the Mau Mau Uprising in Kenya, and was involved in actions in Singapore and the Suez Canal region.[15] The British also occupied parts of northern Germany following the division of the country into zones at the end of the Second World War, and postings to the British Army of the Rhine were common. Increasingly, however, Britain's military commitments and its "men of the world" became a point of debate. From 1946 there was sustained opposition to the introduction of peacetime conscription. In 1950 Labour MP Fenner Brockway (later Baron Brockway, a leading antiwar campaigner and founder of War on Want in 1951) argued in the House of Commons that "these boys of 18 or 19 have grown up in a world for which the older generation is responsible, and . . . the older generation have no right to command these young men to join the Services to kill and be killed when they have had no responsibility for the conditions of the world in which they have grown up."[16] Labour MP Victor Yates opposed conscription on more practical terms: "The country is in economic danger. We need skilled manpower, we need technical training, and while other countries are turning out more technologists and scientists . . . we are engaged in this colossal enterprise of tying up our young men—our national assets—and mailing them to all parts of the world."[17] Nor was such language restricted to the British Left: Conservative Bromley-Davenport opposed the Attlee government's spending on national service and its use of "boys . . . just left school," noting: "We are now in 1951. It is not like 1917–18, when there was a world war and we were suffering the most fearful casualties . . . and we were almost down to our last man."[18] Although resistance to conscription was not unique to the Cold War period (Brockway had, for instance, also founded the No-Conscription Fellowship in November 1914), the debate was couched more than ever in terms of masculinity and generational responsibility: the "boys" of Britain were part of the debate about Britain's military capabilities in the Cold War world. Many asked if Britain had a responsibility (or, indeed, an economic need) to keep up its international role despite diminishing imperial commitments and therefore reconsidered the contribution required of its armed forces.[19]

Debates over masculinity in the Cold War era were also conflated with debates about what it meant to be a democratic citizen. As Penny Summerfield notes, "Citizenship was predicated upon military service in the minds of many nineteenth- and twentieth-century Britons," particularly during the Second World War where men and women excluded from military service would form quasi-military organizations to claim they were legitimate citizens.[20] From world wars to terrorist attacks, Lucy Noakes and Susan Grayzel highlight that citizenship remained persistently gendered in the twentieth century and split along "passive" and "active" lines—"with women and children largely as victims and men as defenders of the home."[21] Furthermore, as Andrew Hammond argues, adjustment to a postwar world did not necessarily mean the complete discontinuation of imperial notions of manhood in British fiction and society, although events like the Suez Crisis (1956) did bring home the scale of imperial curtailment.[22]

Yet the association between men and active (that is, military) roles in the state did not go uncriticized. In *A Brave New World Revisited* Huxley rejected the idea that militaries should be used to protect political freedom, but he nevertheless used the gendered language of active citizenship ("uniformed boys") to root his distaste in a social reality his readers would recognize. Huxley's diatribe also highlights the role of independent thought and therefore, by implication, self-reflexivity within the democratic system. "Thinking" was one of the overarching themes of citizenship in early Cold War Britain.[23] In describing the advances of the 1944 Education Act, the Labour Party Manifesto of 1945 noted that "the great purpose of education is to give us individual citizens capable of thinking for themselves."[24] This capacity had direct implications in the setting of the Cold War. In the War Office film *Two Ways of Life* (1958), a distinct comparison was drawn between the army of Britain and that of the USSR: "Unlike the forces of the USSR, every British serving man has a freedom of thought and choice that would be unthinkable under Communism. He has the right to know the reason for his service in the forces and to be informed on national and foreign policy, and, what is more important, to ask questions on that policy which is more than the Soviet soldier or citizen can or dare do."[25] Thinking and self-awareness were therefore part of how the state defined British manhood and citizenship in opposition to communism.

Others were also coming to terms with what British manhood meant in the post-1945 world. In British film, the gentlemanly characters of the 1930s were increasingly replaced by the Everyman, characterized by wartime Ealing comedies and even by particular actors, such as John Mills, who for many embodied everyday, stoic Englishness.[26] The question of manhood was also being asked in literature. One well-known example is the dystopic novel *Lord of the Flies* (1954) by William Golding, the British Nobel laureate.[27] Rather than engaging in a classic island escapade, full of male daring, exploration, and resourcefulness, Golding's group of schoolboys, washed up on an unspecified island, destroy both each other and the island they live on, constantly dogged by fear of a "beast" in the shadows. In his study of imperialism and boyhood adventure stories, Richard Phillips argues that Golding subverted established masculine tropes with his novel: he "used adventure as a medium in which to negotiate British manliness" but also to "unmap" imperial ambitions and to mark the decline of masculine, imperial endeavors.[28] Moreover, the sketchy background to the island adventure in *Lord of the Flies*, seldom mentioned by the boys, is that they have been forced to flee a postapocalyptic Britain.[29] Their rescue by a uniformed officer at the end of the book brings back some of the stability of their former lives and society, but the boys' future, even off the island, is far from certain.

The Korean War deepened this gendered debate about Britain's role in the world. Veterans have argued that few people in Britain knew where Korea was, still fewer the reasons for fighting there. Although this might have been an exaggeration, there was certainly little awareness of the history of the peninsula. Korea had been occupied by the Japanese from 1911 to 1945, and, following the Second World War, politically divergent regimes had developed on either side of the thirty-eighth parallel. Communist North Korea, known as the Democratic People's Republic of Korea, was supported by the Soviet Union. South Korea, the Republic of Korea, was backed by the United States. By the end of 1950, the People's Republic of China had entered the war to support North Korea and had pushed back the initial UN advance. The first year of the conflict was marked by the rapid movement of troops up and down Korea, whereas the latter two years were marked by static trench warfare and patrols around the thirty-eighth parallel. In July 1950 the Labour government decided to commit British troops in defense of South Korea. As many as 50 percent of the British troops deployed were national servicemen, joined by recalled reservists from the Second World War and a small number of K-Force volunteers from across the Commonwealth.

A range of motives arguably influenced the Attlee government's decision to commit British forces to the UN mission in Korea. The standard explanations are that Britain wished to support the idea of collective security through the UN and to offer the United States assistance to ensure their continued aid to postwar Europe.[30] Sean Greenwood, however, argues that Britain also hoped to soften America's potentially insensitive policy in Korea and toward the People's Republic of China.[31] Some historians maintain that Britain was even able to mediate US policy, particularly through the UN: British representatives suggested important amendments to the wording of UN policy documents on Korea.[32] On July 5, 1950, Attlee evoked the memory of the Second World War when he called for the House of Commons to support both the United States and the UN: "I need not remind the House of the heavy obligation which we have undertaken for the preservation of peace all over the world. . . . As the House knows, we are taking all the steps possible to try to build up conditions in the world which will not provide fruitful soil for Communist propaganda."[33] Attlee argued that "the world is indebted to the Government of the United States for its prompt action. With equal promptitude His Majesty's Government resolved to support this action."[34]

However, the memory of the Second World War and the reassertion of Allied unity intersected with debates over generational responsibility, as the impassioned arguments of Brockway and Yates demonstrate. What then was the significance of the "boys" and "men" debate to policy discussion about Korea, and what were its wider consequences? Historian K. A. Cuordileone argues that, in the US context, such policy stances can reveal more about preoccupations in society at large, particularly gender anxieties. As Aaron Belkin has recently noted, military masculinity can be "a site where irreconcilable political contradictions have been smoothed over [and] . . . where domestic fears of the other have been exaggerated."[35] Was this the case with Britain, and did one of these competing definitions of masculinity become hegemonic?

Gender, Cold War Armies, and Hegemonic Masculinity

Since the end of the Cold War, scholars have increasingly stressed the importance of gender in the conflict's nature and denouement. Marko Dumančić recently highlighted two main avenues of inquiry in this research. First, historians have examined how Cold War politics shaped gender ideals.[36] Gender was one of many areas of debate and rivalry between the United States and the USSR. Nikita Khrushchev and Richard Nixon's famous "kitchen debate" of 1959, in which the two leaders debated the role of women in the modern kitchen at the opening of the American National Exhibition at Sokolniki Park, Moscow, forms an important component in this line of argument. As Dumančić notes, the research of Susan E. Reid and Katherine Pence, for instance, has further advanced our understanding of female consumerism and citizenship in the Soviet Union and the German Democratic Republic.[37] Second, scholars have also shown how gender shaped the Cold War. According to this argument, the parameters of masculinity were a pivotal part of political debate, both nationally and internationally. Defining who and what constituted a man mattered to policy makers amid the tension of the Cold War. For example, Cuordileone provides a detailed case study of American political discourse in the 1950s and argues that "anxieties about sexuality, manhood and the self surfaced in cold war political rhetoric and intersected with anxieties about Communism and national security."[38]

However, there are several other aspects of gender scholarship that warrant further attention. First, recent scholarship has revealed the importance of gender to nonelite men and women. Andrew Hammond, for example, explores the role of gender in British nuclear war fiction from the early Cold War: popular dystopic novels about nuclear disaster frequently focused on men and were written largely by male authors. It was only later in the Cold War, with détente, that female voices emerged and women began to write about the impact of nuclear war on families.[39] Vinen, although seldom mentioning the Cold War directly, argues that gender was part of the lived experience of *fighting* its various wars, asserting that through national service British men gained a particular sense of themselves as men.[40] Underpinning all this scholarship are two clear research imperatives. First, our analysis needs to extend to a range of national and local contexts in order to fully understand the mobilization and use of gender in the Cold War. Dumančić concludes that gender studies have largely focused on US politics and high culture, leaving Soviet and Eastern European contexts profoundly underanalyzed.[41] Second, we should acknowledge that gender was an integral part of both the rhetoric *and* lived experience of the Cold War, as demonstrated by the series of case studies offered in this collection.

Nonetheless, the diversification of Cold War studies is not without controversy. For example, Anders Stephanson and Federico Romero have argued against the broadening definition of the Cold War.[42] Romero asserts that widening the geographical scope of the Cold War has made the very definition of the conflict "more and more indeterminate and amorphous, as the traditional paradigm of a highly specific bipolar conflict . . . is superseded by a complex fabric of disparate interactions."[43] If the Cold War refers to *everything* that happened between 1945 and the early 1990s, then it potentially loses its meaning. How then are we to approach the history of the Cold War if by broadening its definition we dilute it? First, we must consider whether moving beyond the United States and the USSR actually constitutes a real dilution of Cold War studies. One might argue that addressing issues such as gender and the lived experience of the many millions of people who were not high-power diplomats or politicians is rightfully broadening the scope of Cold War studies, not taking it in an alternate direction or making the term useless. Romero is right to insist that we remain historiographically vigilant about the limits of the Cold War, but, as other chapters in this volume show, this does not mean that "collapsing the two dimensions [of a bipolar conflict] in an indistinct global haze" necessarily leads to a "sprawling reading of the Cold War."[44] It is not ahistorical to broaden our analysis beyond the political and beyond the dispute between the United States and the USSR. In fact, as Odd Arne Westad argues, the focus on the United States and its communist adversaries alone is itself the product of Western power politics during the Cold War. He notes, "All hegemonic powers in history have in some way or another attempted to subsume key historical or cultural concepts under their own discourses."[45] Writing US-centric history was an attempt to claim power during and after the Cold War, but such history potentially ignores how the United States engaged with local elites and conditions and the specific ways in which other nations—such as Britain—engaged with communism.

Westad's stance "against hegemony" also has potential consequences for the study of gender in the Cold War: if hegemonic powers do subsume key "cultural concepts" under their own umbrella, then there is a possibility that polities have sought to associate particular masculine traits with their own agenda. In other words, claiming exclusivity over certain definitions of masculinity could be part of claiming power in the Cold War period. To explore this idea further, the much-contested theory of "hegemonic masculinity," a term first coined by sociologist R. W. Connell, is instructive. Connell claimed that certain forms of masculinity are hegemonic at "any given moment," while other forms of masculinity are subordinated (sometimes permanently, other times temporarily). Connell highlighted the role of the soldier in constructing masculine identity: the soldier—"the murderous hero, the supreme specialist in violence"—validated the idea that male violence was somehow "natural."[46] According to Connell, the modern state also venerated military violence wielded in the name of the "common good." In the modern Western world, a particular definition of martial masculinity thus became a "hegemonic masculinity," used to recruit troops and maintain popular support for the state's wars.[47] Belkin argues that, during the twentieth century, military masculinity in the United States was heralded by political figures as the "archetypal expression of democracy."[48] In such a system, femininity is simultaneously subordinated: as Sandra Via argues in her study of hypermasculinity in modern international security firms, "a man (or anyone's) claim to masculinity . . . is a positional claim in opposition to a feminist other that society has constructed to be the lesser of the two binaries."[49] This subordination is not purely abstract; hegemonic masculinity infuses specific institutions and political outlooks. As historian John Tosh notes, the term implies a specific "pecking order" within a structure of control.[50]

In this way, hegemonic masculinity has a concrete impact on how people live, work, and fight. The material elements of hegemonic masculinity originate in the term "hegemony." In using the term hegemonic, Connell was referencing the work of Italian Marxist Antonio Gramsci. Reworking the Marxist interpretation that the economic base and superstructure account for all human actions, Gramsci suggested instead that culture and "common sense" play a role equal to that of the means of production: unequal social relations might also be produced and sustained by society's normative values. But as Tosh notes, Gramsci provided few clues as to how hegemony operated in gender relationships.[51] The prime example Connell uses is the hegemonic masculinity exhibited by the military: "the murderous hero" has underwritten cults of martial masculinity across the Western world, but it has also underwritten daily definitions of power and leadership.[52] According to this view, this cult of martial masculinity directly influences how men view themselves. From Shakespeare's *Henry V* to Samuel Johnson, men who have not been soldiers have supposedly held "their manhoods cheap" or thought "meanly of . . . [themselves] for not having been a soldier."[53] The idea even has an effect on historians themselves: when writing books or interacting with veterans, John Keegan, Richard Holmes, and Jay Winter all describe feeling excluded to some extent by their lack of military service, but they conclude that this should not inhibit historical study.[54]

Hegemonic masculinity has been widely used by researchers from a variety of disciplines since it was first conceptualized.[55] Yet Tosh argues that historians have largely employed the concept uncritically, using it as a catchall to describe the cultural and social ascendancy of men across the ages and to support the concept of patriarchy developed by feminist theorists in the 1980s.[56] Tosh nevertheless holds that patriarchy, a broad term used to describe male ascendancy regardless of historical context, is not the same as hegemonic masculinity. He claims that hegemonic masculinity presents the contemporary historian with a profound problem. For cultural historians, it is too heavily based in economics and the social structures that characterize Marxist history. For social historians, it is too vague to describe the complexity of masculinity and "smacks too much of the naive sexual politics of socialist feminism."[57] Tosh is right to remain cautious because, as with the broadening of the term Cold War, the term hegemonic masculinity loses some of its relevance and piquancy when applied indiscriminately to all forms of masculinity. It loses both its social and economic grounding if simply used to describe cultural expressions of gender inequality without interrogating the context in which those inequalities were produced. Increasingly, historians have highlighted the multiplicity of masculinities in any one period of time: within this mix, one or more definitions may be "hegemonic" and exert a controlling force on other definitions. Furthermore, the focus on the experience of the historical subject and the growing history of selfhood challenge the depiction of one type of masculine figure as dominant. A single hegemonic masculinity does not necessarily operate in a vacuum and is not the sole organizing factor in influencing male subjectivity. This debate begs the question: how then did British servicemen in Korea see themselves in Korea—as "men of the world" or "uniformed boys"?

Masculinity and British Servicemen in the Korean War

To a certain extent servicemen were very aware of the figure of the soldier hero and the model of masculinity expected of them. Culturally, the soldier had long stood for adventure, daring, and masculinity.[58] For younger servicemen, their perception of war was influenced by their fathers' memories of the Second World War. For example, Private Anthony Baker's father wrote to his son in Korea about his memories of the Second World War, and Robin Bruford-Davies, an officer taken as a prisoner of war during Korea, mentioned in an oral history interview that his father, who had been a soldier before him and "had just finished a war, said 'right, you must go out with some proper clothes,'" knowing the particular importance of keeping hands and feet warm.[59] Many young servicemen like Bruford-Davies mention that "everybody else had just had a war" and they had been keen to go to Korea to "do their bit."[60] Some phrased this in terms of male bonding, signing up for Korea because their friends were also going.[61] John Martin, who joined the K-Force volunteers, explained why in his later memoir: "The fascination for the K-Force contract was the combat appeal for those who had missed out on World War II, were bored to tears with civvie street and were missing the shots of adrenalin and comradeship of previous service."[62]

If memory of the Second World War dominated the experiences of younger men in Korea, does this mean that older ideas of masculinity remained hegemonic in the early Cold War? According to Connell, hegemonic masculinity is also underwritten by violence. To some extent military violence was still seen as the most legitimate form of masculine experience. This argument, however, is not unproblematic. As Joanna Bourke writes, gauging violence can be very difficult when analyzing wartime experiences. Moreover, Connell argues, the number of servicemen involved in hand-to-hand killing is comparatively few, given the advances and specialization in military technology.[63] Although the Korean War was itself like many conventional conflicts before it, some scholars maintain that the Cold War at large was even more detached from older established notions of hand-to-hand combat.[64]

Whether the Cold War saw a decline in violence itself (and many historians dispute this claim), older ideas that a soldier's worth was judged only by his performance and proximity to battle remained active during the Korean War and the early Cold War period. We must remember, Bourke argues, that the "characteristic act of war is not dying, it is killing."[65] The persistence of this view is evident from a surprising and overlooked body of source material: the battle experience questionnaire. In 1951, the Questionnaire and War Diary Section of the Directorate of Tactical Investigation at the War Office revived a practice from the Second World War, giving officers returning from Korea a standard form of ten questions.[66] Responses were usually handwritten and completed within four months of the officers' time in Korea; after being completed, they were returned to the War Office for analysis by Major Philip Hugh Godsal.[67] Although historians have previously used this material to analyze the empirical aspects of military experience (as most questions focused on enemy tactics), it is possible to read them instead for what they divulge about subjectivity and how servicemen thought of themselves in the war.[68]

As well as writing "N.K." (not known), officers provided a variety of responses on enemy tactics, equipment shortages, and morale. However, most notably, many officers used these forms to distance themselves from what they saw as the "real" war. Captain G. R. Hill wrote: "During my whole service in Korea I was situated in rear div. area and never actually had battle experience in the sense of the word." Another respondent noted that he had "no real first-hand knowledge of the actual front line tactics except at second hand and occasional visits to the front. I shall avoid 'hearsay' knowledge."[69] These responses show the desire to provide an authentic account of battle, but they also indicate that some officers simply did not see their job in the army as having much relationship to enemy combat at all, let alone to protecting democracy as a dutiful soldier-citizen. For many, the term "battle" entailed a specific action between combatant forces, planned and carried out on an operational level. As Carolyn Steedman notes, soldiers frequently see war and its highfalutin ideals as "not to do with them."[70] Some did their best to reproduce the answers they felt the War Office wanted, despite their lack of personal experience. For instance, one captain admitted at the very bottom of his quite-detailed questionnaire that "much of this pro forma . . . [was] not compiled from personal experience."[71] All these responses demonstrate that officers had an idea that contact with the enemy or actual work on the front line itself is what constituted "battle experience." Military experience and proximity to battle were clearly prized among British servicemen and used as a yardstick against which to measure themselves.

The responses to battle experience forms demonstrate again the enduring importance of the Second World War to British servicemen in the Korean War, influencing how they interpreted their own military experience. When describing the weapons that had the greatest effect on morale, Captain Bergin noted: "The enemy had nothing in my opinion that had any great effect on morale. The general opinion was that their weapons were nothing in comparison to those used against us in 1939–1945."[72] The majority of responses tallied with this statement, although many noted the destabilizing effect of accurate mortar fire, as well as factors such as "lack of info" provided to troops, the weather, lack of support from newspapers at home, and even "the use of women as infantry by the Communist."[73] The cultural memory of the Second World War nevertheless pervades these forms. Furthermore, active frontline fighting is frequently used as the benchmark against which to measure military experience. Servicemen were therefore at least partially aware that the "murderous hero" was the expected model of a soldier—and of a man.

However, this comparison with the older generation is less obviously gendered than other aspects of Korean War experience. The language used by both social commentators and servicemen to describe the war addressed contemporary gender relations as a direct result of the cultural and social realities of 1950s Britain. In the opening paragraph of one of the few British novels on Korea, *A Hill in Korea* by Simon Kent (the pen name of Max Catto), Lieutenant Jeff Butler describes a hill he can see while on patrol as "exactly like a woman's tit," although "he did this with an abstract kind of diffidence, being a literary-minded Winchester man."[74] There are repeated references to the Korean landscape as female and sexualized and to the crass, violent nature of the British men seeking to conquer it.[75] For example, Butler notes to himself that in war "men . . . lost their inhibitions naturally" but that when urinating "it was instinctive to most at such moments to avert their backs." However, one particularly war-battered regular private chose to face the men, "exposing himself, like a horse raising a puddle; and they looked at him coldly, then turned away."[76] In an even more explicit description of a bayonet attack, Kent portrays even the enemy as female: "Clutching the hot foreign face to his in a horrid embrace, he [Butler] pressed the point of the bayonet, twice, rapidly, into the throat. It went in like butter. There was a warm gush of blood and it ran over Butler's face. The man was quivering, but only for a moment: then flaccid. He lay gently in Butler's arms like a satiated lover. The orgasm was over."[77] This fictional representation of the enemy does diverge from the more standard descriptions of the enemy: numerous British servicemen refer to the Chinese Army as a "wave," "red flood," or "hoard," using the racialized nineteenth-century language to describe their enemy and rarely describing contact with particular individuals.[78] Nevertheless, sexual imagery has long been used to describe warfare, and *A Hill in Korea* in no exception. But, as Vinen argues, national service, removing young men from female company, meant that sex became "a matter of words rather than deeds."[79] Sexual language was ubiquitous among younger men and was an ever-present part of British Army speech in the early 1950s. One might argue that such language is not unique to the soldier or young man of this period. However, as Gill Plain argues, this particular type of "banter," originating in public schools and the military, became a crucial part of negotiating "acceptable masculinities" in the postwar era.[80] It is of little wonder, then, that servicemen used it when describing the Korean War. On the voyage to Korea many servicemen mention passing through the exotic Port Said and how many of their fellow soldiers "painted the town a rather lurid colour."[81] Such language was also influenced by changes in health education: as Lesley Hall observes, by 1950 it had become acceptable for authorities like the military to advise on certain aspects of sexual behavior.[82] One serviceman describes in his diary the "endless" lectures on venereal disease they received, warning about the dangers of prostitutes when on leave in Japan.[83] By the 1950s, therefore, sex, sexual language, and sexual education were an acknowledged part of military experience.

However, it is important to acknowledge the variations in sexual language and, crucially, the class differences between British servicemen in Korea. The majority of national service conscripts were working class, and middle-class, grammar-school-educated young men were often shocked by the language used by their fellow recruits.[84] For example, national serviceman Mel Calman recalls a sense of hitherto-unknown manly friendship cultivated through the communal use of foul language to describe women.[85] Likewise, in *A Hill in Korea* it is made clear that the regular soldier who urinated publically was from a different social background than many of the middle-class men in his platoon. Sexual language therefore carried a different significance for young men from particular educational and social backgrounds; these differences highlight the importance of addressing the variety of masculine subjects in this context.

These men's use of gendered language was not restricted to the 1950s: veterans writing in the late 1990s often describe national service as the "making of them," turning them into men. While their fathers' Second World War experiences had, even in the 1950s, eclipsed their own experiences and continued to dominate popular and national discourse, their experience in Korea formed no such shadow over future generations of British men. Many former servicemen lamented modern masculinity at the end of the twentieth century. Penny Summerfield has highlighted the importance of intergenerational relationships in the memory of conflict, specifically the Second World War.[86] The simultaneous sense of obligation to a former generation and bafflement at subsequent generations that Summerfield describes also resonates with the descriptions in Korean War memoirs, particularly those about national service. Korean War veteran Harold Davis wrote in his memoir that national service "is the best thing a young man can do. . . . I can say that being in the Army stands you in good stead for the rest of your life."[87] Some servicemen credited the military with making them into "men."[88] Davis saw duty and discipline as standard markers of masculinity, echoing the definition of active citizenship prevalent in the mid-twentieth century. Interestingly, the gendered subjectivity of the veteran is seldom considered in any great detail by researchers, except by health-care professionals.[89] Ruth Jolly's study of servicemen leaving the military, *Changing Step*, purposefully makes no distinction between male and female veterans.[90] Yet, as Connell contends, the fighting man is an enduring, central image of masculinity in modern society, even given the reduction in military service.[91] It is unlikely that veterans were unaffected by this characterization of masculinity and exclusion from active citizenship once they had grown old. The characteristic image of the veteran is an old, infirm man or a broken body of a young man, both of which evoke impotence and feminization.[92] From this standpoint, then, veterans criticized subsequent generations of young men, showing that particular definitions of masculinity continue to matter after military service.

"Against Hegemony"?

Although forgotten in the United Kingdom today, the Korean War exposes much of the debate about Britain's role in the post-1945 world, a debate that encompassed discussion about masculinity, both within Britain and on an international stage. However, as this chapter has shown, while parliamentarians, novelists, and commentators debated whether Britain's soldiers in Korea were "men" or "boys," masculinity had a profound impact on servicemen and on the subjectivity and writing of veterans. The chapter also raises potential questions about the continued use of hegemony in Cold War historiography and gender studies. Westad's stance "against hegemony" in Cold War history undoubtedly has interesting consequences for scholars of both geopolitical change and gender relations. As is evident from the argument above, the model of hegemonic masculinity fits uneasily with the realities of lived, gendered experience in the Korean War. Vying notions of manhood—the democratic citizen, the imperial adventurer, the ambivalent youth—infused the language of British servicemen in Korea. However, this does not mean that the concept has no use. As Westad notes, any claim to hegemony is a claim to power. Thus, claims that masculinity itself follows one particular model or pattern are used to support the power of particular interest groups. Connell has defended the concept as well, arguing that some "hegemonic masculinities can be constructed [that] do not correspond closely to the lives of any actual men. Yet these models do, in various ways, express widespread ideals, fantasies, and desires. They provide models of relations with women and solutions to problems of gender relations."[93] Hegemonic masculinity is *always* infused with unrealistic expectations and mythologized pasts, but this does not mean that such myths cannot have a direct influence on self-perception. The British Army needed its soldiers to be perceived—and to perceive themselves—as "men of the world" in the threatening years after the Second World War, just as rearmament opponents needed them to be "boys," sent needlessly to a place few British people could find on a map. One might argue that this highlights the fragility of the concept still further: if the state or interest groups *need* to promote particular models of masculinity, then perhaps other models have greater sway. Uniquely perhaps, servicemen in the Korean War readily acknowledged these contradictory definitions and made no claims to the mythologized images of masculinity associated with the previous generation. War had "made them" into men, but the Second World War, so present in popular consciousness, continued to act as the yardstick against which battle experience was measured.

On balance, then, if we are to answer Westad's call and take a stand against hegemony in Cold War historiography, we must first identify when polities, groups, and individuals are seeking to establish it, and then distinguish among variations across space and time. However successful these models were in practice, we must pinpoint when certain gender definitions are purported as dominant or as the norm in particular societies; otherwise, the lived, gendered experience of the historical subject, like Cold War politics beyond the United States, will continue to be sidelined.

Notes

This work was kindly supported by the University of Warwick under the Chancellor's Scholarship scheme. My thanks also go to all the reviewers for their insightful comments.

1. Anthony Perrins, *"A Pretty Rough Do Altogether": The Fifth Fusiliers in Korea, 1950–1951, An Apercu* (Alnwick: Fusiliers Museum of Northumberland, 2004), 337; Russell Frederick Edwards, unpublished memoir, May 2008, National Army Museum, Docs. 19562, 50; Ron Larby, *Signals to the Right, Armored Corps to the Left* (Leamington Spa: Korvet, 1993), 173–74.

2. Charles S. Young, "POWs: The Hidden Reason for Forgetting Korea," *Journal of Strategic Studies* 33, no. 2 (2010): 317–32.

3. James Hinton, *Nine Wartime Lives. Mass-Observation and the Making of the Modern Self* (Oxford: Oxford University Press, 2010), 1; Michael Paris, *Warrior Nation: Images of War in British Popular Culture, 1850–2000* (London: Reaktion, 2000), 221.

4. David Kynaston focuses largely on the economic consequences of the Korean War in his study of the postwar Labour government (1945–1951), and David Edgerton, whose book *Warfare State* puts forward the argument that Britain's economy was still geared up for war—not welfare—after 1945, does not explore Korea in detail. See David Kynaston, *Austerity Britain, 1945–51* (London: Bloomsbury, 2008), 345–51; and David Edgerton, *Warfare State: Britain 1920–1970* (New York: Cambridge University Press, 2006), 5.

5. Gill Plain, *John Mills and British Cinema: Masculinity, Identity and Nation* (Edinburgh: Edinburgh University Press, 2006), 16.

6. Richard Vinen, *National Service: Conscription in Britain 1945–1963* (London: Penguin, 2014), 163.

7. In 1940, the Crown Film Unit (CFU) succeeded the Empire Marketing Board Film Unit (1930–1933) and the General Post Office Film Unit (1933–1940) in making centrally funded documentary films. The CFU was discontinued in 1952 because of criticism over its costs. Central government films were increasingly made by private firms such as the Shell Film Unit from the mid-1940s. See Imperial War Museum, "Personnel Selection in the British Army," prod. Shell Film Unit, 1944, UKY 591;

Jack C. Ellis and Betsy A. McLane, *A New History of Documentary Film* (New York: Continuum, 2005), 154; and Paul Swann, *The British Documentary Film Movement, 1926–1946* (Cambridge: Cambridge University Press, 1989), 164.

8. *Men of the World*, dir. Ronald Clark (Crown Film Unit, 1950); James Blackford, *BFI Central Office of Information (COI) Collection: Films from Britain, vol. 3* (London: BFI, 2010), 6–7.

9. Journalist Andrew Roth argued that the "armed ground soldier is still in the decisive force in modern warfare"; see Andrew Roth, "Persia Turns the Military Scales," article manuscript, September 15, 1950, Bishopsgate Institute Library, Andrew Roth Papers, ROTH/3/20.

10. Brian Harrison, *Seeking a Role: The United Kingdom, 1951–1970* (Oxford: Oxford University Press, 2009), 6.

11. Graham Dawson, *Soldier Heroes: British Adventure, Empire and the Imagining of Masculinities* (London: Routledge, 1994), 53–78; Carolyn Steedman, *The Radical Soldier's Tale: John Pearman, 1819–1908* (London: Routledge, 1988), 39.

12. *Hansard's Parliamentary Debates*, 5th Series, vol. 486, cols. 2143–54.

13. Aldous Huxley, *Brave New World Revisited* (London: Chatto and Windus, 1959), 8.

14. R. W. Connell, "Masculinity, Violence and War," in *Men's Lives*, ed. Michael S. Kimmel and Michael A. Messner (New York: Macmillan, 1992), 179.

15. National Army Museum, *Project Korea: The British Soldier in Korea, 1950–3* (London: NAM, 1988), 8.

16. *Hansard's Parliamentary Debates*, 5th Series, vol. 478, cols. 1410–92.

17. *Hansard's Parliamentary Debates*, 5th Series, vol. 550, cols. 2440–48.

18. *Hansard's Parliamentary Debates*, 5th Series, vol. 484, cols. 408–550.

19. Sean Greenwood, *Britain and the Cold War, 1945–91* (Basingstoke: Macmillan, 2000), 73.

20. Penny Summerfield, "'She Wants a Gun Not a Dishcloth!': Gender, Service and Citizenship in Britain in the Second World War," in *A Soldier and a Woman: Sexual Integration in the Military*, ed. Gerard J. DeGroot and Corinna Peniston-Bird (Harlow: Pearson Education, 2000), 119–20.

21. Lucy Noakes and Susan Grayzel, "Defending the Homeland: Gendering Civil Defence from the First World War to the 'War on Terror,'" in *Gender and Conflict since 1914: Historical and Interdisciplinary Approaches*, ed. Ana Carden-Coyne (New York: Palgrave, 2012), 31.

22. Andrew Hammond, *British Fiction and the Cold War* (Basingstoke: Palgrave, 2013), 159.

23. Anthony Giddens, *Modernity and Self Identity: Self and Society in the Late Modern Age* (Cambridge: Polity, 1991), 244.

24. Labour Party, *Let Us Face the Future: A Declaration of Labour Policy for the Consideration of the Nation* (London: Labour Party, 1945), 9.

25. *Two Ways of Life*, dir. Peter Bryan (War Office, 1958). This film was a War Office Production, Crown copyright July 1958. It was produced for the Army Kinema Corporation by Associated British-Pathé.

26. Plain, *John Mills and British Cinema*, 2.

27. William Golding, *Lord of the Flies* (London: Faber, 1954).

28. Richard Phillips, *Mapping Men and Empire: Geographies of Adventure* (Abingdon: Routledge, 1997), 151.

29. Hammond, *British Fiction and the Cold War*, 60.

30. Callum Macdonald, *Britain and the Korean War* (Oxford: Blackwell, 1990), 27–28.

31. Sean Greenwood, "'A War We Don't Want': Another Look at the British Labour Government's Commitment in Korea, 1950–51," *Contemporary British History* 17, no. 4 (Winter 2003): 1–24.

32. Instructions to UK Representative at the United Nations, June 1950, Bodleian Special Collections, Clement Attlee Papers, MS Attlee 102.227; Statement by the Prime Minister, February 1, 1951, Clement Attlee papers, MS Attlee 118.2–7.

33. *Hansard's Parliamentary Debates*, 5th Series, vol. 477, cols. 485–596.

34. Ibid.

35. Aaron Belkin, *Bring Me Men: Military Masculinity and the Benign Façade of American Empire, 1898–2001* (London: Hurst, 2012), 5.

36. Marko Dumančić, "Spectrums of Oppression: Gender and Sexuality during the Cold War," *Journal of Cold War Studies* 16, no. 3 (2014): 190–91.

37. Susan E. Reid, "Cold War in the Kitchen: Gender and the De-Stalinisation of Consumer Taste in the Soviet Union under Khrushchev," *Slavic Review* 61, no. 2 (2002): 211–52; Katherine Pence, "'You As a Woman Will Understand': Gender and the Relationship between State and Citizenship in the GDR's Crisis of 17 June 1953," *German History* 19, no. 2 (2001): 218–52; also quoted in Dumančić, "Spectrums of Oppression," 190.

38. K. A. Cuordileone, *Manhood and American Political Culture in the Cold War* (New York: Routledge, 2005), xx.

39. Hammond, *British Fiction and the Cold War*, 67–69.

40. Vinen, *National Service*, 162–97.

41. Dumančić, "Spectrums of Oppression," 192.

42. Anders Stephanson, "Cold War Degree Zero," in *Uncertain Empire: American History and the Idea of the Cold War*, ed. Joel Isaac and Duncan Bell (New York: Oxford University Press, 2012), 22; Federico Romero, "Cold War Historiography at the Crossroads," *Cold War History* 14, no. 4 (2014): 685–703.

43. Romero, "Cold War Historiography at the Crossroads," 687.

44. Ibid.

45. Odd Arne Westad, "Exploring Histories of the Cold War. A Pluralist Approach," in Isaac and Bell, *Uncertain Empire*, 52.

46. Connell, "Masculinity, Violence and War," 178.

47. John Hopton, "The State and Military Masculinity," in *Military Masculinities: Identity and State*, ed. Paul Higate (London: Praeger, 2003), 113.

48. Belkin, *Bring Me Men*, 6.

49. Sandra Via, "Gender, Militarism and Globalization: Soldiers for Hire and Hegemonic Masculinity," in *Gender, War and Militarism. Feminist Perspective*, ed. Laura Sjoberg and Sandra Via (Santa Barbara, CA: Praegar, 2010), 43.

50. John Tosh, "Hegemonic Masculinity and the History of Gender," in *Masculinities in Politics and War: Gendering Modern History*, ed. Stefan Dudnik, Karen Hagemann, and John Tosh (New York: Palgrave, 2004), 42.

51. Ibid., 44.

52. Connell, "Masculinity, Violence and War," 178.

53. William Shakespeare, *Henry V*, act 4, scene 3, line 66; Samuel Johnson (1778) is quoted in Yuval Noah Harari, *The Ultimate Experience: Battlefield Revelations and the Making of Modern War Culture, 1450–2000* (Basingstoke: Palgrave, 2008), 1; Joanna Bourke, *An Intimate History of Killing: Face-to-Face Killing in Twentieth-Century Warfare* (London: Granta, 2000), 67.

54. Richard Holmes, *Firing Line* (London: Cape, 1985), 8–9; John Keegan, *The Face of Battle: A Study of Agincourt, Waterloo and the Somme* (London: Pimlico, 1991), 15; Jay Winter, "Representations of War and the Social Construction of Silence," in *Fighting Words and Image: Representing War across the Disciplines*, ed. Elena V. Baraban, Stephan Jaegar, and Adam Muller (Toronto: University of Toronto Press, 2012), 31.

55. R. W. Connell and James W. Messerschmidt, "Hegemonic Masculinity: Rethinking the Concept," *Gender and Society* 19, no. 6 (2005): 833–35.

56. Tosh, "Hegemonic Masculinity and the History of Gender," 45.

57. Ibid., 56.

58. Dawson, *Soldier Heroes*, 53–78; Steedman, *Radical Soldier's Tale*, 39.

59. Papers of Anthony John Baker, December 3, 1950, National Army Museum (henceforth NAM) 1990-12-34; Oral history Interview of Robin Bruford-Davies by David Smurthwaite, February 10, 1989, NAM 1989-05-163.

60. Oral history interview of Robin Bruford-Davies by David Smurthwaite, February 10, 1989, NAM 1989-05-163; Papers of D. F. Barrett, unpublished autobiography, 2000, 4:94, NAM 2000-88-55.

61. Oral history interview of Thomas Ashley Cunningham-Boothe by Conrad Wood, December 8 1999, 19913, Imperial War Museum (henceforth IWM).

62. John Martin, *K-Force: To the Sharp-End* (Leamington Spa: Korvet, 1999), 2–3.

63. Bourke, *Intimate History of Killing*, 9; Connell, "Masculinity, Violence and War," 181.

64. For instance, in 2007 Steven Pinker controversially argued that "today we may be living in the most peaceable era in our species' existence" and that the world had become progressively less violent. See Stephen Pinker, *The Better Angels of Our Nature* (New York: Allen Lane, 2011), xxi. Lawrence Freedman tests the thesis on the Cold War context; see Lawrence Freedman, "Stephen Pinker and the Long Peace: Alliance, Deterrence and Decline," *Cold War History* 14, no. 4 (2014): 657–72.

65. Bourke, *An Intimate History of Killing*, 1.

66. This was extended to eleven questions in the second half of 1952.

67. Godsal was formerly of the Ox and Bucks Light Infantry and was well-known for escaping from a German prisoner-of-war camp in 1917. See Report by Captain P. H. Godsal, April 30, 1917, National Archives (henceforth TNA), Foreign Office, Treatment of British Prisoners of War in Germany, FO 383/266; Letter from Major P. H. Godsal to Captain R. W. B. Oatts, Korea: Battle Experience Questionnaire, May 21, 1952, TNA, War Office (DTI), WO 308.89; Letter from Major P. H. Godsal to Captain F. H. B. Matthews (REME), Essex, Korea: Battle Experience Questionnaire, May 19, 1952, TNA, War Office (DTI), WO 308.89.

68. David French, *Army, Empire and Cold War: The British Army and Military Policy, 1945–1971* (Oxford: Oxford University Press, 2012), 139; Robert Engen, *Canadians under Fire: Infantry Effectiveness in the Second World War* (Montreal: McGill-Queen's University Press, 2009).

69. Captain G. R. Hill, Korea: Battle Experience Questionnaire, 1952 (no exact date given), War Office (DTI), WO 308.90; Lieutenant Marshall, Korea: Battle Experience Questionnaire, December 15, 1952, TNA, War Office (DTI), WO 308.90.

70. Steedman, *Radical Soldier's Tale*, 42.

71. Captain P. Benn, DCLI, Korea: Battle Experience Questionnaire, July 21, 1952, TNA, War Office (DTI), WO 308.90.

72. Captain H. J. Bergin, Korea: Battle Experience Questionnaire, September 11, 1951, War Office (DTI), WO 308.90.

73. Major A. J. S. de S Clayton, Korea: Battle Experience Questionnaire, September 12, 1951, War Office (DTI), WO 308.90; Lieutenant H. L. Ackers, Korea: Battle Experience Questionnaire, September 17, 1952, TNA, War Office (DTI), WO 308.90. In a few limited instances, women did occupy combat roles in Communist armies; see Paul M. Edwards, *Historical Dictionary of the Korean War*, 2nd ed. (Plymouth, MA: Scarecrow, 2010), 337.

74. Simon Kent, *A Hill in Korea* (Watford: Hutchinson University Book Club, 1954), 1.

75. Ibid., 37 and 84.

76. Ibid., 17.

77. Ibid., 112–13.

78. Major J. L. Bromhead, Korea: Battle Experience Questionnaire, April 17, 1952, TNA, War Office (DTI), WO 308.89; Major C. W. Woods, Korea: Battle Experience Questionnaire, August 31, 1952, War Office (DTI), WO 308.90.

79. Vinen, *National Service*, 184.

80. Plain, *John Mills and British Cinema*, 15.

81. Oral history interview of Sebastian "Sam" Mercer by David Smurthwaite, July 18, 1988, NAM 8905.

82. Lesley Hall, *Hidden Anxieties: Male Sexuality, 1900–1950* (Cambridge: Polity, 1991), 170.

83. Papers of C. B. L. Barr, diary, May 11, 1954, IWM, Docs. 7178.

84. Vinen, *National Service*, 92.

85. Mel Calman in B. S. Johnson, *All Bull: The National Servicemen* (London: Quartet Books, 1973), 125.

86. Penny Summerfield, "The Generation of Memory: Gender and the Popular Memory of the Second World War in Britain," in *British Cultural Memory and the Second World War*, ed. Lucy Noakes and Juliette Pattinson (London: Bloomsbury, 2014), 28.

87. Harold Davis, with Paul Smith, *Tougher than Bullets: The Heroic Tale of a Black Watch Survivor of the Korean War* (Edinburgh: Mainstream, 2012), 22.

88. Letter from Ron Laver to Mr. Miller, August 31, 2003, Papers of Ron Laver, NAM 2005–04–19/1.

89. S. M. Frane et al., "Gender Disparities in Veterans Health Administration Care: Importance of Accounting for Veteran Status," *Medical Care* 46, no. 5 (2008): 549–53.

90. Ruth Jolly, *Changing Step: From Military to Civilian Life; People in Transition* (London: Brassey's, 1996), viii.

91. Connell, "Masculinity, Violence and War," 177.

92. R. W. Connell argues that even in training, the inability to complete a given task or to be suitably "soldierly" prompts instructors to call recruits "girls" (or similar expressions) as a term of abuse. See Connell, "Masculinity, Violence and War," 177–79.

93. Connell and Messerschmidt, "Hegemonic Masculinities," 838.

References

Archives

Bishopsgate Institute Library, London, United Kingdom
Bodleian Library, Oxford, United Kingdom
Imperial War Museum, London, United Kingdom
National Archives, Kew, United Kingdom
National Army Museum, London, United Kingdom

Films

Men of the World (dir. Ronald Clark, Crown Film Unit, 1950).
Two Ways of Life (dir. Peter Bryan, War Office, 1958).

Selected Published Works

Belkin, Aaron. *Bring Me Men: Military Masculinity and the Benign Facade of American Empire, 1898–2001*. London: Hurst, 2012.

Bourke, Joanna. *An Intimate History of Killing: Face-to-Face Killing in Twentieth-Century Warfare*. London: Granta, 2000.

Connell, R. W. "Masculinity, Violence and War." In *Men's Lives*, edited by Michael S. Kimmel and Michael A. Messner, 176–83. New York: Macmillan, 1992.

Connell, R. W., and Messerschmidt, James W. "Hegemonic Masculinity: Rethinking the Concept." *Gender and Society* 19, no. 6 (2005): 829–59.

Dawson, Graham. *Soldier Heroes: British Adventure, Empire and the Imagining of Masculinities*. London: Routledge, 1994.

Dumančić, Marko. "Spectrums of Oppression: Gender and Sexuality during the Cold War." *Journal of Cold War Studies* 16, no. 3 (2014): 190–204.

French, David. *Army Empire and Cold War: The British Army and Military Policy, 1945–1971*. Oxford: Oxford University Press, 2012.

Golding, William. *Lord of the Flies*. London: Faber, 1954.

Hammond, Andrew. *British Fiction and the Cold War*. Basingstoke: Palgrave, 2013.

Huxley, Aldous. *Brave New World Revisited*. London: Chatto and Windus, 1959.

Kent, Simon. *A Hill in Korea*. Watford: Hutchinson University Book Club, 1954.

Labour Party. *Let Us Face the Future: A Declaration of Labour Policy for the Consideration of the Nation*. London: Labour Party, 1945.

Noakes, Lucy, and Susan Grayzel. "Defending the Homeland: Gendering Civil Defence from the First World War to the 'War on Terror.'" In *Gender and Conflict since 1914: Historical and Interdisciplinary Approaches*, edited by Ana Carden-Coyne, 53–70. New York: Palgrave, 2012.

Plain, Gill. *John Mills and British Cinema: Masculinity, Identity and Nation*. Edinburgh: Edinburgh University Press, 2006.

Romero, Federico. "Cold War Historiography at the Crossroads" *Cold War History* 14, no. 4 (2014): 685–703.

Steedman, Carolyn. *The Radical Soldier's Tale: John Pearman 1819–1908*. London: Routledge, 1988.

Summerfield, Penny. "'She Wants a Gun Not a Dishcloth!': Gender, Service and Citizenship in Britain in the Second World War." In *A Soldier and a Woman: Sexual Integration in the Military*, edited by Gerard J. DeGroot and Corinna Peniston-Bird, 119–20. Harlow: Pearson Education, 2000.

Tosh, John. "Hegemonic Masculinity and the History of Gender." In *Masculinities in Politics and War: Gendering Modern History*, edited by Stefan Dudnik, Karen Hagemann, and John Tosh, 41–58. New York: Palgrave, 2004.

Vinen, Richard. *National Service: Conscription in Britain 1945–1963*. London: Penguin, 2014.

Westad, Odd Arne. "Exploring Histories of the Cold War. A Pluralist Approach." In *Uncertain Empire: American History and the Idea of the Cold War*, edited by Joel Isaac and Duncan Bell, 51–60. New York: Oxford University Press, 2012.

CHAPTER 13

Yuri Gagarin and Celebrity Masculinity in Soviet Culture

Erica L. Fraser

In April 1961, Yuri Gagarin became the first person to successfully orbit the earth. Seated in the cramped capsule of *Vostok-1*, Gagarin was launched from the Baikonur Cosmodrome in Kazakhstan and executed one full orbit before landing again. He was a twenty-seven-year-old senior lieutenant in the Soviet Air Force with a wife and two young daughters, and his face and name were about to explode onto headlines around the world. Overturning years of secrecy about the cosmonaut training program, the Soviet government publicized Gagarin's historic flight as soon as he landed. Such publicity was partly meant to announce to the United States that Soviet rocket technology had successfully sent a man to space and could, presumably, launch missiles just as far, but the publicity surrounding Gagarin's feat conveyed more than coded military and scientific messages. Not selected for any particular skill on the flight deck, Gagarin was rather a man who, as historian Andrew Jenks has observed, was "straight out of Soviet central casting"—a handsome, articulate, and charismatic young military officer with a famously bright smile.[1]

In cultivating his image both at home and abroad, space program authorities presented a particular image of Soviet masculinity for the Cold War, one that would ideally stabilize masculine authority in flux since World War II. The careful ways in which his masculinized image was packaged and sold in the early 1960s sparked a lasting space-hero cult of celebrity. A space suit on its own can render sex and gender invisible, after all; before the 1960s, both Soviet and Western science fiction featured robotic spacemen with neutral boxed heads and torsos. Advancing space technology that placed humans in the suits opened a path for revealing the contents of the space suit to the public on earth. As cultural critic Stefan Brandt has written of American space culture, "the body of the astronaut [was] increasingly used as a projection screen for anxieties concerning the stability of gender categories."[2] The narrative of Soviet masculinity projected onto Gagarin, the first man in the world to emerge from that suit, reveals anxieties about the gendered cultural terrain of the Soviet Union after World War II, particularly regarding sex, family, authority, and service.

Previous studies of the Soviet cosmonauts have focused on the scientific and political negotiations that led to Gagarin's flight, and, more recently, social historians in both Russia and the West have begun to crack the almost-hagiographic narrative about Gagarin.[3] The gendered aspects of his public persona have not been fully investigated, however. The first part of this chapter will discuss Gagarin's image in Soviet culture as he dominated newspapers, periodicals, films, and other visual media after his flight. The second part will explore Gagarin's image abroad. From the summer of 1961 through much of 1962, Gagarin played the roles of global celebrity, public relations envoy, and cultural attaché, dispatched to nearly every corner of the globe, including Brazil, India, Japan, Canada, the United Kingdom, Bulgaria, Soviet Uzbekistan, Egypt, Afghanistan, Ghana, and Liberia.

Gagarin's domestic and global image drew on understandings of masculinity that anchored Cold War ideology for both Soviet audiences and a variety of global publics. Those understandings included the security of the family, the primacy of military expertise, and the diplomatic acumen to peacefully navigate the new world order. That Gagarin was routinely portrayed as an expert in all these areas is not surprising; as literary critic Lev Danilkin has observed, Gagarin easily "embodied all conceivable manly virtues."[4] Rather, it is the categories themselves that matter. In attaching certain attributes to Gagarin and positioning them as hegemonic in Soviet culture, authorities countered the increasing evidence of plurality in Soviet gender identities since the end of the war, especially for men of Gagarin's generation.

Soviet Masculinities

Since 1917, the Bolshevik revolutionaries had developed the new Soviet state according to particular scripts of masculinity. The foundational civil war that cemented Bolshevik control of the government set the tone for the battle motifs and idealization of masculine soldiering that would follow in Soviet culture, and it influenced the sculpting of healthy male bodies as national symbols in literature, art, and political posters. By the 1930s, Joseph Stalin was able to cultivate support for his dictatorship in part by playing up the paternal image that endeared him as father-comrade of the state. Nationalism relied on the propaganda of masculinized heroes, from Vladimir Lenin and Leon Trotsky during the revolution and civil war to the newly trained tractor drivers of the 1920s, the record-shattering coal miners of the 1930s, and the patriotic soldiers of the 1940s. Socialist iconography of the virile male worker combined with the pervasive patriarchy of the Stalin era to create a heavily masculinized political culture.[5] At the same time, socialist ideology regarding women's equality led to phenomena not widely seen in the West in the first half of the twentieth century, such as most women working outside the home and expansive social services for mothers. During World War II, moreover, Soviet women fought in combat roles and maintained their communities on the home front in the absence of an adequate number of men to fill these roles. By 1946, the deaths of approximately twenty million men in the war had led to the highly visible fact that in the countryside and the cities, in private and public, the Soviet Union had become a country of women.[6] All women soldiers were quickly demobilized after the war, as a major part of the postwar recovery project in Soviet society involved "remasculinizing" the Soviet military and reestablishing masculine role models in the broader society.[7]

Yuri Gagarin and his cosmonaut cohort became leaders in this effort to prescribe Cold War masculinity. Until they were selected for space travel in the late 1950s, proper masculine heroes were difficult for authorities to pin down. Youth in particular had become a troubling category for the Soviet leadership; since the war, young men—especially those who had been too young in the early 1940s to fight—eschewed the traditional scripts for Soviet manhood of labor, service, and sacrifice, instead focusing on consumer goods, leisure, pleasure, and Western music and fashion.[8] Gagarin and the five cosmonauts who followed him into space within two years, known collectively in the press and in participant memoirs as the *shestiorka*, or Group of Six, shared in the instant celebrity that space travel brought them.[9] As historian Slava Gerovitch has shown, the creation of cosmonaut myths and the production of their postflight images were not dictated by any single agency, nor did they preclude the cosmonauts' own involvement.[10] The process relied on a collaborative shaping of cultural understandings of manliness, part of which built on older archetypes (the soldier) and part of which required building up a new masculine hero for the Cold War. According to cosmonaut Gherman Titov, who trained with Gagarin and was also considered for the position of first man in space before fronting the second flight instead, officials wanted the first cosmonaut to be a man "whose will and energy, industriousness and sincere generosity, self-discipline and high feeling of duty were the best example for those who dreamed selflessly to serve the homeland, science, and the people."[11] In practice, these generic attributes translated for Gagarin in his roles as a husband and father, an air force captain, and a savvy diplomat.

Gendering *Sputnik*

Even before Gagarin's flight, public discourse about the machinery of space flight relied on particular formulations of masculinity. In October 1957, the Soviet Union became the first country to successfully launch a satellite, the now-famous *Sputnik*, into space. Links between technological innovation and the success of socialism in the Soviet Union predated the Cold War; the cultural significance of machinery to Soviet industry in the 1920s and 1930s put rocketry into a familiar story in Soviet history. Whereas in the 1920s and 1930s humans were encouraged to become more like machines, in the late 1950s space program representations suggested that machines were becoming more like humans.[12] Technology meant little without a human face. The anthropomorphism of satellites and rockets, moreover, depended on specific visions of masculinity and femininity.

Popular media covering *Sputnik* routinely downplayed the potential military impact of the launch by representing the satellite as an ambitious, enthusiastic, but otherwise harmless little boy. The satirical magazine *Krokodil* consistently published masculinized *Sputnik* imagery in the wake of the satellite's launch. In these cartoons, *Sputnik* was either a male figure itself, or little boys repeatedly

Figure 13.1. "A possible case at the Committee for the Investigation of Un-American Activities. —Do you know, madam, that your son is a communist?" B. Efimov, *Krokodil*, November 10, 1957, 2.

explained its significance to the bewildered women around them. One common female figure in *Sputnik* cartoons was Mother Earth, a proud if passive witness as "her" little boy, *Sputnik*, flew past (fig. 1).[13] In many other cartoons, elderly women failed to appreciate *Sputnik*'s achievement. One cartoon showed a young boy waiting for his grandmother to read him a bedtime story. "Grandmother," he told her, exasperated, "you're telling me stories about flying carpets, when a man-

Figure 13.2. "Grandmother, you're telling me stories about flying carpets, when a man-made satellite is already in flight!" E. Gorokhov, *Krokodil*, October 20, 1957, 2.

made satellite is already in flight!" The grandmother, who did not reply, wore a kerchief tied under her chin, the visual signal of a traditional peasant woman (fig. 2).[14] Another cartoon in the family magazine *Sem'ia i shkola* depicted a young boy in a spacesuit, leaning out the window of a spacecraft. He reached out to a witch riding a broomstick as he passed her. "Come sit, Grandmother, and we will give an old friend a lift," he said.[15] The demonized figure of the babushka, a traditional and sometimes sinister old woman, is well-known in postrevolutionary Soviet culture, particularly in visual representations.[16] The marginalization of feminized elements—peasants, the elderly, and religion—drew on these older cues to cultivate meaning for the Cold War, but they also projected a new vision of male youth as the future of Soviet technological innovation.

Coding *Sputnik* in visual media as not only human but childlike and boyish accomplished two things in addition to marginalizing women from technology and space exploration. First, it downplayed the technology itself. Anthropomorphizing its image suggested to the viewer that the machine was not virile on its own and would not connect with the audiences to which it was being sold. Humanizing the satellite made its launch not only a victory for Soviet science and machinery but for Soviet citizens and workers as well. One image in *Krokodil*, for instance, portrayed *Sputnik* as one of several new satellites waiting to go into orbit. Neatly queued and wearing work clothing and caps, they compared notes about their assignments: one was heading to Mercury, another to Jupiter. Their tasks seemed open to ordinary (male) workers with the enthusiasm to take on a new assignment (fig. 3).[17] Second, casting *Sputnik* as a little boy underlined not only masculinity but youth. As preliminary technology, an achievement in itself but also only a starting point, the satellite had room to mature—both as a scientific project that would pave the way for more sophisticated rocket technology, and as a child whose image could develop into that of an adult man.

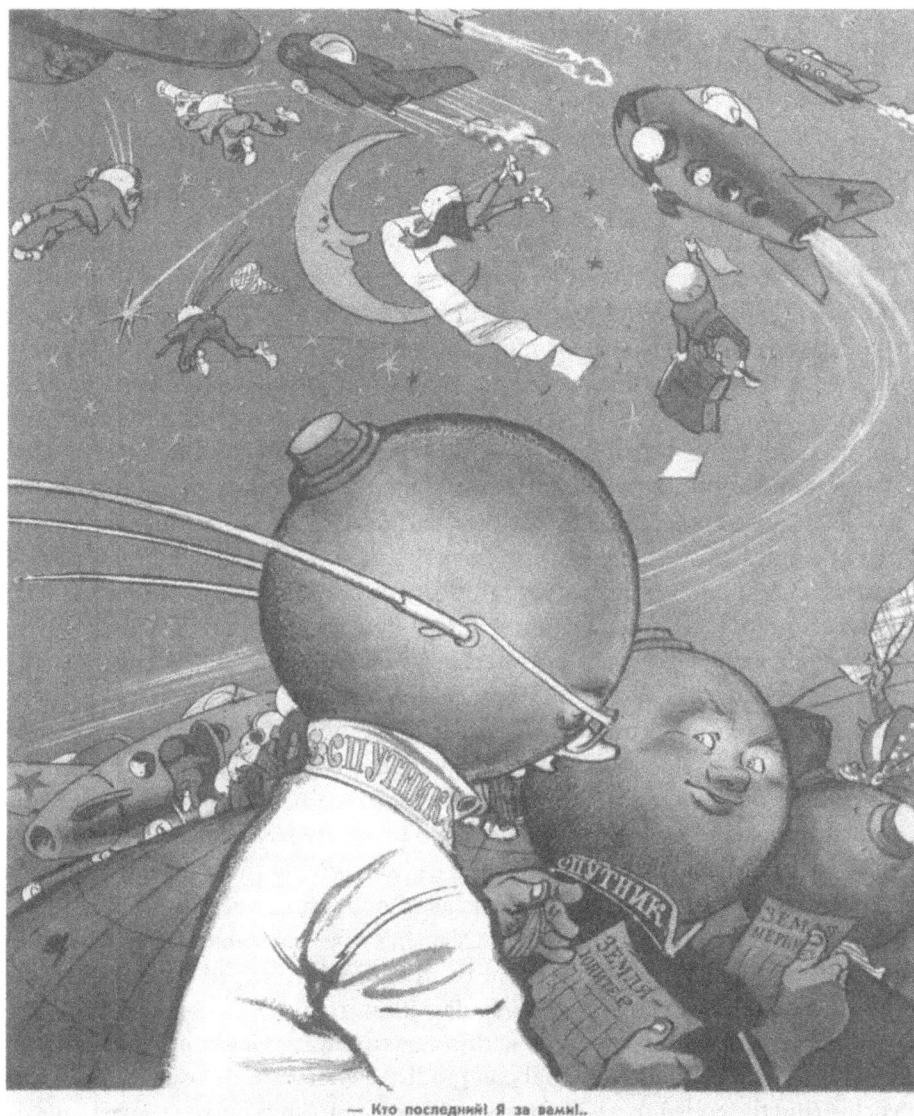

Figure 13.3. "Who's last? I'm after you!" V. Dobrovol'skii, *Krokodil*, November 20, 1957, 1.

Gagarin's Family Values

Less than four years after *Sputnik*, the Soviet government announced its next technological feat: the successful launch, orbit, and landing of Yuri Gagarin's capsule.[18] As his generic flight suit peeled away and the man underneath embarked on a carefully plotted public victory lap, his image as a specific masculine icon came into sharper focus. Like previous Soviet celebrities such as the quota-exceeding coal miner Alexei Stakhanov or the group of pilots who mapped the Arctic in the 1930s, Gagarin's fame relied on his role as an exceptional individual within the collective, a model of a socialist man for the gaze of audiences at home and abroad. Unlike his predecessors, though, the labor of Gagarin's accomplishment was often downplayed in favor of his personality. The cosmonauts in fact neither needed nor were permitted to touch the controls of the spaceship. Maneuvering the actual technology of the flight was not part of their job.[19] The trajectory of Gagarin's fame differed from earlier worker-celebrities in this postwar country still looking to recharge its notions of masculine heroism.

Gagarin as a family man was a crucial theme to his celebrity. This role not only helped establish space travel as a masculine pursuit but also lent a famous face to the government's postwar project of shoring up the war-ravaged Soviet family. While the period of Joseph Stalin's rule from the late 1920s to his death in 1953 is generally seen as much more socially conservative than the eras before and after it, family law after the Second World War largely continued to encourage monogamous marriage alongside parenthood.[20] As an incentive to marry and have children, the 1944 family law decree expanded a 1941 "bachelor tax." Men between the ages of twenty and fifty, and women between the ages of twenty and forty-five, were subject to the tax if they had fewer than three children. At the birth of a third child the tax was no longer levied, and the state began paying mothers a child allowance.[21] Although postwar laws for women provided state and social support for the large number of unmarried mothers in Soviet society after the war, men's legal standing differed significantly. The abolition of paternity laws—as the state took up the role of provider to mothers—meant that all unmarried men were officially childless.[22] In order to escape the bachelor tax, a man had to marry and father at least three children with the same woman, his wife. The law therefore steered men toward monogamous marriage and fatherhood, despite the fact that they were no longer responsible for paternity payments outside of marriage. Particularly at risk, authorities feared, were young men in their late teens and twenties who were susceptible to bachelorhood, aimlessness, and—most worrisome—evasion of military service.[23] Gagarin's role as a stable family patriarch, the country's most famous devoted husband and father, helped cement the value of those roles in Soviet culture and popular discourse.

At the same time, however, and within certain limits, Gagarin was also represented as a desirable (hetero)sexual commodity. Playing on his good looks as well as delivering the coded message that operating a spaceship must be a particularly manly endeavor, space program authorities fashioned Gagarin as a man whom women should desire. In a series of public incidents, Gagarin played right into those expectations, telling a Swedish press conference in which he had been asked about his wife's choice of dresses that "I prefer her without clothing." As historian Andrew Jenks has chronicled, even local hosts on the cosmonauts' postflight tours played into the sexualized image, one Komsomol leader coyly telling a group of women meeting Gagarin and Titov, "You see what kind of boys" they are.[24] Gagarin's appeal was not confined to earth girls, either: a month after his flight, *Krokodil* featured a cartoon of a Martian suitor sneaking up behind his date, causing her to blush as he placed his hands over her eyes. "Gagarin?" she asked hopefully (fig. 4).[25] Despite the trail of female desire that was meant to follow him, however, it was clear in the press that Gagarin was not available. His wife, Valentina, was always portrayed as fully supportive, accompanying him on tours and appearing by his side at public events.

ГДЕ-ТО НА МАРСЕ
— Гагарин!

Figure 13.4. "Somewhere on Mars. —Gagarin?" L. Samoilov, *Krokodil*, May 20, 1961, 12.

Gagarin's safely flirtatious but ultimately conservative image would be mirrored a few years later by the first American astronauts. Although they had a reputation as hard-partying tough guys, owing mostly to their portrayal in Tom Wolfe's famous book *The Right Stuff*, astronauts such as John Glenn played important public roles as family-oriented, well-behaved men humbled in the service of God and country. (Religion would provide the major point of difference between the astronauts and Gagarin's cosmonaut cohort, who used their experiences in space to declare the universe to be man's domain, not God's, and to advance the official atheism of Soviet ideology.)[26] As with the cosmonauts, though, the astronauts' pristine image often masked men who "drove too fast, drank too much, and left their pants in unexpected places."[27]

Soviet space program officials, led by the *shestiorka*'s primary chaperone, General Nikolai Kamanin, went to great lengths to cover up similar activities among the cosmonauts. The most famous incident was not widely known at the time and was revealed only with the publication of Kamanin's diaries in the 1990s. In Crimea with his wife and several other cosmonauts and officials in October 1961, Gagarin was found outside his hotel, unconscious and bleeding from the head in the middle of the night. Emergency surgery saved his life, but he suffered a severe head injury and required three weeks in hospital, which proved difficult to explain to the press. Piecing the story together later, Kamanin concluded that after confirming that his wife was playing cards with others on the trip, an intoxicated Gagarin went upstairs to the room of a twenty-seven-year-old nurse and propositioned her. When his wife knocked on the door looking for him, the nurse later said, he jumped off the balcony to escape, plunging to the courtyard below.[28] When Gagarin continued his tour in India six weeks later, journalists asked him about the scar over his left eyebrow. The question gave Gagarin pause, Kamanin recounted, before his trademark smile returned. On vacation in Crimea in October, he began, he injured himself playing with his younger daughter, Galka. The explanation was rich with descriptions of his wife and daughters, reminding the journalists that Galka was already seven months old and his children were the light of his life.[29] Gagarin's sexuality might have been safely advertised to sell him as a man that men should want to emulate and women should want to marry, but any tales of drunkenness, recklessness, or infidelity were kept carefully from public view.

As part of Gargarin's family-oriented persona, his wife, Valentina, featured prominently in press about him. Public discourse about Valentina Gagarina also helped cement space travel as a masculine endeavor that women could not fully understand or access. After Gagarin's flight, for instance, Soviet leader Nikita Khrushchev acknowledged that neither Gagarin nor other space program officials were permitted to tell Valentina Gagarina the details of the flight, and she did not learn about it until shortly before his departure—owing, she later said, to her advanced pregnancy and the fear of upsetting her.[30] Khrushchev praised her "courage" and "great soul" in supporting her husband unconditionally, despite not knowing the details of his work.[31] In her public role as the cosmonaut's wife, Valentina Gagarina implicitly validated women's domesticity as well as their unsuitability for space flight. "Congratulations to Yuri Alekseevich [Gagarin]'s wife, mother, and sister," one woman wrote to the women's magazine *Rabotnitsa*. "I wish all mothers could experience such great happiness and live through their own Yuri." Another writer thanked Valentina Gagarina, "who was so courageous to see her husband off on this distant path."[32] Other cosmonaut wives were not as supportive, a transgression for which they were publicly judged. Titov, the second man in space, told Khrushchev in the widely reported congratulatory phone call after his flight that his wife had not been pleased to learn of his selection for the flight. "How did your wife feel about [it]?" Khrushchev nudged. "She did not quite approve," Titov admitted, implying that after being told her response was unacceptable for a cosmonaut's wife, "then, she did [approve]."[33]

Documentary films about the Gagarin family were also an important conduit for the domestic coziness that had become key to Gagarin's public masculinity. In one film, whose apparent purpose was only to chronicle the hero's leisure time, Gagarin sunbathed, threw stones into the surf, swam, and went rowing (all without his shirt) while Valentina sat on the beach, happily watching him and rocking a baby carriage.[34] Although the Soviet cosmonaut program also boasted the first woman to travel to space, Valentina Tereshkova, who flew on the sixth mission of the *shestiorka* in 1963, the masculinized character of space travel established through Gagarin's public persona marginalized her achievement.[35] By prominently featuring Gagarin's wife in public discourse about him, authorities cemented Gagarin's image as a family man and also contributed to coding space flight and cosmonaut identity as masculine and normalizing Cold War Soviet masculinity within the family. A profile of Gagarin in the newspaper *Komsomol'skaia pravda* summed it up best:

> He is 27 years old. He lives among us. He sits beside us at films, on Sundays pushing a pram in the park (his family appears to have one more "passenger.") He visits friends, plays basketball and billiards . . . and now he travels to space. Gagarin . . . how many times now has that simple, Russian name been said around the world? And for [Valentina] he is simply Yura. And to Lenochka he is simply papa. And to the world he is a son that we can be eternally proud of.[36]

Cosmonaut Masculinity on Tour

In February 1962, ten months after his flight, Gagarin arrived in Liberia to meet with government officials, tour rubber plantations, and offer sound bites to Soviet, African, and global media about his success. Establishing Gagarin's masculine authority at home was only part of the cultural work Soviet authorities needed him to do. Gagarin and his *shestiorka* colleagues also embarked on a series of world tours, visiting factories in Czechoslovakia, meeting with leaders such as Jawaharlal Nehru in India, and attending receptions with the queen in London.[37] Gagarin's visit to Liberia was only one stop on these tours. While gathered with Liberian government leaders for photographs, Gagarin donned what the Soviet press called the "Liberian national dress" over his ever-present air force uniform, smiling with the group and playing the role in which Soviet authorities had cast him: the celebrity face of science, military honor, and socialism for the consumption of audiences in Cold War battlegrounds around the world, as well as for the Soviet public at home (fig. 5).[38] The exchange of people and cultures through touring was a relatively common feature of the Cold War, at least after Stalin's death, and Gagarin was not the only individual or group deployed for this type of soft power diplomacy. As historian David Caute has shown, during the 1950s and 1960s ballerinas, violinists, chess players, and athletes from all sides of the Cold War traversed the globe to advertise their worldview and way of life.[39] Deploying Gagarin and his cosmonaut cohort, however, also involved selling to a global audience the masculinized persona authorities had constructed at home. That this task was given to a man already famous at home for his sex appeal and family-man persona ensured that masculinity would play a central role in Gagarin's touring. Now added to Gagarin's domestic role as a loyal husband and father was the role of politician and diplomat.

Gagarin's gendered identity mattered to his image as an envoy abroad. The space age was also an era in which a wave of new, young leaders took power in several geo-

Figure 13.5. "Cosmonaut Iu. A. Gagarin in the national dress of Liberia greeting representatives of Liberia, February 1962." A. A. Zvorykin, photographer. RGANTD Fond 173, op. 1, d. 27.

politically strategic states: John F. Kennedy in the United States, Fidel Castro in Cuba, Gamal Nasser in Egypt, and (if only symbolically) Queen Elizabeth II in the United Kingdom. In addition to his use as a propaganda vehicle for marriage and father-hood among Soviet men, Gagarin and, in his wake, the *shestiorka* men became key symbols of youth and virility in government. Maximizing their visual effectiveness in photographs and public appearances, officials either paired the aging Khrushchev with a cosmonaut or allowed the cosmonaut to replace him entirely. Khrushchev met with both John F. Kennedy and Fidel Castro in the summer of 1961, for instance. Meeting Kennedy in Vienna in early June, Khrushchev was photographed with the young president. The images mirror photographs that same spring and summer of Khrushchev with Gagarin, whose youth and megawatt smile matched Kennedy's.[40] Khrushchev's son, reminiscing about Gagarin's welcome in Moscow after his flight, confirms that Khrushchev literally took a backseat to Gagarin's fame:

> [Khrushchev] very much wanted to ride with them in the same car and share their joy; on the other hand, it was their triumph, and, as they say, three's a crowd. It was Gagarin who settled it. He was already in the car, standing there like a marshal about to review his regiments. Yuri smiled at Father and stretched out his hand as though to help him get in. Father took a back seat. Thus they rode the whole route: Leninsky Avenue, the jubilant square that would be named after him, and on to the Kremlin. Yuri and Valentina standing and [Khrushchev] sitting at the back.[41]

In addition to contributing to impressions at home that the Soviet leadership was younger and fresher than was actually the case, Gagarin and his masculine per-sona were dispatched around the world to rebrand the Soviet Union not as an outdated bastion of aged, pensioner-revolutionaries but as a modern, technologically sophisticated state where young, handsome men like Gagarin were building communism and flourishing in the comfortable life it provided.

Deploying Gagarin as a masculine icon, and using his famous smile and charisma to disarm global audiences, also masked the more sinister implications of his space flight. It was well understood in both Soviet and American military circles that, as historian Sue Bridger has pointed out, "Only an extremely powerful missile, one equally capable of delivering a nuclear bomb directly onto American soil, could have propelled *Sputnik* into orbit."[42] The same was true of Gagarin's launch. Gagarin's celebrity image was largely based on his nonthreatening personality as an Everyman who enjoyed vacationing with his family or grabbing a beer with the guys.[43] But in more subtle ways, his fame was also predicated on a careful Soviet script, one in which his military credentials and his performance of soldier masculinity lurked just behind his self-deprecating jokes and casual hand-waves. One key aspect of this second script came in the form of the air force uniform that Gagarin, Titov, and the other men in the *shestiorka* always wore in public. Although no one openly discussed the military uses implicit in rocket technology, it hovered plainly in the background.[44]

On tour, the performance of intellectual and political expertise became a key part of Gagarin's celebrity image. He was sanctioned to act as a surrogate diplomat, routinely scheduled to meet with world leaders at most stops—not only because both sides would have seen the publicity benefits of being photographed together but ostensibly also to discuss major political issues. On a tour through North Africa and West Africa in early 1962, Gagarin's first stop was in Egypt, where he met with Gamal Nasser and spoke about the politically prickly Aswan High Dam project. During a press conference in which Gagarin talked about the Cairo youth festival and the city's new stadium, he also lent support to the dam.[45] Perhaps noting his willingness to comment on political matters, an Egyptian journalist later asked him if he would ever become a deputy to the Supreme Soviet. Gagarin replied, "In our country, deputies to the Soviet parliament are the servants of the people. . . . All Soviet people participate—for peace, labor, freedom, equality, brotherhood, and happiness."[46] It was a moment intended to secure his credibility as a people's diplomat, but it also underscored the fact that he was not a deputy and did not have the credentials or authority to speak with Nasser and the Egyptian public about the Aswan Dam or any other diplomatic issue.

Later on that trip, Gagarin was photographed with Liberian government officials before moving on to Ghana, where he met with one of the most powerful postcolonial leaders of the time, Ghanaian president and pan-African activist Kwame Nkrumah. Ghanaian newspapers suggested that Gagarin's influence had motivated Nkrumah to redouble his government's efforts to promote scientific research.[47] In the Soviet press, meanwhile, Gagarin and Nkrumah became such good friends on the visit that they cemented their intellectual brotherhood by exchanging copies of their respective books—implying that Gagarin's ghostwritten celebrity memoir, *Dawn of the Space Age*, was an equal text to Nkrumah's anti-imperialism manifesto, *I Speak of Freedom*.[48] Both Ghanaian and Soviet journalists played into the myth that Gagarin possessed political, military, and diplomatic credentials that rivaled Nkrumah's, the two men's qualifications rooted in their shared understanding of Cold War masculinity. "I see a powerful man tearing asunder the chains of colonialism with powerful hands," Gagarin told the *Ghanaian Times*, speaking not directly of Nkrumah but of postcolonial Africa as often depicted in Soviet antiracism imagery. "I see before me the image of a man squaring his broad shoulders. His chains have fallen to his feet and his muscular hands, the hands of a worker, are free. I should like to clasp those hands. This is the desire with which I am going to Africa."[49]

Space program authorities repeatedly presented Gagarin as an equal to the world leaders he met. In November 1961, Gagarin met with Jawaharlal Nehru and Indira Gandhi in India, despite later revealing to Indian radio that his political expertise was limited to his certainty that India was a "brother country" to the Soviet Union.[50] In Afghanistan in December 1961, not only did Gagarin address the Kabul Military Academy, fortifying young pilots with his own story of success, but he also met with King Muhammad Zahir Shah.[51] In March 1964, a trip to Sweden was postponed after the KGB found a bomb at Gagarin's destination. Swedish newspapers were quick to pick up on the implication: "A bomb for Gagarin is a bomb for Khrushchev!" headlines blared, further securing his status as a diplomatic proxy for the Soviet government.[52] In the United Kingdom in July 1961 he met with both political and symbolic leaders, speaking with Prime Minister Harold Macmillan and dining with Queen Elizabeth—where he dared to lean forward to touch her leg under their lunch table. Having heard of kings and queens only from fairy tales, he wanted to make sure that she was a "live" queen, he later told a colleague.[53] That particular transgression not only violated royal protocol but might have played, however subtly, into his image as an attractive young man who was entitled access to women's bodies. The queen, of course, was off-limits for such a narrative. Kamanin later described Elizabeth II—who would have turned thirty-five that spring—as a "pleasant middle-aged woman, dressed very simply, without any decorations or traces of make-up."[54] As he was with so many other global leaders, Gagarin was portrayed as the queen's equal, perhaps even her superior, an experienced and charming diplomat. After touching her knee, Gagarin received no rebuke but only a smile from the queen over her coffee cup.[55]

Valentina Tereshkova, the first woman in space, was also deployed on global publicity tours. Her experience with celebrity differed markedly from that of her male colleagues in many ways, including authorities' failure to grant her the diplomatic access to foreign leaders that Gagarin enjoyed. Unlike other touring female celebrities of the time, such as Queen Elizabeth or Jacqueline Kennedy, Tereshkova's publicity tours were not as politicized, and she was not expected to comment on political situations. During her high-profile visit to London in February 1964, Tereshkova was met by cheering crowds. She accepted an award from the British Interplanetary Society, attended a reception at the Great Britain–USSR Association, and briefly met with the queen at Buckingham Palace.[56] Kamanin reported that she had a "meeting with parliament," although the *Times* clarified the nature of that visit: "She was presented with books containing coloured pictures of Parliament and an account of how it works. The party, which included the Soviet ambassador and 12 of his staff, then walked through to the central lobby, where they met Mr. Wilson, Leader of the Opposition." Marking the fortieth anniversary of the opening of diplomatic relations between Britain and the Soviet Union at an event that evening in Tereshkova's honor, the Soviet ambassador and Tereshkova's chaperone, Alexander Soldatov, read a message from Khrushchev aloud.[57] Finally, upon her departure, Tereshkova informed the British press that her favorite stop on the trip had been at Stratford-upon-Avon because she, like many Russians, was an avid Shakespeare reader.[58] In sharp contrast to Gagarin's role as a diplomat armed with mandates to engage in political discussions with foreign leaders, Tereshkova's celebrity as a cosmonaut kept her away from the political realm. Whereas Gagarin often spoke in Khrushchev's place abroad, Tereshkova could only listen while the ambassador spoke on Khrushchev's behalf in London. Despite traveling the world with a similar message of peace and prosperity as spokespeople for international cooperation based on the shared global interest in space exploration, Gagarin and Tereshkova represented vastly different roles for Soviet men and women on the world stage and, by extension, at home.

Gagarin's government meetings abroad buoyed his diplomatic masculinity, but only if he received suitable adoration at each stop. In Ghana in early 1962, Gagarin met a crowd of thousands of Young Pioneers eager for his autograph, their "Pioneer discipline" the only thing apparently keeping them stoic and reserved. Dancing and cheering for him in Accra's main square, the children held up banners in Russian that read, "Hurrah! The man from space is among us!"[59] In Liberia, Gagarin was given the Order of the African Star and taken to see local businesses, construction sites, educational institutions, and plantations. At one point, the Soviet delegation passed a crowd singing "Moscow Nights," a famous Soviet anthem.[60] A guide reportedly told *Pravda* correspondent Nikolai Denisov, who was traveling with Gagarin, "Pass on to Mr. Khrushchev our great thanks that he sent Yuri Gagarin first into space, and then to us, in Liberia!"[61]

Many accounts characterize the stops on these tours as places of otherness that could be brought into the Soviet sphere of influence through the force of Gagarin's personality and achievements alone. Soviet observers focused on Africans' customs such as dance or clothing, positioning Africans as ignorant but attentive as they listened to Gagarin's explanations of the science of space flight. This insinuated lack of science in the African and Asian countries the cosmonauts visited was a repeated theme. Gherman Titov, who often traveled with Gagarin, recounts this story: "One day an Arab journalist asked [Gagarin]: 'Did you have any sort of good-luck charm with you in the cabin of the spaceship *Vostok*?' 'Yes,' answered Gagarin, 'in the pocket of my protective suit was a certificate that I was a citizen of the Soviet Union. That is the most trustworthy good-luck charm!'"[62] The invented contrast between Soviet science and other countries' superstition or mythology came up again in Greece and Cyprus, where the press referred to Gagarin as the "Icarus of the cosmos," a moniker with roots in Greek mythology and its own history in Russian aviation culture as well. In Russian legend, Ivan the Terrible told a serf with dreams of flying that "a man is not a bird. He does not have wings. Those who attach wooden wings to themselves do so in opposition to the will of nature."[63] Conquering the will of nature was part of the promise of Soviet science, and Gagarin reflected on that while speaking to journalists in Cyprus. When asked about the Greek mythological hero, he said, "Icarus had wings made from wax, a material that is not very stable, but Soviet space ships are made from durable modern metals. These metals are produced by the hands of our workers and engineers, our Soviet people—they are the ones who should rightly be called 'Icarus of the cosmos!'"[64] Considering what happened to Icarus in Greek mythology, it is perhaps no wonder that Gagarin was eager to distance himself from the name, but in the process he created a vision of the superstitious other that Soviet science and reason could conquer in the same way they had conquered space.

The idealized masculinity of the conquering hero informed conversations about the tours. *Komsomol'skaia pravda* observed after Gagarin's flight that the work of Jules Verne and other adventure fiction encouraged "boys to dream of setting out for the jungles of Africa, the prairie of South America, to desert islands and unknown lands. . . . And on 4 October 1957, boys on all five continents raised their heads" to watch the stars and dream of becoming cosmonauts.[65] Like Africa or South America, outer space was labeled an unknown land, and it was the duty of Soviet cosmonauts to chart it. Whether in space vessels or on victory tours on earth, cosmonaut celebrity and masculinity were tied not only to notions of peaceful diplomacy but also to a vocabulary of conquest.

Conclusion

Yuri Gagarin's space flight and subsequent publicity tours both at home and abroad attempted to carve out lasting, positive identities for Soviet men of the early Cold War generation while also modeling socialist heroism to the world. Family devotion, military honor, and political diplomacy defined Gagarin's masculinity. At home, his sexually charged but carefully contained image as a desirable but monogamous young man complemented postwar family law policies intent on reestablishing the primacy of marriage and fatherhood for Soviet men. Abroad, being handsome and charismatic was not quite enough; Gagarin also played the role of diplomat in an effort to add intellectual substance to his persona, as well as to attach a fresh face to the Cold War policies of the Soviet administration. Parading Gagarin around the globe and placing him in physical, intellectual, and cultural contrast to the people and places he visited affirmed a Cold War brand of Soviet masculinity that included charisma, diplomatic skill, and authority derived from fronting a technological achievement recognized by a variety of global publics. As a makeshift political leader, his youth and attractiveness trumped the age and experience of leaders before (and concurrent with) him; as a diplomat, his space flight lent legitimacy to his discussions of international affairs on earth; and as a cultural celebrity, he filled a niche in martial masculine heroism missing in Soviet society since World War II.

Notes

1. Andrew Jenks, *The Cosmonaut Who Couldn't Stop Smiling: The Life and Legend of Yuri Gagarin* (Dekalb: Northern Illinois University Press, 2012), 6.
2. Stefan Brandt, "Astronautic Subjects: Postmodern Identity and the Embodiment of Space in American Science Fiction," *Gender Forum* 16 (2006), www.genderforum.org/fileadmin/archiv/genderforum/space2/article_brandt.html.

3. Andrew Jenks and Lev Danilkin have led scholars in asking new questions about Gagarin's legacy. See Jenks, *Cosmonaut Who Couldn't Stop Smiling*; and Danilkin, *Iurii Gagarin* (Moskva: Molodaia gvardiia, 2011). For an early post-Soviet study of Gagarin's persistent appeal in 1990s Russia, see Alexei Yurchak, "Gagarin and the Rave Kids: Transforming Power, Identity, and Aesthetics in Post-Soviet Nightlife," in *Consuming Russia: Popular Culture, Sex, and Society Since Gorbachev*, ed. Adele Marie Barker (Durham, NC: Duke University Press, 1999), 76–109. There have been several other studies of the Soviet space program published in the past few years, including Slava Gerovitch, *Voices of the Soviet Space Program: Cosmonauts, Soldiers, and Engineers Who Took the USSR into Space* (New York: Palgrave Macmillan, 2014); Asif Siddiqi, *The Red Rockets' Glare: Spaceflight and the Soviet Imagination, 1857–1957* (Cambridge: Cambridge University Press, 2010); Asif Siddiqi and James T. Andrews, eds., *Into the Cosmos: Space Exploration and Soviet Culture* (Pittsburgh: University of Pittsburgh Press, 2011); and Eva Maurer, Julia Richers, Monica Rüthers, and Carmen Scheide, eds., *Soviet Space Culture: Cosmic Enthusiasm in Socialist Societies* (New York: Palgrave Macmillan, 2011).

4. Danilkin, *Iurii Gagarin*, 7.

5. Most of the historical work on early Soviet masculinities has been done by literature scholars. See Lilya Kaganovsky, *How the Soviet Man Was Unmade: Cultural Fantasy and Male Subjectivity under Stalin* (Pittsburgh: University of Pittsburgh Press, 2008); Eliot Borenstein, *Men without Women: Masculinity and Revolution in Russian Fiction, 1917–1929* (Durham, NC: Duke University Press, 2000); and John Haynes, *New Soviet Man: Gender and Masculinity in Stalinist Soviet Cinema* (New York: Manchester University Press, 2003). On the policing of heteronormative boundaries for men under Stalin, see Dan Healey, *Homosexual Desire in Revolutionary Russia: The Regulation of Sexual and Gender Dissent* (Chicago: University of Chicago Press, 2001). For an excellent historical collection, see Barbara Evans Clements, Rebecca Friedman, and Dan Healey, eds., *Russian Masculinities in History and Culture* (New York: Palgrave Macmillan, 2002).

6. See Elena Zubkova, *Russia after the War: Hopes, Illusions, and Disappointments, 1945–1957*, trans. Hugh Ragsdale (New York: M. E. Sharpe, 1998); Mie Nakachi, "Population, Politics and Reproduction: Late Stalinism and Its Legacy," in *Late Stalinist Russia: Society between Reconstruction and Reinvention*, ed. Juliane Fürst (London: Routledge, 2006), 37–66. On women in the Soviet military in World War II, see Anna Krylova, *Soviet Women in Combat: A History of Violence on the Eastern Front* (Cambridge: Cambridge University Press, 2010).

7. On Soviet efforts to reclaim martial spaces in society for men after the war, see Erica L. Fraser, "Masculinities in the Motherland: Gender and Authority in the Soviet Union during the Cold War, 1945–1968" (PhD diss., University of Illinois at Urbana-Champaign, 2009).

8. Known as the *stiliagi*, or "stylish guys," this category of youth requires much more scholarly attention. For an excellent overview of their social and political role in late Stalinist society, see Mark Edele, "Strange Young Men in Stalin's Moscow: The Birth and Life of the *Stiliagi*, 1945–1953," *Jahrbücher für Geschichte Osteuropas* 50, no. 1 (2002): 37–61; and Gleb Tsipursky, "Living 'America' in the Soviet Union: The Cultural Practices of 'Westernized' Soviet Youth, 1945–1964," in *The Soviet Union and the United States: Rivals of the Twentieth Century*, ed. Eva-Maria Stolberg (New York: Peter Lang, 2013), 139–64. On Soviet youth after World War II, see Juliane Fürst,

Stalin's Last Generation: Soviet Post-War Youth and the Emergence of Mature Socialism (Oxford: Oxford University Press, 2010).

9. The Group of Six included Yuri Gagarin (flight date April 12, 1961), Gherman Titov (August 6–7, 1961), Andriian Nikolaev (August 11–15, 1962), Pavel Popovich (August 12–15, 1962), Valerii Bykovskii (June 14–19, 1963), and Valentina Tereshkova (June 16–19, 1963). After this cohort, the Soviet manned space program experienced several setbacks that led to less frequent flights until 1967. The Group of Six is also defined by their spacecraft, the *Vostok*, which flew these six missions before the improved *Voskhod* line forced the cancellation of *Vostok* missions 7 to 13.

10. Slava Gerovitch, "'Why Are We Telling Lies?' The Creation of Soviet Space History Myths," *Russian Review* 70, no. 3 (July 2011): 466.

11. Rossiiskii gosudarstvennyi arkhiv nauchno-tekhnicheskoi dokumentatsii (RGANTD) Fond 31, op. 6, d. 340, l. 3.

12. On the early Soviet era, see Rolf Hellebust, *Flesh to Metal: Soviet Literature and the Alchemy of Revolution* (Ithaca, NY: Cornell University Press, 2003); and Eric Naiman, *Sex in Public: The Incarnation of Early Soviet Ideology* (Princeton, NJ: Princeton University Press, 1997).

13. "Vozmozhnyi sluchai v komissii po rassledovaniiu antiamerikanskoi deiatel'nosti" [A possible case at the Committee for the Investigation of Un-American Activities], *Krokodil*, November 10, 1957, 2.

14. "Chto ty mne, babushka, skizki pro kover-samolet rasskazyvaesh', kogda uzhe iskusstvennyi sputnik letaet!" [Grandmother, you're telling me stories about flying carpets, when a man-made satellite is already in flight!], *Krokodil*, October 20, 1957, 2.

15. "Sadis', babushka, pod'ezem po-staromu znakomstvu" [Come sit, Grandmother, and we will give an old friend a lift], *Sem'ia i shkola*, January 1960, 24.

16. See Lynne Viola, *Peasant Rebels under Stalin: Collectivization and the Culture of Peasant Resistance* (Oxford: Oxford University Press, 1996); and Victoria E. Bonnell, *Iconography of Power: Soviet Political Posters under Lenin and Stalin* (Berkeley: University of California Press, 1997).

17. "Kto poslednii! Ia za vami!" [Who is last? I'm behind you!], *Krokodil*, November 20, 1957, 1.

18. Between *Sputnik* and Gagarin, the Soviet space program conducted many other experiments to see whether living creatures could survive in space. For a detailed discussion of the now-famous, and tragic, plight of the Soviet space dogs, see Amy Nelson, "Cold War Celebrity and the Courageous Canine Scout: The Life and Times of the Soviet Space Dogs," in Siddiqi and Andrews, *Into the Cosmos*, 133–55.

19. Slava Gerovitch, "'New Soviet Man' inside Machine: Human Engineering, Spacecraft Design, and the Construction of Communism," in *The Self as Project: Politics and the Human Sciences*, ed. Greg Eghigian, Andreas Killen, and Christine Leuenberger (Chicago: University of Chicago Press, 2007), 136.

20. An important exception to the reinforcement of conservative family law after the war, however, was the decriminalization of abortion in 1955, which Stalin had outlawed in 1936. See Nakachi, "Population, Politics and Reproduction."

21. Rudolf Schlesinger, ed., *The Family in the USSR: Documents and Readings* (London: Routledge and Kegan Paul, 1949), 368, 372.

22. Ibid., 403.

23. On Soviet leaders' anxieties about military service and evasion after World War II, see

Fraser, "Masculinities in the Motherland." On government concerns about unmarried men and absentee fathers after the war, see Nakachi, "Population, Politics and Reproduction."

24. Jenks, *Cosmonaut Who Couldn't Stop Smiling*, 208.

25. "Gde-to na Marse" [Somewhere on Mars], *Krokodil*, May 20, 1961, 12.

26. Victoria Smolkin-Rothrock, "Cosmic Enlightenment: Scientific Atheism and the Soviet Conquest of Space," in Siddiqi and Andrews, *Into the Cosmos*, 163.

27. Matthew H. Hersch, review of *Into that Silent Era: Trailblazers of the Space Era, 1961–1965*, by Francis French et al., *Journal of American Culture* 30, no. 4 (December 2007): 455. For a detailed discussion of masculinity and American space culture, see Dario Llinares, *The Astronaut: Cultural Mythology and Idealised Masculinity* (Newcastle upon Tyne: Cambridge Scholars, 2011).

28. N. Kamanin, *Skrytyi kosmos: Kniga pervaia, 1960–1963 gg* (Moskva: Infortekst IF, 1995), 58–59.

29. N. Kamanin, *Pervyi grazhdanin vselennoi* (Moskva: Molodaia gvardiia, 1962), 106. For further analysis of the ways Gagarin consistently breached boundaries between "truth" and "lies," see Jenks, *Cosmonaut Who Couldn't Stop Smiling*, ch. 8: "Sacred Lies, Profane Truths"; and Gerovitch, "Why Are We Telling Lies?"

30. O. Apenchenko and V. Peskov, "Reportazh iz doma pervogo kosmonavta," *Komsomol'skaia pravda*, April 14, 1961, 2. Their second daughter was born a month before Gagarin's flight.

31. *Sem'ia i shkola*, June 1961, 4.

32. "Pochta" [Mail], *Rabotnitsa*, May 1961, 4.

33. "Beseda N. S. Khrushcheva po telefonu s kosmonavtom G. S. Titovym," *Pravda*, August 7, 1961, 1.

34. RGANTD, *Iu.A. Gagarin vo vremia otdykha v Sochi*, No. 120. Undated, but judging by the baby's age, it seems to be late 1961 or early 1962.

35. On Tereshkova's exclusion from the cosmonauts' cult of masculinity, see Fraser, "Masculinities in the Motherland." In a contrasting argument, Roshanna P. Sylvester has found that Tereshkova's flight was not diminished in significance but in fact helped inspire many Soviet girls to study science and technology. See Sylvester, "She Orbits Over the Sex Barrier: Soviet Girls and the Tereshkova Moment," in Siddiqi and Andrews, *Into the Cosmos*, 195–212.

36. Apenchenko and Peskov, "Reportazh iz doma pervogo kosmonavta," 2.

37. Kamanin kept detailed diaries of the tour stops. See Kamanin, *Skrytyi kosmos*.

38. RGANTD Fond 173, op. 1, d. 27.

39. See David Caute, *The Dancer Defects: The Struggle for Cultural Supremacy during the Cold War* (Oxford: Oxford University Press, 2005). On Cold War–era tourism abroad by ordinary Soviet citizens, see Anne E. Gorsuch, *All This Is Your World: Soviet Tourism at Home and Abroad after Stalin* (Oxford: Oxford University Press, 2011).

40. *Komsomol'skaia pravda*, April 15, 1961, 1, and June 4, 1961, 1.

41. Sergei Khrushchev, "Yesteryear, Yuri Gagarin's Seven Years of Glory," *Moscow News*, no. 15 (2001): 6.

42. Sue Bridger, "The Cold War and the Cosmos: Valentina Tereshkova and the First Woman's Space Flight," in *Women in the Khrushchev Era*, ed. Melanie Ilič, Susan E. Reid, and Lynne Attwood (New York: Palgrave Macmillan, 2004), 224.

43. On Gagarin's "bromance" appeal, see Jenks, *Cosmonaut Who Couldn't Stop Smiling*, 210.

44. Tereshkova, as a civilian, wore dresses, not a uniform, in her public appearances. More work needs to be done on the gendered differences in public discourse between men

and women in the *shestiorka* cohort. For an overview, see Fraser, "Masculinities in the Motherland."

45. RGANTD Fond 31, op. 6, d. 349, ll. 58–59.
46. N. N. Denisov, *Na orbitakh mira i druzhby (Iz zapisnoi knizhki korrespondenta "Pravdy")* (Moskva: Izd-vo "Znanie," 1963), 43.
47. "Major Gagarin's Visit to Ghana Hailed," *Evening News* [Accra], February 5, 1962, 3.
48. On the book exchange, see Denisov, *Na orbitakh mira i druzhby*, 44–45. On the ghostwriting of cosmonaut autobiographies, see Gerovitch, "'Why Are We Telling Lies?,'" 466.
49. "Yuri Gagarin (World's First Spaceman) Hails Ghana's Example in National Construction," *Ghanaian Times*, February 5, 1962, 2.
50. RGANTD Fond 31, op. 6, d. 349, l. 46.
51. RGANTD Fond 31, op. 6, d. 349, l. 54.
52. N. Kamanin, *Skrytyi kosmos: Kniga vtoraia, 1964–1966 gg* (Moskva: Infortekst IF, 1997), 28.
53. Danilkin, *Iurii Gagarin*, 355.
54. Ibid., 352.
55. Ibid., 355.
56. "Woman Cosmonaut at the Palace," *Times* (London), February 6, 1964, 12.
57. "Space Woman Visits Commons," *Times* (London), February 8, 1964, 6.
58. "Woman Cosmonaut Goes Home," *Times* (London), February 11, 1964, 7.
59. Denisov, *Na orbitakh mira i druzhby*, 44–45.
60. Ibid., 45.
61. Ibid., 45–47.
62. RGANTD Fond 31, op. 6, d. 340, l. 14. *Pravda* correspondent Denisov also tells this story. See Denisov, *Na orbitakh mira i druzhby*, 42.
63. Quoted in Scott W. Palmer, *Dictatorship of the Air: Aviation Culture and the Fate of Modern Russia* (Cambridge: Cambridge University Press, 2006), 4.
64. Denisov, *Na orbitakh mira i druzhby*, 20.
65. "Vas zhdet vozdushnyi okean," *Komsomol'skaia pravda*, July 9, 1961. *Sputnik* was launched on October 4, 1957.

References

Archives

Russian State Archive of Scientific-Technical Documentation, Moscow, Russia (RGANTD)

Periodicals

Evening News (Accra)
Ghanaian Times
Komsomol'skaia pravda
Krokodil
Pravda
Rabotnitsa
Sem'ia i shkola
Times (London)

Selected Published Works

Borenstein, Eliot. *Men without Women: Masculinity and Revolution in Russian Fiction, 1917–1929*. Durham, NC: Duke University Press, 2000.

Bridger, Sue. "The Cold War and the Cosmos: Valentina Tereshkova and the First Woman's Space Flight." In *Women in the Khrushchev Era*, edited by Melanie Ilič, Susan E. Reid, and Lynne Attwood, 222–37. New York: Palgrave Macmillan, 2004.

Caute, David. *The Dancer Defects: The Struggle for Cultural Supremacy during the Cold War*. Oxford: Oxford University Press, 2005.

Clements, Barbara Evans, Rebecca Friedman, and Dan Healey, eds. *Russian Masculinities in History and Culture*. New York: Palgrave Macmillan, 2002.

Danilkin, Lev. *Iurii Gagarin*. Moskva: Molodaia gvardiia, 2011.

Denisov, N. N. *Na orbitakh mira i druzhby (iz zapisnoi knizhki korrespondenta "Pravdy")*. Moskva: Izd-vo "Znanie," 1963.

Edele, Mark. "Strange Young Men in Stalin's Moscow: The Birth and Life of the *Stiliagi*, 1945–1953." *Jahrbücher für Geschichte Osteuropas* 50, no. 1 (2002): 37–61.

Fraser, Erica L. "Masculinities in the Motherland: Gender and Authority in the Soviet Union during the Cold War, 1945–1968." PhD diss., University of Illinois at Urbana-Champaign, 2009.

Gerovitch, Slava. *Voices of the Soviet Space Program: Cosmonauts, Soldiers, and Engineers Who Took the USSR into Space*. New York: Palgrave Macmillan, 2014.

———. "'Why Are We Telling Lies?' The Creation of Soviet Space History Myths." *Russian Review* 70, no. 3 (July 2011): 460–84.

Jenks, Andrew L. *The Cosmonaut Who Couldn't Stop Smiling: The Life and Legend of Yuri Gagarin*. Dekalb: Northern Illinois University Press, 2012.

Kaganovsky, Lilya. *How the Soviet Man Was Unmade: Cultural Fantasy and Male Subjectivity under Stalin*. Pittsburgh: University of Pittsburgh Press, 2008.

Kamanin, N. *Pervyi grazhdanin vselennoi*. Moskva: Molodaia gvardiia, 1962.

———. *Skrytyi kosmos: Kniga pervaia, 1960–1963 gg.* Moskva: Infortekst IF, 1995.

———. *Skrytyi kosmos: Kniga vtoraia, 1964–1966 gg.* Moskva: Infortekst IF, 1997.

Nakachi, Mie. "Population, Politics and Reproduction: Late Stalinism and Its Legacy." In *Late Stalinist Russia: Society Between Reconstruction and Reinvention*, edited by Juliane Fürst, 23–45. London: Routledge, 2006.

Siddiqi, Asif, and James T. Andrews, eds. *Into the Cosmos: Space Exploration and Soviet Culture*. Pittsburgh: University of Pittsburgh Press, 2011.

Siddiqi, Asif. *The Red Rockets' Glare: Spaceflight and the Soviet Imagination, 1857–1957*. Cambridge: Cambridge University Press, 2010.

Yurchak, Alexei. "Gagarin and the Rave Kids: Transforming Power, Identity, and Aesthetics in Post-Soviet Nightlife." In *Consuming Russia: Popular Culture, Sex, and Society Since Gorbachev*, edited by Adele Marie Barker, 76–109. Durham, NC: Duke University Press, 1999.

Contributors

Philip E. Muehlenbeck is a professorial lecturer at George Washington University. He has authored *Betting on the Africans: John F. Kennedy's Courting of African Nationalist Leaders* (Oxford University Press, 2012) and *Czechoslovakia in Africa, 1945–1968* (Palgrave Macmillan, 2015), and served as the editor of *Race, Ethnicity and the Cold War: A Global Perspective* and *Religion and the Cold War: A Global Perspective* (Vanderbilt University Press, 2012).

Jeffrey S. Ahlman is an assistant professor of history and African studies at Smith College. His research reflects on issues of decolonization, political and social sovereignty, citizenship, and the Cold War in mid-twentieth-century Africa. His first book, *Living with Nkrumahism: Nation, State, and Pan-Africanism in Ghana*, focuses on the transnational politics of pan-Africanism and global socialism in mid-twentieth-century Ghana and the popular reactions to it, particularly around themes of gender, generation, and labor in the early postcolonial state.

Elisabeth Armstrong is professor and director of the Program for the Study of Women and Gender at Smith College. Her publications include *Gender and Neoliberalism: The All India Democratic Women's Association and Globalization Politics* (Routledge, 2014) and *The Retreat from Organization: U. S. Feminism Reconceptualized* (SUNY Press, 2002).

Benjamin A. Cowan is an assistant professor of history at George Mason University. He is the author of *Securing Sex: Morality and Repression in the Making of Cold War Brazil* (University of North Carolina Press, 2016). His interest in right-wing radicalism, morality, sexuality, and twentieth-century imperialism has led him to research focused on Cold War Brazil, with a specialization in the cultural and gender history of the post-1964 era. He has published articles in *American Quarterly*, *Journal of the History of Sexuality*, *Hispanic American Historical Review*, *Radical History Review*, and other venues.

Marko Dumančić is an assistant professor of Russian and Eastern European history at Western Kentucky University. He has published articles in *Cold War History*, *Men and Masculinities*, *Studies in Russian and Soviet Cinema*, and *Journal of Cold War Studies*, and authored a chapter in the volume *Queer Visibility in Post-socialist Cultures* (Intellect, 2013).

Erica L. Fraser is an adjunct professor at the Institute of European, Russian and Eurasian Studies at Carleton University. Her research interests focus on Russian and Soviet history, gender and masculinity, Cold War culture, military cultures, masculinity in Soviet sports, daily life, and the press in communist states.

Karen Garner is a professor of historical studies at SUNY Empire State College. She is the author of three books: *Precious Fire: Maud Russell and the Chinese Revolution* (University of Massachusetts Press, 2003); *Shaping a Global Women's Agenda: Women's NGOs and Global Governance, 1925–85* (Manchester University Press, 2010); and *Gender and Foreign Policy in the Clinton Administration* (Lynne Rienner, 2013). She also has a book contract with Bloomsbury Publishers to write a textbook on gender and international relations that will cover the twentieth century and the first decade of the twenty-first century.

Patrizia Gentile is an associate professor in the Institute of Interdisciplinary Studies at Carleton University. She holds a PhD from Queen's University in the Department of History. She coauthored *The Canadian War on Queers: National Security as Sexual Regulation* (University of British Columbia Press, 2010) with Gary Kinsman and has coedited with Jane Nicholas, *Contesting Bodies and Nation in Canadian History* (University of Toronto Press, 2013). She is currently completing a manuscript titled, *Queen of the Maple Leaf: Beauty Contests and Settler Femininity in Canada.*

May Hawas is Assistant Professor of English and Comparative Literature at the University of Alexandria (Egypt) and Associate Editor of the *Journal of World Literature* (Brill). She is the author of *The Diaries of Waguih Ghali: An Egyptian Writer in the Swinging Sixties* (AUC Press), and has published a number of articles, edited collections, and short stories. She received her PhD in literature from Leuven University (Belgium) and has been offered visiting scholar positions in France and Germany. She has worked extensively in various NGOs for women's issues and youth employment in Egypt. Her current research project deals with overlaps between theoretical concepts of world history and world literature, and historiography and *belles lettres.*

Grace Huxford is a lecturer in British history in the Historical Studies Department at the University of Bristol (UK). She has researched and published widely the social history of the Korean War and the Cold War in Britain.

Valur Ingimundarson is professor of contemporary history and the chair of EDDA—Center of Excellence in Critical Contemporary Research at the University of Iceland. He received his PhD from Columbia University in New York. He has written extensively on US-European relations during and after the Cold War, Icelandic foreign and security policy, the politics of memory, gender politics, transitional justice, Arctic geopolitics, and postconflict developments in the former Yugoslavia.

Katherine Rossy is a PhD candidate in modern European history at the School of History, Queen Mary University of London. She is a recipient of the Joseph-Armand Bombardier Canada Doctoral Scholarship from the Social Sciences and Humanities Research Council of Canada. Her research interests include the history of children and childhood, war and military occupation, and refugees and statelessness.

Nichole Sanders is a professor of history and director of graduate studies in history at Lynchburg College, in Lynchburg, Virginia. Her monograph, *Gender and Welfare in Mexico: The Consolidation of a Postrevolutionary State*, was published in 2011 by Penn State University Press. She has also coedited a volume with Berghahn Press, *Maternalism Reconsidered: Social Welfare in Twentieth-Century History* (2012). Her research centers on questions of gender, political legitimacy, and economic development.

Kathleen A. Tobin is associate professor of history and department head in the Department of History and Philosophy at Purdue University Northwest. She earned her PhD from the University of Chicago and currently teaches Latin American and United States history. Her recent research addresses population issues and birth control history, and she recently published an article entitled "Population Density and Housing in Port-au-Prince: Historical Construction of Vulnerability" in the *Journal of Urban History*. Her books include *The American Religious Debate over Birth Control, 1907–1937* (McFarland, 2001) and *Politics and Population Control: A Documentary History* (Greenwood, 2004).

Karen Turner is a professor of history at College of the Holy Cross. Her research interests include comparative law, Chinese legal history, Vietnamese history, women and war, law and human rights in Asia, and comparative empires. Her publications include *Even the Women Must Fight: Memories of War from North Vietnam* (Wiley, 1998); *The Limits of the Rule of Law in China* (University of Washington, 2000); and *American Perspectives on Chinese Law*, written in Chinese (Chinese University of Law and Politics, 1994). She was also the producer and director of the documentary film *Hidden Warriors: Voices from the Ho Chi Minh Trail*, now revised with new material, *Sisters of the Blood Road* (forthcoming, 2017).

Index